Reading in a Languag

Cognitive and psycholinguistic issues

Edited by Xi Chen, Vedran Dronjic,
and Rena Helms-Park

Routledge
Taylor & Francis Group

LONDON AND NEW YORK

First published 2016
by Routledge
2 Park Square, Milton Park, Abingdon, Oxon, OX14 4RN

and by Routledge
605 Third Avenue, New York, NY 10017

Routledge is an imprint of the Taylor & Francis Group, an informa business

Library of Congress Cataloging-in-Publication Data
Reading in a second language : cognitive and psycholinguistic issues / edited by Xi Chen, Vedran Dronjic, and Rena Helms-Park.
    pages cm
    Includes bibliographical references and index.
    1. Reading (Higher education)   2. Second language acquisition.
3. English language—Study and teaching (Higher)—Foreign speakers.
4. Reading comprehension.   5. Psycholinguistics.   I. Chen, Xi, 1974–
editor.   II. Dronjic, Vedran, editor.   III. Helms-Park, Rena, editor.
    LB2395.3.R43 2016
    418′.40711—dc23
    2015024839

ISBN: 978-0-415-89392-3 (hbk)
ISBN: 978-0-415-89393-0 (pbk)
ISBN: 978-1-315-88274-1 (ebk)

Typeset in Minion
by Apex CoVantage, LLC

Reading in a Second Language

Reading in a Second Language offers a comprehensive survey of the phenomenon and process of reading in a second language geared towards graduate and upper-level undergraduate students in second language acquisition, psycholinguistics, and applied psychology courses. The book explores reading processes from a number of complementary standpoints, integrating perspectives from fields such as first and second language reading, second language acquisition, linguistics, psycholinguistics, and cognitive neuroscience. The first half examines major factors in second language reading: types of scripts, the cognitive and neural substrates of reading, metalinguistic awareness, word recognition, language transfer, and lexical knowledge. The second part of the book discusses the social and educational contexts in which reading development occurs, including issues related to pedagogy, the use of technology in the classroom, reading disorders, and policy making. *Reading in a Second Language* provides students with a full, logically organized overview of the primary factors that shape reading development and processes in a second language.

Xi Chen is an Associate Professor in the Department of Applied Psychology and Human Development at the University of Toronto. Her research specializes in the language and literacy development of bilingual and English Language Learners.

Vedran Dronjic is an A. W. Mellon Postdoctoral Fellow in the Department of Modern Languages at Carnegie Mellon University, where he teaches in the doctoral program in Second Language Acquisition. His research focuses on the cognitive underpinnings of language knowledge and performance, particularly morphology, the mental lexicon, and reading.

Rena Helms-Park is an Associate Professor of Linguistics at the University of Toronto Scarborough, where she teaches in the Psycholinguistics Specialist program. Her research interests lie in lexical acquisition and cross-linguistic influence.

TO
Kathy
Nadežda & Ante
Mummy & Nani, Tara Helms

Contents

List of illustrations   ix

List of contributors   xi

Preface   xv

Acknowledgements   xix

1 From proto-writing to multimedia literacy:
  scripts and orthographies through the ages   1
  RENA HELMS-PARK, VEDRAN DRONJIC, AND SHAWNA-KAYE TUCKER

2 Reading, brain, and cognition   32
  VEDRAN DRONJIC AND TALI BITAN

3 Development of word recognition in a second language   70
  KEIKO KODA

4 Cross-language transfer of metalinguistic and cognitive
  skills in second language learning   99
  KATHLEEN HIPFNER-BOUCHER AND XI CHEN

5 The role of lexical knowledge in second language reading   133
  BRENT WOLTER AND RENA HELMS-PARK

6 Higher-level processes in second language reading
  comprehension   159
  MIAO LI AND NADIA D'ANGELO

7 The social context of second language literacy and biliteracy   195
   MILA SCHWARTZ AND LIUBOV BALADZHAEVA

8 Problems with reading   236
   CHRISTIE FRASER, ANGELA MASSEY-GARRISON, AND ESTHER GEVA

9 Reading instruction in a technological age   282
   YOUNGMIN PARK AND MARK WARSCHAUER

   Index   303

Illustrations

PLATES

1 The main cortical regions involved in reading in the left hemisphere.
2 Effects of orthographic transparency and familiarity in reading Hebrew.
3 Upper panel: artificial script learned in alphabetical and non-alphabetical training conditions. Middle panel: activation map in three training conditions. Lower panel: performance gains within and between sessions.

FIGURES

1.1	The pointed form of /daˈvaʁ/ "thing".	11
1.2	The pointed form of /diˈbeʁ/ "he spoke".	11
1.3	Diacritics used to mark vowels in Hindi.	12
1.4	A Japanese sentence using kanji, hiragana, and katakana.	13
1.5	Money exchange.	21
1.6	Bookstore.	21
1.7	Street sign.	22
2.1	Different fixation points for the English word *reading*.	37
6.1	The revised working memory model.	163
9.1	VSTF creates cascading patterns that are meant to reflect syntactic hierarchies.	294
9.2	Jenga formatting of text.	294

Contributors

Liubov Baladzhaeva is a PhD student of English language and literature at the University of Haifa, Israel. Her research interests lie in the field of second language acquisition, with the main focus on first language attrition and cross-linguistic influence in multilinguals.

Tali Bitan is a senior lecturer in the Department of Psychology at the University of Haifa. Her area of research is brain plasticity in the acquisition of language skills. She studies the role of procedural and declarative learning in the acquisition of reading and morphological inflections in artificial languages using fMRI.

Xi Chen is an associate professor in the Department of Applied Psychology and Human Development at University of Toronto. Her research focuses on bilingual and English Language Learner (ELL) children's language and literacy development. She is interested in how children develop literacy skills simultaneously in their first language and second language, and whether these skills transfer between the two languages.

Nadia D'Angelo is a PhD candidate at the Ontario Institute for Studies in Education at the University of Toronto. She received her master's degree in developmental psychology at Carleton University. Her research focuses on the associations between higher-level literacy processes and reading comprehension for second language learners with comprehension difficulties.

Vedran Dronjic is an A.W. Mellon postdoctoral fellow in the Department of Modern Languages at Carnegie Mellon University, where he teaches in the doctoral program in second language acquisition. His research focuses on morphological processing, the cognitive bases of language, and the measurement of various components of linguistic and metalinguistic ability in bilinguals and monolinguals, primarily lexical knowledge, morphological awareness, and reading.

Christie Fraser is in the final year of her doctoral studies in the Department of Applied Psychology and Human Development at the University of Toronto. Her research interests include: the cognitive processes involved in learning to read, language and literacy skills in English Language Learners (ELLs) with and without learning difficulties, and reading intervention for struggling readers.

Esther Geva's research, publications, and teaching focus on the development of language and literacy skills in typically developing L2 learners and those with learning difficulties, and on cultural perspectives on children's psychological problems. Professor Geva has published extensively on these topics, presented her work internationally, and served on numerous advisory, policy, and review committees.

Rena Helms-Park is associate professor of linguistics at the University of Toronto Scarborough. She is cross-appointed to the Speech-Language Pedagogy Department at the University of Toronto St. George. Her research interests center on cross-linguistic transfer with a focus on second language lexical acquisition.

Kathleen Hipfner-Boucher is an assistant professor in the Département de didactique des langues at the Université du Québec à Montréal. Her main area of research is in the connection between oral and written language competencies, particularly in second language learners.

Keiko Koda is professor of second language acquisition and Japanese in the Department of Modern Languages at Carnegie Mellon University. Her primary areas of research include second language reading, biliteracy development, and foreign language education.

Miao Li is a SSHRC-funded postdoctoral fellow in the Ontario Institute for Studies in Education at University of Toronto. Her main area of research is in second language reading education, particularly the cognitive processes of reading development in bilingual children.

Angela Massey-Garrison is a PhD student at the Ontario Institute for Studies in Education, University of Toronto. Her research focuses on typical and atypical reading and language development, cognitive processes underlying reading development, and second language learning.

Youngmin Park is a PhD student at the University of California, Irvine, specializing in language, literacy, and technology. Previously a high school teacher and teacher trainer in Korea, she has published and presented on topics related to teaching and learning English as a second or foreign language.

Mila Schwartz is a professor in the Department of Linguistics at the Oranim Academic College of Education, Israel. Her primarily research interests include educational language policies and models of early bilingual education; bilingual teachers' pedagogical development; socio-cultural, language, and cognitive development of early sequential bilinguals; and peer language interaction as a facilitator in L2 learning.

Shawna-Kaye Tucker is a graduate of the University of Toronto Scarborough with a specialization in psycholinguistics. Her research interest lies in second language acquisition, and she has partnered with various psycholinguists and speech pathologists in this area.

Mark Warschauer is professor and associate dean of education at the University of California, Irvine, director of the Digital Learning Lab at UCI, and editor-in-chief of AERA Open. His recent books include *Learning in the Cloud: How (and Why) to Transform Schools with Digital Media* (Teachers College Press).

Brent Wolter is a professor in the Department of English at Idaho State University. His main research interests include L2 vocabulary acquisition and L2 collocations. He is particularly interested in the psychological and psycholinguistic aspects of L2 vocabulary development.

Preface

This book describes the phenomenon and process of reading in a second language from a number of complementary standpoints, including first and second language reading, second language acquisition, psycholinguistics, and cognitive neuroscience. The primary emphasis is on the development of second language reading skills in children and adolescents from diverse backgrounds. The book acknowledges the importance of the social and educational context in which reading development takes place in these populations and keeps in mind the numerous exciting ways in which changes in modern society (e.g., migration, globalization, multiculturalism) and technology are reshaping second language reading. Important pedagogical and planning/policy implications of the surveyed research are highlighted where relevant.

This comprehensive and multidisciplinary survey is intended as a primary text for graduate and upper-level undergraduate courses in second language reading. It is well-suited for courses that aim to present theory and research in an accessible manner, yet also offer practical applications. As such, this book will find use in a variety of academic settings: (1) programs in second language acquisition/education, (2) programs in linguistics which offer specialization in psycholinguistics, (3) programs in educational or applied psychology where second language reading is discussed, and (4) elective subjects in initial teacher education programs. The volume will also be useful to researchers and educators in the fields of reading science, second language acquisition, speech-language pathology, and psycholinguistics as a handy reference volume, providing a detailed account of the latest research findings. Even for seasoned researchers, the volume offers a convenient way to keep abreast of developments in neighboring subfields.

The book is unique in that the three editors come from diverse yet overlapping backgrounds. Dr. Chen has expertise in reading and literacy development, Dr. Dronjic specializes in second and first language processing, and

Dr. Helms-Park is an expert on second language acquisition, particularly in the domains of lexical transfer and vocabulary assessment. Throughout the writing and editing process, we have made every effort to approach important issues from multiple angles. Thus, this book brings together perspectives from a variety of related fields not usually found in a single integrated volume; the authors of the chapters are experts who specialize in cognitive and sociocultural approaches to reading science, second language acquisition, cognitive neuroscience, psycholinguistics, linguistics, and learning technology.

The editors of the book share an interest in how reading works, what its cognitive subcomponents are, and how they come together in a coherent process. We also share a set of common views about language and cognition. We see language, arguably the most sophisticated expression of human cognitive powers, as being grounded in a set of phylogenetically pre-existing cognitive abilities which humans evolved over a long period of time. Most of these cognitive abilities (e.g., auditory perception, memory, attentional control) are shared with related species, had a pre-existing primary function, and were at some point expanded and co-opted for the purpose of supporting linguistic functioning. Some of them (e.g., the ability to combine and recombine elements freely and creatively, the ability to learn a virtually unlimited number of referential words) are likely uniquely human. Consequently, our view is that experience with language use in comprehension and production is the primary driving force behind the process of first and second language acquisition. Competence and performance, if separated, are intricately interrelated; one does not take the back seat to the other.

While humans have had sufficient time during the course of evolution to adapt for the use of language and optimize it, reading is a recent cognitive add-on for which they cannot be evolutionarily adapted. The acquisition of literacy is a lengthy, deliberate, and effortful process, particularly in a second language. We take the componential view of first and second language reading; reading can be broken into a number of linguistic, metalinguistic, and other cognitive processes, including visual perception, phonological and orthographic processing, morphological and syntactic parsing, lexical access and processing, phonological and morphological awareness, working memory, higher-level comprehension processes, strategies, and so on. Expert reading then emerges from a well-balanced interaction among all of these components, with some undertaking more intensive duties to meet task demands. We have structured the volume such that each chapter addresses one major component of the complex process of reading. In addition, we incorporate sociocultural and technological perspectives on literacy. We have attempted to highlight the pedagogical implications of the surveyed theories and research in hopes of facilitating second language reading outcomes.

This volume consists of nine chapters. It opens with a chapter by Rena Helms-Park, Vedran Dronjic, and Shawna-Kaye Tucker, which presents an overview of writing systems and their evolution, and highlights the need to examine scripts when investigating the psycholinguistic and cognitive processes underlying reading. The chapter also discusses the power dynamics emanating from the use of particular scripts, the surge of electronic literacies, and the potential benefits of childhood digraphia (dual orthographies) in certain social contexts. The second chapter, written by Vedran Dronjic and Tali Bitan, examines the cognitive and neural bases of reading in an accessible format and presents the latest eye-tracking, behavioural, and neuroimaging research on reading. It emphasizes the importance of automaticity in the attainment of fluent reading ability. Chapter 3, authored by Keiko Koda, provides a survey of the universal and language-specific aspects of the development of second language word recognition and the resulting cross-language interactions. This delineation is crucial for the understanding of the nature of reading. The fourth chapter, by Kathleen Hipfner-Boucher and Xi Chen, presents an overview of the theoretical frameworks that guide the research on cross-language transfer and a summary of empirical findings. It discusses factors that influence the transferability of linguistic and cognitive skills involved in reading. Chapter 5, written by Brent Wolter and Rena Helms-Park, is an in-depth treatment of the role of lexical knowledge in second language reading. The chapter presents a number of important theoretical constructs pertinent to the study of the mental lexicon and synthesizes existing empirical research.

Chapter 6, by Miao Li and Nadia D'Angelo, focuses on the higher-level cognitive processes that contribute to reading comprehension (e.g., working memory, background knowledge, inference making). The chapter discusses the implications of these processes for second language reading instruction. The seventh chapter of this book, contributed by Mila Schwartz and Liubov Baladzhaeva, addresses the role of social and cultural factors in the development of second language literacy. The chapter pays particular attention to immigrant communities in the North American context and suggests a variety of instructional and curricular strategies to serve these communities. Chapter 8, written by Christie Fraser, Angela Massey-Garrison, and Esther Geva, synthesizes the research on reading difficulties in second language learners, examines it in light of a variety of theoretical frameworks, and presents a discussion of the complexity of the identification of reading difficulties in second language learners. The chapter also presents two case studies which highlight some of the challenges in identifying second language students experiencing difficulties with reading. The book concludes with a chapter by Youngmin Park and Mark Warschauer that discusses the integration of digital media into L2 reading instruction. These tools can be used for such important purposes as activating background knowledge, learning vocabulary, and improving reading fluency.

Acknowledgements

At the end of this long and occasionally challenging process, we are delighted that this volume is now complete and ready to be presented to colleagues and students. We are acutely aware of the fact that our effort alone would have been insufficient to produce this comprehensive work. We are extremely grateful to the authors for their willingness to contribute their time, hard work, and expertise to this joint effort. In particular, we wish to thank Kathleen Hipfner-Boucher for her energy and extraordinary generosity of spirit. It bears noting that some of the authors graciously agreed to serve as internal reviewers. We should also take this opportunity to thank our external reviewers, Elizabeth Hirshorn, Sihui Ke, Poh Wee Koh, Chin-Hsi Lin, and Charles Perfetti. We would also like to express our gratitude to Kelly-Ann Blake, Irene Delicano, Kyung-Jin Jinny Ihn, Kathy Leung, Melissa Marasigan, and Connie Ting for their assistance with editing and proofreading, as well as Michael Scott Brown and Irene Delciano for their artistic input. Finally, we express our gratitude to Ivy Ip, Leah Babb-Rosenfeld and Elysse Preposi at Routledge. Their endless patience and continued support gave us the strength to complete this project.

From proto-writing to multimedia literacy
Scripts and orthographies through the ages

*Rena Helms-Park, Vedran Dronjic,
and Shawna-Kaye Tucker*

---

1. INTRODUCTION

We begin this book on reading in a second language with an examination of scripts. Apart from the obvious fact that the reader needs to decode and interpret a text written in a particular script, there are more compelling reasons for examining the systems used to represent linguistic structures in writing. Perhaps foremost among these is the *interplay* of cognitive skills required to recognize language-specific words, which have their own structural characteristics, in a specific script, which also has its own structural peculiarities. While the "visual word form area" has been shown to be script-neutral (Nakamura, Dehaene, Jobert, Le Bihan, & Kouider, 2005), there are differences in the areas of the brain that are engaged while reading even when the script used is the same, as with Italian and English (Paulesu et al., 2000). The visual word form area responds differentially to differences in bigrams (grapheme pairs in languages), displaying greater partiality to high-frequency pairings in an L1 script than to low-frequency or non-existent ones (Vinckier et al., 2007); the same predilection is displayed when responding to stimuli from one's own script versus an unknown one (Baker et al., 2007). Thus, it is not surprising that reading in a second script demands proficiency not only in the second language (L2) linguistic code but also in the special ways in which this code is represented in writing. Without some degree of automatization of L2 visual word recognition skills, higher-level processing of a text – and probably even sentence-level comprehension – is either laborious or unachievable. Furthermore, L1 strategies continue to exert an influence on L2 reading at various levels of proficiency, as seen in various behavioural studies (e.g., Chikamatsu, 1996; Cook & Bassetti, 2005; Koda, 2005; Muljani, Koda, & Moates, 1998; Wang & Geva, 2003) as well as L1-L2 brain studies (e.g., Nakada, Fujii, & Kwee, 2001; Tan et al., 2003). Examining the attributes of the scripts in question affords the learner, instructor, or researcher an opportunity to hypothesize what mechanisms are at play in particular cases of biliteracy.

Section 2 provides a history of writing over the last five thousand years. Section 3 presents a description of the world's scripts, divided into two broad categories: phonographic and morphographic. This section ends with an overview of the orthographic depth hypothesis (Frost, 2005; Katz & Frost, 1992). Section 4 focuses on the sociolinguistic, political, and educational issues surrounding the use of certain scripts by nations or communities, as exemplified by two interesting case studies: digraphic Serbo-Croatian and Jamaican Creole (Patois), a code with a flexible orthography and eminently suitable for "textspeak".

2. THE HISTORY OF WRITING

2.1 The brain's filters for representing written symbols

There is some consensus in current times that, unlike neural circuits that are heavily engaged in oral language representation and processing (e.g., those found in cortical areas traditionally referred to as Broca's area or Wernicke's area), no brain centers have evolved explicitly for the purpose of facilitating reading and writing. Rather, the area that evolved in prehistory to recognize objects (but not faces) is said to have provided the architectural infrastructure for recognizing what are now graphemes in scripts (Changizi, Zhang, Ye, & Shimojo, 2006; Dehaene, 2009; Wolf, 2007). Through a cross-linguistic statistical examination of scripts, Changizi et al. (2006) concluded that certain junctions of lines and ensuing shapes, such as an "L" and "T", appear with great frequency across scripts. In other words, neurons dedicated to respond to specific shapes ("shape filters") for the purposes of object recognition were assigned to create and recognize the graphemes of scripts ("neuronal recycling") (Dehaene, 2009). Scripts have evolved in line with what is "learnable" by the brain, but, in keeping with Dehaene's neuronal recycling hypothesis, literacy skills require instruction and practice, as opposed to speaking and listening.

2.2 Beginnings of writing and earliest scripts

Writing – in the sense of internally structured systems of visual marks intended to communicate thought among humans by encoding language in an unambiguous and systematic way (Fischer, 2004; Rogers, 2005) – has been invented independently several times in human history, though the number of instances is still not exactly clear (Chrisomalis, 2009). At least two kinds of "recording devices" (Daniels, 1996, p. 21) are known to have existed before the advent of writing: the Neolithic symbols found on objects produced by the Vinča culture (5700–4500 BCE) in present-day Serbia – which visually resemble letters but cannot, at present, be conclusively shown to be a script – as well as Near Eastern clay tokens dating as far back as 8000 BCE, likely used for bookkeeping purposes (Daniels, 1996). In fact, writing systems have had a tendency to emerge in conjunction with numerical notation systems, which have appeared independently at least five times in human history: in Mesopotamia, Egypt, China, Lowland Mesoamerica, Peru, and possibly on a few other occasions.

Scripts independently developed in Mesopotamia, China, Lowland Mesoamerica, and likely also in Egypt and the Indus Valley (Chrisomalis, 2009; Fischer, 2004). The Indus Valley script has not yet been deciphered, and it is not known what language it might have represented, nor is there universal agreement that it is linguistic in nature. Statistical analysis by Rao et al. (2009) claims to demonstrate that Indus Valley inscriptions have a conditional entropy comparable to that of other linguistic systems, particularly early cuneiform, but the validity of this analysis has been questioned (e.g., Sproat, 2014). (For another undeciphered case of possible early writing, see Macri, 1996b, for an account of *rongorongo* or "recitation" that once existed on Easter Island.) Meanwhile, the Egyptian script was originally believed to have been an application of the abstract principle of writing developed in Mesopotamia, but there are now indications that writing developed roughly simultaneously in Egypt and Mesopotamia (Cruz-Urube, 2001), with no agreement as to whether one writing system slightly predates the other (Michalowski, 1996). It is noteworthy that, despite the two areas' relative proximity, Mesopotamian numbers used a variety of notation systems and numerical bases, while the Egyptian numerical notation system used a base of ten and, unlike the case in Mesopotamia, did not serve the same broad bookkeeping purposes (Chrisomalis, 2009; Michalowski, 1996).

The first written Mesopotamian texts appear on clay tablets dated around 3200–3000 BCE and originate from Uruk, situated on the Euphrates River in present-day Iraq. Since early Mesopotamian writing was pictographic in nature (i.e., it did not represent sound but rather meaning), it is difficult to deduce what language is represented on the clay tablets. However, the few known cases of phonological complementation in this early period reveal that the language recorded is Sumerian (Michalowski, 1996). Mesopotamian writing evolved in stages, from tokens being impressed upon a clay envelope; to, possibly, the clay envelope becoming a flat tablet; to the symbols for tokens being drawn on the tablet with a stylus (Michalowski, 1996; Rogers, 2005).

Since dragging the stylus through clay was not practical, triangular styluses came to be used to make impressions in the clay, thus giving the script its name, *cuneiform* or "wedge-shaped" (Rogers, 2005).

The earliest cuneiform symbols were also pictographic in nature, being either an iconic visual representation of the object they stood for (e.g., the picture of a head for the word SAG, "head"), or an abstract representation (e.g., a cross in a circle for the word UDU, "sheep") (Cooper, 1996). Semantic extension was common. For instance, the symbol depicting a foot was extended to represent the words DU "go" and GUB "stand". Many symbols were iconic in a metonymic way, such as the symbol for A "water", which was a depiction of a stream (Rogers, 2005). At any rate, the original pictographic symbols quickly became more stylized (e.g., undergoing a ninety-degree rotation) and eventually became purely symbolic (Cooper, 1996; Rogers, 2005). The symbols were also phonetically extended. For example, the aforementioned symbol for "water", A, also started being used to mean "in", since the two words were homophonous. Then finally, the symbol simply came to stand for the syllable /a/ in general.

Cuneiform gradually evolved to represent the complex morphological structure of Sumerian. Symbols for certain affixes appear after 2900 BCE but are consistently found only in the early second millennium, when the language was probably no longer spoken (Cooper, 1996). Eventually, a fairly complex situation evolved in written Akkadian, in which some symbols could stand for morphemes, others for sound units, such as morae (explained in Section 3 ahead) or syllables (often with various phonemic contrasts being disregarded), and yet others for semantic complements, used to disambiguate among homographs; often, the same symbol could stand for a meaning and a sound unit (Rogers, 2005).

Egyptian writing existed in three basic styles. The oldest is hieroglyphic, whose graphemes are the well-known pictographic representations of objects (a vulture, a hand, a hill, etc.). Hieratic appeared at a similar time as hieroglyphic and is a direct cursive simplification of the hieroglyphs; various forms of it evolved over time. Demotic was the most cursive and least formal of the three styles (Ritner, 1996). Hieroglyphs were spatially arranged as convenient, while hieratic and demotic scripts were always written right to left. Based on the rebus principle, hieroglyphic writing used a mixture of the phonographic (sound-representing) and morphographic (morpheme-representing) principles. Only consonants were written, while the position of the vowels was inferable from context to readers proficient in the language; Egyptian had a templatic morphological structure similar to that found in other branches of Afro-Asiatic, with mostly triconsonantal discontinuous roots interwoven with derivational and inflectional morphemes. When the phonographic principle was used, graphemes could stand for one, two, or three consonants, but sound was often represented redundantly as well. Homonyms were disambiguated by adding a semantic complement, which was a grapheme that pointed at the intended meaning (Rogers, 2005). Today, a small number of demotic graphemes survive in the mostly Greek-based alphabet used to write Coptic, the last stage of the Egyptian language, and which is also the liturgical language used by the Coptic Orthodox Church of Alexandria.

Chronologically, the next script to be independently invented was the Chinese script, which was first attested – already in a mature form capable of representing the entirety of the Old Chinese language – in inscriptions found on ox bones and turtle shells known as oracle bone inscriptions; these are dated at around 1200 BCE, the Shang dynasty period. While much earlier inscriptions have been found on fragments of pottery, dating as far back as approximately 4800 BCE, these cannot be shown to be related to oracle bone inscriptions or to be linguistic in nature (Boltz, 1996). All later forms of Chinese characters are descended from the oracle bone script.

The script was based on the morphographic principle (also known as the logographic principle), in which meaning was represented, not sound. The characters stood for syllable-sized units, which mostly corresponded to morphemes in Old Chinese, with some exceptions. However, the lexicon mostly consisted of monosyllabic, monomorphemic words and the language had an isolating morphology (Branner, 2001; Norman, 1988). Characters could either be simple ("unit characters") or compound. Unit characters developed from pictographic representations of the referents of the words they stood for. Later, they began to be used to write other, non-visual words, either by semantic or phonetic extension. This would have resulted in a modicum of ambiguity. Compound characters were developed in response to this situation by adding a second element, which was meant to indicate which word was being written by hinting at the intended meaning or pronunciation (Boltz, 1996). The Chinese writing system will be discussed in more detail ahead, in the section on types of scripts.

A final region where full-fledged writing unambiguously developed independently is Mesoamerica. The earliest attested and confirmed Mesoamerican writing system is the Zapotec script, dated at about 600–400 BCE (Macri, 1996a; Robinson, 2014). An even earlier set of symbols is associated with the Olmec culture and has been dated at about 900 BCE (Martínez et al., 2006), but there is still no agreement on whether this system was a script. Chronologically following Zapotec is the Epi-Olmec (or Isthmian) script, attested on archaeological artefacts dated to be from the 2nd century CE (Justeson & Kaufman, 1993; Kaufman & Justeson, 2001). Related to Epi-Olmec is the best-known (and largely deciphered) Mesoamerican system, the Mayan script, which is traditionally described as being attested in its fully developed form in 3rd century CE. This date has been significantly pushed back by the discovery of Maya writing at the ruins of San Bartolo in Guatemala, with inscriptions that can be dated at 300–200 BCE (Saturno, Stuart, & Beltrán, 2006). The Mayan script was made up of glyphs, which were roughly square in shape and consisted of symbols that could stand for morphemes, consonant-vowel sequences, phonological complements, and, though rarely, semantic complements. Similar to Egyptian, the same word could be written in different ways, often with redundancy of representation and, unlike Egyptian, without writers settling on one conventionalized form per word. This variation was even common with proper nouns and may have been a consequence of aesthetic preferences (Rogers, 2005). It also bears noting that while writing in Mesopotamia developed in the context of commerce and Egyptian writing was closely associated with religious purposes, Mesoamerican writing may have emerged, at least partially, out of a desire to maintain a record of astronomical knowledge (Macri, 1996a).

For an accessible yet systematic overview of the world's writing systems with a linguistic focus, the reader is referred to Rogers (2005), while one good source of more extensive information, often with an archaeological focus, would be the edited volume by Daniels and Bright (1996).

3. TYPES OF SCRIPTS

Although there are numerous ways of classifying scripts (e.g., Rogers, 2005, pp. 269–288), we are adapting a taxonomy used by Coulmas (1999) and Cook and Bassetti (2005) to serve as an organizational framework for Section 3.1. At the highest level of organization are *phonographic and morphographic writing systems*, since these are fundamental mechanisms by which written forms systematically encode language – that is, by representing sounds (i.e., phonographic systems) or meanings (i.e., morphographic systems). Within each of these systems are *script types*; for example, the phonographic system encompasses alphabets, abjads, abugidas, and syllabaries/moraic scripts. Within each script type are specific scripts, a set of graphemes or units of writing used as physical written instantiations of a language or languages (Cook & Bassetti, 2005). However, even when languages share a script they have language-specific orthographies, or conventions for spelling as well as mechanics, such as punctuation and capitalization. Thus, we can say that English and French use different orthographies, but share the Latin script (with minor divergences), which is a type of alphabetic script within the phonographic system.

We should note, however, that while the terms *phonographic system, morphographic system, script,* and *orthography* are being used to organize the information in Section 3.1 of this chapter, the term "script" is used more generally elsewhere in the chapter and, for that matter, in much of the literature on writing; thus it can cover system, script, and orthography. In fact, many experts use these terms interchangeably or use one as an umbrella terms for all three (as in the case of "*orthographic* depth hypothesis"). Similarly "system" can be used for all scripts and orthographies since they are systematic to some degree. As stated by Rogers (2005, p. 272), "writing systems are taxonomically 'messy'", and this also applies to an extent to the terminology used by various researchers.

3.1 Phonographic and morphographic systems

There are two broad options for how scripts can encode human languages. Following the phonographic principle, graphemes represent sound units in various fashions. Following the morphographic principle, graphemes most closely correspond to morphemes, or units of meaning. (While the term "logographic" is commonly used to represent a system of grapheme-word correspondences, Rogers points out that the more accurate term is "morphographic" since the scripts in question are best characterized as using grapheme-morpheme correspondences.) We should note that there is no extant script that is entirely morphographic or phonographic in nature (Rogers, 2005). Rather, various amounts of meaning-based and sound-based information are encoded by all scripts.

Most of today's sound-based scripts owe their existence to the discovery of the phonographic principle in Mesopotamia and (marginally, if seen as a separate discovery) Egypt. Currently, most of the world's languages are written using various phonographic scripts: *alphabets* (e.g., English, Indonesian, Swahili); *abugidas*, scripts that encode consonant-vowel sequences in a systematic way, where a consonant grapheme is modified with a vowel diacritic (e.g., Hindi, Amharic, Thai); *abjads*, scripts that encode mostly or exclusively consonants (e.g., Arabic, Hebrew, Farsi); and *moraic/syllabic* scripts (e.g., Japanese, as part of its mixed orthography, Cherokee, Yi). Rogers (2005), based on a 1992 conference talk by William Poser, notes that many scripts traditionally referred to as syllabic in fact typically encode morae, phonological units that may or may not coincide with the syllable; some syllables contain one mora, others contain two, and on rare occasions a syllable contains three. In Japanese kana, a mora is either a syllable onset plus a nucleus or a coda, but when the nucleus is a long vowel, it constitutes two morae (Rogers, 2005, p. 54).

Finally, Chinese, Japanese (partially), and Zhuang are examples of languages that currently use a script originally based on the morphographic principle; all three cases use a system based on Chinese characters. Japanese, in fact, uses a mixed writing system, based on both morphographic and phonographic (moraic) principles. Morphographic scripts have historically evolved via the pictographic principle, whereby a pictorial representation of an object, such as a picture of a house, would come to represent the word "house". Some examples of morphograms in the current English script are "&" and "4".

In continuation, we present a brief sketch of the aforementioned types of writing systems. The aim is certainly not to achieve any degree of extensive coverage, but rather to familiarize the reader with the basic principles of writing that are currently in use. For more details, the reader is referred to Rogers (2005), Daniels and Bright (1996), and the multitude of works cited therein.

3.1.2 The phonographic principle

Alphabets. In alphabetic writing systems, graphemes tend to represent phonemes. Unlike abjads, which represent only consonants (or consonants and some vowels), alphabets represent both vowel and consonant phonemes (but often still imperfectly, such that the number of graphemes and the number of phonemes typically do not coincide). Most alphabetic orthographies currently in use, such as Greek, various versions of the Latin script, and various versions of the Cyrillic script, can historically be traced back to the Semitic abjad (most probably its Phoenician version), which was itself likely developed under the influence of a simplified form of Egyptian writing (Rogers, 2005).

Alphabetic scripts vary along a cline of orthographic depth, with certain systems being fairly shallow (meaning that the writing principle is mainly phonographic and that there is a fairly straightforward relationship between spelling and pronunciation), and others being relatively deep (meaning that the writing principle is at least partially morphographic or etymological, and the relationship between spelling and pronunciation is not always straightforward). These variations will be discussed ahead.

Serbian, one standard version of Serbo-Croatian, can be written in a Latin or Cyrillic alphabet and is an example of a shallow orthography. Each Serbian consonant grapheme corresponds to exactly one phoneme. The five vowel graphemes can represent a long or a short vowel phoneme. Vowel length, as well as pitch accent (a type of lexical tone), can be indicated by diacritics, which are not used in most everyday contexts. Thus, the written form *sedi* (Latin) or *седи* (Cyrillic) can stand for the following forms: (1) /sêdi/ "sit down" (imperative, second person singular), (2) /sê:di/ "the grey-haired one" (masculine), (3) /sědi/ "sits/is sitting", (4) /sě:di/ "turns/is turning grey-haired". There are very few other irregularities in the orthography, mostly due to a mild morphographic principle, such as the words *šesto/шесто* "sixth" (neuter, singular, nominative) and *šeststo/шестсто* "six hundred"; both are pronounced /şê:sto/.

English sits at the opposite end of the orthographic depth continuum. Its orthography has not kept up to date with its phonology, and, as a consequence, a single grapheme can represent multiple phonemes (e.g., A for /æ/, /ej/, /ɑ/, /ə/, and /ɛ/), and a single phoneme can be written in various ways (/k/ can be K, C, CK, CH, KK, QU, and Q). While this creates an enormous amount of irregularity and difficulty for individuals learning how to read and write in English, it does have the advantage of a strong tendency to preserve the identity of morphemes. For instance, the morpheme {nat-}, found in words such as *native, nativity, nation,* and *national,* counts /'neɪt/, /nət/, /'neɪʃ/, and /ˌnæʃ/ among its allomorphs, yet is always written as *nat-*. Similarly, homophonous morphemes, such as those found in the words *sale* and *sail,* are distinguished in written form. It is often remarked that the English orthography is most regular in terms of how it codes syllable onsets and syllable rhymes, and that it is at this level where learners extract the most regularities. However, the orthography is far from consistent in this respect, with numerous irregularities, which have frequently been sung in popular (often anonymous) poems, such as this short excerpt (author unknown):

> When the English tongue we speak
> Why is break not rhymed with weak?
> Won't you tell me why it's true
> We say sew, but also few?

Between these two extremes, there are various degrees of orthographic depth in alphabetic scripts. For instance, Spanish is often cited as an entirely shallow or transparent system (e.g., Frost, 2005), but it actually contains quite a few examples of many-to-one, one-to-many, and one-to-zero correspondences (e.g., I, Y = /i/; G, J = /x/; G = /g/, /x/; H is not pronounced in *hablo* "I speak"; U is not pronounced in *qué* "what"). Greek is similar due to the partially etymological/morphographic character of its orthography; to illustrate, the phoneme /o/ can be written O or Ω, /e/ can be E and AI, and /i/ can be I, H, Υ, EI, or OI. However, both orthographies are easy to decipher once the basic grapheme-phoneme correspondence rules are known, which is much more difficult to achieve in truly deep orthographies, such as English.

Hangul: a featural alphabetic system. The invention of the Korean alphabet, *hangul* (as it is known in South Korea) or *chosongul* (as it is known in North Korea) – both meaning "Korean script" – is traditionally attributed to 15th-century king Sejong, but it is more accurate to say that the king "took a strong personal interest in its development" (Rogers, 2005, p. 70). At the time of hangul's invention, Koreans were already well-versed in writing; in fact, Chinese characters (called *hanja* in Korean) were the main way of writing Korean.

Hangul is a script of striking originality. Its consonant symbols are based on phonetic illustrations and are systematically related based on phonetic features. For instance, the symbol for /k/ ~ /g/ is ㄱ, illustrating the velar nature of the sound it represents (i.e., tongue raised against the velum). The related aspirated phoneme, /kʰ/, is represented by an additional stroke, hence, ㅋ, and a third related phoneme, the "tense" /k̰/, is represented by reduplicating the symbol for /k/, hence, ㄲ. The apical/alveolar character of /n/ is shown in the grapheme ㄴ, illustrating the tip of the tongue raised against the alveolar ridge. The grapheme representing /s/ is a stylized representation of a lower incisor, ㅅ, and the grapheme for /m/ is a representation of the lips/mouth, ㅁ. The labial stop series is derived from the symbol for /m/; thus ㅂ for /p/ ~ /b/, ㅍ for aspirated /pʰ/, ㅃ for "tense" /p̰/, and so forth (Ledyard, 1997). Hangul is the only alphabet in which the graphemes are grouped into syllabic blocks (see, e.g., Rogers, 2005, for the rules, which depend on syllable structure as well as the types of strokes in the graphemes); thus, the word "hangul", consisting of the graphemes ㅎ /h/, ㅏ /a/, ㄴ /n/, ㄱ /k/ ~ /g/, ㅡ /ɯ/, and ㄹ /ɾ/ ~ /l/, is written 한글. Due to phonological change, hangul has become a relatively deep orthography in the course of its history, requiring knowledge of morphophonemic rules in order for text to be decoded properly (Rogers, 2005).

Abjads. Abjads are alphabetic writing systems which, in their purest form, encode only consonants while vowels are ignored. The two best-known examples are the Arabic script (and its derivatives) and the Hebrew script. Abjads focus on consonants at the expense of vowels due to the fact that they evolved for the writing of Egyptian and various Semitic languages, which, as mentioned earlier, are characterized by templatic morphology. Most of a word's meaning in these languages is represented by a discontinuous root, often consisting of three consonants, while various derivational and inflectional forms are chiefly arrived at by interweaving (also discontinuous) transfixes (patterns) with the roots, as well as by adding prefixes and suffixes.

As an example, the Hebrew written form דבר (from right to left: /d/ + /b/ ~ /v/ + /ʁ/) could stand for /daˈvaʁ/ "thing", /daˈbeʁ/ "speak" (imperative, 2nd person singular), /diˈbeʁ/ "he spoke", /duˈbaʁ/ "was spoken", or /ˈdeveʁ/ "plague" (examples adapted from Frost & Bentin, 1992). A skilled Hebrew reader arrives at the correct form by relying on contextual cues present in the text being read and, of course, by drawing on lexical and grammatical knowledge.

It is possible to indicate the precise identity of the word being written by adding additional diacritics. Called *nikud* "pointing" or *nekudot* "points" in Modern Hebrew, these diacritics are written below, inside, or next to consonant graphemes and serve to indicate vowels and to disambiguate between ambiguous graphemes (e.g., ב, or *bet*, which stands for both /b/ and /v/ when "unpointed"). Thus, /daˈvaʁ/ "thing", normally written דבר, is rendered as shown in Figure 1.1 in "pointed" Hebrew, while /diˈbeʁ/ "he spoke" (also

FIGURE 1.1 The pointed form of /daˈvaʁ/ "thing".

FIGURE 1.2 The pointed form of /diˈbeʁ/ "he spoke".

normally written as רבד), is rendered as shown in Figure 1.2. Pointed Hebrew print is used mostly in texts for beginner readers, poetry, religious texts, grammars, and dictionaries, among others. A similar system of diacritics exists in the Arabic script and has similarly restricted uses.

In their modern form, both the Hebrew and Arabic abjads encode certain vowels. Which instances of which vowels are written and which are not depends on the history of each individual language/script pair.

Abugidas. Abugidas, or alphasyllabaries, are phonographic writing systems that primarily encode consonants, with vowels indicated by diacritics applied to the consonants to modify them in a more or less systematic way. Presently, there are four geographic areas where abugidas are widespread: the Indian subcontinent, Southeast Asia, Ethiopia and Eritrea, and Canada. The very term *abugida* (አቡጊዳ) comes from Ge'ez, the classical language of Ethiopia; like the words *alphabet* and *abjad*, the term was created by stringing along the names of the initial graphemes of the script; in the case of *abugida*, there were four graphemes. In India, the earliest attested abugidas, *Kharoṣṭhī* and *Brāhmī*, date back to 3rd century BCE and were used to write Prakrit, the descendant of Sanskrit, and, in the case of *Brāhmī*, later also Sanskrit (Rogers, 2005). The *Brāhmī* script later evolved into all modern Indic abugidas, the Tibetan abugida, and most abugidas of Southeast Asia. The details of the origins of *Kharoṣṭhī* and *Brāhmī* are debated, but it is likely that they were inspired by Semitic abjads, most likely Aramaic (Rogers, 2005).

In abugidas, an unmodified consonant grapheme usually has an inherent vowel (e.g., /ə/ in Hindi), while other vowels are explicitly marked by diacritics. Abugidas vary in the predictability of the final visual form of the consonant + vowel combination. For instance, in the Ethiopic abugida, the vowel diacritics have merged with the consonant symbols to such an extent that there are irregularities, although the compositionality of the consonant + vowel combinations is still obvious (Rogers, 2005). The absence of a vowel can be indicated in abugidas either via a vowel syncope rule, whereby the inherent vowel is not pronounced in certain contexts, or via a special diacritic. Abugidas also tend to have a certain number of consonantal diacritics. In Canada, a family of abugidas is used to write aboriginal languages, such as the Cree languages and Inuktitut. In these abugidas, vowels are indicated not by diacritics but by rotating the basic consonantal symbol (e.g., Inuktitut ∧ /pi/, > /pu/, < /pa/ and ∩ /ti/, ⊃ /tu/, C /ta/). In addition, there are diacritics that can be used to indicate the consonant in the coda of a closed syllable as well as vowel length. There are also symbols for vowels without a preceding consonant (Rogers, 2005).

In continuation, in Figure 1.3 we illustrate how abugidas with diacritics work using the devanāgarī script. Currently one of the most used writing systems in the world, the script is used to write Hindi (one of the largest languages in the world) alongside other Indian languages, such as Nepali, Marathi, Konkani, and Sindhi.

Moraic scripts and syllabaries. Moraic scripts and syllabaries are similar to abugidas in that they encode units of sound larger than the phoneme. Unlike abugidas, however, the graphemes are not compositional, and there is no predictable relationship between graphemes that share a consonant or a vowel they encode. Take, for instance, these two sets of graphemes from the Cherokee syllabary, an almost exclusively moraic script invented in the 19th century by Sequoyah, a native speaker of Cherokee (Rogers, 2005): R stands for /e/, Ᏺ for /ge/, δ for /le/, and Ꭽ for /me/; Ꮲ stands for /gi/, A for /go/, and J for /gu/. No visual component of the graphemes in the first set can be identified that could be said to represent the phoneme /e/, nor is there a shared component among the graphemes in the second set that can be said to represent the phoneme /g/; rather, the characters must be memorized as a whole. This contrasts with the following characters from the Ethiopic abugida: ጀ stands for /ge/, ለ for /le/, and ␣ for /me/; ጊ stands for /gi/, ጎ for / go/, and ጉ for /gu/. It is apparent that the component of each grapheme that stands for /g/ is the part resembling a hook or an upside-down Latin grapheme J, while the diacritic for /e/ is shaped like a loop or a small Latin letter D.

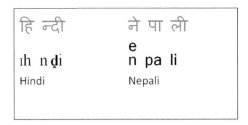

FIGURE 1.3 Diacritics used to mark vowels in Hindi.

FIGURE 1.4 A Japanese sentence using kanji, hiragana, and katakana (LOC = locative, INAN = inanimate, CON = continuative).

The largest and best-known modern language that uses the moraic principle of writing is Japanese. Japanese has a mixed writing system of considerable complexity (see, e.g., Rogers, 2005 for details), in which most texts consist of graphemes belonging to three scripts: (1) *kanji*, based on Chinese characters, which is morphographic in nature and used to write monomorphemic and multimorphemic lexical (content) elements; (2) *hiragana*, which is moraic and largely used to write grammatical morphemes; and (3) *katakana*, which is moraic and mostly used to write loan words. In addition, the Latin script can be used to write certain loan words, acronyms, and brand names.

Figure 1.4 shows a simple Japanese sentence using all three scripts (*Sunshine 60* is the name of a skyscraper in Tokyo). *Tokyo* is written in kanji; both characters are pronounced with their "on" readings, meaning that they are pronounced approximating how they sounded in Chinese at the time when they were borrowed into Japanese. *Sunshine*, obviously borrowed from English, is written in katakana. The remainder of the sentence, which consists of grammatical morphemes, is written in hiragana. It can also be seen from this example that the two kana scripts are moraic rather than syllabic in character.

3.1.3   *The morphographic principle*

Hànzì: a morphographic system. The Chinese writing system, known as 汉字 (in traditional characters: 漢字) or *hànzì* ("Chinese characters"), sharply sets itself apart from most other writing systems currently in use by its morphographic nature. A single Chinese character roughly, but not perfectly, corresponds to a single syllable and a single morpheme. For example, the character 猫 *māo* ("cat") corresponds to one syllable, one free lexical morpheme, and, therefore, a word. There are also polysyllabic morphemes, such as 葡萄 *pútao* ("grape"), written with two characters that do not have a meaning and are never used on their own or in other morphemes and words.

Other polysyllabic morphemes, such as 沙发 *shāfā* ("sofa"), are written with characters that ordinarily stand for other morphemes (in this example, "sand" and "distribute"), but are merely used for their sound in such cases. The typical Mandarin Chinese lexical morpheme, however, is the bound root; such morphemes must obligatorily appear with another root or with a suffix (of which Mandarin does not have many) in order to make up a word. One such root is 房 *fáng* ("house"); it appears in words like 房子 *fángzi* ("house/building/room") and 平房 *píngfáng* ("bungalow") (examples are from Dronjic, 2011). 儿 /ɻ/ is a subsyllabic suffix with a diminutive meaning (e.g., 一点 *yīdiǎn* "a little" (as a quantifier), 一点儿 *yīdiǎnr* "a little.DIMINUTIVE"). More than 70% of Mandarin vocabulary consists of disyllabic, dimorphemic compounds (Institute of Language Teaching and Research, 1986), with compounds making up around 80% of all words (Xing, 2006) and 95% of all neologisms (Ceccagno & Basciano, 2007).

Due to the history of Mandarin and other Sinitic languages, in which syllable structure has been drastically simplified, homophony is rampant. For instance, some of the meanings and ways of writing *xī* are the following: 西 "west", 溪 "creek", 希 "expect", 夕 "evening", 膝 "knee", 稀 "rare", 吸 "inhale", and so forth. These morphemes would have sounded very different in Old Chinese. According to one recent reconstruction (Baxter & Sagart, 2014), 西 "west" could have been /s-nˤər/, 溪 "creek" /kʰˤe/, and 膝 "knee" /s-tsik/. Homophonous morphemes may even share a character, as is the case with 华 *huá*, which means both "Chinese" and "magnificent". Sometimes, different morphemes are just homographs without sharing sound, such as *liǎo* ("know") and *le* ("PERFECTIVE ASPECT"), both written as 了.

Traditionally, Chinese characters have been divided into various categories based on their structure (Xǔ Shèn's ~1st-century CE 六书 *liùshū* "six writings"). Since not all of these categories are relevant in Modern Standard Chinese, this classification is somewhat simplified. As mentioned earlier, Chinese characters have a pictographic origin, and this pictographic nature is still visible in some graphemes. To illustrate, 山 *shān* "mountain" is a stylized depiction of a mountain, and 木 *mù* "wood" is a stylized tree. Other pictograms (sometimes referred to as ideograms) are illustrations of abstract concepts, such as 上 *shàng* "up" and 下 *xià* "down". Such abstract pictograms can also be combined into compound abstract pictograms: for example, 卡 *kǎ* "get stuck/block", which is a combination of "up" and "down" meant to evoke the idea of not being able to go up or down. 卡 is also an example of a semantic-semantic compound (Rogers, 2005), a type of character in which two simple characters are combined based on their meanings to yield a new meaning. Another example of this principle is 明 *míng* "bright" ("sun" + "moon", both concrete pictograms).

The most common type of character is the semantic-phonetic compound. These are characters in which one part indicates meaning and the other indicates sound, created in order to disambiguate earlier phonetic extensions. One well-known example of such a character is 妈 *mā* "mother", which has the semantic component 女*nǚ* "female" and the phonetic component 马 *mǎ* "horse" ("something related to women that sounds like the word for horse" = "mother"). Apart from their regular (free) form, some characters have also developed a bound form, which is used in compound characters. For instance, 人 *rén* "person" has the bound form 亻, as seen in 休 *xiū*, a semantic-semantic compound meaning "rest" (i.e., man leaning against a tree). Due to the significant phonological changes that all Sinitic languages have undergone since the invention of hànzì, phonetic radicals are nowadays only imperfect indicators of pronunciation: Disregarding tone, 26% of phonetic elements faithfully represent the segments of the intended pronunciation (Fan, Gao, & Ao, 1984).

3.2 The impact of script differences on word recognition

3.2.1 The concept of orthographic depth

While it has been suggested that languages end up with writing systems that are optimized for their structure (Frost, 2012), such claims are too strong. It is much closer to the truth that languages have scripts that are compatible with their structure to some extent, but the fact remains that scripts are often adopted though accidents of history – for example, the adoption of the Latin script for languages without a script, thanks to English (Behme, 2012; Seidenberg, 2012). Moreover, as outlined in Treiman and Kessler (2005), in light of the complexities and changing nature of languages and speech, a script cannot be a complete or fully accurate representation of oral language; there need to be trade-offs between learnability and complexity, morphological constancy and phonemic transparency, and the like.

Although the concept of orthographic depth has been characterized variously, virtually all experts envisage depth as a continuum. As discussed in the preceding section, some scripts, for example, Serbo-Croatian, Turkish, or Finnish, are very consistent in how graphemes represent sounds. These scripts are considered shallow. In plain language, this means that it is easy to predict how a word is pronounced on the basis of its spelling. Those scripts with inconsistencies of sundry kinds (e.g., English, Scots Gaelic) or missing graphemes (e.g., abjads such as unvowelized Hebrew or Arabic) are considered deep. Rogers (2005) proposes that depth be assessed according to whether graphemes represent phonemes (a shallow script) versus morphograms (as in Chinese) or "morphophonemes" (i.e., with phonological changes at the morpheme boundary, as in English "electric" and "electricity"). (See also Frost & Katz, 1992.)

Grabe (2009) highlights factors related to consistency, regularity, and completeness in spelling to be considered in an evaluation of orthographic depth.

An excellent addition to these concepts of depth, at least for phonographic scripts, comes from Seymour, Aro, and Erskine (2003), who add the dimension of syllable complexity to the formula for depth. Thus Germanic languages (e.g., German, Danish, English), with a variety of allowable consonant clusters both (phonologically and graphemically) in their onsets and codas (e.g., "strengths"), would be deep in this respect, while Finnish, Italian, and Spanish would be shallow.

The orthographic depth hypothesis (Frost, 2005; Frost & Katz, 1992) posits a continuum of shallow to deep orthography and predicts that the depth of a script has an impact on the processes governing lexical access and, therefore, word recognition. There are numerous models of lexical access, some with dual routes for phonological and visual processing (e.g., Coltheart, 1978) and, more commonly in recent times, with a single route (e.g., Frost, 2005; Seidenberg & McClelland 1989). Most of the debate in this area revolves around when word phonology is activated (pre-lexically, post-lexically, or at-lexically) and to what extent phonology plays a role in lexical access (see Frost, 2005, for a detailed overview).

3.2.2   The orthographic depth hypothesis and L1 reading

Various studies have indicated that the nature of the L1 script has an impact on the cognitive skills used by children when learning to read. A frequently cited study by Hanley and Huang (1997) suggested that, while phonological awareness skills were strongly tied to reading proficiency among English-speaking children, visual processing skills (elicited through a visual paired associates test) were better predictors of reading performance among Chinese-speaking children. However, contrary to theoretical views in earlier decades, phonological awareness has been found to be useful to L1 Chinese-speaking readers – for example, to glean information from the phonetic component of characters, often helpful for pronunciation purposes (Koda, 2005).

To account for the differences in the average ages at which children with L1s with a variety of scripts and orthographies can recognize words effectively, Ziegler and Goswami (2006) propose a "psycholinguistic grain size" theory of reading. Children learning a shallow orthography tend to rely on grapheme-phoneme correspondence rules. English orthography forces readers to adopt multiple recoding strategies (grapheme-phoneme correspondence rules, onset-rhyme patterns, as in "rain" and "pain", and whole-word reading, as in "choir"). The need to juggle different grains during the lexical access process provides one explanation for the fact that English-speaking children lag behind their European counterparts in terms of the time taken to achieve reliable word recognition skills (Ziegler & Goswami, 2006), often remaining at a "partial alphabetic" stage while their counterparts have moved on to a "full alphabetic stage" (Ehri, 2005).

3.2.3   The influence of L1 reading skills on L2 reading skills

Extensive exposure to a particular script appears to mold the brain for reading in that script (Baker et al., 2007; Nakada et al., 2001; Tan et al., 2003). Research has demonstrated that this type of cognitive specialization influences subsequent reading acquisition through memory and visual processes as well as phonological awareness. In general, similarities in L1 and L2 scripts are facilitative, and differences create a few obstacles (Cook & Bassetti, 2005; Koda, 2005).

Thus it is not surprising that Chinese-speaking children coming from a morphographic system tend to show different patterns from their English counterparts when reading regular, irregular, and pseudowords in English (Wang & Geva, 2003). Furthermore, when processing an L2 phonographic script, readers whose L1 scripts are phonographic tend to outperform their counterparts whose L1 scripts are morphographic (Chikamatsu, 1996; Durgunoğlu, Nagy, & Hancin-Bhatt, 1993). The influence of not only a phonographic system but also syllable structure can be seen in Muljani et al.'s (1998) study in which Indonesian-as-L1 readers outperformed Chinese-as-L1 readers in an English word recognition task, especially when the target word was phonotactically allowable in Indonesian.

Chapters 2 and 4 continue the discussion of the influence of script on cognitive and neurolinguistic processing.

4.   SCRIPTS, CULTURE, AND POWER: IMPLICATIONS FOR L1 AND L2 LITERACY

4.1   The democratization of literacy

Much has been written about the democratization of literacy resulting from royal decrees, historical events, government policies, and the like. History has also taken note of the spread of literacy through new technologies – for example, printing presses invented in China, Korea, and Europe, mechanized typesetting in the 19th century, and in the last few decades, computer programming and computerized digital typesetting, which have allowed text to be read on a variety of electronic gadgets (Crystal, 1997; Ong, 2012; Wolf, 2007). (Chapter 9 covers some of the electronic resources available to developing L1 and L2 readers.)

Decisions regarding which scripts should or must be used in a given community often have great symbolic value and far-reaching consequences. When Sejong the Great encouraged the use of the phonographic *hangul* script in Korea (see also Section 3.1.2), the move did not win the approval of the elite literati, who preferred the continued use of morphographic *hanja* and feared that common people, and especially women, could now become literate and disturb the status quo. However, hangul did facilitate the spread of literacy across the less-privileged milieu of the Korean population (Kim-Renaud, 2000; Rogers, 2005). Likewise, Atatürk's replacement of the Ottoman Turkish alphabet (derived from the Arabic script and closely connected to religion) with the Latin script for writing in Turkish marked not only the seculariza-tion of Turkey but also a new wave of literacy in the country, albeit with complications in intergenerational communication through the expunging of Arabic and Persian words (Coulmas, 1989). Interestingly, religion can be the source of the introduction of a new script, as when the combined impact of Catholicism and colonization (by the French) led to the Latinization of the Vietnamese script (formerly *chữ nôm*, a Chinese-derived script, and now *quốc ngữ*) (see Section 3.1.3) (Haudricourt, 1949). Here, too, the use of the Latin-based Vietnamese alphabet has contributed to very high literacy levels in Vietnam, but, as is to be expected, at the expense of a rich classical literature written in *chữ nôm* (Pears, 2004).

While literacy was generally "owned" by an elite minority in the past, whether by scribes, clergy, royalty, or colonizers, today there is widespread agreement that all children should have access to literacy through schooling (Ong, 2012; Wolf, 2007). Those who prevent equal access to education, and thereby literacy, are generally viewed as extremely regressive and chauvinistic. In the words of Malala Yousafzai ("Malala", 2015), "Education is neither eastern nor western. Education is education and it's the right of every human being." The last decades of the 20th century have also marked a transition to "people power" in the area of publishing, with the exception of parts of the world where freedom of speech is significantly curtailed or poverty prevents access to electronic media. People generally do not need to belong to an elite class to publish electronically in blogs, newspapers, e-books, forums, social media, and so on. In line with the view that "electronic literacies" should be available to all citizens of the world (Warschauer, 1999), there are organizations such as Internet.org whose mission it is to provide Internet access to those still lacking it (Internet.org, n.d.).

One of the outcomes of the spread of Internet access worldwide is the proliferation of the Latin script to encode text in not only English but also indigenous languages with non-Latin scripts (e.g., writing Urdu or Greek in the Latin script, as documented in Rosowsky, 2010, and Koutsogiannis, 2015, respectively). While such use of the Internet potentially facilitates reading in an L2 that uses a Latin script – for example, English, French, or Spanish – this also could further marginalize indigenous scripts, and, perhaps temporarily, create new elite groups among school-age children who have access to digital media and, therefore, special opportunities to gain media literacy and use digraphia creatively (Koutsogiannis, 2015). While there have also been attempts to curb the domination of the Latin script – for instance, via the use of Unicode, facilitating the use of most scripts on the Internet and allowing domain names to be written in non-Latin scripts – 55% of websites still use English, with Russian and German remaining a distant second, at less than 6% (w3techs, n.d.).

As for the effect of electronic communication on orthographic conventions, the rules are generally created as needed, mostly on the basis of sociolinguistic, pragmatic, and logistical criteria. Here we see the results of what Ong (2012) called "secondary orality", which coexists with literacy but also influences it with some of the attributes of oral traditions, especially in the areas of style and register. For example, texting, posting on social media, commenting on articles and posts, and similar activities have led to greater informality in writing, as well as both simplifying English orthography and adding a new quirkiness to it. At times, spelling follows the alphabetic principle more closely, as in the use of *tonite* for "tonight", but there also is prolific use of pictograms like <3 (heart symbol) for "love" or <}} for "ice cream". In other cases, the alphabetic and morphographic systems meet, as in *gr8* for "great". An extreme example of anticipated changes in literacy norms in the age of "secondary orality" appear in Penguin's newly released *OMG Shakespeare*, consisting of *YOLO Juliet*, *srsly Hamlet*, *Macbeth #killingit*, and *A Midsummer Night #nofilter*, written in "textspeak" and *emoji* icons (e.g., Juliet tells Romeo to text instead of talking "i don't want my family to [picture of 🐍] you yelling, they'll be srsly upset, I'm talking, like, pissed [picture of frown ☹]") (Flood, 2015).

In light of how scripts and/or orthographies will inevitably change as new generations engage in rapidly evolving digital communication, there is potential for promoting literacy, including digital literacy, through various types of childhood digraphia. In the case of "Greeklish" (Greek written using the Latin script, and often claimed by children to be easier to spell), the solution proposed by Koutsogiannis (2015 p. 90.) is to transport the school literacy curriculum to the digital age and serve both the children whose homes are wired and those who are not: "Schools have to bridge this gap between creative children's out of school literacy practices and monotonous school reality."

The following section presents two vignettes, the first about Serbo-Croatian and the two scripts learned by children in Serbian-speaking areas (the official Serbian Cyrillic alphabet, and the Latin script). The second is about Jamaican-English and Jamaican Creole (Patois). The tug-of-war between the two codes exemplifies a home-school gap (of a different kind from the one described by Koutsogiannis, 2015, earlier) arising from divided opinions about the status of Jamaican Creole as a linguistic code in its own right. Numerous studies have underlined the importance of children becoming literate in the linguistic code that they have oral proficiency in (Lesaux & Geva, 2006). This is especially important in the case of Jamaican Creole, which is often the only code that children are fluent in, but which is often dismissed as being "broken English" with a non-standardized orthography. Yet, Jamaican Creole is an immensely popular medium of electronic communication (Hinrichs, 2006), especially among young people, and thus holds the potential for being the route to child literacy in both Jamaican Creole and Jamaican English.

4.2   Childhood digraphia: reality and potential

4.2.1   *The case of Serbian*

Serbian Digraphia

Serbian, one of the standard versions of the polycentric Serbo-Croatian language, is a rare example of a language extensively written in two equivalent writing systems within the same "sociolinguistic ecosystem". Traditionally, Serbian has been written in the Serbian version of the Cyrillic alphabet, but it has also come to be written in the Latin alphabet used to write the Croatian and Bosnian standard varieties of Serbo-Croatian.

The Serbian constitution stipulates that the Serbian language and the Cyrillic alphabet are official, while the use of other languages and scripts is to be regulated by law (Ivković, 2013). Ivković remarks that both alphabets are in use in Serbia for a variety of reasons: (1) The Latin script was used as a concession to Croats and Bosniaks in the Yugoslav period; (2) The global dominance of the Latin script; and (3) The Serbs, as the largest ethnic group in Yugoslavia, may have been more secure in their cultural identity and therefore have felt little threat from the introduction of the Latin alphabet.

Currently, although the Cyrillic alphabet is the only alphabet with official status in Serbia, government web sites typically appear in two versions: Cyrillic and Latin. Both alphabets can also appear on official documents. For instance, the current version of the Serbian passport has *РЕПУБЛИКА СРБИЈА* (Latin script: *Republika Srbija*; "Republic of Serbia") and *ПАСОШ* (*pasoš*; "passport") written on its cover page, both only in Serbian and in Cyrillic. If one looks at the identification page, the line indicating the bearer's citizenship reads *Држављанство* (Latin script: *državljanstvo*)/*Nationality*/*Nationalité* in Serbian, Cyrillic, English, and French, but the nationality itself is indicated as *SRPSKO* ("Serbian", in the Latin scipt only).

Some general patterns of use in the two alphabets are as follows: Advertisements and packaging are almost exclusively in the Latin alphabet; books, magazines, newspapers, and Internet content tend to be in the Latin alphabet; street signs can appear in both alphabets (Ivković, 2013); road signs tend to appear in both scripts; content associated with the Serbian Orthodox religion and nationalist discourse appears in Cyrillic; and elementary and high school textbooks are in Cyrillic (Ivković, 2013). However, individual writers' choice of alphabet may depend on convenience as well as political and ideological convictions, among other factors.

Figures 1.5, 1.6, and 1.7 illustrate Serbian digraphia (all three photos were taken by Dejan Ivković and are being published here with permission). Figure 1.5 shows the entrance to a currency exchange. The word *currency exchange* appears in both alphabets, as *menjačnica* and *мењачница*; the *open* sign, *отворено* (*otvoreno*), is in Cyrillic, and the two signs that give details about services offered are in the Latin alphabet. Figure 1.6 shows a bookstore called *Азбука* (*Azbuka*), which is the word for the Cyrillic alphabet; the name of

FIGURE 1.5 Money exchange.

FIGURE 1.6 Bookstore.

the business is in Cyrillic, but the word *bookstore* appears in the Latin script: *knjižara*. Similarly, the name of the business next door appears in Cyrillic, but the word *loto* ("lotto") appears in the Latin alphabet. Figure 1.7 shows the name of the longest street in Belgrade; *Bulevar Revolucije* ("Revolution Boulevard") is what the street used to be called during the socialist Yugoslav period. The name was later changed to the original/traditional name: *Булевар Краља Александра* (*Bulevar Kralja Aleksandra*, "King Alexander Boulevard"),

FIGURE 1.7 Street sign.

which appears in Cyrillic. The sign in the middle is the name of the company
that insures the building and appears in Cyrillic.

In sum, the case of the Serbian standard of Serbo-Croatian, where one
language yields literacy in two scripts, is a kind of digraphia that could be
potentially facilitative when readers educated in Serbia, Montenegro, and
parts of Bosnia and Herzegovina begin to read in an L2 that has a Latin or
Cyrillic script. For example, while Serbian Cyrillic and Russian Cyrillic do
not share all of their graphemes and grapheme-phoneme correspondences,
have differing grapheme combinations (mostly due to the phonological

differences between the languages), and differ in certain graphic details (e.g., in cursive and italic styles), a child schooled in the Serbian alphabet could start decoding Russian Cyrillic, or, for that matter, its Bulgarian or Ukrainian counterparts, with some additional learning and practice. (This ability, however, would not necessarily imply comprehension of the texts being decoded.)

Similarly, those schooled in both the Inuktitut syllabary (abugida) and Latin script (as outlined in Section 3.1.2) have the potential advantage of using a language-specific and culturally significant script as well as the more widely used Latin one. (Note that Inuttitut, the dialect spoke in Labrador, is under threat and neither the syllabary nor the Latin script is used to read and write in Inuttitut, as outlined in Sherkina-Lieber & Helms-Park, 2014.)

A potentially greater advantage when reading in a second language might be enjoyed by children in many parts of the Mandarin-speaking world who learn both Mandarin characters and *pinyin* since absorbing the principles underlying the phonographic pinyin alphabet seems to facilitate learning a second-language phonographic script (Cheung, Chen, Lai, Wong, & Hills, 2001; Wang, Perfetti, & Liu, 2005). While a far from perfect system, pinyin is also helpful when non-Chinese speakers are learning L2 Mandarin since being able to pronounce new Mandarin words through pinyin appears to facilitate word learning (Everson, 1998). (For literacy-related facilitative transfer across languages and scripts, see Chapters 3 and 4 of this book.) The use of dual scripts in a situation where each belongs to a fundamentally different writing system – that is, phonographic versus morphographic – poses the thorny question of whether phonographic scripts, by virtue of being more widespread, easier on learners' memories, and more Internet-friendly, will ultimately threaten the existence of the morphographic one (as has been witnessed in Vietnam and Korea in previous eras) (Crystal, 1997, p. 315).

Conversely, there are cases where speakers of near-identical or similar languages use very different scripts. For example, Hindi and Urdu are considered by many to be the same language for morphosyntactic purposes (e.g., Helms-Park, 2001). However, they are separated by minor aspects of their sound systems and some aspects of their lexicon, but more significantly by their scripts (Kachru, 2009). (While the Urdu script is based on the Persian one, which, in turn, derives from the Arabic script, the Hindi script belongs to the devanāgarī group of scripts.) The demographic realities of the region are as follows: Urdu is mostly the language of the Muslims in Pakistan and India, and Hindi and other Indic languages are mostly spoken by other groups in North India; being biliterate in the Urdu and devanāgarī scripts is rare. The one way in which Hindi and Urdu can be mutually intelligible in written form is when they are encoded in the Latin script, learned through English.

4.1.2   The case of Jamaican English and Patois

JAMAICAN CREOLE

As Jamaican is a primarily spoken language, and the government has not implemented an official and accepted orthography; spelling conventions tend to vary across the island as individuals write based on what they perceive as well as their knowledge of English conventions.

The example below shows how one greeting was found to be generally written over text messaging by Jamaicans.

Standard English greeting: *"What's going on?"*

Jamaican Creole greeting:

- **What** *a gwaan?*

- **Wah** *gwaan?*

- **Wha** *gwaan?*

- *What a* **gwan?**

- *Wah* **gwan?**

- *Wha* **gwan?**

In 2012, the New Testament of the Bible was published in Jamaican Creole, entitled *'Di Jamiekan Nyuu Testiment.'*

Below is an example from the text:

Mark 4: 39 Jesus Calms the Storm.

In English it reads, 'Jesus stood up and commanded the wind, "Be quiet!" and he said to the waves, "Be still!"'

In Patois this now reads, 'So Jiizas get op an taak chrang tu di briiz, an tel di sii fi sekl dong.'

Source: United Bible Societies (2012).

With a long history of struggle for status, Jamaican Creole, often referred to as *Patois*, coexists with the nation's official language, English. The linguistic situation in Jamaica parallels those of neighbouring Caribbean island nations once under European colonial rule. Typically, the official language is currently a European language, such as English, Spanish, French or Dutch, while a native creole, often perceived to be of lower status and suitable only for informal communication, is also widely used as a vernacular. Jamaican Creole was born out of the languages in contact during the time of the slave trade: the African languages of the slaves (primarily Akan languages, but also Bantu and Kwa languages) and British English, the language of the slave owners (Patrick, 2006).

In Jamaica today, many perceive Jamaican Creole as "broken English" instead of as a language in its own right since it is an English-based creole and exists alongside English in Jamaica. An added complication is that the Jamaican language situation is often represented along a continuum, with speakers ranging from Standard (Jamaican) English, to various combinations of Patois and Standard English, and to "complete Patois" (Patrick, 1999). An unfortunate outcome of the creole continuum concept, while one way of representing the existence of the two codes, is the connotation that with special training, Patois can "become" standard Jamaican English and that speakers of Patois, the majority in Jamaica, are therefore "semilingual" (Devonish, 2015).

As it is a primarily spoken language, individuals therefore write Jamaican Creole on the basis of what they perceive or invent creatively instead of following an established orthography. Thus, we have what Chang (2012) refers to as Jamaican written the English way and Jamaican written the Jamaican way. When writing Jamaican Creole, many use the known conventions of English orthography to guide their spelling, named "etymological" orthography as it stays true to the traditional lexifier language, English. In contrast, the Cassidy-LePage system, developed in 1961, puts forward an orthographic system for Jamaican Creole that stays true to its phonology (i.e., has clear-cut grapheme-phoneme correspondences) without using Standard English as a reference point (Siegel, 2005). However, it is the minority, made up of linguists and few others, who generally use the phonemic orthographic system, as the Jamaican government has not acknowledged it as the official orthography of Jamaican Creole.

Efforts to create a standardized Jamaican Creole orthography over the years have often been hampered by negative attitudes toward the language itself (i.e., that it does not deserve a fixed orthography). On the other hand, Haitian Creole enjoys a far more favourable status since it was made an official language alongside French in 1987, and to date is used in primary schools as the language of instruction through grades 1–4. In addition, there is an accepted standardized official orthography, "Otograf IPN", that is used, which allows for consistency in spelling practices (Siegel, 2005).

As the Jamaican diaspora in the North American societies continues to grow exponentially, resulting in more speakers of Jamaican Creole moving into schools and workplaces, closer attention needs to be given to policies governing English language literacy instruction for these speakers. Often such children are placed in English-as-a-Second-Language classes, which Bryan (2004), among others, debunks as a poor solution since such classes cater to newcomers to North America with very little English: "Any form of teacher action that embraces stereotypical or undifferentiated language teaching and learning practices will fail these children" (p. 87).

According to Devonish (2015), what the Jamaican Ministry of Education, Youth and Culture's Language Education Policy (2001) promotes is "monoliterate, transitional bilingualism". His claim is that the policy seems to envision a Patois-speaking child becoming fluent and literate in Jamaican English and then mostly abandoning Patois. What Devonish advocates instead is a bilingual and digraphic approach to language instruction and support in Jamaica, in keeping with the belief that both the home code and the school one can develop in harmony (Corson, 2001; Craig, 1976), and furthermore, literacy is best acquired in the language that the child has greatest proficiency in. In this regard, standardizing the orthography of Jamaican Creole would be advantageous. Meanwhile, the possible good news for digraphia in Jamaica is that, while Jamaican English has "overt prestige", Patois has "covert prestige" (Hinrichs, 2006, p. 14), something that is probably helped by its widespread, felicitous use in digital communication.

5. CONCLUSION

The scholarly examination of scripts has moved from being mainly the domain of philology, classical anthropology, and (historical) linguistics to also being central to the investigation of the cognitive, psycholinguistic, and neurolinguistic processes underlying reading, both in primary and non-primary languages. The study of scripts is an especially exciting area of research in the new millennium, which will see traditional forms of literacy and new electronic literacies coexisting peaceably at times and doing battle at others. In short, the very nature of literacy is changing and the processes governing reading in a first or second language script will continue to provide rich material for future research on literacy. Furthermore, rapidly evolving technologies serving language-related research should be able to provide newer and more sophisticated ways of examining the interaction of scripts and literacy.

REFERENCES

Baker, C.I., Liu, J., Wald, L.L., Kwong, K.K., Benner, T., & Kanwisher, N. (2007). Visual word processing and experiential origins of functional selectivity in human extrastriate cortex. *Proceedings of the National Academy of Sciences, 104*(21), 9087–9092.

Baxter, W.H., & Sagart, L. (2014). *Old Chinese: A new reconstruction.* New York: Oxford University Press.

Behme, C. (2012). Can evolution provide perfectly optimal solutions for a universal model of reading? *Behavioral and Brain Sciences, 35,* 279–280.

Boltz, W.G. (1996). Early Chinese writing. In P.T. Daniels & W. Bright (Eds.), *The world's writing systems* (pp. 191–199). New York: Oxford University Press.

Branner, D.P. (2001). Chinese languages: Classical Chinese. In J. Garry & C.R. Galvez Rubino (Eds.), *Facts about the world's languages* (pp. 134–138). New York: Wilson.

Bryan, B. (2004). Language and literacy in a creole-speaking environment: A study of primary schools in Jamaica. *Language, Culture and Curriculum, 17,* 87–96.

Ceccagno, A., & Basciano, B. (2007). Compound headedness in Chinese: An analysis of neologisms. *Morphology, 17,* 207–231.

Chang, L. (2012). Aatagrafi. Retrieved from http://www.jumieka.com/

Changizi, M., Zhang, Q., Ye, H., & Shimojo, S. (2006). The structures of letters and symbols throughout human history are selected to match those found in objects in natural scenes. *The American Naturalist, 167*(5), 117–139.

Cheung, H., Chen, H.C., Lai, C.Y., Wong, O.C., & Hills, M. (2001). The development of phonological awareness: Effects of spoken language experience and orthography. *Cognition, 81*(3), 227–241.

Chikamatsu, N. (1996). The effects of L1 orthography on L2 word recognition: A study of American and Chinese learners of Japanese. *Studies in Second Language Acquisition, 18*(4), 403–432.

Chrisomalis, S. (2009). The origins and co-evolution of literacy and numeracy. In D.R. Olson & N. Torrance (Eds.), *The Cambridge handbook of literacy* (pp. 59–74). Cambridge: Cambridge University Press.

Coltheart, M. (1978). Lexical access in simple reading tasks. In G. Underwood (Ed.), *Strategies of information processing* (pp. 151–216). New York: Academic Press.

Cook, V., & Bassetti, B. (2005). An introduction to researching second language writing systems. In V. Cook & B. Bassetti (Eds.), *Second language writing systems* (pp. 1–67). Clevendon: Multilingual Matters.

Cooper, J.S. (1996). Sumerian and Akkadian. In P.T. Daniels & W. Bright (Eds.), *The world's writing systems* (pp. 37–57). New York: Oxford University Press.

Corson, D. (2001). *Language diversity and education*. Mahwah, NJ: Erlbaum.

Coulmas, F. (1989). *Writing systems of the world*. Oxford: Blackwell.

Coulmas, F. (1999). *The Blackwell encyclopedia of writing systems*. Oxford: Blackwell.

Craig, D.R. (1976). Bidialectal education: Creole and standard in the West Indies. *International Journal of the Sociology of Language, 1976*(8), 93–136.

Cruz-Urube, E. (2001). Scripts: An overview. In D.B. Redford (Ed.), *The Oxford encyclopedia of ancient Egypt* (Vol. 3, pp. 192–188). New York: Oxford University Press.

Crystal, D. (1997). *The Cambridge encyclopedia of language* (2nd revised ed.). Cambridge: Cambridge University Press.

Daniels, P.T. (1996). *The first civilizations*. In P.T. Daniels & W. Bright (Eds.), *The world's writing systems* (pp. 21–32). New York: Oxford University Press.

Daniels, P.T., & Bright, W. (Eds.). (1996). *The world's writing systems*. New York: Oxford University Press.

Dehaene, S., (2009). *Reading in the brain: The new science of how we read*. New York: Penguin.

Devonish, H. (2015). Stop demonizing Patois – From a semi-lingual to a bilingual Jamaica. Retrieved June 15, 2015, from http://jamaica-gleaner.com/gleaner/20120826/cleisure/cleisure2.html

Dronjic, V. (2011). Mandarin Chinese compounds, their representation, and processing in the visual modality. *Writing Systems Research, 3*, 5–21.

Durgunoğlu, A.Y., Nagy, W.E., & Hancin-Bhatt, B.J. (1993). Cross-language transfer of phonological awareness. *Journal of Educational Psychology, 85*(3), 453.

Ehri, L.C. (2005). Development of sight word reading: Phases and findings. In M.J. Snowling & C. Hulme (Eds.), *The science of reading: A handbook* (pp. 135–154). Oxford: Blackwell.

Everson, M. E. (1998). Word recognition among learners of Chinese as a foreign language: Investigating the relationship between naming and knowing. *The Modern Language Journal, 82*(2), 194–204.

Fan, K. Y., Gao, J. Y., & Ao, X. P. (1984). Pronunciation principles of the Chinese character and alphabetic writing scripts. *Chinese Character Reform, 3*, 23–27.

Fischer, S. R. (2004). *History of writing*. London: Reaktion Books.

Flood, A. (2015, June 12). Shakespeare goes textspeak. *The Guardian*. Retrieved from http://www.theguardian.com/culture/2015/jun/12/omg-shakespeare-penguin-random-house-yolo-juliet-srsly-hamlet-textspeak

Frost, R. (2005). Orthographic systems and skilled word recognition processes in reading. In M. J. Snowling & C. Hulme (Eds.), *The science of reading: A handbook* (pp. 272–295). Oxford: Blackwell.

Frost, R. (2012). Towards a universal model of reading. *Behavioral and Brain Sciences, 35*, 263–279.

Frost, R., & Bentin, S. (1992). Reading consonants and guessing vowels: Visual word recognition in Hebrew orthography. *Advances in Psychology, 94*, 27–44.

Grabe, W. (2009). *Reading in a second language: Moving from theory to practice*. Cambridge: Cambridge University Press.

Haudricourt, A. (1949). L'origine des particularités de l'alphabet vietnamien [The origin of the peculiarities of the Vietnamese alphabet]. *Dân Việt-Nam, 3*, 61–68. Retrieved from https://halshs.archives-ouvertes.fr/file/index/docid/920064/filename/Haudricourt1949_Peculiarities_MonKhmerStudies2010.pdf

Helms-Park, R. (2001). Evidence of lexical transfer in learner syntax. *Studies in Second Language Acquisition, 23*(1), 71–102.

Hinrichs, L. (2006). *Codeswitching on the Web: English and Jamaican creole in e-mail communication*. Amsterdam: Benjamins.

Huang, H. S., & Hanley, J. R. (1997). A longitudinal study of phonological awareness, visual skills, and Chinese reading acquisition among first-graders in Taiwan. *International Journal of Behavioral Development, 20*(2), 249–268.

Institute of Language Teaching and Research. (1986). 现代汉语频率词典 [Modern Chinese frequency dictionary]. 北京语言学院出版社 [Beijing: Beijing Language Institute Press].

Internet.org. (n.d.). Making the Internet affordable. Retrieved June 6, 2015, from https://internet.org/about

Ivković, D. (2013). Pragmatics meets ideology: Digraphia and non-standard orthographic practices in Serbian online news forums. *Journal of Language and Politics, 12*, 335–356.

Justeson, J. S., & Kaufman, T. (1993). A decipherment of epi-Olmec hieroglyphic writing. *Science, 259*, 1703–1711.

Kachru, Y. (2009). Hindi-Urdu. In B. Comrie (Ed.), *The world's major languages* (2nd ed., pp. 470–489). New York: Routledge.

Katz, L., & Frost, R. (1992). The reading process is different for different orthographies: The orthographic depth hypothesis. In R. Frost & L. Katz (Eds.), *Orthography, phonology, morphology and meaning* (pp. 67–84). Amsterdam: Elsevier Science.

Kaufman, T., & Justeson, J. (2001). Epi-Olmec hieroglyphic writing and texts. In *The proceedings of the Maya hieroglyphic workshop: The coming of kings; Epi–Olmec writing, March 10–11, 2001, University of Texas at Austin* (pp. 93–224). Available at: http://www.albany.edu/pdlma/EOTEXTS.pdf

Kim-Renaud, Y. (2000). Sejong's theory of literacy and writing. *Studies in the Linguistic Sciences, 30*(1), 13–46.

Koda, K. (2005). *Insights into second language reading: A cross-linguistic approach.* New York: Cambridge University Press.

Koutsogiannis, D. (2015). Translocalization in digital writing, orders of literacy, and schooled literacy. In S. Bulfin, N. Johnson, & C. Begum (Eds.), *Critical perspectives on technology and education* (pp. 183–200). New York: Palgrave Macmillan.

Laufer, B. (1997). What's in a word that makes it hard or easy? Intralexical factors affecting the difficulty of vocabulary acquisition. In N. Schmitt & M. McCarthy (Eds.), *Vocabulary: Description, acquisition and pedagogy* (pp. 140–155). Cambridge: Cambridge University Press.

Ledyard, G. (1997). The international linguistic background of the correct sounds for the instruction of the people. In Y.K. Kim-Renaud (Ed.), *The Korean alphabet: Its history and structure* (pp. 31–87). Honolulu: University of Hawai'i Press.

Lesaux, N.K., & Geva, E. (2006). Synthesis: Development of literacy in language-minority students. In D. August & T. Shanahan (Eds.), *Developing literacy in second-language learners* (pp. 53–74). Mahwah, NJ: Erlbaum.

Macri, M.J. (1996a). Maya and other Mesoamerican scripts. In. P.T. Daniels & W. Bright (Eds.), *The world's writing systems* (pp. 172–182). New York: Oxford University Press.

Macri, M.J. (1996b). Rongorongo of Easter Island. In P.T. Daniels & W. Bright (Eds.), *The world's writing systems* (pp. 183–188). New York: Oxford University Press.

Malala Yousafzai. (2015). The Biography.com website. Retrieved June 4, 2015, from http://www.biography.com/people/malala-yousafzai-21362253

Martínez, M.D.C.R., Ceballos, P.O., Coe, M.D., Diehl, R.A., Houston, S.D., Taube, K.A., & Calderón, A. D. (2006). Oldest writing in the New World. *Science, 313*, 1610–1614.

Michalowski, P. (1996). Mesopotamian cuneiform: Origin. In P.T. Daniels & W. Bright (Eds.), *The world's writing systems* (pp. 33–36). New York: Oxford University Press.

The Ministry of Education, Youth and Culture. (2001). *Language education policy.* Kingston, Jamaica: Ministry of Education, Youth and Culture.

Muljani, D., Koda, K., & Moates, D.R. (1998). The development of word recognition in a second language. *Applied Psycholinguistics, 19*(1), 99–113.

Nakada, T., Fujii, Y., & Kwee, I. (2001). Brain strategies for reading in the second language are determined by the first language. *Neuroscience Research, 40*(4), 351–358.

Nakamura, K., Dehaene, S., Jobert, A., Le Bihan, D., & Kouider, S. (2005). Subliminal convergence of Kanji and Kana words: Further evidence for functional parcellation of the posterior temporal cortex in visual word perception. *Journal of Cognitive Neuroscience, 17*(6), 954–968.

Norman, J. (1988). *Chinese.* Cambridge: Cambridge University Press.

Ong, W.J. (2012). *Orality and literacy: The technologizing of the word.* New York: Routledge.

Patrick, P. (1999). *Urban Jamaican creole: Variation in the mesolect.* Amsterdam: Benjamins.

Patrick, P. (2006). Language in Jamaica. In K. Brown (Ed.), *Encyclopedia of language and linguistics* (2nd ed., Vol. 6, pp. 88–90). Amsterdam: Elsevier.

Paulesu, E., McCrory, E., Fazio, F., Menoncello, L., Brunswick, N., Cappa, S.F., & Frith, U. (2000). A cultural effect on brain function. *Nature Neuroscience, 3*(1), 91–96.

Pears, P. (2004). *Remnants of empire in Algeria and Vietnam: Women, words, and war.* Oxford: Lexington Books.

Rao, R.P., Yadav, N., Vahia, M.N., Joglekar, H., Adhikari, R., & Mahadevan, I. (2009). Entropic evidence for linguistic structure in the Indus script. *Science, 324*, 1165–1165.

Ritner, R.K. (1996). Egyptian writing. In P.T. Daniels & W. Bright (Eds.), *The world's writing systems* (pp. 73–87). New York: Oxford University Press.

Robinson, A. (2014). The New World begins to write: The Zapotec and Isthmian scripts (Mexico). In C. Moseley (Ed.), *Writing systems* (Vol. 1, pp. 136–151). New York: Routledge.

Rogers, H. (2005). *Writing systems: A linguistic introduction.* Malden, MA: Blackwell.

Rosowsky, A. (2010). "Writing it in English": Script choices among young multilingual Muslims in the UK. *Journal of Multilingual and Multicultural Development, 31*(2), 163–179.

Saturno, W.A., Stuart, D., & Beltrán, B. (2006). Early Maya writing at San Bartolo, Guatemala. *Science, 311*, 1281–1283.

Seidenberg, M.S. (2012). Writing systems: Not optimal, but good enough. *Behavioral and Brain Sciences, 35*, 305–307.

Seidenberg, M.S., & McClelland, J.L. (1989). A distributed, developmental model of word recognition and naming. *Psychological Review, 96*(4), 523.

Seymour, P.H., Aro, M., & Erskine, J.M. (2003). Foundation literacy acquisition in European orthographies. *British Journal of Psychology, 94*(2), 143–174.

Sherkina-Lieber, M. & Helms-Park, R. (prepublished). A prototype of a receptive lexical test for a polysynthetic heritage language: The case of Inuttitut in Labrador. *Language Testing.* Prepublished 15/15/2014, DOI: 10.1177/0265532214560799

Siegel, J. (2005). Literacy in pidgin and creole languages. *Current Issues in Language Planning, 6*(2), 143–163.

Sproat, R. (2014). A statistical comparison of written language and nonlinguistic symbol systems. *Language, 90*, 457–481.

Tan, L.H., Spinks, J.A., Feng, C.M., Siok, W.T., Perfetti, C.A., Xiong, J., & Gao, J.H. (2003). Neural systems of second language reading are shaped by native language. *Human Brain Mapping, 18*(3), 158–166.

Treiman, R., & Kessler, B. (2005). Writing systems and spelling development. In M. J. Snowling & C. Hulme (Eds.), *The science of reading: A handbook* (pp. 120–134). Oxford: Blackwell.

United Bible Societies. (2012). *Some examples Bible in Patois from the new Jamaican New Testament.* Retrieved from http://www.biblesociety.org.uk/press/uploads/Some-examples-Bible-in-Patois-from-the-new-Jamaican-New-Testament_10082628.pdf

Vinckier, F., Dehaene, S., Jobert, A., Dubus, J.P., Sigman, M., & Cohen, L. (2007). Hierarchical coding of letter strings in the ventral stream: dissecting the inner organization of the visual word-form system. *Neuron, 55*(1), 143–156.

w3techs. (n.d.). Usage of content languages for websites. Retrieved June 13, 2015, from http://w3techs.com/technologies/overview/content_language/all

Wang, M., & Geva, E. (2003). Spelling performance of Chinese children using English as a second language: Lexical and visual orthographic processes. *Applied Psycholinguistics, 24*, 1–25.

Wang, M., Perfetti, C.A., & Liu, Y. (2005). Chinese-English biliteracy acquisition: Cross-language and writing system transfer. *Cognition, 97*(1), 67–88.

Warschauer, M. (1999). *Electronic literacies: Language, culture, and power in online education*. Mahwah, NJ: Erlbaum.

Wolf, M. (2007). *Proust and the squid: The story and science of the reading brain*. Cambridge: Icon.

Xing, J. Z. (2006). *Teaching and learning Chinese as a foreign language: A pedagogical grammar*. Hong Kong: Hong Kong University Press.

Ziegler, J., & Goswami, U. (2006). Becoming literate in different languages: similar problems, different solutions. *Developmental Science*, 9(5), 429–36.

2

Reading, brain, and cognition

Vedran Dronjic and Tali Bitan

INTRODUCTION

In this chapter, we survey the neurocognitive underpinnings of reading. It is often remarked that, unlike spoken language, which evolved in humans over an extremely long period of time and has likely been around in its modern form for at least 100,000 years, reading and writing are relatively recent additions to our cognitive repertoire. The oldest confirmed writing systems are approximately 5,000 years old (see Chapter 1, this volume), and literacy has become truly widespread only over approximately the last century. This means that, while our brains had a chance on an evolutionary time scale to adapt to language, reading is a process that we are forced to perform with whatever cognitive resources are available. It is also often remarked that, while spoken language is acquired by all normally developing and healthily socialized children, with no explicit instruction required, learning how to read is a laborious and deliberate process that requires extensive instruction and practice. With this in mind, it is quite remarkable that reading functions as seamlessly as it does in skilled readers.

The chapter begins with an overview of the basic anatomical and physiological facts pertaining to the human visual system, tracing the visual signal from the environment to the brain's primary visual cortex. We then present a survey of how readers' eyes move around the page while deciphering written language and what properties of the text and of the reader influence the pattern of eye movements and fixations during the course of reading. We rely on data coming from studies conducted with novice and skilled first language readers and in various languages and scripts. While eye tracking has recently started to be used in second language processing research, it currently serves as a proxy for studying various aspects of language processing rather than as an object of inquiry in its own right.

Next, we turn our attention to the issue of the complexity of language and reading and to the automaticity of processing as the primary cognitive prerequisite for efficient reading. These issues are considered against the backdrop of what the nature and limitations of the human memory system mean for linguistic functioning in native and non-native languages across the lifespan.

We then address the topic of the neural network underlying reading in a first language, followed by a survey of what is known about the neural basis of second language reading and of reading in various scripts. The topic of the neural evidence for interactions between the first and second languages in the brain is also addressed. (For behavioural aspects of transfer in reading, see Chapter 5, this volume. For more on how different types of writing systems encode language and a brief summary account of the implications this has for reading processes, see Chapter 1.) The chapter concludes with a brief discussion of the implications all of the foregoing has for reading instruction as well as some directions for future research. We limit the scope of this review to lower-level reading processes because the neurocognitive underpinnings of these aspects of reading are currently better understood than those of higher-level processes, such as text comprehension and inferencing. (For a review of higher-level processes from a reading science perspective, see Chapter 6, this volume.)

THE VISUAL SYSTEM

Vision is the complex process of converting the four-dimensional reality of space-time via three-dimensional spatial scenes in individual moments in time to two-dimensional images at the back of our eyes and then perceiving these two-dimensional images as three-dimensional and, ultimately, with the addition of the time factor, four-dimensional again in our mind (Palmer, 1999).

The human eye gathers light reflected off the surfaces of objects and converts it into electrochemical neural activity. The cornea and lens have the function of focusing light on the back of the eye, where the retina is located. The retina contains photoreceptors, cells that are capable of converting light into neural activity, of which two types are of interest – rods and cones. Rods are extremely sensitive to light, but cannot detect colour, while cones require much more light in order to produce a response, but are highly responsive to colour and fine detail.

Photoreceptors pass on their neural signal to ganglion cells, whose axons converge at the back of the eye to form the optic nerve at what is referred to as the optic disk or the blind spot, since it contains no photoreceptors. There is a spot right at the back of the eye which contains a high concentration of cones, called the fovea. It is at this spot, which covers only approximately 2 degrees (or 1%) of our visual field, that the acuity of our vision is the highest (Lauwereyns, 2012; Palmer, 1999). The fovea is crucially important for most vision, including reading. The rest of our visual field, which includes the parafoveal (4 degrees left and right of the foveal region) and peripheral fields of vision, is mostly covered by rods (with a much smaller proportion of cones), and, consequently, as will be seen ahead, can be of only limited use in visual tasks that hinge on high levels of precision, such as reading.

Visual information from the left half of the retina in the left eye and the left half of the retina in the right eye, containing information about the right visual field, is directed toward the left hemisphere of the brain. Conversely, information from the left visual field, collected by the right half of the retina in each eye, is directed toward the right cerebral hemisphere. Thus, optic nerve fibres from the inner half of each retina need to cross over to the opposite side of the head. This happens at the optic chiasm (or chiasma). Beyond this point, the neural fibres carrying visual information (now from the left or right visual field exclusively) toward the brain are referred to as the optic tract. Past the optic chiasm, a very small proportion of visual information is diverted toward the superior colliculi of the midbrain, a pair of structures in the brainstem that plays a role in detecting movement in the visual field and orienting us toward that movement, including participation in the programming of eye movements.

Most of the visual information reaches the two lateral geniculate nuclei of the thalamus, structures anatomically adjacent to the superior colliculi. The thalamus directs visual information on to the primary visual cortex in the brain's occipital lobe. This cortex is organized topographically, such that visual information originating in adjacent regions of the retina is processed in adjacent regions of the primary visual cortex (Banich, 2004; Palmer, 1999), but inverted both vertically and horizontally. Moreover, many more neurons in the primary visual cortex are dedicated to processing foveal relative to peripheral information, a phenomenon known as cortical magnification. The visual cortex plays a role in initial visual processing – for instance, the detection of lines and edges (and, consequently, form), spatial frequency, orientation, movement, and colour (Palmer, 1999; also Banich, 2004; Farah, 2000). It passes on its inputs to higher-order visual cortical areas and also receives feedback from them, which serves to modify its activity. We return to details of the neural underpinnings of reading later in this chapter.

EYE MOVEMENTS DURING READING

In normal daily functioning, humans are constantly moving their eyes. Despite our impression that visual perception is smooth and continuous, our eyes jump from point to point while examining any visual scene. In fact, our eyes are incapable of keeping perfectly still even when we are fully intent on staring at a single point in space. There are three different kinds of eye movements which occur during eye fixation (typically referred to as fixational eye movements): drift, tremor, and microsaccades. Drift comprises small, slow eye movements that take place during fixation, while tremor consists of even smaller eye movements that occur during drift. Microsaccades are small, involuntary, jerky, high-velocity eye movements which occur a few times per second, interrupting the slower drift movements. When an image is experimentally kept perfectly still on our retinae, it quickly disappears from vision, a phenomenon known as perceptual fading. The available research suggests that drift and microsaccades play a joint role in preventing perceptual fading and controlling fixation position (Rolfs, 2009).

The basic mechanics of reading

In the process of reading, fixations are the periods when our eyes rest on a portion of the text we are viewing and extract relevant visual information about the identity of the words we are attempting to recognize. Fixations range in duration from 50 to 500 milliseconds, with the mean typically falling somewhere in the range of 200 to 280 milliseconds (Engbert, Longtin, & Kliegl, 2002; Staub & Rayner, 2007).

While fixational eye movements, discussed earlier, are of great interest in vision science and psychophysics, they do not serve as a source of information in eye-tracking investigations of reading. Reading research is primarily concerned with saccades, eye movements which occur between fixations, and which help bring different portions of the text into the foveal field of vision, where they can be recognized. Saccades are very fast eye movements; a saccade during reading lasts about 20–50 milliseconds (Rayner & Juhasz, 2006; Staub & Rayner, 2007) and takes about 150 milliseconds to program. The programming of saccades happens in parallel with lexical processing (Engbert et al., 2002), and their execution is ballistic in nature, which means that once a saccade is programmed and initiated, its course and destination cannot be altered, although it is always possible to plan and execute an additional compensatory saccade in the event of undershoot or overshoot (Palmer, 1999).

The length of the average saccade for readers of English is between 7 and 9 letters, but with considerable variability, ranging from 1 to 20 characters (Staub & Rayner, 2007). Saccades are shorter in scripts with more densely packed information, such as Hebrew, Arabic, Japanese, and Chinese. Most saccades move the eyes forward. In skilled readers, about 10% to 15% of the saccades move the eyes backwards in order to resolve processing difficulties (Rayner & Juhasz, 2006). These backward saccades are referred to as regressions. Return sweeps are large backward saccades used to move the eyes from the end of one line of text to the beginning of the next, and they precede as many as 20% of all fixations in reading (Hofmeister, Heller, & Radach, 1999).

The brain deceives the reader

It is worth noting that there are many points during the process of visual perception (which includes reading) when the brain intervenes in a top-down fashion to alter perception. For instance, we do not normally perceive the blind spots in our vision caused by the two optic discs in our eyes, nor do we perceive the dense network of blood vessels superimposed on our retinae. Under normal conditions, the brain compensates for these discontinuities in our visual field and fills them in. Another example of top-down compensation for discontinuity in our vision is the fact that fixational eye movements and saccades do not disrupt our perception of the world around us as a seamless, perfectly focused picture. Nor do we perceive a blur during saccades, a phenomenon referred to as saccadic suppression.

Various accounts of saccadic suppression have been advanced, such as: (1) the masking of the blurred perception by the sharp and well-focused images received by the brain, although it is not clear exactly how this masking would happen (Palmer, 1999), (2) the inhibition of certain types of visual information during saccades (for more details, see Banich & Scalf, 2003), and (3) certain neurons reversing their usual pattern of activity to effectively cancel out the impression of movement generated by other neurons (Thiele, Henning, Kubischik, & Hoffmann, 2002). While it is possible that saccadic suppression results from a combination of mechanisms such as the ones listed here, recent research suggests that it is largely due to an active neural mechanism (Knöll, Holl, & Bremmer, 2013), but the exact link between neural activity and the behavioural reality of saccadic suppression is as yet unclear (Ibbotson & Krekelberg, 2011).

Where to fixate a word

What follows provides a good illustration of the makeshift nature of reading alluded to at the opening of this chapter. In fluent reading, we program saccades so that the eyes will land in a certain location within the word. However, we routinely miss this position and land in a different spot. Moreover, neither of the two locations actually corresponds to the place in the word that is optimal for word recognition! (See Figure 2.1.)

In languages with alphabetic writing systems, saccades in reading seem to be aimed at the middle of the word that is to be fixated (Deutsch & Rayner, 1999). Blank spaces between words are crucial in saccade programming (Staub & Rayner, 2007). For Chinese text, written without word boundaries, there are indications that the programming of saccades depends on whether parafoveal segmentation of words is successful; if the right boundary of the word can be determined, a saccade is launched with respect to the center of the word, and if not, the initial fixation is at the beginning of the word (Yan, Kliegl, Richter, Nuthmann, & Shu, 2010). In reading Chinese, saccade programming does not appear to depend on word length, but seems to be the product of a complex interaction of character and word properties (Li, Liu, & Rayner, 2011).

The optimal viewing position (OVP) is the point in a word at which the word needs to be fixated to yield optimal recognition as indicated by lexical decision, word naming, and perceptual identification performance. In normal reading, the eyes do not tend to land in the OVP; this is achieved only in experiments where the fixation point is manipulated by researchers. In alphabetic scripts written left to right, the OVP is left of the middle of the word (Shillcock, 2007). Success at word identification with respect to fixation point follows an inverted J-shaped curve, with best identification at the OVP, somewhat worse performance at the beginning of the word, and the worst performance toward the end of the word.

In Arabic and Hebrew, languages written from right to left, in which mostly consonants are orthographically represented, there is no OVP asymmetry (Deutsch & Rayner, 1999; Farid & Grainger, 1996). This is likely a consequence of these languages' templatic morphology, in which discontinuous roots are interwoven with inflectional and derivational patterns (transfixes) largely consisting of vowels, many of which are not written. It has also been shown that the presence of a prefix in Arabic moves the OVP toward the left and the presence of a suffix moves it toward the right, while the effect of morphology is much subtler in French (Farid & Grainger, 1996). Deutsch and Rayner demonstrate that, similar to Arabic, the location of the OVP in Hebrew also depends on morphology (specifically the position of the root within a word), but that attentional, hemispheric dominance and morphological factors also play a role. There is also an OVP asymmetry toward the beginning of the word in the Japanese hiragana syllabary, written from left to right or

FIGURE 2.1 Different fixation points for the English word *reading*. The "X" indicates the programmed fixation point, the triangle indicates the optimal viewing point (OVP), and the circle indicates where the fixation may actually tend to occur in fluent reading – the preferred viewing location (PVL).

top to bottom, and it is more pronounced in the vertical text alignment (Kajii & Osaka, 2000).

As mentioned earlier, readers' eyes usually land neither at the middle of the word nor at the OVP, but in alphabetic writing systems written from left to right, in a position to the left of the OVP, referred to as the preferred viewing location (PVL). This is assumed to happen due to saccadic under-shoot. The position of the initial fixation is computed based on attentional and word-length factors, but is not determined by morphological structure (Deutsch & Rayner, 1999). The preference for fixating words left of the middle emerges as early as one year into the learning-to-read process (Ducrot, Lété, Sprenger-Charolles, Pynte, & Billard, 2003). In Hebrew, the PVL is located toward the beginning (the right-hand side) of the word (Deutsch & Rayner, 1999).

Variability, change, and adaptation

The number and duration of fixations made on any given word in normal reading depend on factors such as: word length, word frequency, morphologi-cal structure, lexical semantic factors, inter-word transition probabilities, syntactic structure, and discourse organization (Brysbaert & Vitu, 1998; Rayner & McConkie, 1976; Staub & Rayner, 2007). The average fixation lasts between 200 and 250 milliseconds (Rayner & Juhasz, 2006), with quite a bit of variability, ranging anywhere from 100 to over 450 milliseconds. Most of the duration of the fixation is not spent on visual processing but rather on linguistic and conceptual processing (Staub & Rayner, 2007). Experienced readers do not obtain useful visual information equally on both sides of the fixation point. Rather, this area is skewed in the direction of the script, such that it is larger to the right of the fixation for scripts written left to right and to the left of the fixation for scripts written right to left. This skew is not due to perceptual but rather to attentional factors (Pollatsek, Bolozky, Well, & Rainer, 1981); it is not evident in novice readers, but emerges as early as one year after beginning to learn how to read (Rayner & Juhasz, 2006). This asymmetrical area of text from which readers are able to extract visual infor-mation is referred to as the perceptual span. In English, it extends 3 to 4 characters to the left of the fixation and 14 or 15 characters to the right. In writing systems in which information is more densely packed, the percep-tual span is narrower. For experienced Chinese readers, the span is 1 character to the left and 2 to 3 characters to the right of the fixation when the text is oriented left to right (Inhoff & Liu, 1998).

There is a narrower region within the perceptual span from which infor-mation useful for word recognition can be obtained, usually referred to as the word identification span, which ranges, in English text, from the left boundary of the perceptual span to about 7 or 8 letter spaces right of the fixation (Underwood & McConkie, 1985), and thus includes the foveal (3 or 4 letters to the left and to the right of the fixation) and parafoveal regions. Phonological information can be extracted from the parafoveal region (Pollatsek, Lesch, Morris, & Rayner, 1992), but not morphological or semantic information (Rayner & Juhasz, 2006), at least not in linearly written alphabetic orthographies (see next paragraph), whereas the peripheral region of vision can provide only very general visual information about the layout of the text, including estimations of word length (Staub & Rayner, 2007). The amount of information available from the parafoveal word preview depends on the word currently being fixated and the context it occurs in, such that less information is obtained from the parafovea when the word is difficult to process due to low frequency or syntactic complexity of the sentence (Henderson & Ferreira, 1990).

More recent findings indicate that, contrary to what was believed earlier, semantic information can be extracted from the parafoveal preview in Chinese and Korean (Kim, Radach, & Vorstius, 2012; Yan, Richter, Shu, & Kliegl, 2009; Yang, Wang, Tong, & Rayner, 2012). While the Chinese orthography is morphosyllabic in character and is predominantly meaning-based, the Korean writing system is alphabetic, but written in syllabic blocks which visually superficially resemble Chinese characters. Both writing systems are informationally dense. For Chinese, the parafoveal semantic effect may be due to information density, the semantic nature of the writing system, and the need for the reader to predict whether the following character is an independent word or part of a morphologically complex word (in order to facilitate saccade programming). For Korean, the preview effect may be a consequence of information density and may be further catalyzed by the right-branching syntax of the language, which may increase the need for rapid structural disambiguation (Kim, Radach, & Vorstius, 2012).

Under normal conditions, skilled readers fail to fixate about 20% of the content words and well over 50% of the function words in a text (Carpenter & Just, 1983). In general, shorter words, more frequent words, and more familiar words (n.b., these dimensions tend to covary and are partially conflated), and words predictable from context are skipped more often, with the availability of visual information from parafoveal preview still being the most important factor (Staub & Rayner, 2007).

Eye movements during reading show clear developmental trends. Compared to novice readers, skilled readers perform longer saccades, shorter fixations, fewer fixations, and fewer regressions and refixations (Rayner, 1998). The same set of contrasts in saccades and fixations can be evoked by presenting a reader with texts of varying levels of difficulty, with difficult texts triggering behaviour that mirrors the behaviour of less skilled readers (Rayner & Juhasz,

2006). Novice readers also show more variability in eye movement behaviour (McConkie et al., 1991).

A note on eye movements in L2 reading

As can be seen from the foregoing, there is a considerable amount of eye movement research in L1 reading that has had eye movement behaviour as its primary focus. In other words, eye tracking has been both the instrument and the object of study in this type of research. There is also a separate and sizeable literature in which eye movements during reading are used to investigate various aspects of language processing other than the mechanics of reading proper, such as lexical access, the organization of the mental lexicon, morphological processing, syntactic processing, and discourse processing. On the other hand, eye tracking has only recently started being used in second language processing research (Keating, 2014; Roberts & Siyanova-Chanturia, 2013; Winke, Godfroid, & Gass, 2013). While the number of studies is growing rapidly, the focus of this work has been L2 lexical processing, the organization of the bilingual mental lexicon, and L2 syntactic processing rather than the mechanics of eye movements during reading as an object of inquiry in their own right. Since the focus of this section is on eye movements themselves rather than on more general aspects of language processing, the existing L2 research will not be elaborated on here (but see, e.g., Roberts & Siyanova-Chanturia, 2013, for a recent review).

Overwhelmingly, the assumption in this emerging L2 research has been that shortcomings in L2 knowledge and processing (relative to the L1 baseline) will have behavioural manifestations similar to those found in novice readers or observed when skilled readers engage with texts of increasing difficulty. In other words, difficulties in L2 processing, as well as, presumably, lower as opposed to higher levels of L2 proficiency, should be reflected in longer fixation durations, a greater number of fixations and refixations, more regressions, and shorter saccades.

While these are reasonable assumptions, differences between L1 and L2 readers are bound to be not only quantitative but also qualitative. A number of additional factors must be considered when using eye movements in L2 research, such as the inevitable variability in L2 users' proficiency levels, processing efficiency (i.e., fluency), learning history, other languages spoken (particularly the writing systems that these languages use), and the nature and amount of exposure to L2 print. It is at present unclear to what extent the foregoing affects the validity and reliability of the existing L2 research. Research on L2 reading eye movement behaviour itself and how this varies with all of the factors discussed earlier is needed and, at present, unavailable.

AUTOMATICITY AND FLUENCY IN
LANGUAGE AND READING

We owe our ability to do much of what we are able to accomplish to the fact that we do not have to focus on the details of executing the vast majority of complex tasks – that is, the structure of the required operations, their sequencing, and timing. For instance, when walking, we do not have to think about what muscles to activate, in what way, to what extent, and in what temporal sequence. In all normally functioning individuals, all that is required is an intention to walk. The process takes care of itself once initiated. If we were forced to focus on the details of every complex operation we attempted to perform, we would be overwhelmed to the point of being unable to function.

The human brain's ability to store information over extended periods of time (long-term memory) is vast and, for all practical intents and purposes, boundless. On the other hand, our ability to store information over very short periods, on the time scale of a few seconds (short-term memory), is severely limited. Similarly limited is our ability to shift the focus of our attention between two temporarily stored sets of information or between a temporarily stored set of information and the demands of an ongoing cognitive task, typically referred to as working memory (e.g., Baddeley, 2000; Baddeley & Hitch, 1974; Engle, Kane, & Tuholski, 1999). The precise nature of this bottleneck in our cognition is still not well understood, neither in terms of the exact processing capacity of working memory (Miller, 1956; also, Cowan, 2001, 2005; Oberauer, 2002; Verhaeghen, Cerella, & Basak, 2004), nor in terms of the exact mechanism that gives rise to the limitations (Engle, Cantor, & Carullo, 1992; Halford, Wilson, & Philips, 2001; Towse, Hitch, & Hutton, 1998; see also Dehn, 2008).

Using language is possibly the most sophisticated cognitive task regularly performed by humans. Regardless of whether we are producing language or interpreting it, the complexity of the undertaking is striking; apart from creating and comprehending complex messages, in which concepts and ideas are predicated onto one another, specified, complemented, modified, and then structured into cohesive and coherent, pragmatically appropriate discourse, we also encode and decode these complex messages using a cognitive system of enormous intricacy.

Whether speaking, comprehending speech, reading, or writing, with very high accuracy, we retrieve just the words we require from a mental store of many tens of thousands of items almost instantaneously, an endeavour which entails linking a meaning and a set of abstract sound units (phonemes). We figure out how these abstract units are mapped onto specific acoustic features, and we link specific acoustic features to sequences of motor programs, all while simultaneously constructing or interpreting complex grammatical (syntactic and morphological) structures that specify numerous properties of the various parts of the utterance (e.g., gender, number, case, animacy, evidentiality, tense, voice, mood, aspect, specificity, definiteness).

All this happens at a breakneck pace; when using language at a normal speed, competent speakers utter or comprehend at least 15 sounds (or five syllables) per second and are able to utter or comprehend a proposition (a complete simple thought) in about 1.5 seconds, all while keeping track of discourse and monitoring themselves and the interlocutor for errors, and remaining able to correct errors and understand such corrections, to maximize the efficiency of the communicative exchange, and to repair communication breakdowns when these occur. And, of course, all of the foregoing happens against a rich backdrop of countless other cognitive processes taking place in the brain simultaneously.

Reading entails numerous additional processes: (1) the rapid recognition of graphemes, which can range in number from under thirty to several thousand and can occur in innumerable visual variations (e.g., bold, cursive, different fonts, different handwriting), (2) the rapid retrieval of the sound information encoded by the written form of the word, and (3) the rapid activation of the meaning associated with the orthographic and phonological form of the word.

The retrieval of meaning can follow a number of different routes (see also Chapter 3, this volume; Carreiras, Armstrong, Perea, & Frost, 2014; Norris, 2013; Rastle, 2007; Stanovich, 1980). We can convert graphemes to phonological units (phonemes, onsets and rhymes, syllables) and assemble these into the spoken form of the word. We can see a word and retrieve its sound in a more holistic fashion, such as when we read the digit "4" or the Chinese character "风", in which no specific part of the written form corresponds to any particular part of the spoken form. We can also link the word's visual form and its meaning directly. Finally, morphemes, the smallest meaningful (or consistently recurring) units of language, also play a role in word recognition and present us with another possible route for retrieving word meanings while we read (see, e.g., Kuperman, Schreuder, Bertram, & Baayen, 2009; also Dronjic, 2011; Marslen-Wilson, 2007).

Language processing, including reading, is made possible by the fact that the myriad cognitive processes involved are able to run in parallel, without interfering with each other or dipping into our limited pool of attentional resources. Current neurologically plausible models of language representation in the brain (Paradis, 2004; Ullman, 2004, 2015) posit that languages acquired from birth (and whose acquisition is not interrupted until adulthood) largely rely on two at least partially distinct kinds of long-term memory for storage and computation. Declarative long-term memory, typically involving awareness, relies on bilateral medial temporal lobe structures, the hippocampi and parahippocampal cortices, as well as temporal and other distributed neocortical structures. It is said to underlie lexical semantic as well as sociopragmatic knowledge. Procedural long-term memory, involved in the learning of skills, including sequences of motor and cognitive operations, is able to function independently of awareness and relies on neural circuits connecting left prefrontal and other cortical areas, the left basal ganglia and thalamus, with inputs from the cerebellum. It is said to underlie combinatorial and probabilistic aspects of language knowledge, such as syntax, at least certain aspects of morphology, phonology, and knowledge about transitional probabilities (Paradis, 2004; Ullman, 2004, 2007, 2015). However, just as is the case in motor learning, in many learning experiences procedural learning and declarative learning occur in parallel and may interact and complement each other (Robertson, 2009; Song, 2009). The declarative system is quick to learn (often after just one exposure), but it is also more prone to decay and forgetting (Drosopoulos, Wagner, & Born, 2005; Fenn & Hambrick, 2013). The procedural system, on the other hand, is slow to learn, but is also more resistant to forgetting and interference (Ghilardi, Moisello, Silvestri, Ghez, & Krakauer, 2009). However, in the field of motor learning, it has been shown that adults tend to rely more on declarative memory, while children tend to rely more on procedural learning for a given task (Nemeth, Janacsek, & Fiser, 2013; Thomas & Nelson, 2001). If applied to language learning, this may have critical implications for the effect of age on second language acquisition.

Much of the core language processing L1 speakers do, such as mapping the acoustic signal on phonology, decoding orthography (in skilled readers), and parsing morphological and syntactic structure, unfolds without a need for conscious awareness, and, indeed, without relying on verbal short-term and working memory as typically measured by tests such as forward and backward digit span and reading span (Caplan & Waters, 1999; Gathercole, 2007; Martin, 2005). In L1 processing, our limited short-term and working memory resources come into play only in second-pass reinterpretation of already processed material, in the building of semantic models of text and discourse comprehension, and in guiding behaviour based on comprehended instructions. They are also important for lexical acquisition (Gathercole, 2007; also Ellis, 2005; Perani, 2005).

Processing that operates below the threshold of consciousness and without the involvement of working memory is considered to be automatized. A cognitive process is said to be automatic when it has the following characteristics: (1) it is rapid; (2) it is ballistic (i.e., unstoppable once it has been initiated); (3) it does not require conscious attention and, therefore, does not compete for working memory resources; and (4) it is consistent (i.e., reliable, accurate, displays low time-course variability) (see, e.g., Segalowitz, 2010).

Second language learners are typically required to perform in the L2 almost immediately despite the fact that automatized knowledge emerges only very slowly, following extensive exposure to stimuli and a considerable amount of repetition. They manage to perform by relying on the declarative system to deal with even those types of language knowledge that would otherwise preferentially be delegated to procedural memory – that is, grammatical knowledge (Clahsen & Felser, 2006; Paradis, 2009; Ullman, 2015) – at least over the initial and intermediate stages of second language learning (Caffarra, Molinaro, Davidson, & Carreiras, 2015; Morgan-Short, Finger, Grey, & Ullman, 2012; Paradis, 2009; Ullman, 2015). Such compensatory, effortful, and deliberate processing also inevitably involves working memory.

This means that, apart from having to deal with higher-order communicative processes, such as strategic planning, monitoring, reinterpretation, building discourse models, and so on, L2 users', including L2 readers', attentional resources are additionally taxed by the conscious, effortful nature of much of the ongoing lower-level processing, including word recognition, morphological parsing, and syntactic parsing. This leads to the types of inconsistent and dysfluent, non-native-like language performance that is typically observed in L2 learners.

In reading, L2 learners' difficulties are compounded by less efficient word decoding skills (LaBerge & Samuels, 1974; Perfetti, 1988). The retrieval of the phonological, morphological, and semantic aspects of a visually presented word is much less efficient and consistent in a second language, even when the L1 and L2 have very similar writing systems, but even more so when these systems are different (Dronjic, 2013; Favreau & Segalowitz, 1983; Segalowitz & Freed, 2004; Segalowitz & Segalowitz, 1993; Tzeglov, Henik, Sneg, & Baruch, 1996). Similarly, even advanced second language readers' processing of inflectional and derivational morphology during L2 sentence reading and its integration into syntactic context is demonstrably less automatic than native speakers' (Dronjic, 2013).

Reading fluency is typically conceived of as involving accuracy, automaticity, and the accurate use of prosody (Kuhn, Schwanenflugel, & Meisinger, 2010) and is considered to be "a critical component of reading development" (p. 230). In reading aloud, the presence of natural-sounding prosody, with appropriate intonation, stress, and pauses, is seen as an indicator of automatized lexical, morphological, and syntactic processing. The speed and accuracy of decoding are typically tested by having participants read lists of isolated words or lists of sentences in a given amount of time. Moreover, they can be evaluated by using experimental psycholinguistic techniques, such as various versions of primed and unprimed lexical decision tasks, word-naming tasks, self-paced reading tasks, eye tracking, mouse tracking, and so forth.

Fluency of visual word recognition critically hinges on multiple opportunities to successfully recognize a word (Logan, 1997). Fluency instruction, such as massive exposure to print and various assisted reading techniques, has been shown to improve fluency as well as text comprehension in children who are learning to read (Kuhn & Stahl, 2003). Fluency, both in terms of increased speed and in terms of increased automaticity of lexical access, has also been shown to improve through L2 study, both in at-home and in study-abroad contexts (Segalowitz & Freed, 2004).

To sum up, fluent, automatic processing of vocabulary (including visual word decoding), morphology, and syntax is crucial for efficient L2 reading. Due to the nature of learning ability and human memory, the only way that automaticity can be attained is through massive amounts of practice, which can be ensured via continuous exposure to the second language. The effect of age on second language acquisition, including learning to read, is still an open question. At present, adult L2 learners' ability to make significant gains in the fluency of L2 lexical access is the least contentious. It also appears that learners are able to automatize the processing of L2 grammar (see, e.g., Caffarra et al., 2015; Morgan-Short, Finger, Grey, & Ullman, 2012), and there are also preliminary indications that positive transfer from the first language may play an additional facilitative role (Dronjic, 2013). The upper bounds of adult learners' ability to ultimately attain native-like patterns of L2 representation and processing are currently unknown, but the picture is not as discouraging as traditionally assumed. Patterns of brain activity in L2 processing appear to converge on L1 patterns with increased experience with a language and with higher proficiency levels (Abutalebi, Cappa, & Perani, 2005). Behavioural studies have not as yet identified a single domain of second language processing in which late starters are not able to attain native-like levels of performance, but they have also not been able to identify an individual who performs in the native range across all tested areas (Abrahamsson & Hyltenstam, 2009).

THE BRAIN NETWORK UNDERLYING SKILLED READING AND READING ACQUISITION IN A FIRST LANGUAGE

The introduction of neuroscientific imaging methodologies toward the end of the 20th century had a dramatic effect on our understanding of the neural and cognitive basis of reading and reading acquisition. The most influential neuroimaging methods for reading research include *structural* imaging in MRI, enabling us to localize brain lesions, quantify grey and white matter volume in specific areas, track connecting pathways of white matter, and measure their integrity. Methods measuring brain *function* include the earlier positron emission tomography (PET) and later functional magnetic resonance imaging (fMRI), providing localization of brain activation during task performance, as well as event-related potentials (ERP) and magnetoencephalography (MEG), providing higher-resolution measures of temporal changes in brain signals. Earlier neuropsychological reading models, which relied on ex-vivo pathological studies of brains of patients with acquired reading disorders, consisted of a simple linear model which included, besides Broca's area (that corresponds to parts of the left inferior frontal gyrus) and Wernicke's area (the posterior part of the left superior temporal gyrus), the visual cortex and the left angular gyrus, suggested to be the "written word form area" by Dejerine (1892, quoted in Dehaene, 2009, p. 75). In comparison to this rather simple model, the host of brain regions suggested to be involved in different aspects of reading in current models is much larger and more complex (see Plate 1).

The area whose discovery is mostly attributed to technological developments in neuroimaging methods is the left ventral occipito-temporal cortex (vOT), an extrastriate region in the left mid-fusiform gyrus. This area is part of the ventral visual stream, on the ventral surface of the brain, which includes regions associated with visual object and face recognition. It is consistently activated when visual words are presented (Turkeltaub, Eden, Jones, & Zeffiro, 2002), it is left lateralized (McCandliss, Cohen, & Dehaene, 2003), and its activity is invariant to the font or case of written letters, suggesting its representation of graphemes is abstract (Dehaene et al., 2001). It was therefore termed the "visual word form area" (VWFA) (Cohen & Dehaene, 2004; Cohen et al., 2000), suggesting its unique involvement in the orthographic processing of familiar words and word parts (Dehaene & Cohen, 2011). The VWFA is the left anterior tip of a bilateral stream of visual regions, organized along a posterior-anterior gradient, with growing selectivity to units of larger size, from individual letters and bigrams in posterior parts of the occipital lobe to larger chunks of familiar words in anterior parts of the temporal lobe (Vinckier et al., 2007). However, the selectivity of the anterior vOT to words over pictures of objects, and whether it represents orthographic processing or generic advanced visual processing, is still under debate (Price, 2012; Price & Devlin, 2003; Schlaggar & McCandliss, 2007).

As mentioned earlier, given the recency of the invention of writing in the timeline of human evolution, brain regions involved in reading could not be innately adapted to this task, but rather to more ancient functions, such as visual object recognition and spoken language (Dehaene & Cohen, 2007; McCandliss et al., 2003). Expertise for reading must therefore be acquired from the individual's reading experience. Indeed, developmental studies have shown increased selectivity in activation in vOT, and increase in left lateralization of this region with age and acquisition of reading experience (Brown et al., 2005; Schlaggar et al., 2002; Shaywitz et al., 2007; Turkeltaub, Gareau,

Flowers, Zeffiro, & Eden, 2003). The connectivity from this region and its effect on phonological processing regions, even in non-phonological tasks, also increase with age (Booth, Mehdiratta, Burman, & Bitan, 2008), suggesting a growing automaticity in the connections from orthography to phonology with reading experience. Activation in vOT increases with reading instruction even when illiterate adults learn to read in their first language (Dehaene et al., 2010). Finally, activation in left vOT is reduced in individuals with developmental dyslexia, across orthographies (Brunswick, McCrory, Price, Frith, & Frith, 1999; Paulesu et al., 2001). These findings, together with evidence for the role of vOT in the fluent reading of connected text (Benjamin & Gaab, 2012), show the critical role of this region in acquiring skilled reading regardless of age.

Consistent with cognitive models of visual word recognition, such as the dual route model (Coltheart, Rastle, Perry, Langdon, & Ziegler, 2001) and connectionist models (e.g., Plaut, McClelland, Seidenberg, & Patterson, 1996), suggesting that orthographic processing is connected to both phonological and semantic processing, neuroimaging studies show that the left vOT interacts with both semantic and phonological processing networks. The ventral lexical semantic stream includes the inferior and middle temporal gyri (ITG and MTG), and inferior frontal (IFG) pars orbitalis and pars triangularis, while the dorsal phonological stream includes the superior temporal gyrus (STG), supramarginal gyrus (SMG) inferior parietal lobule (IPL), and inferior frontal gyrus (IFG), pars opercularis (Booth et al., 2008; Dehaene, 2009; Jobard, Crivello, & Tzourio-Mazoyer, 2003; Mechelli et al., 2005; Yoncheva, Zevin, Maurer, & McCandliss, 2010). The existence of both forward and feedback connections between the left vOT and these regions suggests that the left vOT integrates bottom-up visual orthographic information with top-down phonological and semantic effects (Dehaene & Cohen, 2011; Price, 2012; Schlaggar & McCandliss, 2007).

Mapping from the orthography to the phonology of visually presented words is typically associated with the left supramarginal gyrus (SMG) and the dorsal part of the left IPL (Graves, Desai, Humphries, Seidenberg, & Binder, 2010; Jobard et al., 2003). These areas are more active when reading pairs of English words with inconsistent spelling-to-sound correspondence (Bitan et al., 2007). The left IPL has been consistently shown to be affected in individuals with developmental dyslexia, showing hypoactivation in functional imaging studies (Maisog, Einbinder, Flowers, Turkeltaub, & Eden, 2008; Shaywitz et al., 2002; Temple et al., 2003) and reduced integrity of the underlying white matter pathways in structural imaging studies (Beaulieu et al., 2005; Ben-Shachar, Dougherty, & Wandell, 2007). Other areas associated with the phonological processing of visually presented words are the left STG also involved in the phonological processing of spoken words (Turkeltaub et al.,

2002), and the left IFG pars opercularis, also involved in articulatory planning for speech production (Fiez & Petersen, 1998). All these regions (left opercularis, left SMG, and left STG) show greater activation for phonological than for semantic decisions on written words (McDermott, Petersen, Watson, & Ojemann, 2003; Price & Mechelli, 2005) and for reading pseudowords compared to words (Binder et al., 2003; Fiebach, Friederici, Muller, & von Cramon, 2002; Vigneau et al., 2006).

Semantic processing of visually presented words is carried out by the same network of regions involved in the semantic processing of spoken words (Vigneau et al., 2006). An MEG study comparing visual and auditory words showed overlap in the pathways from about 400 milliseconds after stimulus presentation, in left anterior temporal and inferior prefrontal regions (Marinkovic et al., 2003). Another area critically involved in mapping orthography to semantics is the left angular gyrus, in the posterior part of the temporo-parietal junction (Graves et al., 2010; Seghier, 2013). The angular gyrus is also involved in non-linguistic functions, such as number processing or the default mode network, indicating that it is a cross-modal hub, integrating multisensory information in order to comprehend events. Finally, lexical semantic retrieval is strongly associated with activation in the anterior part of the left IFG, pars orbitalis (BA 47) (Vigneau et al., 2006), while the triangularis part of the left IFG has been associated with lexical retrieval as well as semantic working memory (Fiebach et al., 2002; Jobard et al., 2003). Overall, activation during semantic processing in lateral temporal and prefrontal regions appears to be more bilateral than activation during phonological processing (Vigneau et al., 2011), with activation in the right temporal lobe typically associated with semantic integration and comprehension processes, such as drawing inferences (Jung-Beeman, 2005). Finally, activation in the left pars orbitalis (BA 47) and in the left MTG during reading also increases with age and with reading experience (Turkeltaub et al., 2003).

EVIDENCE FROM THE BRAIN ON READING IN
A SECOND LANGUAGE

Our knowledge about the brain network underlying reading in skilled readers and beginners can provide some insights into the cognitive basis of reading in a second language. Some of the questions that have been the focus of interest of neuroscientific research in this field are: Do bilinguals and monolinguals apply different mechanisms to reading in a given orthography? Do bilinguals employ different reading pathways when reading in each of their languages? Do these differences depend on the properties of the orthography and the structure of the corresponding spoken languages? Or are they determined by the individual's order and age of acquisition of each orthography and the individual's reading fluency in this orthography? What are the inter-actions between the first and second languages during reading? Does reading in one language affect reading in another language?

Differences between orthographies

Before discussing the effects of reading in first compared to second languages, it is important to consider differences and similarities in the brain mechanisms supporting reading in different orthographies even as they are read by native speakers. Previous research has shown that a large portion of the reading network is common across readers of different orthographies (Bolger, Perfetti, & Schneider, 2005; Dehaene, 2009). It has even been suggested that the con-straints of the brain's visual perceptual system have shaped the evolution of writing systems, so that they all share the same basic properties, such as having high density and high contrast marks, being combined hierarchically into larger and more complex units, and being connected to both sounds and meaning (Changizi et al., 2006). These properties best fit the organization and capabilities of the extrastriate visual perceptual cortex, adapted for visual object recognition during evolution, and its connections with regions associ-ated with phonological and semantic processing (Dehaene, 2009). The shared features across orthographies can, in turn, explain some of the universalities found in the neural processing of written language.

Despite the shared network underlying reading in different languages, there are also some important differences, which can be attributed to properties of the writing systems, such as alphabetic versus logographic writing systems, or orthographies with different levels of transparency (or depth). Other dif-ferences in the reading process are attributed to differences in the structure of the spoken language, such as the linearity of morphemes, the semantic transparency of morphemes, or the proportion of homophones in the lan-guage (Bick, Goelman, & Frost, 2011; Frost, 2012). Although such differences between orthographies can also manifest themselves when comparing groups of monolinguals reading in their respective native languages, such comparisons are confounded by individual and cultural differences, as well as differences in educational and reading instruction policies. Some of these confounds can be avoided when studying bilinguals reading in two languages, although, of course, these studies have their own set of confounds, such as the order and age of reading acquisition in each language, and the relative reading compe-tency in the two languages.

Many fMRI studies, including three meta-analyses (Bolger et al., 2005; Tan, Laird, Li, & Fox, 2005; Zhu, Nie, Chang, Gao, & Niu, 2014), compared reading in alphabetical and Chinese logographic writing systems (n.b., the Chinese script is more accurately characterized as morphosyllabic, although it is commonly cited as a surviving example of the logographic writing principle; see Chapter 1, this volume). These studies consistently show activation unique for alphabetical writing systems in left superior temporal and temporo-parietal cortices suggested to be involved in mapping orthography to phonology (Bolger et al., 2005; Tan et al., 2005). In contrast, activation unique for reading in logographic writing systems was found in the left middle frontal gyrus, interpreted as reflecting greater reliance on motor spelling representations, to facilitate memorizing the large number of characters in the script (Bolger et al., 2005; Tan et al., 2005; Zhu et al., 2014). Finally, activation in the vOT, associated with orthographic processing of visual words (Dehaene, Le Clec, Poline, Le Bihan, & Cohen, 2002), is left lateralized in readers of alphabetical orthographies and is more bilateral in logographic writing systems (Bolger et al., 2005; Tan et al., 2005). One interpretation for this difference suggests that the left vOT supports local visual processing, which is required for distinguishing between characters in both types of scripts, whereas the right vOT supports global visual spatial processing, which is required more for processing the global shape of Chinese characters and the spatial relations among radicals within them (Nelson, Liu, Fiez, & Perfetti, 2009). Alternatively, the difference in lateralization may be related to differences in orthographic transparency (Mei et al., 2013) or to attentional differences in the size of mapping units from orthography to phonology (Yoncheva, Blau, Maurer, & McCandliss, 2010), with smaller, grapheme-phoneme units in alphabetical orthographies and larger units in logographic writing systems.

Even within alphabetical writing systems, orthographic transparency (depth) may have an effect on the reading process. Transparent (shallow) orthographies, such as Spanish or Italian, with consistent mapping of orthography to phonology, have been suggested to enhance the readers' reliance on mapping of orthography to phonology, compared to more opaque (deep) orthographies, like English. A classic PET study in English and Italian monolinguals (Paulesu et al., 2000) showed greater activation in the left STG, associated with phonological processing, in Italian readers and greater activation in the left ITG, and the left ventral IFG, associated with lexical retrieval, in English readers. A similar effect of orthographic transparency was found in Spanish-English bilinguals, showing greater activation for the more transparent Spanish orthography in the left STG (Meschyan & Hernandez, 2006). However, this difference is confounded by the fact that bilinguals in this study were less proficient in Spanish compared to English, which could account for increased activation. Another study that examined early Spanish-English bilinguals with matched proficiency across languages did not find differences in these regions (Jamal, Piche, Napoliello, Perfetti, & Eden, 2012).

MANY WAYS TO READ YOUR VOWELS: EFFECTS OF ORTHOGRAPHIC TRANSPARENCY AND FAMILIARITY ON READING HEBREW WORDS

One approach used to study effects of orthographic transparency within individuals is examining Semitic languages, such as Arabic and Hebrew, with dual script versions (Bourisly, Haynes, Bourisly, & Mody, 2013; Weiss, Katzir, & Bitan, 2015). In the pointed version of the Hebrew script (and in vowelized Arabic text) diacritic marks represent vowels in a transparent manner, whereas in the unpointed version (and unvowelized Arabic) vowels are only sparsely represented by vowel letters, which can also represent consonants. In a recent study with adult Hebrew readers (Weiss et al., 2015) we examined the effect of reading with and without diacritic marks in addition to comparing the reading of words with and without vowel letters. It should be noted that although diacritic marks, which provide full and unambiguous vowel information, are used in the early stages of Hebrew reading instruction, they are not typically used in texts read after Grade 4. In contrast, vowel letters, which provide sparse and ambiguous vowel information, are nevertheless frequently used in some Hebrew words throughout the reader's lifespan. Indeed our results showed that diacritic marks did not facilitate word recognition behaviourally. Diacritics also *increased* brain activation in the left SMG and the left IPL associated with mapping orthography to phonology and in the left IFG, pars triangularis, associated with lexical retrieval, suggesting that diacritics increased the demands of reading in both of these pathways (see Plate 2.A). In contrast, vowel letters, which facilitate reading of unpointed words behaviourally, showed an opposite effect of *decreased* activation in the same regions (see Plate 2.B and 2.C), indicating reduced effort in mapping orthography to phonology and lexical retrieval. Altogether, these results suggest that the effect of familiarity overrides the effect of orthographic transparency and that adult skilled readers benefit from increased orthographic transparency in reading only when this does not interfere with the familiarity of the word forms. The critical effect of familiarity and the amount of practice will also be evident in the effect of proficiency in reading a second language, as discussed in the following section.

Proficiency and effort

When considering differences in the brain network supporting reading in first and second languages, a critical factor, beyond differences in the structure of the orthography, is the individual's level of proficiency in the two written and spoken languages. Neuroimaging studies of spoken language processing in bilinguals show that participants' proficiency and amount of language exposure determine brain activation in a second language more than the order or the age of acquisition of the languages (Chee, Hon, Lee, & Soon, 2001; Mechelli et al., 2004; Perani et al., 1998, 2003). Similarly, neuroimaging studies of reading in a first language show more activation for words with low familiarity, frequency, and imageability (Ischebeck et al., 2004; Pugh et al., 2008). Consistent with this literature, reading studies in bilinguals often find greater activation for reading in the less proficient language, indicating more effortful processing and greater involvement of explicit control mechanisms (Rao, Mathur, & Singh, 2013). Although there is some evidence for increased activation in visual areas for reading in the more familiar language (Vingerhoets et al., 2003), and increased activation in the vOT during learning new letter-sound associations (Hashimoto & Sakai, 2004), most studies show the reversed pattern – namely, reduced activation with increased proficiency. For example, Japanese English low-proficiency bilinguals showed greater activation in reading English compared to Japanese words (both Kanji and Hiragana) in the left ventral IFG (BA 47) and the left angular gyrus, suggesting greater effort in word retrieval in the low-proficiency language (Buchweitz, Mason, Hasegawa, & Just, 2009). Similar results were shown in an fMRI study of semantic and syntactic processing of German written sentences, comparing L1 German speakers to Russian-German bilinguals with lower proficiency in German. L2 German speakers showed more activation than L1 speakers in the left IFG, MTG, and STG, indicating greater effort for reading their less proficient L2 (Rueschemeyer, Zysset, & Friederici, 2006).

Further evidence for the greater processing demands required for reading in a second, less proficient language comes from structural imaging studies, measuring the integrity of white matter connecting pathways. These studies show that in comparison to English monolinguals, Chinese-English bilinguals showed stronger correlation between English reading and white matter integrity under the anterior cingulate gyrus associated with response conflict monitoring (Cummine & Boliek, 2013). Chinese-English bilinguals also showed a stronger correlation between English reading and right hemisphere pathways connecting language homologue regions (Bakhtiari, Boliek, & Cummine, 2014). Although these findings can also be attributed to the higher cognitive demands associated with reading a second language, they can also suggest that mechanisms associated with reading Chinese are recruited for reading their second language, as will be discussed ahead.

Interactions between first and second languages in reading

An important piece of the puzzle for understanding reading in a second language is the extent to which reading in a second language activates representations of the native language. The question of activating representations of the non-target language in bilinguals has been widely studied in relation to spoken language. These studies typically show that lexical and phonological representations of the non-target language are activated not only when the target language is the second language but also even when processing in their native language (Spivey & Marian, 1999; van Hell & Dijkstra, 2002). The specific question related to reading is whether orthographic representations of the non-target language have a similar status to semantic and phonological representations and whether they are automatically accessed when reading in a second language. In such studies it is important to control the setting of the experiment and to have only a single language tested per session, because a multilingual context and shifting between languages might enhance the tendency to activate the non-target language. This was done in ERP studies of Chinese-English bilinguals reading in their second language (English) (Thierry & Wu, 2007; Wu & Thierry, 2010). Participants performed a semantic judgment task on pairs of English words, with an implicit manipulation on the Chinese translations of these words: some of the pairs contained either a sound or a spelling repetition. The results show modulation of the ERP signal when the Chinese translation of the presented English words contained a sound repetition but not a character repetition (Wu & Thierry, 2010). These results suggest that participants activate the phonological but not the orthographic representations of words in their native language when reading in their second language, at least in languages with different orthographies, such as English and Chinese.

Given the automatic activation of lexical and phonological representation of the non-target language, it may be expected that bilinguals would develop enhanced processing abilities relative to monolinguals, even for processing their native language. The continuous need to exert control and inhibit competition from the irrelevant language in bilinguals has been suggested to result in the "bilingual advantage" (Bialystok, Craik, Klein, & Viswanathan, 2004), a higher capacity than in monolinguals to control interference, which is manifested even in non-linguistic tasks. Specifically for reading, bilinguals show greater activation in language areas compared to monolinguals even when reading in their native language (Jones et al., 2012), which may reflect greater efforts required for suppressing interference from the second language. An fMRI study of Italian-English and English-Italian bilinguals shows a positive correlation between proficiency in their second language and activation during reading words in their first language in the left IFG pars orbitalis, associated with word retrieval (Nosarti, Mechelli, Green, & Price, 2010). These results suggest that being a proficient reader in a second language (perhaps especially one that is written with the same writing system as the first language) increases the competition and interference from the second language with respect to lexical semantic access in the first language. Thus, the stronger activation for proficient second language readers reflects the effort it takes to suppress interference from this language.

Accommodation and assimilation

The concepts of "accommodation" and "assimilation", suggested by Perfetti et al. (2007), summarize some of the complexities found in reading a second language, as they address both the effects of properties of the writing systems and the order of reading acquisition in the two languages. In assimilation, the same brain mechanisms associated with reading the first language are applied to reading a second language, resulting in minimal differences between languages within bilingual readers. However, because both languages are read with the mechanisms relevant to the first language, the critical factor that determines the reading process is the order – namely, which language was read first. In contrast, accommodation is the process by which the brain mechanisms applied for reading in a second language are different from those applied for reading in the first language. This may be a result of unique requirements of the second language orthography, resulting in differences between languages, regardless of the order of language acquisition.

The processes of assimilation and accommodation are both evident in the pattern of activation in the vOT, associated with orthographic processing, in English-Chinese and Chinese-English bilinguals. Comparisons of monolingual speakers of these languages showed more bilateral activation in this region in Chinese readers and left lateralization in English readers (Bolger et al., 2005; Tan et al., 2005). However, bilingual readers show different patterns of activation in the vOT depending on which language is more dominant. An fMRI study compared two groups of bilinguals: proficient Chinese-English bilinguals and low-proficiency English-Chinese bilinguals (Nelson et al., 2009). They found that proficient Chinese-English bilinguals activated bilateral vOT when reading in both languages, whereas non-proficient English-Chinese bilinguals activated the left vOT when reading English words and bilateral vOT when reading in Chinese. The authors conclude that the results in the proficient Chinese-English bilinguals reflect the processes of assimilation, because they applied the mechanisms used for reading in their first language to their second language. In contrast, the results of the English-Chinese group reflect the process of accommodation, because they use a different reading mechanism to read in each one of their languages, adapting to the requirements of the newly learned Chinese orthography. The authors suggest that the writing system of readers' first language has a critical role in how their reading network adapts to reading in a new writing system. Chinese orthography requires both local visual processing (identifying strokes in radicals) and global visual processing (identifying spatial relationships between radicals in characters), whereas reading English requires mostly local visual processing. Therefore, visual orthographic processes developed for Chinese can assimilate the reading processes of English, but not vice versa; hence the assimilation process is asymmetrical (Nelson et al., 2009; Perfetti et al., 2007). It should be noted, however, that the two bilingual groups in the aforementioned study differed both in order of language acquisition and in proficiency in the second language. Therefore, it is not yet clear which one of these factors is critical in determining the processes of assimilation and accommodation.

Other studies have also found combined effects of the properties of the orthography and language dominance on the neural mechanisms applied in reading (Das, Padakannaya, Pugh, & Singh, 2011; Ibrahim & Eviatar, 2009; Tan et al., 2003). Another example of assimilation is related to the left middle frontal gyrus, uniquely activated in reading Chinese as compared to alphabetical orthographies (Bolger et al., 2005; Tan et al., 2005; Zhu et al., 2014). In an fMRI study (Yokoyama et al., 2013), Chinese and Korean native speakers were compared when learning to read Japanese words. Japanese words were written in the kana script, which is a phonographic writing system, similar to the Korean writing system (albeit syllabic rather than alphabetic), and unlike Chinese. The results showed greater activation in the left middle frontal gyrus for native Chinese speakers compared to native Korean speakers while they were reading Japanese words. These findings suggest that native Chinese readers assimilated the reading process for L2 Japanese words into the existing mechanisms that serve for reading in their first language, demonstrating the critical role of the dominant language, at least in early stages of reading acquisition in a second language. A different study shows the process of accommodation in late proficient Indonesian-Chinese bilinguals, in a measure of functional connectivity between language regions. These bilinguals showed stronger connectivity between the left STG and left IFG when reading Indonesian (which has an alphabetic orthography) relative to reading Chinese words, presumably due to more reliance on phonological processing (Huang et al., 2014).

LEARNING TO READ IN A NOVEL LANGUAGE:
THE EFFECT OF READING INSTRUCTION ON
THE BRAIN MECHANISMS INVOLVED IN
READING A NEW ORTHOGRAPHY

What is the most effective instruction method for learning to read in a second language? Does the instruction method determine the types of reading mechanisms that develop? These questions were addressed in a study with adult participants receiving multisession training in reading an artificial orthography using Morse-like graphemes consisting of two symbols each. Participants were trained in one of three conditions: (1) Letter-Alph – practice reading alphabetical words with prior direct letter instruction; (2) Word-Alph – practice reading alphabetical words with only whole-word instruction; (3) Word-Arb – practice reading non-alphabetical words which cannot be decomposed into letters. Results show that direct letter instruction (Letter-Alph) resulted in the highest level of generalization to reading untrained words composed of the same letters (Bitan & Booth, 2012; Bitan & Karni, 2004) and a strong activation in the left IFG pars opercularis, associated with phonological segmentation, indicating the development of decoding skills for the new script (see Plate 3) (Bitan, Manor, Morocz, & Karni, 2005). In contrast, whole-word instruction (Word-Alph and Word-Arb) resulted in bilateral occipital and parietal activation, regardless of whether the words were alphabetical. Furthermore, only direct letter instruction (Letter-Alph) resulted in improvement between training sessions (see Plate 3), indicating more effective consolidation processes and suggesting greater reliance on procedural learning (Bitan & Booth, 2012). These findings are consistent with the advantage found for "phonics" instruction in educational studies of reading acquisition in children learning to read in their first language (Foorman, 1995). They extend this advantage to adults learning to read in a second language, and suggest a neurocognitive basis for this advantage in terms of the learning mechanism involved in reading acquisition.

Directions for future research

Many questions about the mechanisms underlying reading in a second language remain open, and require more research using both behavioural and neuroscientific measures – for example:

- To what extent can it be assumed that the mechanics of eye movements in second language reading mirror those in first language reading? What characteristics and patterns of eye movements in a second language might be due to variability in levels of proficiency, exposure to the second languages, others languages and scripts known, automaticity and fluency of second language processing, and so forth?
- What are the behavioural benchmarks of automatic processing? What amount of variability of performance (e.g., reaction times and accuracy) is characteristic of automatized processing, and what amount of variability can be taken as an indicator of a non-automatic process? Will this depend on the process being evaluated?
- Is there an upper limit of automatization and proceduralization of second language knowledge that adult learners of second languages are able to achieve, and, if there is, where does it lie?
- What learning conditions are the most conducive to the automatization of processes involved in second language reading?
- What is the effect of age and order of acquisition of the languages on reading in a second language? Do these factors affect reading fluency beyond the amount of language exposure? How do they affect processes of accommodation and assimilation beyond language proficiency?
- Despite evidence for activation of phonological and lexical representations of the non-target language during the processing of both spoken and written language in bilinguals, the findings related to automatic activation of orthographic representations are less consistent (Nosarti et al., 2010; Wu & Thierry, 2010). This raises the question of the conditions under which orthographic representations of the non-target language would also be activated automatically. A closely related question is the effect of a shared writing system between two languages in bilinguals on the competition between these languages during reading. Neuroimaging methods can help reveal whether the source of such competition and interference is at the orthographic, phonological, or lexical level of processing.
- Despite the increasing amount of studies on bilingual processing of spoken and written language, very few studies examined the learning process itself, and how it is affected by other factors. For example, one important question is about the interactions between reading in two orthographies learned at the same time, and whether they interfere or facilitate each other. A related issue is the effect of reading in more than one language on the ability and mechanisms involved in learning to read in yet another language. These questions are all related to a larger question of whether we have some generalized learning ability, which could be improved and then applied to different languages and orthographies regardless of their specific structure.

Educational implications

Despite the many open questions, evidence from the last two decades has shown a tremendous amount of plasticity in the brain throughout the lifespan. Research in illiterate adults learning to read in their first language shows that the same brain regions are recruited for reading regardless of age (Dehaene et al., 2010). Similarly, research in bilingual spoken language shows that language proficiency plays a more important role than age of acquisition in the brain regions involved in processing the language (Perani et al., 1998). These findings suggest that the role of age in determining a person's ability to learn a new language should not be overemphasized. In contrast, a critical factor that has been shown to play an important role in mechanisms underlying the reading process is the amount of experience the reader has in reading the language. This factor affects the amount of effort exerted by the brain during the reading process. It is also reflected in the robust effects of familiarity and frequency, which facilitate the reading process and override differences in the properties of orthographies, such as orthographic transparency.

Finally, research shows the critical role of reading instruction in a second language, even for adults who are familiar with the alphabetic principle and are experienced at reading in their native language. Similar to findings in children learning to read in their first language, explicit instruction on the smallest units of writing (letters in alphabetic orthographies) is very important. It promotes better decoding skills, better generalization to new words, and more stable representations over time. Apart from decoding, promoting the efficiency (i.e., automaticity and fluency) of cognitive processes such as lexical access, morphological processing, and syntactic processing can ensure that valuable cognitive resources are left for higher-level processing (see Chapter 6, this volume). Research to date suggests that this is best achieved via extensive practice with using the language; for instance, fluency of lexical access for reading is best promoted via reading practice (both unguided and guided), while morphological and syntactic fluency can be expected to benefit from both reading and listening practice. Finally, there is a possibility that computerized tasks incorporating lexical access and sentence and text comprehension under time pressure could foster reading fluency, but at present such tasks await testing in laboratory and classroom studies.

REFERENCES

Abrahamsson, N., & Hyltenstam, K. (2009). Age of onset and nativelikeness in a second language: Listener perception versus linguistic scrutiny. *Language Learning, 59,* 249–306.
Abutalebi, J., Cappa, S. F., & Perani, D. (2005). What can functional neuroimaging tell us about the bilingual brain? In J. F. Kroll & A.M.B. de Groot (Eds.), *Handbook of*

bilingualism: Psycholinguistic approaches (pp. 497–515). New York: Oxford University Press.

Baddeley, A. D. (2000). The episodic buffer: A new component of working memory? *Trends in Cognitive Sciences, 4,* 417–423.

Baddeley, A. D., & Hitch, G. (1974). Working memory. In G. Bower (Ed.), *The psychology of learning and motivation* (Vol. 8, pp. 47–90). New York: Academic Press.

Bakhtiari, R., Boliek, C., & Cummine, J. (2014). Investigating the contribution of ventral-lexical and dorsal-sublexical pathways during reading in bilinguals. *Frontiers in Human Neuroscience, 8,* 1–10. doi:10.3389/fnhum.2014.00507

Banich, M. T. (2004). *Cognitive neuroscience and neuropsychology.* Boston: Houghton Mifflin.

Banich, M. T., & Scalf, P. E. (2003). The neurocognitive bases of developmental reading disorders. In M. T. Banich & M. Mack (Eds.), *Mind, brain, and language: Multidisciplinary perspectives* (pp. 283–306). Mahwah, NJ: Erlbaum.

Beaulieu, C., Plewes, C., Paulson, L. A., Roy, D., Snook, L., Concha, L., & Phillips, L. (2005). Imaging brain connectivity in children with diverse reading ability. *NeuroImage, 25*(4), 1266–1271.

Benjamin, C.F.A., & Gaab, N. (2012). What's the story? The tale of reading fluency told at speed. *Human Brain Mapping, 33*(11), 2572–2585. doi:10.1002/hbm.21384

Ben-Shachar, M., Dougherty, R. F., & Wandell, B. A. (2007). White matter pathways in reading [Review]. *Current Opinion in Neurobiology, 17*(2), 258–270. doi:10.1016/j.conb.2007.03.006

Bialystok, E., Craik, F.I.M., Klein, R., & Viswanathan, M. (2004). Bilingualism, aging, and cognitive control: Evidence from the Simon task. *Psychology and Aging, 19*(2), 290–303. doi:10.1037/0882–7974.19.2.290

Bick, A.S., Goelman, G., & Frost, R. (2011). Hebrew brain vs. English brain: Language modulates the way it is processed. *Journal of Cognitive Neuroscience, 23*(9), 2280–2290. doi:10.1162/jocn.2010.21583

Binder, J.R., McKiernan, K.A., Parsons, M.E., Westbury, C.F., Possing, E.T., Kaufman, J.N., & Buchanan, L. (2003). Neural correlates of lexical access during visual word recognition. *Journal of Cognitive Neuroscience, 15*(3), 372–393.

Bitan, T., & Booth, J.R. (2012). Offline improvement in learning to read a novel orthography depends on direct letter instruction. *Cognitive Science, 36*(5), 896–918. doi:10.1111/j.1551–6709.2012.01234.x

Bitan, T., Burman, D.D., Chou, T., Lu, D., Cone, N.E., Cao, F., . . . & Booth, J.R. (2007). The interaction between orthographic and phonological information in children: An fMRI study. *Human Brain Mapping, 28*(9), 880–891.

Bitan, T., & Karni, A. (2004). Procedural and declarative knowledge of word recognition and letter decoding in reading an artificial script. *Cognitive Brain Research, 19*(3), 229–243.

Bitan, T., Manor, D., Morocz, I.A., & Karni, A. (2005). Effects of alphabeticality, practice and type of instruction on reading an artificial script: An fMRI study. *Cognitive Brain Research, 25*(1), 90–106.

Bolger, D.J., Perfetti, C.A., & Schneider, W. (2005). Cross-cultural effect on the brain revisited: Universal structures plus writing system variation. *Human Brain Mapping, 25*(1), 92–104. doi:10.1002/hbm.20124

Booth, J.R., Mehdiratta, N., Burman, D.D., & Bitan, T. (2008). Developmental increases in effective connectivity to brain regions involved in phonological processing during tasks with orthographic demands. *Brain Research, 1189*, 78–89.

Bourisly, A.K., Haynes, C., Bourisly, N., & Mody, M. (2013). Neural correlates of diacritics in Arabic: An fMRI study. *Journal of Neurolinguistics, 26*(1), 195–206. doi:10.1016/j.jneuroling.2012.07.004

Brown, T.T., Lugar, H.M., Coalson, R.S., Miezin, F.M., Petersen, S.E., & Schlaggar, B.L. (2005). Developmental changes in human cerebral functional organization for word generation. *Cereb Cortex, 15*(3), 275–290.

Brunswick, N., McCrory, E., Price, C.J., Frith, C.D., & Frith, U. (1999). Explicit and implicit processing of words and pseudowords by adult developmental dyslexics – A search for Wernicke's Wortschatz? *Brain, 122*, 1901–1917.

Brysbaert, M., & Vitu, F. (1998). Word skipping: Implications for theories of eye movement control in reading. In G. Underwood (Ed.), *Eye guidance in reading and scene perception* (pp. 125–147). Oxford: Elsevier Science.

Buchweitz, A., Mason, R.A., Hasegawa, M., & Just, M.A. (2009). Japanese and English sentence reading comprehension and writing systems: An fMRI study of first and second language effects on brain activation. *Bilingualism-Language and Cognition, 12*(2), 141–151. doi:10.1017/s1366728908003970

Caffarra, S., Molinaro, N., Davidson, D., & Carreiras, M. (2015). Second language syntactic processing revealed through event-related potentials: An empirical review. *Neuroscience and Biobehavioral Reviews, 51*, 31–47.

Caplan, D., & Waters, G.S. (1999). Verbal working memory and sentence comprehension. *Behavioural and Brain Sciences, 22*, 77–126.

Carpenter, P.A., & Just, M.A. (1983). What your eyes do while your mind is reading. In K. Rayner (Ed.), *Eye movements in reading: Perceptual and language processes* (pp. 275–307). New York: Academic Press.

Carreiras, M., Armstrong, B.C., Perea, M., & Frost, R. (2014). The what, when, where, and how of visual word recognition. *Trends in Cognitive Sciences, 18*, 90–98.

Changizi, M.A., Zhang, Q., Ye, H., & Shimojo, S. (2006). The structures of letters and symbols throughout human history are selected to match those found in objects in natural scenes. *American Naturalist, 167*, E117–E139.

Chee, M.W., Hon, N., Lee, H.L., & Soon, C.S. (2001). Relative language proficiency modulates BOLD signal change when bilinguals perform semantic judgments. Blood oxygen level dependent. *Neuroimage, 13*(6, Pt. 1), 1155–1163.

Clahsen, H., & Felser, C. (2006). Grammatical processing in language learners. *Applied Psycholinguistics, 27*, 3–42.

Cohen, L., & Dehaene, S. (2004). Specialization within the ventral stream: The case for the visual word form area. *NeuroImage, 22*(1), 466–476.

Cohen, L., Dehaene, S., Naccache, L., Lehericy, S., Dehaene-Lambertz, G., Henaff, M.A., & Michel, F. (2000). The visual word form area: Spatial and temporal characterization of an initial stage of reading in normal subjects and posterior split-brain patients. *Brain, 123* (Pt. 2), 291–307.

Coltheart, M., Rastle, K., Perry, C., Langdon, R., & Ziegler, J. (2001). DRC: A dual route cascaded model of visual word recognition and reading aloud. *Psychological Review, 108*(1), 204–256.

Cowan, N. (2001). The magical number 4 in short-term memory: A reconsideration of mental storage capacity. *Behavioral and Brain Sciences, 24*(1), 87–114.

Cowan, N. (2005). *Working memory capacity.* New York: Erlbaum.

Cummine, J., & Boliek, C.A. (2013). Understanding white matter integrity stability for bilinguals on language status and reading performance. *Brain Structure & Function, 218*(2), 595–601. doi:10.1007/s00429–012–0466–6

Das, T., Padakannaya, P., Pugh, K.R., & Singh, N.C. (2011). Neuroimaging reveals dual routes to reading in simultaneous proficient readers of two orthographies. *Neuroimage, 54*(2), 1476–1487. doi:10.1016/j.neuroimage.2010.09.022

Dehaene, S. (2009). *Reading in the brain.* New York: Penguin.

Dehaene, S., & Cohen, L. (2007). Cultural recycling of cortical maps [Review]. *Neuron, 56*(2), 384–398. doi:10.1016/j.neuron.2007.10.004

Dehaene, S., & Cohen, L. (2011). The unique role of the visual word form area in reading. *Trends in Cognitive Sciences, 15*(6), 254–262. doi:10.1016/j.tics.2011.04.003

Dehaene, S., Le Clec, H.G., Poline, J.B., Le Bihan, D., & Cohen, L. (2002). The visual word form area: A prelexical representation of visual words in the fusiform gyrus. *Neuroreport, 13*(3), 321–325.

Dehaene, S., Naccache, L., Cohen, L., Bihan, D.L., Mangin, J.F., Poline, J.B., & Riviere, D. (2001). Cerebral mechanisms of word masking and unconscious repetition priming. *Nat Neurosci, 4*(7), 752–758.

Dehaene, S., Pegado, F., Braga, L.W., Ventura, P., Nunes, G., Jobert, A., . . . Cohen, L. (2010). How learning to read changes the cortical networks for vision and language. *Science, 330*(6009), 1359–1364. doi:10.1126/science.1194140

Dehn, M.J. (2008). *Working memory and academic learning: Assessment and intervention.* Hoboken, NJ: Wiley.

Deutsch, A., & Rayner, K. (1999). Initial fixation location effects in reading Hebrew words. *Language and Cognitive Processes, 14*, 393–421.

Dronjic, V. (2011). Mandarin Chinese compounds, their representation, and processing in the visual modality. *Writing Systems Research, 3*, 5–21.

Dronjic, V. (2013). *Concurrent memory load, working memory span, and morphological processing in L1 and L2 English* (Unpublished doctoral dissertation). University of Toronto, Toronto.

Drosopoulos, S., Wagner, U., & Born, J. (2005). Sleep enhances explicit recollection in recognition memory. *Learning & Memory, 12*(1), 44–51. doi:10.1101/kfg.mu-luebeck.de

Ducrot, S., Lété, B., Sprenger-Charolles, L., Pynte, J., & Billard, C. (2003). The optimal viewing position effect in beginning and dyslexic readers. *Current Psychology Letters: Behaviour, Brain & Cognition, 1*(10).

Ellis, N.C. (2005). At the interface: Dynamic interactions of explicit and implicit language knowledge. *Studies in Second Language Acquisition, 27*, 305–352.

Engbert, R., Longtin, A., & Kliegl, R. (2002). A dynamical model of saccade generation in reading based on spatially distributed lexical processing. *Vision Research, 42*, 621–636.

Engle, R.W., Cantor, J., & Carullo, J.J. (1992). Individual differences in working memory and comprehension: A test of four hypotheses. *Journal of Experimental Psychology: Learning, Memory, and Cognition, 18*, 972–992.

Engle, R.W., Kane, M.J., & Tuholski, S.W. (1999). Individual differences in working memory capacity and what they tell us about controlled attention, general fluid intelligence, and functions of the prefrontal cortex. In A. Miyake & P. Shah (Eds.), *Models of working memory: Mechanisms of active maintenance and executive control* (pp. 102–134). New York: Cambridge University Press.

Farah, M.J. (2000). *The cognitive neuroscience of vision*. Malden: Blackwell.

Farid, M., & Grainger, J. (1996). How initial fixation position influences visual word recognition: A comparison of French and Arabic. *Brain and Language, 53*, 351–368.

Favreau, M., & Segalowitz, N.S. (1983). Automatic and controlled processes in the first- and second-language reading of fluent bilinguals. *Memory & Cognition, 11*, 565–574.

Fenn, K.M., & Hambrick, D.Z. (2013). What drives sleep-dependent memory consolidation: Greater gain or less loss? *Psychonomic Bulletin & Review, 20*(3), 501–506. doi:10.3758/s13423–012–0366-z

Fiebach, C.J., Friederici, A. D., Muller, K., & von Cramon, D.Y. (2002). fMRI evidence for dual routes to the mental lexicon in visual word recognition. *Journal of Cognitive Neuroscience, 14*(1), 11–23.

Fiez, J.A., & Petersen, S.E. (1998). Neuroimaging studies of word reading. *Proceedings of the National Academy of Sciences of the United States of America, 95*(3), 914–921.

Foorman, B.R. (1995). Research on "The Great Debate": Code-oriented versus whole language approaches to reading instruction. *School Psychology Review, 24*(3), 376–392.

Frost, R. (2012). Towards a universal model of reading. *Behavioral and Brain Sciences, 35*, 263–329.

Gathercole, S.E. (2007). Working memory and language. In M. G. Gaskell (Ed.), *The Oxford handbook of psycholinguistics* (pp. 757–769). Oxford: Oxford University Press.

Ghilardi, M.F., Moisello, C., Silvestri, G., Ghez, C., & Krakauer, J.W. (2009). Learning of a sequential motor skill comprises explicit and implicit components that consolidate differently. *Journal of Neurophysiology, 101*(5), 2218–2229. doi:10.1152/jn.01138.2007

Graves, W.W., Desai, R., Humphries, C., Seidenberg, M.S., & Binder, J.R. (2010). Neural systems for reading aloud: A multiparametric approach. *Cerebral Cortex, 20*(8), 1799–1815. doi:10.1093/cercor/bhp245

Halford, G.S., Phillips, S., & Wilson, W.H. (2001). Processing capacity limits are not explained by storage limits. *Behavioral and Brain Sciences, 24*, 123–124.

Hashimoto, R., & Sakai, K.L. (2004). Learning letters in adulthood: Direct visualization of cortical plasticity for forming a new link between orthography and phonology. *Neuron, 42*(2), 311–322.

Henderson, J.M., & Ferreira, F. (1990). Effects of foveal processing difficulty on the perceptual span in reading: Implications for attention and eye movement control. *Journal of Experimental Psychology: Learning, Memory, and Cognition, 16*, 417–429.

Henke, K. (2010). A model for memory systems based on processing modes rather than consciousness. *Nature Reviews Neuroscience, 11*, 523–532.

Hofmeister, J., Heller, D., & Radach, R. (1999). The return sweep in reading. In W. Becker, H. Deubel, & T. Mergner (Eds.), *Current oculomotor research: Physiological and psychological aspects* (pp. 349–357). New York: Kluwer Academic/Plenum.

Huang, P., Jin, H., Mo, L., Zhou, Y., Cai, M.X., Li, L., & Fang, X.Y. (2014). An fMRI functional connectivity study on first and second language reading in late proficient Indonesian-Chinese bilinguals. *Research Journal of Biotechnology, 9*(8), 1–7.

Ibbotson, M., & Krekelberg, B. (2011). Visual perception and saccadic eye movements. *Current Opinion in Neurobiology, 21*, 553–558.

Ibrahim, R., & Eviatar, Z. (2009). Language status and hemispheric involvement in reading: Evidence from trilingual Arabic speakers tested in Arabic, Hebrew, and English. *Neuropsychology, 23*(2), 240–254. doi:10.1037/a0014193

Inhoff, A.W., & Liu, W. (1998). The perceptual span and oculomotor activity during the reading of Chinese sentences. *Journal of Experimental Psychology: Human Perception and Performance, 24*, 20.

Ischebeck, A., Indefrey, P., Usui, N., Nose, I., Hellwig, F., & Taira, M. (2004). Reading in a regular orthography: An fMRI study investigating the role of visual familiarity. *Journal of Cognitive Neuroscience, 16*(5), 727–741.

Jamal, N.I., Piche, A.W., Napoliello, E.M., Perfetti, C.A., & Eden, G.F. (2012). Neural basis of single-word reading in Spanish-English bilinguals. *Human Brain Mapping, 33*(1), 235–245. doi:10.1002/hbm.21208

Jobard, G., Crivello, F., & Tzourio-Mazoyer, N. (2003). Evaluation of the dual route theory of reading: A metanalysis of 35 neuroimaging studies. *NeuroImage, 20*(2), 693–712.

Jones, O.P., Green, D.W., Grogan, A., Pliatsikas, C., Filippopolitis, K., Ali, N., . . . Price, C.J. (2012). Where, when and why brain activation differs for bilinguals and monolinguals during picture naming and reading aloud. *Cerebral Cortex, 22*(4), 892–902. doi:10.1093/cercor/bhr161

Jung-Beeman, M. (2005). Bilateral brain processes for comprehending natural language. *Trends Cognitive Science, 9*(11), 512–518.

Kajii, N., & Osaka, N. (2000). Optimal viewing position in vertically and horizontally presented Japanese words. *Perception & Psychophysics, 62*, 1634–1644.

Keating, G.D. (2014). Eye-tracking with text. In J. Jegerski & B. VanPatten (Eds.), *Research methods in second language psycholinguistics* (pp. 69–92). London: Taylor & Francis.

Kim, Y.S., Radach, R., & Vorstius, C. (2012). Eye movements and parafoveal processing during reading in Korean. *Reading and Writing, 25*, 1053–1078.

Knöll, J., Holl, P., & Bremmer, F. (2013). Saccadic suppression comprises an active binocular mechanism. *Journal of Vision, 13*, 108–108.

Kuhn, M.R., Schwanenflugel, P.J., & Meisinger, E.B. (2010). Aligning theory and assessment of reading fluency: Automaticity, prosody, and definitions of fluency. *Reading Research Quarterly, 45*, 230–251.

Kuhn, M.R., & Stahl, S.A. (2003). Fluency: A review of developmental and remedial practices. *Journal of Educational Psychology, 95*, 3–21.

Kuperman, V., Schreuder, R., Bertram, R., & Baayen, R.H. (2009). Reading of polymorphemic Dutch compounds: Towards a multiple route model of lexical processing. *Journal of Experimental Psychology: Human Perception and Performance, 35*, 876–895.

LaBerge, D., & Samuels, S.J. (1974). Toward a theory of automatic information processing in reading. *Cognitive Psychology, 6*, 293–323.

Lauwereyns, J. (2012). *Brain and the gaze: On the active boundaries of vision*. Cambridge: MIT Press.

Li, X., Liu, P., & Rayner, K. (2011). Eye movement guidance in Chinese reading: Is there a preferred viewing location? *Vision Research, 51*, 1146–1156.

Logan, G.D. (1997). Automaticity and reading: Perspectives from the instance theory of automatization. *Reading & Writing Quarterly: Overcoming Learning Difficulties, 13*, 123–146.

Maisog, J.M., Einbinder, E.R., Flowers, D.L., Turkeltaub, P.E., & Eden, G.F. (2008). A metes-analysis of functional neuroimaging studies of dyslexia. In G. F. Eden & D. L. Flower (Eds.), *Learning, skill acquisition, reading, and dyslexia* (Vol. 1145, pp. 237–259). Oxford: Blackwell.

Marinkovic, K., Dhond, R.P., Dale, A. M., Glessner, M., Carr, V., & Halgren, E. (2003). Spatiotemporal dynamics of modality-specific and supramodal word processing. *Neuron, 38*(3), 487–497. doi:10.1016/s0896–6273(03)00197–1

Marslen-Wilson, W.D. (2007). Morphological processes in language comprehension. In M. G. Gaskell (Ed.), *The Oxford handbook of psycholinguistics* (pp. 175–193). Oxford: Oxford University Press.

Martin, R.C. (2005). Components of short-term memory and their relation to language processing: Evidence from neuropsychology and neuroimaging. *Current Directions in Psychological Science, 14*, 204–208.

McCandliss, B.D., Cohen, L., & Dehaene, S. (2003). The visual word form area: Expertise for reading in the fusiform gyrus. *Trends in Cognitive Sciences, 7*(7), 293–299.

McConkie, G.W., Zola, D., Grimes, J., Kerr, P. W., Bryant, N.R., & Wolff, P. M. (1991). Children's eye movements during reading. In J. E Stein (Ed.), *Vision and visual dyslexia* (pp. 251–262). London: Macmillan Press.

McDermott, K.B., Petersen, S.E., Watson, J.M., & Ojemann, J.G. (2003). A procedure for identifying regions preferentially activated by attention to semantic and phonological relations using functional magnetic resonance imaging. *Neuropsychologia, 41*(3), 293–303.

Mechelli, A., Crinion, J.T., Long, S., Friston, K.J., Ralph, M.A.L., Patterson, K., . . . Price, C.J. (2005). Dissociating reading processes on the basis of neuronal interactions. *Journal of Cognitive Neuroscience, 17*(11), 1753–1765.

Mechelli, A., Crinion, J.T., Noppeney, U., O'Doherty, J., Ashburner, J., Frackowiak, R.S., & Price, C.J. (2004). Structural plasticity in the bilingual brain – Proficiency in a second language and age at acquisition affect grey-matter density. *Nature, 431*(7010), 757–757. doi:10.1038/431757a

Mei, L.L., Xue, G., Lu, Z.L., He, Q.H., Zhang, M.X., Xue, F., . . . Dong, Q. (2013). Orthographic transparency modulates the functional asymmetry in the fusiform cortex: An artificial language training study. *Brain and Language, 125*(2), 165–172.

Meschyan, G., & Hernandez, A.E. (2006). Impact of language proficiency and orthographic transparency on bilingual word reading: An fMRI investigation. *NeuroImage, 29*(4), 1135–1140.

Miller, G.A. (1956). The magical number seven, plus or minus two: Some limits on our capacity for processing information. *Psychological Review, 63*, 81–97.

Morgan-Short, K., Finger, I., Grey, S., & Ullman, M.T. (2012). Second language processing shows increasing native-like neural responses after months of no exposure. *PLoS ONE, 7*, 1–18.

Nelson, J.R., Liu, Y., Fiez, J., & Perfetti, C.A. (2009). Assimilation and accommodation patterns in ventral occipitotemporal cortex in learning a second writing system. *Human Brain Mapping, 30*(3), 810–820. doi:10.1002/hbm.20551

Nemeth, D., Janacsek, K., & Fiser, J. (2013). Age-dependent and coordinated shift in performance between implicit and explicit skill learning. *Frontiers in Computational Neuroscience, 7*, 1–13. doi:10.3389/fncom.2013.00147

Norris, D. (2013). Models of visual word recognition. *Trends in Cognitive Sciences, 17*, 517–524.

Nosarti, C., Mechelli, A., Green, D. W., & Price, C. J. (2010). The impact of second language learning on semantic and nonsemantic first language reading. *Cerebral Cortex, 20*(2), 315–327. doi:10.1093/cercor/bhp101

Oberauer, K. (2002). Access to information in working memory: Exploring the focus of attention. *Journal of Experimental Psychology: Learning, Memory, and Cognition, 28*, 411–421.

Palmer, S. E. (1999). *Vision science: Photons to phenomenology*. Cambridge: MIT Press.

Paradis, M. (2004). *A neurolinguistic theory of bilingualism*. Amsterdam: Benjamins.

Paradis, M. (2009). *Declarative and procedural determinants of second languages*. Amsterdam: Benjamins.

Paulesu, E., Demonet, J. F., Fazio, F., McCrory, E., Chanoine, V., Brunswick, N., . . . Frith, U. (2001). Dyslexia: Cultural diversity and biological unity. *Science, 291*(5511), 2165–2167.

Paulesu, E., McCrory, E., Fazio, F., Menoncello, L., Brunswick, N., Cappa, S. F., . . . Frith, U. (2000). A cultural effect on brain function [see comment]. *Nature Neuroscience, 3*(1), 91–96.

Perani, D. (2005). The neural basis of language talent in bilinguals. *Trends in Cognitive Sciences, 9*, 211–213.

Perani, D., Abutalebi, J., Paulesu, E., Brambati, S., Scifo, P., Cappa, S. F., & Fazio, F. (2003). The role of age of acquisition and language usage in early, high-proficient bilinguals: An fMRI study during verbal fluency. *Human Brain Mapping, 19*(3), 170–182.

Perani, D., Paulesu, E., Galles, N. S., Dupoux, E., Dehaene, S., Bettinardi, V., . . . Mehler, J. (1998). The bilingual brain: Proficiency and age of acquisition of the second language. *Brain, 121*(Pt. 10), 1841–1852.

Perfetti, C. A. (1988). Verbal efficiency in reading ability. In M. Daneman, G. E. Mackinnon, & T. G. Waller (Eds.), *Reading research: Advances in theory and practice* (Vol. 6, pp. 109–143). San Diego, CA: Academic Press.

Perfetti, C. A., Liu, Y., Fiez, J., Nelson, J., Bolger, D. J., & Tan, L. H. (2007). Reading in two writing systems: Accommodation and assimilation of the brain's reading network. *Bilingualism-Language and Cognition, 10*(2), 131–146. doi:10.1017/s1366728907002891

Plaut, D. C., McClelland, J. L., Seidenberg, M. S., & Patterson, K. (1996). Understanding normal and impaired word reading: Computational principles in quasi-regular domains. *Psychological Review, 103*(1), 56–115.

Pollatsek, A., Bolozky, S., Well, A. D., & Rayner, K. (1981). Asymmetries in the perceptual span for Israeli readers. *Brain and Language, 14*, 174–180.

Pollatsek, A., Lesch, M., Morris, R. K., & Rayner, K. (1992). Phonological codes are used in integrating information across saccades in word identification and reading. *Journal of Experimental Psychology: Human Perception and Performance, 18*, 148–162.

Price, C. J. (2012). A review and synthesis of the first 20 years of PET and fMRI studies of heard speech, spoken language and reading [Review]. *Neuroimage, 62*(2), 816–847. doi:10.1016/j.neuroimage.2012.04.062

Price, C. J., & Devlin, J. T. (2003). The myth of the visual word form area. *Neuroimage, 19*(3), 473–481.

Price, C. J., & Mechelli, A. (2005). Reading and reading disturbance. *Current Opinion in Neurobiology, 15*(2), 231–238.

Pugh, K. R., Frost, S. J., Sandak, R., Landi, N., Rueckl, J. G., Constable, R. T., . . . Mencl, W. E. (2008). Effects of stimulus difficulty and repetition on printed word identification: An fMRI comparison of nonimpaired and reading-disabled adolescent cohorts. *Journal of Cognitive Neuroscience, 20*(7), 1146–1160.

Rao, C., Mathur, A., & Singh, N. C. (2013). "Cost in transliteration": The neurocognitive processing of Romanized writing. *Brain and Language, 124*(3), 205–212. doi:http://dx.doi.org/10.1016/j.bandl.2012.12.004

Rastle, K. (2007). Visual word recognition. In M. G. Gaskell (Ed.), *The Oxford handbook of psycholinguistics* (pp. 71–87). Oxford: Oxford University Press.

Rayner, K. (1998). Eye movements in reading and information processing: 20 years of research. *Psychological Bulletin, 124*, 372–422.

Rayner, K., & Juhasz, B. (2006). Reading processes in adults. In K. Brown (Ed.), *Encyclopedia of language & linguistics* (pp. 89–105). Oxford: Elsevier.

Rayner, K., & McConkie, G. W. (1976). What guides a reader's eye movements? *Vision Research, 16*, 829–837.

Roberts, L., & Siyanova-Chanturia, A. (2013). Using eye-tracking to investigate topics in L2 acquisition and L2 processing. *Studies in Second Language Acquisition, 35*, 213–235.

Robertson, E. M. (2009). From creation to consolidation: A novel framework for memory processing. *PLoS Biology, 7*(1), e1000019.

Rolfs, M. (2009). Microsaccades: Small steps on a long way. *Vision Research, 49*, 2415–2441.

Rueschemeyer, S. A., Zysset, S., & Friederici, A. D. (2006). Native and non-native reading of sentences: An fMRI experiment. *Neuroimage, 31*(1), 354–365. doi:10.1016//j.neuroimage.2005.11.047

Schlaggar, B. L., Brown, T. T., Lugar, H. M., Visscher, K. M., Miezin, F. M., & Petersen, S. E. (2002). Functional neuroanatomical differences between adults and school-age children in the processing of single words. *Science, 296*(5572), 1476–1479.

Schlaggar, B. L., & McCandliss, B. D. (2007). Development of neural systems for reading. *Annual Review of Neuroscience, 30*, 475–503. doi:10.1146/annurev.neuro.28.061604.135645

Segalowitz, N. (2010). *Cognitive bases of second language fluency.* New York: Routledge.

Segalowitz, N., & Freed, B. F. (2004). Context, contact, and cognition in oral fluency acquisition: Learning Spanish in at home and study abroad contexts. *Studies in Second Language Acquisition, 26*, 173–199.

Segalowitz, N., & Segalowitz, S. J. (1993). Skilled performance, practice, and the differentiation of speed-up from automatization effects: Evidence from second-language word recognition. *Applied Psycholinguistics, 14*, 396–385.

Seghier, M. L. (2013). The angular gyrus: Multiple functions and multiple subdivisions. *The Neuroscientist, 19*(1), 43–61. doi:10.1177/1073858412440596

Shaywitz, B. A., Shaywitz, S. E., Pugh, K. R., Mencl, W. E., Fulbright, R. K., Skudlarski, P., . . . Gore, J. C. (2002). Disruption of posterior brain systems for reading in children with developmental dyslexia. *Biological Psychiatry, 52*(2), 101–110.

Shaywitz, B. A., Skudlarski, P., Holahan, J. M., Marchione, K. E., Constable, R. T., Robert, K. F., . . . Sally, E. S. (2007). Age-related changes in reading systems of dyslexic children. *Annals of Neurology, 61*(4), 363–370.

Shillcock, R. (2007). Eye movements and visual word recognition. In M. G. Gaskell (Ed.), *The Oxford handbook of psycholinguistics* (pp. 327–359). Oxford: Oxford University Press.

Song, S.B. (2009). Consciousness and the consolidation of motor learning. *Behavioural Brain Research, 196*(2), 180–186. doi:10.1016/j.bbr.2008.09.034

Spivey, M.J., & Marian, V. (1999). Cross talk between native and second languages: Partial activation of an irrelevant lexicon. *Psychological Science, 10*(3), 281–284. doi:10.1111/1467–9280.00151

Stanovich, K.E. (1980). Effects of explicit teaching and peer tutoring on the reading achievement of learning disabled and low-performing students in regular classrooms. *Reading Research Quarterly, 16*, 32–71.

Staub, A., & Rayner, K. (2007). Eye movements and on-line comprehension processes. In M. G. Gaskell (Ed.), *The Oxford handbook of psycholinguistics* (pp. 327–359). Oxford: Oxford University Press.

Tan, L.H., Laird, A.R., Li, K., & Fox, P.T. (2005). Neuroanatomical correlates of phonological processing of Chinese characters and alphabetic words: A meta-analysis. *Human Brain Mapping, 25*(1), 83–91. doi:10.1002/hbm.20134

Tan, L.H., Spinks, J.A., Feng, C.M., Siok, W.T., Perfetti, C.A., Xiong, J., . . . Gao, J.H. (2003). Neural systems of second language reading are shaped by native language. *Human Brain Mapping, 18*(3), 158–166.

Temple, E., Deutsch, G.K., Poldrack, R.A., Miller, S.L., Tallal, P., Merzenich, M.M., & Gabrieli, J.D.E. (2003). Neural deficits in children with dyslexia ameliorated by behavioral remediation: Evidence from functional MRI. *Proceedings of the National Academy of Sciences of the United States of America, 100*(5), 2860–2865. doi:10.1073/pnas.0030098100

Thiele, A., Henning, P., Kubischik, M., & Hoffmann, K.P. (2002). Neural mechanisms of saccadic suppression. *Science, 295*, 2460–2462.

Thierry, G., & Wu, Y.J. (2007). Brain potentials reveal unconscious translation during foreign-language comprehension. *Proceedings of the National Academy of Sciences of the United States of America, 104*(30), 12530–12535. doi:10.1073/pnas.0609927104

Thomas, K.M., & Nelson, C.A. (2001). Serial reaction time learning in preschool- and school-age children. *Journal of Experimental Child Psychology, 79*(4), 364–387.

Towse, J.N., Hitch, G.J., & Hutton, U. (1998). A reevaluation of working memory capacity in children. *Journal of Memory and Language, 39*, 195–217.

Turkeltaub, P.E., Eden, G.F., Jones, K.M., & Zeffiro, T.A. (2002). Meta-analysis of the functional neuroanatomy of single-word reading: method and validation. *Neuroimage, 16*(3 Pt. 1), 765–780.

Turkeltaub, P.E., Gareau, L., Flowers, D.L., Zeffiro, T.A., & Eden, G.F. (2003). Development of neural mechanisms for reading. *Nature Neuroscience, 6*(7), 767–773.

Tzelgov, J., Henik, A., Sneg, R., & Baruch, O. (1996). Unintentional word reading via the phonological route: The Stroop effect with cross-script homophones. *Journal of Experimental Psychology: Learning, Memory, and Cognition, 22*, 336–349.

Ullman, M.T. (2004). Contributions of memory circuits to language: The declarative/procedural model. *Cognition, 92*, 231–270.

Ullman, M.T. (2007). The biocognition of the mental lexicon. In M. G. Gaskell (Ed.), *The Oxford handbook of psycholinguistics* (pp. 267–286). Oxford: Oxford University Press.

Ullman, M. T. (2015). The declarative/procedural model: A neurobiologically motivated theory of first and second language. In B. VanPatten & J. Williams (Eds.), *Theories in second language acquisition: An introduction* (2nd ed., pp. 135–158). New York: Routledge.

Underwood, N. R., & McConkie, G. W. (1985). Perceptual span for letter distinctions during reading. *Reading Research Quarterly, 20*, 153–162.

van Hell, J. G., & Dijkstra, T. (2002). Foreign language knowledge can influence native language performance in exclusively native contexts. *Psychonomic Bulletin & Review, 9*(4), 780–789.

Verhaeghen, P., Cerella, J., & Basak, C. (2004). A working memory workout: How to expand the focus of serial attention from one to four items in 10 hours or less. *Journal of Experimental Psychology: Learning, Memory, and Cognition, 30*, 1322–1337.

Vigneau, M., Beaucousin, V., Herve, P. Y., Duffau, H., Crivello, F., Houde, O., . . . Tzourio-Mazoyer, N. (2006). Meta-analyzing left hemisphere language areas: Phonology, semantics, and sentence processing. *NeuroImage, 30*(4), 1414–1432.

Vigneau, M., Beaucousin, V., Herve, P.-Y., Jobard, G., Petit, L., Crivello, F., . . . Tzourio-Mazoyer, N. (2011). What is right-hemisphere contribution to phonological, lexico-semantic, and sentence processing?: Insights from a meta-analysis. *NeuroImage, 54*(1), 577–593.

Vinckier, F., Dehaene, S., Jobert, A., Dubus, J. P., Sigman, M., & Cohen, L. (2007). Hierarchical coding of letter strings in the ventral stream: Dissecting the inner organization of the visual word-form system. *Neuron, 55*(1), 143–156. doi:10.1016/j.neuron.2007.05.031

Vingerhoets, G., Van Borsel, J., Tesink, C., van den Noort, M., Deblaere, K., Seurinck, R., . . . Achten, E. (2003). Multilingualism: An fMRI study. *Neuroimage, 20*(4), 2181–2196. doi:10.1016/j.neuroimage.2003.07.029

Weiss, Y., Katzir, T., & Bitan, T. (2015). *Many ways to read your vowels – Neural processing of diacritics and vowel letters in Hebrew.* Manuscript in preparation.

Winke, P. M., Godfroid, A., & Gass, S. M. (2013). Eye-movement recordings in second language research. *Studies in Second Language Acquisition, 35*, 205–212.

Wu, Y. J., & Thierry, G. (2010). Chinese-English bilinguals reading English hear Chinese. *Journal of Neuroscience, 30*(22), 7646–7651. doi:10.1523/jneurosci.1602–10.2010

Yan, M., Kliegl, R., Richter, E. M., Nuthmann, A., & Shu, H. (2010). Flexible saccade-target selection in Chinese reading. *The Quarterly Journal of Experimental Psychology, 63*, 705–725.

Yan, M., Richter, E. M., Shu, H., & Kliegl, R. (2009). Readers of Chinese extract semantic information from parafoveal words. *Psychonomic Bulletin & Review, 16*, 561–566.

Yang, J., Wang, S., Tong, X., & Rayner, K. (2012). Semantic and plausibility effects on preview benefit during eye fixations in Chinese reading. *Reading and Writing, 25*, 1031–1052.

Yokoyama, S., Kim, J., Uchida, S., Miyamoto, T., Yoshimoto, K., & Kawashima, R. (2013). Cross-linguistic influence of first language writing systems on brain responses to second language word reading in late bilinguals. *Brain and Behavior, 3*(5), 525–531. doi:10.1002/brb3.153

Yoncheva, Y. N., Blau, V. C., Maurer, U., & McCandliss, B. D. (2010). Attentional focus during learning impacts N170 ERP responses to an artificial script. *Developmental Neuropsychology, 35*(4), 423–445.

Yoncheva, Y.N., Zevin, J.D., Maurer, U., & McCandliss, B.D. (2010). Auditory selective attention to speech modulates activity in the visual word form area. *Cerebral Cortex, 20*(3), 622–632. doi:10.1093/cercor/bhp129

Zhu, L., Nie, Y., Chang, C., Gao, J.-H., & Niu, Z. (2014). Different patterns and development characteristics of processing written logographic characters and alphabetic words: An ALE meta-analysis. *Human Brain Mapping, 35*(6), 2607–2618. doi:10.1002/hbm.22354

3

Development of word recognition in a second language

Keiko Koda

INTRODUCTION

The ultimate goal of reading is to construct text meanings based on the linguistic information encoded in print. Word recognition entails an assortment of operations, including analyzing a grapheme, extracting phonological and morphological information from the grapheme, identifying its lexical entry, and retrieving its meaning. Efficient word recognition necessitates lexical and sub-lexical knowledge, and, perhaps more critically, the ability to use the knowledge effortlessly for extracting and integrating visually presented information in printed words. Although word recognition is universally required, the subskills it requires vary widely across languages. Such variation has a significant implication for second language (L2) reading research because L2 reading development is jointly affected by the language-specific demands imposed by the properties of two languages. This chapter provides a brief overview of the universal and language-specific constraints on L2 word recognition development and resulting cross-linguistic interactions in L2 lexical information processing.

Word recognition refers to the process of retrieving the context-appropriate meaning of words. As building blocks in text meaning construction, retrieved word meanings must be aligned with emerging local text meanings. Semantic "alignment" thus is an additional, but crucial, operation in word recognition. How this multi-faceted competence develops is a chief concern among reading researchers. A large number of studies, with both children and adults, have addressed the core issue in visual word recognition – that is, how graphically encoded information is extracted, integrated, and linked to stored knowledge of word forms, meanings, and real-life experiences.

Building on models of reading acquisition, this chapter discusses how word recognition subskills develop in a second language, and how their development is affected by learners' previous language and literacy learning experiences. By way of background, the chapter begins by relating word recognition to local text meaning construction. The chapter also describes the component operations of word recognition, including orthographic, phonological, morphological, and semantic processes. It then discusses how word recognition subskills are acquired and refined in a second language, and how the formation of L2 subskills is affected jointly by the language-specific demands imposed by the properties of two languages.

WORD RECOGNITION AND TEXT
MEANING CONSTRUCTION

Reading entails integrative interactions between text information and the reader's knowledge. Such interactions are achieved through several interlinked operations, including phonological and morphological information extraction, word meaning retrieval, local text meaning construction (textbase construction), lexical alignment, and knowledge incorporation (situation model building). Supported by a large body of empirical studies, the prevailing view in the current literature indicates that word recognition encompasses the first three operations (Adams, 1990; National Reading Panel, 2000; Perfetti & Stafura, 2014; Roberts, Christo, & Shefelbine, 2011).

In word recognition, reader-text interactions occur when lexical information extracted from print is linked, through word forms and meanings, to the reader's world knowledge. The sections that follow describe how word recognition operations jointly and uniquely interact with local text meanings construction. Based on widely acknowledged definitions of vocabulary knowledge (Anderson & Nagy, 1991; Nation, 2001; Schmitt, 2014), the sections then discuss what it means to know a word and how this knowledge bridges printed words in text and the reader's real-life experiences during reading.

Reader-text interactions: shifting views

The centrality of the bidirectional relationship between word-level information processing and text-level information integration has been widely acknowledged (Adams, 1990; Nassaji, 2014). However, the way their relationship is conceptualized has changed dramatically over the past 40 years. In early studies, the top-down conceptualization dominated reading research.

As seen in the "psycholinguistic guessing game" model (Goodman, 1973), the reader's primary task is to generate hypotheses regarding the forthcoming text content. Word meaning retrieval, in this interpretation, is necessary only to confirm the hypotheses, because the basis for text meaning construction was thought to be the reader's prior knowledge. Reflecting the prevalence of the conceptually driven view, in the 1970s and early 1980s, word recognition received less attention in reading research relative to knowledge activation and integration (Anderson & Pearson, 1984).

The tide has turned, however. In the subsequent years, the availability of technologically sophisticated apparatuses allowed researchers to measure processing behaviours during word recognition with greater precision. Their findings provided little support for the strong top-down claims that the reader's knowledge is an exclusive force in driving text comprehension. Eye movement studies, as an illustration, repeatedly showed that most content words received direct visual fixation (Balota, Pollasek, & Rayner, 1985; Just & Carpenter, 1980, 1987), that the absence of even a single letter was disruptive, heavily diminishing reading efficiency (McConkie & Zola, 1981; Rayner & Bertera, 1979), and that text comprehension was impeded by a single anomalous word (Kintsch, 1998). Contrary to the predictions from the top-down conceptualization, these findings indicate that the majority of words in a text are thoroughly processed during reading, and that emerging text interpretations do not easily override incoming lexical information extracted from text.

Reading development studies uniformly demonstrate that poor readers have difficulty in extracting phonological information from print, and that deficiency in phonological processing is directly linked to poor comprehension (Fowler & Liberman, 1995; Perfetti, 1985; Stanovich, 1993). The ability to analyze the morphological structure of words is known to be another strong predictor, independent of phonological skills, of reading achievement (Carlisle, 2003; Deacon & Kirby, 2004). Given the evidence supporting the reader's continual engagement in print information processing and heavy reliance on lexical information during reading, word recognition should be regarded as critical as prior knowledge because it enables the reader to bring stored information – be it linguistic or conceptual – into text meaning construction.

Relationships among word forms, word meanings, and prior knowledge

Word meaning retrieval plays a pivotal role in linking word forms to word meanings, word meanings with text meanings, and word meanings with prior knowledge. As such, it interacts directly and reciprocally with every one of the other operations in reading. As an illustration, word meaning retrieval depends on accurate and speedy lexical and sub-lexical information extraction. At the same time, it relies on local text meanings for deriving the context-appropriate meaning of individual words. Additionally, word meanings connect the written form of words with stored knowledge representations. Such mediation is necessary because word forms have an arbitrary relation to knowledge representations. Word meanings in a way serve as passcodes to stored knowledge bases as they include "information about the things to which words refer – be they related to the external world or to internal states of the mind" (Schreuder & Flores d'Arcais, 1992, p. 422).

To disentangle these complex interactions, we must first understand the nature of the knowledge of word meanings. Anderson and Nagy (1991) contend that conventional models of word meanings equate word meanings with definitions under the assumption that the knowledge of word meanings is stored in the form of a generalization that defines the set of entities or events to which a word refers. However, real-life world knowledge is less abstract than definitions because it includes the representations of the contexts in which a word appears. This implies that definitions do not map well onto real-life experiences. If word meanings consist only of definitions, we must assume that they have a restricted role in linking the words in a text with the reader's prior knowledge. Anderson and Nagy argue that a viable model of word meanings, particularly in the context of reading research, must incorporate both (a) context-free abstract meanings for the commitment to parsimony of representation and (b) context-bound meanings for the preservation of their connections to real-life world knowledge.

In exploring an alternative conceptualization of word meaning knowledge, Anderson and Nagy (1991) suggest four distinctions by incorporating language function (pointing and attributing) and context specificity (context-bound and context-free). The terms "reference" and "sense" are used to describe the context-bound meaning representations. The "reference" of a word is defined as the thing or things "picked out" by the word on a particular occasion. The sense of a word, on the other hand, indicates the attributes that the word conveys in a specific situation. The terms "denotation" and "connotation" are used to describe context-free meaning representations. The denotation of a word alludes to the entire set of all potential referents for a word, while the connotation of a word refers to the distinction for determining whether an action, object, or event belongs to the set that makes up the denotation of the word. If, for example, "cat" constitutes a given denotation, some algorithm, or rule, must be used to distinguish between specific cats with different attributes, such as Persian and Siamese, as well as to distinguish cats from other similar-looking animals.

As a complex construct, word meaning knowledge emerges gradually through repeated encounters with a word referring to a particular object,

event, or property in particular situations. As noted earlier, words display
different meanings in different contexts. Meaning retrieval during word recognition therefore must include the selection of the sense that best fits the
context in which a word appears. For example, the word "house" can evoke
all the different images of houses included in the reader's denotation –
ranging, perhaps, from a large mansion to a decrepit shack with a leaking
roof. The selection of the context-appropriate meaning of the word "house"
depends on the emerging interpretation of the local text meaning. Anderson
and Nagy (1991) underscore the importance of flexibility in word meaning
selection during reading comprehension by stating that "really knowing a
word . . . always means being able to apply it flexibly but accurately in a range
of new contexts and situations" (p. 721).

Aitchison (1994) likens the development of word meaning knowledge to
performing three interrelated, but distinct, tasks: labeling (what concept is
conveyed by the word); packaging (what real-life experiences are abstracted
in this concept); and network building (what other words can also be used
to convey this, or related, concepts).

Relationships among vocabulary knowledge, vocabulary learning, and text comprehension

Although word meanings are central to vocabulary knowledge, it has been
agreed that this knowledge comprises other dimensions that are equally
essential for text meaning construction. Nation (2001) identifies three dimensions of vocabulary knowledge: form, meaning, and use. The "form" dimension
includes knowledge of a word's spoken and written forms, whereas the "use"
dimension entails an understanding of its collocational behaviour (knowing
which words co-occur with the word – e.g., "auspicious" collocates with
"event"), grammatical functions, and usage constraints (where, when, and
how often the word can appear). The "meaning" dimension, similar to the
distinction described earlier, includes knowledge of the connections between
word forms and meanings, as well as those between word meanings and real-
life experiences.

Nation (2001) underscores the critical role that a word's morphosyntactic
and phonological properties play in language production and comprehension.
Building on Levelt's speech production model (1989), he explains that the
processes – involved in converting pre-verbal message segments, or fragmented
thoughts, into internal speech plans – are lexically driven. A possible implication is that the grammar, morphology, and phonology of the intended message
are largely determined by the particular words chosen. Thus, knowledge of
a word's morphosyntactic features is as essential as that of its semantic properties for language production and, by logical extension, comprehension.

Thus, text meaning construction necessitates the full spectrum of vocabulary knowledge. The extensive range of information included in this knowledge develops at varying rates and in different sequences (Durso & Shore, 1998; Nagy & Scott, 2000). Studies involving adult L2 learners consistently suggest that possessing one knowledge dimension does not guarantee the acquisition of others (Laufer & Patribakht, 1998; Schmitt, 1998). Acquisition modes are also likely to differ among different dimensions of vocabulary knowledge. Ellis (1994) maintains that word forms and meanings entail contrasting modes of learning. While knowledge of word forms is acquired primarily through implicit learning, knowledge of word meanings evolves through more explicit, conscious learning. Ellis contends that implicit learning requires attention to recurring structural regularities implicit in language input, but not any particular conscious operations, and as such, it is strongly affected by input frequency. In contrast, explicit learning involves searching and applying rules, and thus is seriously influenced by both amounts of attention and quality of mental operations.

Vocabulary knowledge, because of its multi-faceted nature, cannot be attained in an all-or-nothing fashion. The knowledge expands incrementally through incessant expansions and refinements of stored lexical information (Nagy & Scott, 2000). For such modifications to happen, words must be repeatedly encountered in a variety of forms, with different functions, and in diverse contexts. At each encounter, a new feature of a word – be it semantic, formal, or functional – must first be recognized as such. If, for example, the reader recognizes that the past tense of a known verb is marked by an irregular form (e.g., "went"), the form-meaning connection of the word ("go") is expanded to incorporate the new formal and semantic features into the stored connection. The context-appropriate meaning/sense of the word, in the given form, must also be selected. When the selected word meaning/sense is aligned with the local text meaning into which it is integrated, the function of the word's new feature is likely to be incorporated as an additional property of the word in lexical memory. Thus, each instance of incidental word learning provides an opportunity to augment stored lexical information and strengthen the links that connect an assortment of information linked with word.

Finally, incidental vocabulary learning and text comprehension share much of their underlying processes. Vital to both is the ability to infer the meaning of an unfamiliar word encountered in text by selectively using and integrating all the information available to the reader, including phonological, orthographic, and morphological information pertaining to the word, syntactic information pertaining to the surrounding sentences, local text meanings, and real-life world knowledge. Contextual word learning and comprehension thus are functionally interrelated through a number of subskills involved in lexical inferencing.

Their relationship is symbiotic as well. While text comprehension necessitates a full range of vocabulary knowledge for text meaning construction, vocabulary learning relies on accurately constructed local text meanings. Such reciprocity attests to the centrality of word recognition in both textbase construction and situation model building.

COMPONENT OPERATIONS

To reiterate, word recognition involves four major operations: (1) analyzing a word's graphemic features, (2) extracting phonological and morphological information, (3) retrieving its meaning, and (4) aligning the word meaning with contextual (sentence and discourse-level) information. The sections ahead describe these operations and their subskills.

Orthographic processing

Fluent reading requires rapid and effortless access to context-appropriate word meanings. It may seem that good readers recognize words instantly and access their meanings and spoken sounds without letter-by-letter processing. However, word recognition studies have repeatedly shown that skilled readers are, through automaticity, capable of segmenting and assembling sub-lexical phonological information effortlessly (Ehri, 1998; Shankweiler & Liberman, 1972). Competent readers are adept at pronouncing both individual letters and nonsense letter strings (Hogaboam & Perfetti, 1978; Siegel & Ryan, 1988; Wagner, Torgesen, & Rashotte, 1994). What seems like seamless holistic performance is not attributable to whole-word retrieval, but rather to children's accumulated knowledge of the orthography in their writing system (Adams, 1990; Ehri, 1994, 1998, 2014; Seidenberg & McClelland, 1989). Orthographic processing entails "the formation of letter-sound connections to bond the spellings, pronunciations, and meanings of specific words in memory" (Ehri, 2014, p. 5). Once formed, orthographic representations are responsible for sight word reading, spelling, and vocabulary learning.

Within connectionist premises, Seidenberg and McClelland (1989) define English orthographic knowledge as "an elaborate matrix of correlations among letter patterns, phonemes, syllables, and morphemes" (p. 525). They contend that this knowledge evolves over time through the cumulative experience of decoding and encoding lexical information in print. The clear implication is that the more frequently a particular pattern of letter sequences is experienced, the stronger the connections that hold the letters together in the sequence. Ultimately, it is the strength of connections that brings about effortless word recognition performance. As Ellis (2002) puts it, performance efficiency is directly tied to input frequency and practice.

Phonological processing

Phonological decoding refers to the processes involved in accessing, storing, and manipulating phonological information (Torgesen & Burgess, 1998). Studies consistently document that poor readers are handicapped in a variety of phonological tasks. Their deficiencies tend to be "domain-specific, longitudinally predictive, and relatively unaffected by non-phonological factors – such as general intelligence, semantic, or visual processing" (Share & Stanovich, 1995, p. 9). It is generally agreed that the ability to extract phonological information from written words is causally related to reading achievement. The primary function of phonological decoding is thought to afford quick access to stored meanings of familiar spoken words (Frost, 1998). Word naming performance is a powerful predictor of reading success among children in the initial grades (Bowers, Golden, Kennedy & Young, 1994; Share & Stanovich, 1995; Torgesen & Burgess, 1998).

Efficient phonological decoding also enhances the functioning of working memory (Kleiman, 1975; Levy, 1975). According to Gathecole and Baddeley (1993), the phonological loop – a major component of working memory – mediates the formation and retention of phonological representations. The durability of phonologically encoded information enhances the capacity of working memory by providing more stable space for linking extracted word forms to word meanings, as well as integrating word meanings incrementally into emerging text meanings.

Morphological processing

Morphemes are the smallest functioning unit in the composition of words. In learning to read, children rely on their emerging knowledge of morpheme functions and concatenation rules. This knowledge has been shown to play an important role in word recognition in English and other languages whose writing systems partly represent morphological information (Ehri, 2014; Frost, 2012; Nunes & Bryant, 2006). As an illustration, the English orthography is alphabetic in nature, and generally bound by phonemic constraints. However, its strong tendency to preserve morphological information allows phonemic constituents to account for its orthographic conventions only partially. For example, distinct orthographic patterns are used to differentiate two unrelated morphemes sharing the same pronunciation, such as "sale" and "sail". Conversely, shared morphemes are spelled identically despite their distinct pronunciations, as in "anxious/anxiety" and "electric/electricity", or the past tense marker "-ed" (e.g., /-d/ in moved, /-t/ in talked, /-ɪd/ in visited).

Morphological processing skills become more central to reading comprehension and incidental word learning as children move through the grades in school.

According to Nagy and Anderson (1984), roughly 60% of the new words children encounter in printed school materials are structurally transparent multi-morphemic words, such as "fire-fight-er" and "un-lady-like". This implies that the meaning of at least half the new words could be inferred by segmenting a word into its morphological constituents. Morphological skills thus bolster the capacity for identifying familiar elements in an unfamiliar word as a whole, and in so doing, enable children to extract partial information from the unknown word (Ku & Anderson, 2003). Without such competence, it is virtually impossible to fill semantic gaps created by unfamiliar words during text comprehension, making incidental word learning exceedingly challenging.

Semantic processings

As described earlier, semantic processing in reading entails three processes: retrieving a word's semantic information, linking it to real-life world knowledge, and selecting the context-appropriate meaning. Since most words have multiple denotations references that are linked to real-life experiences, meaning selection, more or less, is necessary for virtually all words presented in text (Adams, 1990; Nagy, 1997). This should not be taxing if local text meanings impose sufficient constraints on possible interpretations of incoming words. The meaning of the homonymous word form *bank* is neither confusing nor ambiguous in the following sentences: "I deposited three checks at the bank" and "I ran along the bank."

There is a long-standing controversy as to how context facilitates word meaning selection. Under the semantic constraint perspective, the emerging interpretation of the context expedites meaning selection by narrowing down a range of possible meanings of the word to be integrated into the context. In this view, the contextual facilitation is assumed to occur *after* the word's meaning have been retrieved. In the conceptually driven (top-down) view, however, context facilitation is thought to occur *before* word meaning selection. If the preceding context creates sufficient semantic constraints, the less-relevant meanings of the forthcoming word are not likely to be activated. Should this be the case, word recognition, let alone meanings selection, is an optional process – necessitated only when contextual constraints are insufficient.

The empirical evidence currently available in the literature favours the view that all of a word's known meanings are activated by its grapheme even when the context creates strong constraints (Seidenberg, Tanenhouse, Leiman, & Bienkowski, 1982). It is also worth noting that word recognition performance among less skilled readers is affected by context to a far greater extent than that of skilled readers (Allington & Fleming, 1978; Becker, 1985; Biemiller, 1979; Perfetti, 1985; Stanovich, 1993), and that contextual effects on word recognition decrease as reading proficiency improves (Becker, 1985; Pring & Snowling, 1986; Stanovich, 1986).

In brief, successful word recognition necessitates skillful phonological and morphological information extraction, speedy lexical access, efficient word meaning retrieval, accurate local text meaning construction, and adroit context-appropriate meaning/sense selection. When these operations are executed successfully in tandem, word recognition can contribute to linking graphically encoded text information to various knowledge representations – linguistic and conceptual – internally available to the reader.

CROSS-LINGUISTIC VARIATION IN WORD RECOGNITION

Before considering cross-linguistic variation, it is necessary to acknowledge that multiple recognition methods are used by single readers, as well as by different readers within the same language. Ehri (1998) maintains that there are five methods of reading words in English:

- assembling letters into a blend of sounds
- pronouncing and blending familiar spelling patterns
- retrieving sight words from memory
- analogizing to words already known by sights
- using context cues to predict words.

(1998, p. 7)

She contends that children learn to use all five methods as they develop reading proficiency. Good readers are adept at using all five, as well as capable of selecting the method best suited to a word based on the context in which it appears, its internal structure, and their familiarity with the word's sub-lexical constituents. Diversity in approaches to word recognition is associated neither with developmental stages nor with reading ability differences. Assuming that multiple methods are also available in other languages, cross-linguistic variation is likely to be observable in the methods themselves, as well as in relative reliance on particular methods within the repertoire that are available in a particular language.

One way of conceptualizing cross-linguistic variation is to analyze how diverse writing systems encode their spoken languages. Writing systems currently in use evolved over time through the process of optimizing their capacity of representing the range of expressions that their respective users wish to convey (Coulmas, 1989). Consequently, writing systems differ in the basic unit of representation (i.e., the linguistic unit represented by each graphic symbol) and the relative proportions of phonological and morphological information encoded in graphemes. As an illustration, Chinese has a large number of homophones. In speech, many are distinguished by lexical tone. In writing, however, tonal information is not graphically encoded. Instead, morphological distinction is signaled by a character's graphic component that indicates the semantic category of the word the character stands for, as shown in 功 (/g ʊ ŋ ˥/, "strength") and 貢 (/g ʊ ŋ ˩/, "tribute"). The characters share one component, 工, which specifies their pronunciation. Their morphological identity is distinguished by the other component in each character (力 "power" in 功 and 貝 "money" in 貢) (Taylor & Taylor, 1995). Explicit morphological distinction in the grapheme makes Chinese characters a powerful tool for communication among speakers of mutually unintelligible languages and dialects in China. The prominence of the grapheme-morpheme linkage in Chinese characters has two implications for reading acquisition: (1) a large number of graphic symbols must be memorized; and (2) word recognition relies heavily on visual orthographic analysis as it necessitates character segmentation into the two functionally distinct graphic components.

The orthographic depth hypothesis (ODH) explains how regularity in grapheme-phoneme correspondences affects phonological information extraction in diverse alphabetic systems (Katz & Frost, 1992). In "shallow" orthographies, the grapheme-phoneme relationships are highly regular, and thus transparent. In Serbo-Croatian, for example, each letter corresponds to one phoneme and each phoneme is represented by one grapheme, thereby constituting a phonologically regular system with highly consistent and reliable grapheme-phoneme correspondences. The English orthography, in contrast, is characterized as a phonologically "deep" system. As described earlier, its tendency to preserve morphological information in the grapheme violates one-to-one grapheme-phoneme correspondences.

According to the ODH, in "shallow" orthographies, phonological information is assembled primarily through letter-by-letter, symbol-to-sound translation. Conversely, in "deep" orthographies, phonological information may not always be obtained before a letter string has been identified as a lexical entry. Phonological information extraction in those systems may occur after a word's lexical identity is established via memory search. The major contention is that orthographic depth is directly related to the degree to which phonological decoding depends on lexical information. In the transparent sound-symbol relationships seen in shallow orthographies, rule-based computation seems to be the most efficient procedure. Decoding necessitates word-specific orthographic information to a far lesser extent than deep orthographies. In support of the prediction, Frost, Katz, and Bentin (1987) demonstrated differential impacts of word frequency on word naming speed in three writing systems with varying orthographic depths: unpointed Hebrew (deepest), English (deep), and Serbo-Croatian (shallow). Naming is a commonly used technique to measure efficiency in the the grapheme-to-phonology mappings. In naming, participants are asked to pronounce visually presented words or nonsense letter strings. Frost et al. reported that Hebrew readers were affected by word frequency to the greatest extent, followed by English and Serbo-Croatian readers. The differential frequency impacts imply that varying amounts of lexical information are necessitated for the extraction of phono-logical information in the three writing systems.

The psycholinguistic grain size theory (Ziegler & Goswami, 2005, 2006) represents a more recent attempt to explain how the amount of orthographic information necessary for decoding is directly related to the size of phono-logical unit (e.g., phoneme, rime, syllable) used as the basis of the grapheme-to-phonology mappings in different orthographies. According to the theory, in spoken language development, children are initially sensitized to larger phonological units, such as spoken word and syllable. They gradually fine-tune the initial sensitivity to smaller intra-syllabic units necessary for distin-guishing similarly sounding words. In learning to read, children continue to refine phonological sensitivity through grapheme-to-phonology mapping experience and eventually discover the orthographic unit that is most consis-tently and reliably corresponds to the phonological unit it represents.

The main contention of the theory is that orthographic depth is directly related to the grain sizes that are optimal for phonological decoding in typologi-cally diverse writing systems. "Grain size" refers to the amount of orthographic information that is necessary for the extraction of phonological information. In shallow orthographies, phonological decoding necessitates little orthographic information. The grain sizes required in phonologically highly regular orthog-raphies are small at the phonemic level. In contrast, phonologically deep orthog-raphies demand more orthographic information corresponding to larger phonological units, such as syllables, rimes, and morphemes, for decoding.

These predictions have been tested in studies involving children learning to read in diverse languages and writing systems. For instance, Korean children develop sensitivity to both syllables and phonemes, and the skills to manipulate phonemes and syllables are strong predictors of their word reading ability (McBride-Chan, Wagner, Muse, Chow, & Shu, 2005). Their phonological sensitivity clearly reflects the dual-unit (syllable and phoneme) representations in the hangul script, where individual symbols, each representing a distinct phoneme, must be packed into blocks to form syllables.

Hebrew is a root-derived language, and a word's base is a root morpheme. Root morphemes generally consist of three consonants (e.g., *gdl*) that convey abstract semantic information (e.g., "largeness"). Hebrew words are formed by intertwining root morphemes with word-pattern morphemes. Each word-pattern morpheme comprises built-in slots for the root's consonants to fit into. The Hebrew orthography encodes consonantal root morphemes, certain vowels (represented by letters that can also stand for consonants), and consonants that appear in patterns, prefixes, and suffixes. Reflecting the visible grapheme-consonant linkage, children learning to read Hebrew are known to develop stronger sensitivity to consonants than vowels (Geva, 2008; Tolchinsky & Teberosky, 1998). Studies involving adult readers, however, present a more complex picture, by demonstrating that word recognition is affected by lexical factors, such as word frequency (Frost et al., 1987), letter sequence (2012), and morphological structural transparency (Feldman, Frost, & Pnini, 1995). These findings would seem to suggest that Hebrew readers rely on solid lexical representations to supply the unspecified information in graphemes in identifying the lexical entry of printed words.

In morphosyllabic Chinese, most characters map directly onto morphemes. Phonological information can be obtained directly through graphemes or via morphemes. As such, a character's lexical entry can be identified directly through orthographic analysis (or visual character segmentation). Because of the privileged grapheme-morpheme connection in Chinese, morphological awareness is shown to be a stronger predictor of children's initial reading success than is phonological awareness (Ku & Anderson, 2003; Li, Anderson, Nagy, & Zhang, 2002).

Collectively, these findings provide empirical support for the postulation that learning to read entails a command of the cognitive mechanisms that detect structural regularities in printed words, and then adapt to the specific demands imposed by the structural properties. From a diachronic perspective, orthographic variations can be seen as an inevitable consequence of the interaction between an external force (e.g., culture) that places pressure on users to optimize shared tools for specific uses in a particular context and internal mechanisms that actualize desired refinements in response to external pressure. In writing systems, as a shared cultural tool, such optimization was achieved by balancing the proportions of orthographic, phonological, and morphological information encoded in written words to accelerate lexical access and meaning retrieval (Frost, 2012). Thus, orthographic variations are neither random nor accidental. They emerged through "the complex interaction of writing system and language structure with history and cultural environment" (Beveridge & Bak, 2012, p. 280). Reading acquisition in a particular orthography does have significant and lasting impacts.

DEVELOPMENT OF L2 WORD RECOGNITION

Reading acquisition, be it in L1 or L2, is similarly constrained by a set of principles that are derived from the universal properties of reading. As noted earlier, the language constraint on writing systems, one such principle, stipulates that all writing systems encode spoken languages, and in so doing specifies the initial task in learning to read. In all languages, children must make links between the spoken language and its writing system. L1 reading research has accumulated overwhelming evidence that sensitivity to the abstract structure of words provides substantial facilitation in acquiring the skills needed for the requisite grapheme-to-language mappings. As an abstract representation, such structural insight is known to be less language-specific (Bialystok, 2001), and as an outgrowth of regularity detection and abstraction, it is shown to be relatively independent of linguistic knowledge (Koda, 2005, 2007). Once acquired in one language, therefore, metalinguistic awareness is available in another language as a cross-linguistically shareable resource. Over the past two decades, a large number of studies involving school-age L2 learners have examined the intra-lingual and inter-lingual contributions of metalinguistic awareness to the development of L2 word recognition.

Reading acquisition, as mentioned earlier, is also constrained by the language-specific demands stemming from the properties of the language and its writing system. From a language-specific perspective, much of L2 research has addressed systematic variations in L2 word recognition, as well as possible factors explaining the observed variations, including (a) L1 orthographic properties, (b) inadequate L2 linguistic knowledge, (c) L1-L2 orthographic distance, and (d) cross-linguistic interactions between L1 skills and L2 orthographic properties.

Collectively, a growing body of L2 research has shown that L1 word recognition skills are involved in L2 print information processing, and that L2 skills emerge through the dynamic interplay between linguistically conditioned L1 skills and the linguistic demands imposed by the properties specific to the second language. The subsequent sections examine how L2 word recognition development is constrained by reading universals, previous language and literacy learning experiences, and the language-specific properties of the target language.

CROSS-LINGUISTIC CONTRIBUTIONS OF METALINGUISTIC AWARENESS

Phonological awareness

In view of the strong contribution of phonological awareness (PA) to reading development in a variety of languages, the general consensus in the literature is that a portion of PA – children's growing understanding of the segmental nature of spoken words – is shared across languages. Since the concept of word segmentation is not specific to any particular language, once developed, it should be readily available in another language. If so, two questions are pertinent: (1) to what extent does L1 PA contribute to the development of L2 PA and decoding?, and (2) how does L1 and L2 orthographic distance alter the cross-linguistic relationships in PA and decoding?

A large number of studies involving school-age L2 learners have provided considerable support for the shareability of PA across languages. Early studies investigated whether PA in either L1 or L2 relates to L2 word reading ability. In a study on Spanish-dominant bilingual first-grade students, Durgunoglu, Nagy, and Hancin (1993) demonstrated that L1 PA is a powerful predictor of decoding development in both languages. In a more recent study, Naka-mura, Koda, and Joshi (2014) extended these early findings by showing that L1 PA, as the sole predictor of L2 decoding, contributed to L2 text compre-hension two years later indirectly through L2 decoding.

Using larger batteries of parallel tasks in two languages, subsequent studies explored cross-linguistic relationships in PA and decoding. Their findings gen-erally suggest that L1 and L2 PA are closely related, and that poor readers are uniformly weak in phonological skills in both languages (Abu-Rabia, 1995; August, Calderon, & Carlo, 2001; Carlisle & Beeman, 2000; Cormier & Kelson, 2000; da Fontoura & Siegel, 1995; Verhoeven, 2000; Wade-Woolley & Geva, 2000). A recent meta-analysis study (Melby-Lervag & Lervag, 2011) indeed demonstrated significant relationships in L1 and L2 PA (n = 16, r = .64), L1 and L2 decoding (n = 22, r = .54), and L1 PA and L2 decoding (n = 14, r = .45).

Other studies have addressed more specific issues concerning construct validity and generalizability of the earlier findings. As a case in point, in a large-scale study involving 812 Spanish-English bilingual kindergarten chil-dren, Branum-Martin et al., (2006) tested the construct validity of three commonly used PA tasks (blending, segmentation, and deletion). Although the three tasks defined a unitary construct in each language, deletion was less strongly related to the construct. Removing deletion, the remaining tasks in both languages loaded on a single factor, implying that although there are some language-specific dimensions, PA in English and PA in Spanish largely overlap.

The vast majority of PA studies cited earlier involved children learning to read two phonographic (alphabetic and alpha-syllabic) writing systems. It is less certain whether similar cross-linguistic relationships are observable in PA and decoding between two typologically diverse writing systems. A small but growing body of evidence suggests that PA is systematically related between Chinese and English (Bialystok, McBride-Chang, & Luk, 2005; Wang, Perfetti, & Liu, 2005), providing further support for the contention that PA is readily shareable across languages.

Morphological awareness

In recent years, interest in morphological awareness (MA) is escalating. Because, as noted earlier, the morpheme is the smallest functional unit of words, isolating MA and vocabulary knowledge is methodologically challenging.

Their distinction is necessary, however, to clarify the precise nature of the facilitation stemming from previous literacy learning experience. Empirical explorations on MA in L2 reading development have just begun, and the empirical database is growing but still heavily limited. Given the inherent complexities of the construct stemming from the diversity in its forms, its functions, and their relationships, a clearer picture of MA's role in L2 word recognition has yet to emerge.

Thus far, only a handful of studies have addressed the contribution of L2 MA to L2 reading subskills in school-age L2 learners, including decoding (Geva & Wang, 2001; Ramirez, Chen, Geva, & Kiefer, 2010; Wang, Ko, & Choi, 2009), vocabulary knowledge (Chen, Ramirez, Luo, & Ku, 2012; Kieffer & Lesaux, 2012), lexical inferencing (Zhang, 2010; Zhang & Koda, 2012), and reading comprehension (Jeon, 2011; Koda, Lu, &, Zhang, 2013; Lam, Chen, Geva, Luo & Li, 2012; Wang et al., 2009; Zhang & Koda, 2013). Reflecting the complexity of the construct, the findings are not always consistent. For example, some studies found significant intra-lingual effects of MA only on decoding speed (Marcolini, Traficante, Zoccolotti, & Burani, 2011), while others have shown its contributions to both decoding speed and accuracy when whole-word frequency and sub-lexical morpheme frequency were controlled (Verhoeven & Schreuder, 2011). In examining cross-linguistic effects of MA, Ramirez et al. (2010) demonstrated a significant direct contribution of L1 MA to L2 decoding in L1 dominant Spanish-English bilingual children. It is less than certain to what extent such cross-linguistic contributions of MA can be generalized to other bilingual groups whose literacy learning involves two typologically distinct languages and writing systems.

Zhang (2010), for example, investigated the relative shareability of two word formation processes (derivation and compounding) in Grade 6 Mandarin-speaking children learning English as a foreign language in China. His data revealed that the two facets of MA were differentially related between the two languages. The cross-linguistic relationship was stronger in compound awareness (used in both languages) than derivational awareness (dominant only in L2). He also found that L1 compound awareness contributed to L2 lexical inferencing only indirectly through L2 compound awareness and L1 lexical inferencing ability, but such (indirect, yet significant) facilitation was not observable in L1 derivational awareness. His findings seem to suggest that the shareability of MA and the resulting cross-linguistic contributions vary across distinct MA facets.

In sum, the empirical findings make it plain that (1) metalinguistic awareness – PA, in particular – plays a recognizable role in L2 word recognition development, (2) PA is more strongly and consistently related between two languages than MA, and (3) the cross-linguistic contribution of MA is more restricted and language-specific than that of PA. Given the close links between MA and linguistic knowledge (vocabulary and grammar, in particular), the restricted shareability of MA across languages is not surprising. Further research is needed to disentangle two competing forces that determine the utility of previously acquired subskills in L2 word recognition development: linguistic restrictions on the shareability of skills across languages and facilitation from universally required competencies.

VARIATIONS IN L2 WORD RECOGNITION DEVELOPMENT

L1 orthographic properties

L1 orthographic effects have been investigated by the magnitude of the effect of a particular experimental manipulation on word recognition performance among L2 learners with contrasting L1 orthographic backgrounds. For example, ESL learners with alphabetic and morphosyllabic backgrounds can be contrasted in their reliance on phonemic analysis during phonological processing. Because alphabetic literacy requires segmenting and manipulating phonemic information, alphabetic readers rely heavily on intra-syllabic phonological analysis. In contrast, morphosyllabic systems involve syllables and morphemes. Phonological decoding in those systems does not entail intra-syllabic analysis. The contrast has led to a hypothesis that blocking visual access to intra-syllabic information induces different reactions among ESL learners with alphabetic and morphosyllabic L1 backgrounds. While decoding efficiency among alphabetic learners would be seriously impaired when intra-syllabic information is made unavailable, phonological processing of morphosyllabic learners would be affected by this manipulation to a far lesser extent.

The studies testing this and other similar hypotheses generally confirm that L2 learners with diverse L1 orthographic backgrounds respond differently to a variety of experimental manipulations (Akamatsu, 2003; Brown & Haynes, 1985; Green & Meara, 1987; Koda, 1998, 1999), and that the observed differences are consistent with the predicted variations directly associated with the participants' respective L1 orthographic systems (Koda, 1989, 1990, 1993; Ryan & Meara, 1991). Viewed collectively, these results indicate that L1 orthographic experience has lasting impacts on L2 reading development and is responsible, in part, for procedural variations in phonological information extraction among linguistically diverse L2 learners.

L2 linguistic knowledge

As a process of converting print into phonological and morphological information, word recognition heavily depends on linguistic knowledge.

In most instances, L2 learners begin to read before they develop adequate linguistic foundations. Inefficient word recognition is known to be a major characteristic of low-proficiency readers. As shown earlier, moreover, L2 word recognition is also affected by L1 orthographic properties. To better understand its subskills development, it is vital to unravel the complex dual-language constraints in L2 word recognition research (Koda, 2012). For example, clarification of the specific linguistic demands of distinct word recognition subskills should allow us to estimate differences in the amount of facilitation stemming from L1 experience across subskills, as well as differences in the amount of L2 linguistic knowledge necessary for reshaping cross-linguistically shared L1 subskills. To date, however, dual-language constraints remain largely unexplored, and little is known about the specific role of linguistic knowledge in the development of L2 word recognition subskills. Only a few studies have addressed the relationship between oral language proficiency and word recognition subskills.

In a sequence of studies, Segalowitz and his associates (Favreau & Segalowitz, 1982, 1983; Segalowitz, 1986; Segalowitz, Poulsen, & Komoda, 1991) found that lexical decision efficiency varied considerably among otherwise fluent adult bilingual speakers. They also found that the observed variance in lexical decision efficiency was closely related to reading comprehension performance. These results corroborate those from L1 reading research, suggesting that oral language competence alone is insufficient for developing fluency in word recognition. Even more pronounced dissociation was found between oral language proficiency and word reading development in studies involving school-age learners (August, Calderon, & Carlo, 2000, 2001; Durgunoglu, Nagy, & Hancin, 1993). Their results consistently demonstrated minimum impacts of L2 linguistic knowledge on L2 decoding performance. Caution is necessary in interpreting the results, however, because, in all studies, word reading ability was operationalized as decoding – the ability that is relatively independent of knowledge of grammar and vocabulary. Given that word-specific orthographic knowledge is essential for sight word reading, spelling, and word learning (Ehri, 2014), we have much to learn from examinations of the relationship between L2 linguistic knowledge and word recognition subskills that are involved in morphological and semantic information processing.

L1-L2 orthographic distance

L1-L2 orthographic distance constitutes another significant factor affecting the reshaping of transferred L1 skills in L2 word recognition development. Orthographic distance refers to the degree of structural similarity between two writing systems. Assuming that shared structural properties pose similar processing demands, it has been hypothesized that transferred L1 skills would be functional in L2 word recognition with minimum adjustment when the two languages employ similar orthographies. Thus, orthographic distance should be responsible at least in part for differences in L2 processing efficiency at a given point in time among linguistically diverse L2 learners. Studies comparing word recognition performance among learners with similar and dissimilar L1 orthographic backgrounds attest to the hypothesized facilitation stemming from L1 skills that are attuned to structurally similar L1 orthographic systems (Akamatsu, 1999; Green & Meara, 1987; Koda, 1988, 1989).

In a study, Muljani, Koda, and Moates (1998) demonstrated how orthographic distance affects L2 intraword sensitivity, which, in turn, explains differences in lexical access efficiency. By comparing lexical decision performance among proficiency-matched adult ESL learners with similar (Indonesian employing a Roman-alphabetic script) and dissimilar (Chinese using a morphosyllabic system) L1 orthographic backgrounds, the researchers found that only Indonesian participants benefited from intraword structural congruity (i.e., spelling patterns consistent between English and Indonesian). Their superiority, however, was far less pronounced with incongruent items whose spelling patterns were unique to English. These findings would seem to suggest that although the orthographic distance has general facilitative impacts, accelerated efficiency is observable only in the items whose demands are identical to those imposed by the learner's first language. Thus, the distance effect is far more localized and particular than has been previously assumed. Two implications arise from such localization: (1) L2 word recognition development is jointly constrained by L1 and L2 orthographic properties, and (2) the reshaping of L1 skills involves pattern detection and matching both within the target language and between the two languages.

Similar findings have been reported in studies comparing morphological segmentation among ESL learners with related (Korean: alphabetic, concatenative) and unrelated (Chinese: morphosyllabic, non-concatenative) first-language backgrounds (Koda, 2000; Koda, Takahashi, & Fender, 1998). Not surprisingly, Korean learners were more efficient in morphological segmentation than their proficiency-matched Chinese counterparts, but their efficiency gap was substantially reduced when they were confronted with items whose structural properties are unique to English. Clearly, segmentation efficiency in the items that are structurally unique to the target language is far less affected by linguistic distance presumably because their analysis requires insights unavailable to either Korean or Chinese ESL learners. Here again, the findings suggest that the distance effect is item-specific, and thus evident only in words sharing structural similarity between L1 and L2. In brief, L1-induced facilitation and any variation therein are systematic and specific and, therefore, can be predicted, with reasonable accuracy, through finely tuned cross-linguistic analysis of the structural properties of words in two languages.

Cross-linguistic interactions

As noted earlier, dual-language involvement is one of the defining character-istics of L2 reading. Understanding how L2 print information processing is constrained by the two languages involved is of the utmost importance. Of late, interest in such interactions has increased. Initial studies have explored the relative impact of L1 and L2 orthographic factors on L2 semantic infor-mation processing, using a variety of experimental tasks, including semantic category judgment (Wang, Koda, & Perfetti, 2003), associative word learning (Hamada & Koda, 2008), and word identification (Wang & Koda, 2005). To isolate the impact stemming from either L1 or L2 factors in these studies, L2 stimulus words were manipulated in one way or another, and the magnitude of the effect of such manipulations was compared between two learner groups, each representing a distinct first language. In such a design, the extent to which a particular manipulation affects both groups is used as the basis for gauging the impact of the L2, and the extent to which the effect of the manipulation varies between the groups of learners serves as an index of the L1 impact.

As an illustration, through semantic category judgments, Wang et al. (2003) compared the relative impact of phonological and graphic manipulations on semantic processing among proficiency-matched ESL learners with alphabetic (Korean) and morphosyllabic (Chinese) L1 orthographic backgrounds. In the study, participants were first presented with a category description, such as "flower," then showed a target word, and then asked to decide whether the word was a member of the shown category. The task would have been simple if the students had been shown the target words. In the experiment, however, the targets were either their homophones (e.g., "rows" for "rose") or their similarly spelled counterparts (e.g., "fees" for "feet"). The primary hypothesis was that the two ESL groups would respond differently to the two types of manipulation: Korean participants would be more likely to accept homo-phones as category members, while Chinese participants would make more false positive responses to graphically similar targets. The data showed that both phonological and graphic manipulations significantly interfered with category judgment performance among ESL learners regardless of their first-language backgrounds. However, the magnitude of interference stemming from each type of manipulation varied between the groups. As predicted, Korean learners made more errors with homophonous (phonologically manipulated) items, while more serious interference occurred with similarly spelled (graphically manipulated) targets among Chinese learners. These results seem to indicate that (a) proficiency-matched ESL learners are equally sensitized to L2 orthographic properties (L2 effects); (b) the two groups rely upon different information during semantic information processing of L2 words (L1 effects); and (c) these differences reflect the variations predicted from the properties specific to the scripts used by their respective first languages.

Similarly, Hamada and Koda (2008) compared impacts of L1 orthographic experiences on decoding and intentional word learning between two groups of proficiency-matched adult ESL learners with alphabetic (Korean) and non-alphabetic (Chinese) L1 backgrounds. It was hypothesized that congruity in L1 and L2 orthographic experiences would facilitate L2 decoding efficiency, which, in turn, would affect semantic information encoding and retention of new words. The Korean group performed significantly better than the Chinese group in both decoding and word learning, suggesting the facilitative impact of congruent orthographic experiences in two languages. The data also showed that spelling regularity of stimulus words (L2 effects) was a more powerful predictor than orthographic congruity (L1 effects) of both decoding and word learning performances. Taken as a whole, these findings seem to suggest that L1 and L2 orthographic factors jointly influence L2 decoding and intentional word learning.

To sum up, the emerging evidence provides strong empirical support for complex cross-linguistic interactions transpiring during L2 word recognition. Findings generally suggest that L1 orthographic experience has lasting impacts on L2 word recognition development, and that proficiency-matched L2 learners are similarly affected by L2 language-specific properties. In all studies comparing joint influences of two languages, L2 variables were found to have a stronger impact, overriding the variance attributable to L1 orthographic experience. While L2 word recognition development is guided by structural insights formed through language and literacy learning experiences in two languages, L2 structural properties and the demands they impose appear to be a dominant force in shaping L2 word recognition subskills.

SUMMARY AND FUTURE RESEARCH DIRECTIONS

The importance of word recognition is widely acknowledged in reading research. Four conclusions can be drawn from a substantial body of evidence: (1) phonological and morphological processing skills have direct relationships with reading ability; (2) knowledge of word forms and their linkages to the sound and meaning of words facilitates efficient retrieval of context-appropriate word meanings; (3) such knowledge evolves gradually through cumulative experience with decoding and encoding lexical information in print; and (4) vocabulary knowledge, as a broad, multi-dimensional construct, mediates the connections between word forms and meanings, as well as those between word meanings and real-life world knowledge.

In conceptualizing word recognition in a second language, the chapter has considered, from both universal and language-specific perspectives, four additional factors uniquely associated with L2 reading: (1) L1 orthographic effects, (2) L2 proficiency effects, (3) L1 and L2 orthographic distance, and (4) cross-linguistic interactions. Taken as a whole, the emerging evidence has yielded some promising insights: (a) metalinguistic awareness (PA, in particular), once acquired in one language, serves as a potentially useful resource for L2 reading development; (b) L1-induced facilitation occurs only in the operations wherein L1 and L2 pose similar processing demands; and (c) variations in L2 word recognition are systematic and can be predicted reasonably well by estimating the language-specific demands imposed by the properties of L1 and L2 writing systems.

In light of the collective implications of the findings, three directions appear to hold strong potential for extending current undertakings in L2 word recognition research. The areas of further explorations include (1) cross-linguistic contributions of MA; (2) developmental changes in L1-L2 orthographic distance effects; and (3) connections between word meaning knowledge and real-life world knowledge. These directions are briefly discussed in what follows.

First, there is overwhelming evidence that PA serves as a cross-linguistically shared resource for learning to read in a second language. In contrast, far less is known about the role of MA in L2 reading development. This, in part, is due to the multi-dimensionality of the construct and its close relationship with linguistic knowledge. In light of the centrality of morphological processing in decoding, meaning retrieval, and word learning, the relative contributions of L1 and L2 MA to L2 word recognition deserve serious research attention. Further explorations of MA will serve us well in understanding the nature of cross-linguistic resource sharing in L2 reading development.

Second, extant research demonstrates that L2 word recognition development is constrained by language-specific demands stemming from the orthographic properties of the L1 and L2, and that, of the two, L2 demands appear to be the dominant force in shaping L2 recognition subskills. To date, however, little is known about how L2-induced constraints alter processing efficiency over time both quantitatively and qualitatively. Future research would do well to focus on dynamic changes arising from successive restructuring that may occur as a result of increased L2 linguistic sophistication.

The knowledge of content-specific word meanings plays a critical role in connecting individual word meanings and the reader's real-life world knowledge. In the current literature, vocabulary knowledge is conceptualized primarily as the abstract core semantic information of words. Reflecting such narrow conceptualization, vocabulary knowledge is estimated based on a variety of measures designed to assess the knowledge of word definitions. Given the criticality of the context-specific meaning representations in word meaning knowledge, broadening the current definition-focused conceptualization would be of considerable advantage. An expanded view of word meaning knowledge, such as the one outlined by Anderson and Nagy (1991), would instigate a new line of research that will certainly yield significant insight into the role of vocabulary knowledge in bringing the reader's real-life world knowledge into text meaning construction. There is much to be learned from such broader, integrative approaches to L2 reading research in general and word recognition studies in particular.

REFERENCES

Abu Rabia, S. (1995). Learning to read in Arabic: Reading, syntactic, orthographic and working memory skills in normally achieving and poor Arabic readers. *Reading Psychology, 16*, 351–394.

Adams, M.J. (1990). *Beginning to read.* Cambridge, MA: MIT Press.

Aitchison, J. (1994). *Words in the mind* (2nd ed.). Oxford: Blackwell.

Akamatsu, N. (1999). The effects of first language orthographic features on word recognition processing in English as a second language. *Reading and Writing, 11*, 381–403.

Akamatsu, N. (2003). The effects of first language orthographic features on second language reading in text. *Language Learning, 53*(2), 207–231.

Allington, R.L., & Fleming, J.T. (1978). The misreading of high frequency words. *Journal of Special Education, 12*, 417–421.

Anderson, R.C., & Nagy, W.E. (1991). Word meaning. In R. Barr, M.L. Kamil, P. Mosenthal, & P.D. Pearson (Eds.), *Handbook of reading research* (Vol. 2, pp. 690–724). New York: Longman.

Anderson, R.C., & Pearson, P.D. (1984). A Schema-theoretic view of reading comprehension. In P.D. Pearson (Ed.), *Handbook of reading research* (pp. 255–291). New York: Longman.

August, D., Calderon, M., & Carlo, M. (2000). *Transfer of skills from Spanish to English: A study of young learners* (ED-98-CO-0071). Washington, DC: Center of Applied Linguistics.

August, D., Calderon, M., & Carlo, M. (2001). *Transfer of skills from Spanish to English: A study of young learners* [Updated review of current literature]. Washington DC: Center for Applied Linguistics.

Balota, D., Pollasek, A., & Rayner, K. (1985). The interaction of contextual constraints and parafoveal visual information in reading. *Cognitive Psychology, 17*, 364–390.

Becker, C.A. (1985). What do we really know about semantic context during reading? In D. Besner, T. Waller, & G. MacKinnon (Eds.), *Reading research: Advances in theory and practice* (Vol. 5, pp. 125–166). New York: Academic Press.

Beveridge, M.E.L., & Bak, T.H. (2012). Beyond one-way streets: The intersection of phonology, morphology, and culture with orthography. *Behavior and Brain Sciences, 35*, 280–281.

Bialystock, E. (2001). *Bilingualism in development.* Cambridge: Cambridge University Press.

Bialystok, E., McBride-Chang, C., & Luk, G. (2005). Bilingualism, language proficiency, and learning to read in two writing systems. *Journal of Educational Psychology, 97,* 580–590.

Biemiller, A. (1979). Changes in the use of graphic and contextual information as functions of passage difficulty and reading achievement level. *Journal of Reading Behavior, 11,* 307–319.

Bowers, P., Golden, J., Kennedy, A., & Young, A. (1994). Limits upon orthographic knowledge due to processes indexed by naming speed. In V.W. Berninger (Ed.), *The varieties of orthographic knowledge I: Theoretical and developmental issues* (pp. 173–218). Dordrecht, the Netherlands: Kluwer.

Branum-Martin, L., Fletcher, J.M., Carlson, C.D., Ortiz, A., Carlo, M., & Francis, D.J. (2006). Bilingual phonological awareness: Multilevel construct validation among Spanish-speaking kindergarteners in transitional bilingual education classrooms. *Journal of Educational Psychology, 98,* 170–81.

Brown, T., & Haynes, M. (1985). Literacy background and reading development in a second language. In T.H. Carr (Ed.), *The development of reading skills* (pp. 19–34). San Francisco, CA: Jossey-Bass.

Carlisle, J.F. (2003). Morphology matters in learning to read: A commentary. *Reading Psychology, 24,* 291–322.

Carlisle, J.F., & Beeman, M.M. (2000). The effects of language of instruction on the reading and writing achievement of first-grade Hispanic children. *Scientific Studies of Reading, 4,* 331–353.

Chen, X., Ramirez, G., Luo, Y.C., Geva, E., & Ku, Y.-M. (2012). Comparing vocabulary development in Spanish- and Chinese-speaking ELLs: The effects of metalinguistic and sociocultural factors. *Reading and Writing: An Interdisciplinary Journal, 25,* 1991–2020.

Cormier, P., & Kelson, S. (2000). The roles of phonological and syntactic awareness in the use of plural morphemes among children in French immersion. *Scientific Studies of Reading, 4,* 267–294.

Coulmas, F. (1989). *The writing systems of the world.* Cambridge, MA: Basil Blackwell.

Da Fontoura, H.A., & Siegel, L.S. (1995). Reading syntactic and memory skills of Portuguese-English Canadian children. *Reading and Writing: An International Journal, 7,* 139–153.

Deacon, S.H., & Kirby, J.B. (2004). Morphological awareness: Just "more phonological"? The roles of morphological and phonological awareness in reading development. *Applied Psycholinguistics, 25,* 223–238.

Durgunoglu, A.Y., Nagy, W.E., & Hancin, B.J. (1993). Cross-language transfer of phonemic awareness. *Journal of Educational Psychology, 85,* 453–465.

Durso, F.T., & Shore, W.J. (1998). Partial knowledge of word meanings. *Journal of Experimental Psychology: General, 120,* 190–202.

Ehri, L.C. (1994). Development of the ability to read words: Update. In R. Ruddell, M. Ruddell, & H. Singer (Eds.), *Theoretical models and processes of reading* (4th ed., pp. 323–358). Hillsdale, NJ: Erlbaum.

Ehri, L.C. (1998). Grapheme-phoneme knowledge is essential to learning to read words in English. In J.L. Metsala & L.C. Ehri (Eds.), *Word recognition in beginning literacy* (pp. 3–40). Mahwah, NJ: Erlbaum.

Ehri, L.C. (2014). Orthographic mapping in the acquisition of sight word reading, spelling memory, and vocabulary learning. *Scientific Studies of Reading, 18*, 5–21.

Ellis, N.C. (1994). Vocabulary acquisition: The implicit ins and outs of explicit cognitive mediation. In N.C. Ellis (Ed.), *Implicit and explicit learning of language* (pp. 211–282). London: Academic Press.

Ellis, N. (2002). Frequency effects in language processing: A review with implications for theories of implicit and explicit language acquisition. *Studies in Second Language Acquisition, 24*, 143–188.

Favreau, M., & Segalowitz, N. (1982). Second language reading in fluent bilinguals. *Applied Psycholinguistics, 3*, 329–341.

Favreau, M., & Segalowitz, N. (1983). Automatic and controlled processes in the first- and second-language reading of fluent bilinguals. *Memory and Cognition, 11*, 565–574.

Feldman, L.B., Frost, R., & Pnini, T. (1995). Decomposition words into their constituent morphemes: Evidence from English and Hebrew. *Journal of Experimental Psychology: Learning, Memory and Cognition, 21*, 1–14.

Fowler, A.E., & Liberman, I.Y. (1995). The role of phonology and orthography in morphological awareness. In L.B. Feldman (Ed.), *Morphological aspects of language processing* (pp. 157–188). Hillsdale, NJ: Erlbaum.

Frost, R. (1998). Towards a strong phonological theory of visual word recognition: True issues and false trails. *Psychological Bulletin, 123*, 71–99.

Frost, R. (2012). Towards a universal model of reading. *Behavioral and Brain Sciences, 35*, 263–329.

Frost, R., Katz, L., & Bentin, S. (1987). Strategies for visual word recognition and orthographic depth: A multilingual comparison. *Journal of Experimental Psychology: Human Perception and Performance, 13*, 104–115.

Gathecole, S., & Baddeley, D. (1993). *Working memory and language.* Hove, UK: Erlbaum.

Geva, E. (2008). Facets of metalinguistic awareness related to reading development in Hebrew: Evidence from monolingual and bilingual and bilingual children. In K. Koda & A.M. Zehler (Eds.), *Learning to read across languages: Cross-linguistic relationships in first and second language literacy development* (pp. 154–187). Mahwah, NJ: Erlbaum.

Geva, E., & Wang, M. (2001). The development of basic reading skills in children: A cross-language perspective. *Annual Review of Applied Linguistics, 21*, 182–204.

Goodman, K.S. (1973). Psycholinguistic universals of the reading process. In F. Smith (Ed.), *Psycholinguistics and reading* (pp. 21–29). New York: Holt, Rinehart and Winston.

Goodwin, A.P., Gilbert, J.K., & Cho, S-J. (2013). Morphological contributions to adolescent word reading: An item response approach. *Reading Research Quarterly, 48*, 39–60.

Green, D.W., & Meara, P. (1987). The effects of script on visual search. *Second Language Research, 3*, 102–117.

Hamada, M., & Koda, K. (2008). Influence of first language orthographic experience on second language decoding and word learning. *Language Learning, 58*, 1–31.

Hogaboam, T.W., & Perfetti, C.A. (1978). Reading skill and the role of verbal experience in decoding. *Journal of Educational Psychology, 70*, 717–729.

Hossein, N., & Geva, E. (1999). The contribution of phonological and orthographic processing skills to adult ESL reading: Evidence from native speakers of Farsi. *Applied Psycholinguistics, 20*, 241–267.

Hussein, N. (2014). The role and importance of lower-level processes in second language reading. *Language Teaching, 47*, 1–37.

Jeon, E. H. (2011). Contribution of morphological awareness to K2 reading comprehension. *Modern Language Journal, 95*, 217–235.

Just, M. A., & Carpenter, P. A. (1980). A theory of reading: From eye fixation to comprehension. *Psychological Review, 87*, 329–354.

Just, M. A., & Carpenter, P. A. (1987). *The psychology of reading and language comprehension.* Boston: Allyn & Bacon.

Katz, L., & Frost, R. (1992). Reading in different orthographies: The orthographic depth hypothesis. In R. Frost & L. Katz (Eds.), *Orthography, phonology, morphology, and meaning* (pp. 67–84). Amsterdam: Elsevier.

Kieffer, M. J., & Lesaux, N. K. (2012). Development of morphological awareness and vocabulary knowledge in Spanish-speaking language minority learners: A parallel process latent growth curve model. *Applied Psycholinguistics, 33*, 23–54.

Kintsch, W. (1998). *Comprehension: A paradigm for cognition.* New York: Cambridge University Press.

Kleiman, G. M. (1975). Speech recording in reading. *Journal of Verbal Learning and Verbal Behavior, 14*, 323–339.

Koda, K. (1988). Cognitive process in second language reading: Transfer of L1 reading skills and strategies. *Second Language Research, 4*, 133–156.

Koda, K. (1989). The effects of transferred vocabulary knowledge on the development of L2 reading proficiency. *Foreign Language Annals, 22*, 529–542.

Koda, K. (1990). The use of L1 reading strategies in L2 reading. *Studies in Second Language Acquisition, 12*, 393–410.

Koda, K. (1993). Transferred L1 strategies and L2 syntactic structure during L2 sentence comprehension. *Modern Language Journal, 77*, 490–500.

Koda, K. (1998). The role of phonemic awareness in L2 reading. *Second Language Research, 14*, 194–215.

Koda, K. (1999). Development of L2 intraword structural sensitivity and decoding skills. *Modern Language Journal, 83*, 51–64.

Koda, K. (2000). Cross-linguistic variations in L2 morphological awareness. *Applied Psycholinguistics, 21*, 297–320.

Koda, K. (2002). Writing systems and learning to read in a second language. In W. Li, J. S. Gaffiney, & J. L. Packard (Eds.), *Chinese children's reading acquisition: Theoretical and pedagogical issues* (pp. 225–248). Boston: Kluwer Academic.

Koda, K. (2005). *Insights into second language reading.* New York: Cambridge University Press.

Koda, K. (2007). Reading and language learning: Cross-linguistic constraints on second-language reading development. *Language Learning, 57*, 1–44.

Koda, K. (2012). L2 reading. In S. M. Gass & A. Mackey (Eds.), *Handbook of second language acquisition* (pp. 303–318). New York: Routledge.

Koda, K., Takahashi, E., & Fender, M. (1998). Effects of L1 processing experience on L2 morphological awareness. *Ilha do Desterro, 35*, 59–87.

Koda, K., Zhang, D., & Lu, C. (2013). The role of metalinguistic awareness in biliteracy development. In X. Chen, Q. Wang, & C. L. Yang (Eds.), *Reading development and difficulties in monolingual and bilingual Chinese children* (pp. 141–170). New York: Springer.

Ku, Y-M., & Anderson, R.C. (2003). Development of morphological awareness in Chinese and English. *Reading and Writing: An Interdisciplinary Journal, 16,* 399–422.

Lam, K., Chen, X., Geva, E., Luo, Y.C., & Li, H. (2012). The role of morphological awareness in reading achievement among young Chinese-speaking English language learners: A longitudinal study. *Reading and Writing: An Interdisciplinary Journal, 25,* 1847–1872.

Laufer, B., & Patribakht, S.T. (1998). The relationship between passive and active vocabularies: Effects of language learning context. *Language Learning, 48,* 365–391.

Levelt, W.J.M. (1989). *Speaking: From intention to articulation.* Cambridge, MA: MIT Press.

Levy, B.A. (1975). Vocalization and suppression effects in sentence memory. *Journal of Verbal Learning and Verbal Behavior, 14,* 304–316.

Li, W., Anderson, R.C., Nagy, W., & Zhang, H. (2002). Facets of metalinguistic awareness that contribute to Chinese literacy. In W. Li, J.S. Gaffiney, & J.L. Packard (Eds.), *Chinese children's reading acquisition: Theoretical and pedagogical issues* (pp. 87–106). Boston: Kluwer Academic.

Marcolini, S., Traficante, D., Zoccolotti, P., & Burani, C. (2011). Word frequency modulates morpheme-based reading in poor and skilled Italian readers. *Applied Psycholinguistics, 32,* 513–532.

McBride-Chan, C., Wagner, R. K., Muse, A., Chow, B.W.-Y., & Shu, H. (2005). The role of morphological awareness in children's vocabulary acquisition in English. *Applied Psycholinguistics, 26,* 415–435.

McConkie, G.W., & Zola, D. (1981). Language constraints and the functional stimulus in reading. In A. M. Lesgold & C.A. Perfetti (Eds.), *Interactive process in reading* (pp. 155–175). Hillsdale, NJ: Erlbaum.

Melby-Lervag, M., & Lervag, A. (2011). Cross-linguistic transfer of oral language, decoding, phonological awareness and reading comprehension: A meta-analysis of the correlational evidence. *Journal of Research in Reading, 34,* 114–135.

Muljani, M., Koda, K., & Moates, D. (1998). Development of L2 word recognition: A connectionist approach. *Applied Psycholinguistics, 19,* 99–114.

Nagy, W. (1997). On the role of context in first- and second-language vocabulary learning. In N. Schmitt & M. McCarthy (Eds.), *Vocabulary: Description, acquisition and pedagogy* (pp. 64–83). Cambridge: Cambridge University Press.

Nagy, W., & Anderson, R.C. (1984). How many words are there in printed school English? *Reading Research Quarterly, 19,* 304–330.

Nagy, W.E., & Scott, J.A. (2000). Vocabulary processes. In M.L. Kamil, P.B. Mothenthal, P.D. Pearson, & R. Barr (Eds.), *Handbook of reading research* (Vol. 3, pp. 269–284). Mahwah, NJ: Erlbaum.

Nakamura, P., Koda, K., & Joshi, M. (2014). Biliteracy acquisition in Kannada and English: A developmental study. *Writing System Research, 6,* 132–147.

Nassaji, H. (2014). The role and importance of lower-level processes in second language reading. *Language Teaching, 47,* 1–37.

Nation, I.S.P. (2001). *Learning vocabulary in another language.* Cambridge: Cambridge University Press.

National Reading Panel. (2000). *Teaching children to read: An evidence-based assessment of the scientific research on reading and its development for reading instruction.* Washington, DC: National Institute of Child Health and Human Development.

Nunes, T., & Bryant, P. (2006). *Improving literacy by teaching morphemes*. London: Routledge.

Perfetti, C.A. (1985). *Reading ability*. New York: Oxford University Press.

Perfetti, C.A. (2003). The universal grammar of reading. *Scientific Studies of Reading, 7*, 3–24.

Perfetti, C.A., & Stafura, J. (2014). Word knowledge in a theory of reading comprehension. *Scientific Studies of Reading, 18*, 22–37.

Pring, L., & Snowling, M. (1986). Developmental changes in word recognition: An information-processing account. *Quarterly Journal of Experimental Psychology, 38*, 395–418.

Ramirez, G., Chen, X., Geva, E., & Kiefer, H. (2010). Morphological awareness in Spanish-speaking English language learners: Within and cross-language effects on word reading. *Reading and Writing: An Interdisciplinary Journal, 23*, 337–358.

Rayner, K., & Bertera, J.H. (1979). Reading without a fovea. *Science, 206*, 468–469.

Roberts, T.A., Christo, C., & Shefelbine, J.A. (2011). Word recognition. In M.L. Kamil, P.D. Pearson, E. Birr Moje, & P. Mosenthal (Eds.), *Handbook of reading research* (Vol. 4, pp. 229–258). New York: Longman.

Ryan, A., & Meara, P. (1991). The case of invisible vowels: Arabic speakers reading English words. *Reading in a Foreign Language, 7*, 531–540.

Schmitt, N. (1998). Tracking the incidental acquisition of second language vocabulary: A longitudinal study. *Language Learning, 48*, 281–317.

Schmitt, N. (2014). Size and depth of vocabulary knowledge: What the research shows. *Language Learning, 64*, 913–951.

Schreuder, R., & Flores d'Arcais, G.B. (1992). Psycholinguistic issues in the lexical representation of meaning. In W. Marslen-Wilson (Ed.), *Lexical representation and process* (pp. 409–436). Cambridge, MA: MIT Press.

Segalowitz, N.S. (1986). Skilled reading in the second language. In J. Vaid (Ed.), *Language processing in bilinguals: Psycholinguistic and neurological perspectives* (pp. 3–19). Hillsdale, NJ: Erlbaum.

Segalowitz, N.S., Poulsen, C., & Komoda, M. (1991). Lower level components or reading skill in higher level bilinguals: Implications for reading instruction. *AILA Review, 8*, 15–30.

Seidenberg, M.S., & McClelland, J.L. (1989). A distributed, developmental model of word recognition and naming. *Psychological Review, 96*, 523–568.

Seidenberg, M.S., Tanenhaus, M.K., Leiman, J.M., & Bienkowski, M. (1982). Automatic access of the meanings of ambiguous words in context: Some limitations of knowledge-based processing. *Cognitive Psychology, 14*, 489–537.

Shankweiler, D., & Liberman, I.Y. (1972). Misreading: A search for causes. In J.F. Kavanaugh & I.G. Mattingly (Eds.), *Language by eye and by ear* (pp. 293–317). Cambridge, MA: MIT Press.

Share, D., & Stanovich, K.E. (1995). Cognitive processes in early reading development: Accommodating individual differences into a model of acquisition. In J.S. Carlson (Ed.), *Issues in education: Contributions from psychology* (Vol. 1, pp. 1–57). Greenwich, CT: JAI.

Siegel, L.S., & Ryan, E.B. (1988). Development of grammatical sensitivity, phonological, and short-term memory in normally achieving and learning disabled children. *Developmental Psychology, 24*, 28–37.

Stanovich, K. E. (1986). Matthew effects in reading: Some consequences of individual difference in the acquisition of literacy. *Reading Research Quarterly, 21,* 360–406.

Stanovich, K. E. (1993). The language code: Issues in word recognition. In S. R. Yussen and M. C. Smith (Eds.), *Reading across the life span* (pp. 111–136). New York: Springer-Verlag.

Taylor, I., & Taylor M. M. (1995). *Writing and literacy in Chinese, Korean, and Japanese.* Philadelphia: Benjamins.

Tolchinsky L., & Teberosky, A. (1998). The development of word segmentation and writing in two scripts. *Cognitive Development, 13,* 1–25.

Torgesen, J. K., & Burgess, S. R. (1998). Consistency of reading-related phonological processes throughout early childhood: Evidence from longitudinal-correlational and instructional studies. In J. L. Metsala & L. C. Ehri (Eds.), *Word recognition in beginning literacy* (pp. 161–188). Mahwah, NJ: Erlbaum.

Verhoeven, L. (2000). Components in early second language reading and spelling. *Scientific Studies of Reading, 4,* 313–330.

Verhoeven, L., & Schreuder, R. (2011). Morpheme frequency effects in Dutch complex word reading: A developmental perspective. *Applied Psycholinguistics, 32,* 483–498.

Wade-Woolley, L., & Geva, E. (2000). Processing novel phonemic contrasts in the acquisition of L2 word reading. *Scientific Studies of Reading, 4,* 295–311.

Wagner, R. K., Torgesen, J. K., & Rashotte, C. A. (1994). The development of reading-related phonological processing abilities: New evidence of bi-directional causality from a latent variable longitudinal study. *Developmental Psychology, 30,* 73–87.

Wang, M., Ko, I. Y., & Choi, J. (2009). The importance of morphological awareness in Korean-English biliteracy acquisition. *Contemporary Educational Psychology, 34,* 132–142.

Wang, M., & Koda, K. (2005). Commonalities and differences in word identification skills among learners of English as a second language, *Language Learning, 55,* 71–98.

Wang, M., Koda, K., & Perfetti, C. A. (2003). Alphabetic and non-alphabetic L1 effects in English semantic processing: A comparison of Korean and Chinese English L2 learners. *Cognition, 87,* 129–149.

Wang, M., Perfetti, C. A., & Liu, Y. (2005). Chinese-English biliteracy acquisition: Cross-language and writing system transfer. *Cognition, 97,* 67–88.

Zhang, D. (2010). *Print experiences, transfer of L1 morphological awareness and development of L2 lexical inference ability in young EFL readers* (Unpublished doctoral dissertation). Carnegie Mellon University, Pittsburgh, PA.

Zhang, D., & Koda, K. (2012). Morphological awareness, lexical inferencing vocabulary knowledge and L2 reading comprehension: Testing direct and indirect effects. *Reading and Writing, 25,* 1195–1216.

Zhang, D., & Koda, K. (2013). Morphological awareness and reading comprehension in a foreign language: A study of young Chinese EFL learners. *System, 41,* 901–931.

Ziegler, J. C., & Goswami, U. (2005). Reading acquisition, developmental dyslexia, and skilled reading across languages: A psycholinguistic grain size theory. *Psychological Bulletin, 131,* 3–29.

Ziegler, J. C., & Goswami, U. (2006). Becoming literate in different languages: Similar problems, different solutions. *Developmental Sciences, 9,* 425–436.

4

Cross-language transfer of metalinguistic and cognitive skills in second language learning

Kathleen Hipfner-Boucher and Xi Chen

INTRODUCTION

There is a general consensus among researchers and educators that learning is influenced by the prior knowledge and skills that the learner brings to the learning task (Bransford, Brown, & Cocking, 1999). This general learning principle has been applied to the processes of second language (L2) learning and biliteracy acquisition. A substantial body of research attests to the influence linguistic competencies gained in the first language (L1) have on learning to read in an additional language (for a review, see Genesee, Geva, Dressler, & Kamil, 2006). Moreover, while studies examining L2 influences on L1 learning outcomes are more limited in number, they provide some evidence that competencies developed initially in the L2 may have an impact on L1 language and literacy learning (e.g., Chen, Xu, Nguyen, Hong, & Wang, 2010). The influence of prior knowledge and skill on subsequent learning is accounted for in terms of cross-language transfer.

Elsewhere, decades of empirical research have led to an understanding that learning to read is first and foremost a metalinguistic endeavour (Nagy & Anderson, 1995). Metalinguistic awareness refers to the ability to isolate and manipulate abstract linguistic units and to reflect on the structural properties of language (e.g., Nagy & Anderson, 1999). The emerging reader must develop the insight that oral language is represented in print, identify the segments of spoken language that are represented in written language (i.e., phonemes, morphemes, sub-syllabic units, or syllables, depending on the script), and develop the skills needed to map one onto the other quickly and accurately (Koda, 2000). Thus, learning to read requires children to approach language from a very unique perspective. Whereas the listener attends exclusively to the meaning conveyed by the message, the reader initially attends to its linguistic and structural features, temporarily setting semantics aside.

This chapter discusses cross-language transfer of four metalinguistic competencies that are associated with literacy development: phonological awareness, morphological awareness, orthographic processing, and cognate awareness. Phonological awareness and morphological awareness have been shown to be key determinants of reading achievement (e.g., Adams, 1990; Carlisle, 1995). In addition, orthographic processing has been shown to relate to reading and spelling outcomes (Stanovich, West, & Cunningham, 1991; Wagner & Barker, 1994), although its status as an independent construct and as a causal force in reading and spelling is subject to debate (e.g., Burt, 2006; Deacon, 2012; Deacon, Benere, & Castles, 2012). Finally, a fairly small body of empirical evidence suggests that cognate awareness, a component of metalinguistic awareness that is available uniquely to bilinguals whose two languages are etymologically related,[1] may play a role in L1 and L2 reading outcomes (e.g., Ramírez, Chen, & Pasquarella, 2013).

While extensive research has examined the impact of metalinguistic skills on children's reading development, there is increasing evidence that cognitive abilities in different domains (e.g., memory, reading fluency, visual processing) are also important for reading (e.g., Ferretti, Mazzotti, & Brizzolara, 2008; Liu, Chen, Chung, & Wang, in press; Vidyasagar & Pammer, 2010), although the roles of these constructs remain underexplored in both L1 and L2 reading. In this chapter, we discuss cross-language transfer of working memory and reading fluency, which are, to our knowledge, among the few cognitive skills that have been examined in transfer studies.

In the present chapter, we summarize research evidence that (a) evaluates the effects that metalinguistic and cognitive skills developed in either L1 or L2 have on the emergence of the same skills in the other language, (b) examines the impact of metalinguistic and cognitive skills assessed in either L1 or L2 on reading outcomes in the other language, and (c) identifies factors that condition cross-language transfer of metalinguistic and cognitive skills (e.g., L1/L2 language proficiency, language typology, instruction). Understanding cross-linguistic influences on learning to read is important since these influences distinguish biliteracy acquisition from monolingual literacy acquisition (Koda, 2008). Furthermore, evidence of cross-language transfer of a particular metalinguistic or cognitive skill implies that it is universally relevant to reading. As a result, research on transfer informs reading theory and instructional practice pertinent to L2 learners.

THEORETICAL FRAMEWORKS OF CROSS-LANGUAGE TRANSFER

The notion of transfer has long been a central concern for researchers in second language acquisition who used it to describe the effects of the native language on the interlanguage of L2 learners. For the earliest among them, cross-language transfer was largely construed as "negative" or as "interference" that was due for the most part to structural (e.g., phonological, morphological, syntactic, lexical) differences between the target language and the native language (e.g., Fries, 1945; Lado, 1957; Weinreich, 1953). From this perspective, firmly embedded in the behaviourist tradition, evidence of cross-linguistic influence was observed in production errors in the L2 that could be traced to the L1 (e.g., spelling errors in the L2 that reflect L1 orthography, such as the *sh/ch* confusion common among English-French bilinguals). Indeed, much of the research conducted within this early contrastive framework sought to determine which elements of a given L2 would be challenging to learn for speakers of a specific L1 (Geva, 2014).

While the central notion that typological distance between languages impacts L2 acquisition has endured, the contrastive framework as originally proposed did not stand up well to the test of rigorous empirical examination. Its predictive power was undermined by findings that L2 errors often reflect developmental constraints that are paralleled in L1 acquisition (Bailey, Madden, & Krashen, 1974; Luk & Shirai, 2009). Furthermore, its emphasis on observable linguistic behaviours made it unsuitable for elucidating cross-language relationships that are more psychological in nature or for accounting for transfer across domains (e.g., transfer of L1 phonological awareness to L2 word reading) (Genesee et al., 2006).

Subsequently, the research community shifted its focus of attention to include the effects of "positive" transfer, also referred to as "facilitation". From this perspective, competencies acquired in one language were hypothesized to support (rather than interfere with) the acquisition of both language (e.g., Odlin, 1990; Ringbom, 1987) and literacy skills in another language (e.g., Cummins, 1979, 1981; Genesee et al., 2006; Koda & Zehler, 2008). Moreover, the scope of inquiry was broadened to consider not only the linguistic but also the cognitive (e.g., working memory, phonological processing), socio-affective (e.g., motivation), developmental, and contextual (e.g., language input, instruction) factors that promote facilitation in L2 learners and contribute to individual differences not only in L2 language learning but also in L2 literacy acquisition (Geva, 2014). For example, a later iteration of the contrastive framework was the script-dependent hypothesis, which proposed that the processes implicated in literacy acquisition may differ across languages as a function of characteristics of the writing systems that represent them (Geva, Wade-Woolley, & Shany, 1997).

Another influential theoretical framework to conceptualize facilitation is Cummins's (1981) *linguistic interdependence hypothesis*. Cummins formulated the hypothesis as follows:

> To the extent that instruction in a certain language is effective in promoting proficiency in that language, transfer of this proficiency to another language will occur, provided there is adequate exposure to that other language (either in the school or environment) and adequate motivation to learn that language.

> (1981, p. 29)

Thus, Cummins introduced the notion of bidirectional facilitation of linguistic proficiency that was contingent on the attainment of a threshold level of linguistic competence in the source language. The linguistic interdependence hypothesis further distinguished skills in terms of their relative cognitive demands. The development of higher-order decontextualized skills, such as reading, was hypothesized to be founded on underlying proficiencies common to all languages that undergird cross-language transfer, although the construct of common underlying proficiencies was vaguely defined.

A primary criticism of the interdependence framework is its inability to identify the specific skills and abilities that transfer across languages (Genesee et al., 2006). This is problematic, as reading is increasingly viewed as a task that draws on a constellation of related yet disparate component processes (e.g., working memory, phonological processing) and skills (e.g., phonological and morphological analysis) (Geva, 2014). Furthering the linguistic interdependence hypothesis, recent research on transfer has attempted to identify the sub-skills that do and do not demonstrate cross-language effects (e.g., Geva & Ryan, 1993). For example, Geva and colleagues have proposed that *common underlying cognitive processes*, such as working memory, phonological awareness, and rapid naming, are part of a child's general cognitive makeup and account for individual differences in the rate and success of learning both the L1 and L2.

This body of research typically distinguishes *language-general* versus *language-specific* processes implicated in L2 literacy development. Language-general competencies are common to all languages; as such, they may facilitate reading across languages (e.g., Geva & Siegel, 2000; Stanovich, Cunningham, & Feeman, 1984). Conversely, language-specific competencies are determined by the unique features of a language/script, so they need to be learned separately for each one (e.g., Katz & Frost, 1992; Saiegh-Haddad & Geva, 2008). Empirical evidence gathered to date suggests that learning to read in an L2 involves both language-general and language-specific processes and that any given metalinguistic skill may exhibit both universal and language-specific patterns of influence (e.g., Geva & Siegel, 2000; Ramírez, Chen, Geva, & Luo, 2011; Saiegh-Haddad & Geva, 2008). For example, a skill assessed in L1 may not correlate with a parallel skill assessed in L2, but significantly predict an aspect of L2 literacy.

The hypothesized effects of language-general versus language-specific skills on biliteracy were elaborated in the transfer facilitation model proposed by Koda (2005, 2007). Koda (2007) defines transfer as "automatic activation of well-established L1 competencies (mapping patterns) triggered by L2 input" (p. 17). In other words, the extent to which L1 metalinguistic awareness can transfer and facilitate L2 metalinguistic awareness development reflects both impact of L1 language properties and adjustment through L2 experience. Koda (2007) further maintains that transfer is non-volitional and non-selective, in that it occurs regardless of learners' intent and cannot be easily controlled. The transfer facilitation model can be applied to explain the patterns of transfer reported for various aspects of metalinguistic awareness. For example, because English and French share certain morphological features (e.g., inflections, derivations), inflectional and derivational awareness acquired through exposure to one language would be expected to transfer to the other, thereby facilitating reading development in that language. Conversely, tone awareness acquired as a speaker/reader of Chinese would not be expected to transfer to either English or French since lexical tones are not features of phonology in these languages.

TRANSFER PATTERNS OF METALINGUISTIC AND COGNITIVE SKILLS

In recent years, cross-language transfer has generated increasing interest among researchers seeking to understand whether and how insights gained in one language can be transferred to facilitate the development of reading and its related abilities in another language (D. Zhang & Koda, 2012). Three distinct empirical perspectives have been applied to the study of cross-language transfer of metalinguistic and cognitive skills. Collectively, these studies aim to distinguish language-universal and language-specific competencies and to ascertain the factors that facilitate or constrain their transfer across languages. At the same time, many test the direction of cross-language influence, attempting to determine whether transfer occurs from the L1 to the L2 only, or whether reverse transfer (i.e., from the L2 to the L1) is in evidence. In doing so, these studies seek to identify the component skills and processes that must be accounted for in elaborating a comprehensive model of biliteracy acquisition.

The first empirical perspective focuses on comparisons of performance on a certain skill in L2 across different L1 groups. The objective of these studies is to determine the extent to which features of an L1 influence the development of a skill in that language and condition transfer to parallel skill in an additional language. The second perspective considers transfer at the construct level. These studies employ a correlational approach to test the hypothesis that a skill acquired in one language is associated with (i.e., is significantly and positively correlated with) parallel skill in another language. Of course, it is essential to keep in mind when interpreting these studies that correlations do not imply causality. Finally, the third perspective examines the transfer of metalinguistic and cognitive skills acquired in one language to reading in another language. Using correlation-based statistical procedures (regression, structural equation modeling), these studies quantify the amount of variance accounted for by specific skills in predicting word-level or text-level reading outcomes across languages. The most stringent measure of transfer is provided in studies that first accounted for within-language effects of the skill under investigation, allowing the cross-language effect to be tested over and above L1 competency in the particular skill.

In what follows, we will define six metalinguistic and cognitive competencies (phonological awareness, morphological awareness, orthographic processing, cognate awareness, memory, and reading fluency), and refer very briefly to the research evidence involving monolingual children that relates each to word reading and/or reading comprehension. We then turn to a review of the L2 literature examining cross-language transfer of each of these competences, situating them within one of the three empirical perspectives outlined earlier.

Phonological awareness

Phonological awareness, defined as the ability to manipulate and reflect on sound units in language, has received considerable attention in the research literature because of the pivotal role it plays in the development of word reading ability in English, as in all alphabetic languages. Study after study has shown that readers who are able to attend to sub-syllabic sound units – individual phonemes in particular – are better able to map written symbols (i.e., letters, letter combinations) onto sound units. As a result, they are able to learn to decode words more readily (Bradley & Bryant, 1983; Kirby, Parilla, & Peiffer, 2003; Wagner, Torgesen, & Rashotte, 1994). Moreover, the relationship between phonemic awareness and word reading is reciprocal: phonemic awareness promotes increased skill in word reading, which in turn heightens awareness of the phonemic structure of words (Perfetti, Beck, Bell, & Hughes, 1982; Wagner & Torgesen, 1987). Research demonstrates a progression in the order in which English-speaking children acquire phonological awareness, such that awareness of larger speech segments (words, syllables) precedes awareness of smaller segments (onsets and rimes, phonemes) (Goswami, 1999; Lonigan, Burgess, Anthony, & Baker, 1998; Schuele & Boudreau, 2008).

A limited number of studies have investigated cross-language transfer of phonological awareness from the comparative perspective, examining patterns of performance exhibited by bilingual versus monolingual children on English phonological awareness tasks (Bialystok, McBride-Chang, & Luk, 2005; Bruck & Genesee, 1995; Caravolas & Bruck, 1993; Chen et al., 2010). Overall, these studies revealed that phonological awareness abilities are influenced by the phonological characteristics of the language to which children are exposed, including the language of instruction. For example, in a study aimed at examining the effect of oral and written language input on the development of phonological awareness, Caravolas and Bruck (1993) compared the performance of 4- to 6-year-old Czech-English bilinguals and English monolinguals on awareness of complex onsets measured in English. Relative to English, Czech contains a greater variety and frequency of complex syllabic onsets, making these phonological units highly salient features of the language. Moreover, Czech is represented by a more transparent orthography than English. Consequently, the bilingual children were expected to show higher levels of awareness than their monolingual peers for complex onsets in English prior to formal schooling and more advanced spelling skills by the end of Grade 1. The results were consistent with these hypotheses, suggesting that the development of phonological awareness is partly conditioned by phonological input. Furthermore, the results demonstrated transfer of L1-induced awareness to the L2, which in turn facilitated the acquisition of L2 literacy competencies.

Studies reported by Chen et al. (2010) also examined transfer of phonological awareness from a comparative perspective, this time examining the influence of phonological awareness acquired through instruction in the L2 (English) on parallel L1 (Mandarin) outcomes in languages that were typologically distant. Working with a sample of Mandarin-speaking children exposed to varying amounts of English-language instruction in Grades 1 through 3, the authors tested the hypothesis that learning English would accelerate the development of Chinese onset-rime and phonemic awareness through cross-language transfer. In addition, they expected that the extent of facilitation would depend on proficiency levels achieved as a function of amount of exposure over time to English. Results were consistent with their hypotheses. Notably, the pattern of cross-language transfer reflected the features of the source language such that additional English instruction had its strongest effect on Chinese phonemic awareness and its weakest effect on tone awareness. Again, these results suggested that quantity of language input is a determinant of facilitation. Parallel findings were reported by Bruck and Genesee (1995) in a study involving English-French bilinguals.

A more substantial body of research has examined concurrent and/or longitudinal transfer of phonological awareness from the second perspective (i.e., at the construct level) in both typologically close (Cárdenas-Hagan,

Carlson, & Pollard-Durodola, 2007; Cisero & Royer, 1995; Dickinson, McCabe, Clark-Chiarelli, & Wolf, 2004; Quiroga, Lemos-Britton, Mostafapour, Abbott, & Berninger, 2002) and distant languages (Gottardo, Yan, Siegel, & Wade-Woolley, 2001; Keung & Ho, 2009; Luo, Chen, & Geva, 2014; Roberts & Corbett, 1997; Saiegh & Geva, 2008; Wang, Park, & Lee, 2006; Wang, Perfetti, & Liu, 2005). All studies reported a statistically significant association between phonological awareness skills assessed in the L1 and the L2 that was interpreted as evidence of cross-language transfer. In the study by Cisero and Royer (1995), for example, Spanish (L1) and English (L2) rime detection and initial and final phoneme detection skills were assessed in Hispanic-American children attending a bilingual education program at the beginning and end of Grade 1. The findings revealed evidence of cross-language transfer, in that Time 1 phonological awareness assessed in the L1 and L2 predicted Time 2 phonological awareness in both languages. Thus, transfer was demonstrated from the stronger to the weaker language, as well as from the weaker to the stronger language.

The vast majority of studies investigating cross-language transfer of phonological awareness are situated within the third empirical perspective, that of assessing the impact of phonological awareness acquired in one language on literacy outcomes in another. Among these, researchers have placed particular emphasis on investigating the contribution of phonological awareness to word and/or pseudo-word reading because of its demonstrated link to decoding ability. As a result, cross-language relations between phonological awareness and word-level reading skills have been firmly established in a number of language combinations. These include language pairs that are related, such as French and English (e.g., Haigh, Savage, Erdos, & Genesee, 2011; Jared, Cormier, Levy, & Wade-Woolley, 2012; Lafrance & Gottardo, 2005; MacCoubrey, Wade-Woolley, Klinger, & Kirby, 2004), and Spanish and English (e.g., Cisero & Royer, 1995; Durgunoğlu, Nagy, & Hancin-Bhatt, 1993; Lindsey, Manis, & Bailey, 2003; Manis, Lindsey, & Bailey, 2004; Quiroga et al., 2002), as well as unrelated language pairs, such as Hebrew and English (Wade-Woolley & Geva, 2000), Chinese and English (e.g., Chow, McBride-Chang, & Burgess, 2005; Gottardo, Chiappe, Yan, Siegel, & Gu, 2006; Gottardo et al., 2001; Hipfner-Boucher, Lam, & Chen, 2014; Marinova-Todd, Zhao, & Bernhardt, 2010; Wang et al., 2005), and Korean and English (Wang, Park, et al., 2006).

While the bulk of the evidence attests to the facilitative effect of L1 phonological awareness on L2 word reading, indicating transfer from the more proficient to the less proficient language, there is evidence of the reverse effect (i.e., L2 phonological awareness on L1 reading) (Comeau, Cormier, Grandmaison, & Lacroix, 1999; Keung & Ho, 2009). In their landmark study, Comeau et al. (1999) reported that phonological awareness skills in English and in

French were significantly correlated with English and French word reading one year later among English (L1) children educated in French (L2). Notably, the cross-language relationships were as strong as the within-language relationships, even after controlling for factors such as age, gender, and general cognitive ability. Similarly, Keung and Ho (2009) demonstrated that English rime detection uniquely predicted Chinese word reading in Cantonese-speaking second graders learning English as an L2 after controlling for within-language phonological skills. Thus, there is limited evidence that phonological awareness acquired in the L2 may facilitate L1 word reading in languages varying in typological distance.

While the cross-language effect of phonological awareness on word reading has been established, there is little evidence of its contribution to reading comprehension outcomes (Haigh et al., 2011; Manis et al., 2004). Haigh et al. (2011) demonstrated transfer of kindergarten English (L1) phonological awareness to Grade 2 French (L2) reading comprehension after controlling for age, general cognitive ability, and kindergarten English word reading as a baseline reading measure. However, when letter-name knowledge replaced word reading as the baseline reading measure in the regression equation, phonological awareness was no longer a significant predictor. Conversely, a facilitative effect of L2 phonological awareness on L1 reading comprehension was reported in a study involving Hispanic-American children of limited English proficiency receiving bilingual instruction. Manis et al. (2004) found that phonological awareness assessed in English (L2) in Grade 1 was a unique predictor of Spanish (L1) reading comprehension assessed in Grade 2 after controlling for print knowledge. The authors interpreted this finding as evidence that in a language with highly consistent spelling-sound correspondences, such as Spanish, phonological skills are the key predictor of reading ability. Clearly, future research is needed to elucidate the role of cross-language transfer of phonological awareness in supporting children's understanding of written text.

Taken together, studies examining the transfer of phonological awareness from the three research perspectives converge on the finding that L1 and L2 phonological awareness skills transfer across languages even among children with relatively limited L2 proficiency and in cases where the child's two languages share few phonological or orthographic features. Moreover, cross-language transfer of phonological awareness is a key determinant of word-level reading outcomes among bilingual children, and its facilitative effect is evident across languages whether assessed in the L1 or the L2, although evidence for reverse transfer is more limited. The results of these studies clearly indicate that phonological awareness is a language-universal construct (Ziegler & Goswami, 2005). Deacon, Chen, Luo, and Ramírez (2013) speculate that this may be due to the universality of the units of phonology (i.e., syllable, onset, rime, phoneme) across languages and in spite of variations in the level at which phonology is encoded in print. At the same time, the development of phonological awareness and its transfer across languages have been shown to interact with features of the L1 and L2 so that its specific contribution to reading outcomes may vary somewhat from language to language (Saiegh-Haddad & Geva, 2010).

Morphological awareness

The English writing system is morphophonemic, meaning that it encodes not only phonemes but also morphemes (Chomsky & Halle, 1968). For example, the silent "g" in the word *sign* is maintained to reflect the word's semantic relationship to the words *signature, signal,* and *signatory.* It is not surprising then that morphological awareness plays an important role in English reading since it can help children to see the semantic relations between words despite differences in phonological structure (Carlisle, 1995; Kuo & Anderson, 2006). Morphological awareness refers to the ability to reflect on and manipulate morphemes, and to use word formation rules (i.e., rules governing inflections, derivations, and compounding) to produce and understand multi-morphemic words (Kuo & Anderson, 2006). The ability to make use of morphemic constituents to facilitate fast, accurate word identification supports reading comprehension and has been shown to distinguish successful and less successful readers (Berninger et al., 2003). In particular, the morphologically aware child is able to apply knowledge of morphemic relations to deduce the meaning of unfamiliar morphologically complex words (Carlisle, 2000). For example, the meaning of the word *piglet* can be deduced by extracting the base word *pig* and the suffix – *let* by way of analogy to *booklet.*

Transfer of morphological awareness implies that the basic insight that words can be segmented into smaller units of meaning acquired as a speaker of one language facilitates the emergence of parallel insight in another language. To our knowledge, very few studies have investigated transfer of morphological awareness from the perspective of language group comparisons, that is, by examining patterns of performance exhibited by groups of bilingual children relative to one another or to a monolingual English L1 (EL1) group on English morphological awareness tasks (Kieffer & Lesaux, 2012; Koda, 2000; Ramírez et al., 2011). The study conducted by Ramírez et al. (2011) reported that English monolinguals and Spanish-speaking English Language Learners (ELLs) in Grades 4 and 7 outperformed Chinese-speaking ELLs on a test of English derivational awareness. Conversely, the Chinese-speaking ELLs and English monolinguals demonstrated equivalent performance on a test of English compound awareness, while the performance of the Spanish ELLs was significantly poorer than that of their monolingual peers. These findings suggest that transfer of morphological awareness depends on the presence of shared structural features (e.g., derivations in Spanish and English, compounding in Chinese and English) between the source and target language. Similarly, a study by Koda (2000) involving Chinese- and Korean-speaking university students assessed on measures of derivational awareness in English found evidence that transfer of morphological awareness is contingent on the presence of shared morphological structures. The students performed best on the English morphological skill that had a parallel in their native language and to which they would be expected to have had the most exposure. The author interpreted this finding as confirmation of the influence of L1 processing experiences on L2 morphological awareness development, an influence that manifests itself in specific and predictable ways.

A limited number of studies have examined concurrent and/or longitudinal transfer of inflectional and derivational morphological awareness from the second empirical perspective (i.e., at the construct level). Overall, studies reporting correlational data derived from measures of inflectional (Deacon, Wade-Woolley, & Kirby, 2007) and derivational awareness (Ramírez, Chen, Geva, & Keifer, 2010) in languages that are typologically close to English provide evidence of cross-language transfer at the construct level. Notably, Deacon et al.'s (2007) results suggest that L1-L2 associations may be somewhat unstable over time, perhaps because they are contingent on factors such as language experience and proficiency. Conversely, studies reporting correlations between morphological awareness in English and a typologically distant language show mixed results. Saiegh-Haddad and Geva (2008) found no association between scores on Arabic and English derivational measures in a sample of Arabic ELLs living in Canada. The authors suggested that the morphologically opaque quality of Arabic relative to English, in conjunction with task difficulty, might explain this finding. On the other hand, Schiff and Calif (2007) found scores on Hebrew and English derivational awareness tasks to be moderately correlated among Israeli children learning English as a second language.

Likewise, previous research has produced mixed results with respect to transfer of compound awareness at the construct level in Chinese-English bilinguals. Studies conducted by Wang et al. (Wang, Cheng, & Chen, 2006; Wang, Yang, & Cheng, 2009) failed to find an association between compound awareness assessed in Chinese and English. Conversely, a number of other studies observed significant cross-language relationships between the two constructs (Cheung et al., 2010; Chung & Ho, 2010; Luo et al., 2014; Pasquarella, Chen, Lam, Luo, & Ramírez, 2011). The most compelling evidence of transfer of compound awareness at the construct level comes from J. Zhang et al. (2010), who implemented an intervention among Grade 5 students learning English as a foreign language in China. Students received a 45-minute training session on either Chinese or English compound morphology. Following the intervention, students instructed in Chinese morphology outperformed a no-treatment control group on an English compound awareness task, indicating transfer of compound awareness from Chinese to English. Reverse transfer from English to Chinese was detected among students with high levels of English reading proficiency only. The results of J. Zhang et al.'s study point to a causal link between Chinese and English compound awareness. They also suggest that a threshold of L2 linguistic proficiency may be required for transfer of specific linguistic skills to take place (Haddad & Geva, 2010).

The majority of studies examining cross-language transfer of morphological awareness are situated within the third empirical perspective, that of assessing the contribution of morphological awareness acquired in one language to literacy outcomes in another. Among these, studies have primarily focused on word-level reading as the outcome variable. Again, these studies involve languages that are both typologically close to English (Deacon et al., 2007; Ramírez et al., 2010) and typologically distant (Chung & Ho, 2010; Luo et al., 2014; Pasquarella et al., 2011; Ramírez et al., 2011; Saiegh-Haddad & Geva, 2008; Schiff & Calif, 2007; Wang, Ko, & Choi, 2009; Wang, Yang, et al., 2009). For example, derivational awareness was found to transfer from L1 to L2 word reading among Hebrew-speaking Israeli children who were learning English as a foreign language (Schiff & Calif, 2007). Overall, the research literature provides evidence of cross-language relations between morphological awareness and word reading skills, although it suggests that it may be contingent upon shared L1 and L2 morphological structures.

One exception to the general pattern of findings in support of cross-language transfer of morphological awareness to word reading comes from a study by Tong and McBride-Chang (2010). The authors found that Chinese visual-orthographic skills and phonological awareness accounted for unique variance in English word reading among second and fifth graders learning English as an L2 in Hong Kong. Chinese compound awareness, on the other hand, was not a significant predictor. The "look and say" approach to English reading instruction favoured by Hong Kong schools was cited as a possible explanation for these findings, suggesting that instructional factors may interact with transfer of metalinguistic competencies.

The possibility of bidirectional transfer of morphological awareness to word reading skill has also been evaluated (Chung & Ho, 2010; Deacon et al., 2007; Wang, Cheng, et al., 2006; Wang, Ko, et al., 2009; Wang, Yang, et al., 2009). Deacon et al. (2007) administered past tense analogy tasks to measure English and French inflectional awareness among a group of EL1 children educated in French every year from Grade 1 to Grade 3. In addition, they administered word reading measures in English and French at each time point. Results revealed bidirectional transfer: While English inflectional

awareness in Grades 1 and 2 explained unique variance in French word reading concurrently and longitudinally, French inflectional awareness in Grades
2 and 3 accounted for unique variance in English word reading both concurrently and longitudinally. The relations persisted after controlling for several
relevant variables, including within-language morphological awareness. The
authors concluded that morphological awareness can be applied to reading
across orthographies, although the relationship is influenced by relative levels
of L1 and L2 language and literacy proficiencies. Conversely, Chung and Ho
(2010) found no support for bidirectional transfer of compound awareness
to word reading among children in Hong Kong learning English as an L2 at
school. Whereas L1 compound awareness was found to facilitate L2 word
reading, no L2 to L1 effect was found. Likewise, Wang, Cheng, et al. (2006)
and Wang, Yang, et al. (2009) found transfer of English compound awareness
to Chinese word reading only in a sample of Chinese American children.
Again, proficiency would appear to play a role in conditioning transfer of
morphological awareness.

With respect to the cross-language transfer of morphological awareness to
reading comprehension, Pasquarella et al. (2011) found English compound
awareness to be a significant predictor of Chinese reading comprehension in
a cross-section of first-, second-, and fourth-grade Canadian English-Chinese
bilinguals, after controlling for a number of variables, including Chinese
compound awareness. On the other hand, Chinese compound awareness did
not predict English reading comprehension. The authors argued that this
transfer is likely based on the shared compounding structure between Chinese
and English. However, because it is a more salient feature of Chinese morphology than English morphology, it plays a key role in Chinese reading only.
This opened the door to transfer of compounding skill acquired in English
to Chinese reading but constrained the role played by Chinese compound
awareness in English reading comprehension. Thus, it would appear that the
direction of morphological awareness transfer may be conditioned by the
morphological structure of the language of the outcome variable.

Overall, studies examining transfer of morphological awareness suggest
that it is implicated in the process of learning to read across typologically
distinct languages. However, there is considerable evidence suggesting that
transfer of morphological awareness across languages may be more constrained than is the transfer of phonological awareness. It is constrained first
and foremost by typology, since it is dependent on the presence of shared
structural features between the source and target languages and may be
influenced by the salience of those features in the target language. In addition,
there is some evidence that transfer of morphological awareness is constrained
by language experience, and that it may be contingent on attainment of a
threshold level of L1 and L2 language proficiency.

Orthographic processing

English is represented in print by a "deep" or "opaque" (versus "transparent") orthography, meaning that phonemes can map onto multiple graphemes (Katz & Frost, 1992). For example, the phoneme /f/ can be represented by the letter "f" as in *fish*, the consonant doublet "ff" as in *office*, or the digraphs "ph" and "gh" as in *phantom* and *tough*, respectively. Furthermore, rules govern the position of certain spelling patterns within words. In English, for example, consonant doublets are "illegal" at the beginning of a word except in a small set of borrowed words – for example, *llama*. Sensitivity to spelling patterns in written language and to the rules governing them is referred to as orthographic processing. There is a growing body of empirical research providing evidence of a relationship between orthographic processing skill and word-level reading ability among monolingual English-speaking children (Barker, Torgesen, & Wagner, 1992; Deacon, 2012; Roman, Kirby, Parrila, Wade-Woolley, & Deacon, 2009; Stanovich et al., 1991), although the direction of causality is not entirely clear (Deacon et al., 2012). Typically these studies employ forced decision tasks in which the child is asked to choose which of two options, a word or its pseudo-homophone, is spelled correctly (e.g., *rane – rain*) or to choose the more "word-like" of two pseudo-words (e.g., *daik – dayk*, where only *aik* may occur as a word ending in English) (Commissaire, Pasquarella, Chen, & Deacon, 2014). The former assesses lexical-level orthographic processing and the latter sub-lexical-level processing.

Relative to phonological and morphological awareness, cross-language transfer of orthographic processing has received little attention in the research literature. Once considered a strictly language-specific skill (e.g., Abu-Rabia, 2001), researchers have only recently begun to consider the potential effects of transfer of orthographic processing in greater depth, and to assess the role that factors such as orthographic proximity and grain size (i.e., lexical versus sub-lexical units) may play in facilitating or constraining its transferability.

Studies examining cross-language transfer of orthographic processing at the construct level among learners of languages represented by different scripts have yielded very little evidence of transferability. The language pairs investigated to date include English and Chinese (Gottardo et al., 2001; Wang et al., 2005; Wang, Yang, et al., 2009), English and Korean (Wang, Park, et al., 2006), and English and Russian (Abu-Rabia, 2001). Conversely, studies involving languages represented by a common script, such as English and French or Spanish, have revealed cross-language transfer of orthographic processing at the construct level (Commissaire, Duncan, & Casalis, 2011; Commissaire et al., 2014; Deacon, Commissaire, Chen, & Pasquarella, 2013; Deacon, Wade-Woolley, & Kirby, 2009; Sun-Alperin & Wang, 2011; but see Deacon, Chen, et al., 2013). However, a study involving Farsi-English bilingual children growing up in Canada reported moderate correlations between orthographic processing outcomes in the two languages (Arab-Moghaddam & Sénéchal, 2001), despite the fact that Farsi is based on the Arabic script and English the Roman script. Thus, more research is needed to investigate transfer of orthographic processing across languages represented by different scripts.

Like studies examining cross-language transfer at the construct level, a small but growing body of work has reported cross-language transfer of orthographic processing to word reading in languages that share the same script (Deacon et al., 2009; Deacon, Chen, et al., 2013; Deacon, Commissaire, et al., 2013; Sun-Alperin & Wang, 2011). For example, Deacon et al. (2009) reported cross-language relationships for second-grade EL1 children educated in French. English and French orthographies, like those of English and Spanish, are both alphabetic and are based on the Roman alphabet. Lexical-level orthographic processing predicted concurrent word reading across languages, after controlling for phonological awareness, vocabulary, and within-language orthographic processing. Notably, the relationship was bidirectional.

In a subsequent study, this time involving a sample of first-grade EL1 and English-dominant children educated in French, the authors reported bidirectional cross-language transfer of both lexical and sub-lexical orthographic processing to word reading (Deacon, Commissaire, et al., 2013). A number of interesting findings emerged from this study. First, scores were higher on items with letter patterns that were shared between English and French as compared with items with language-specific letter patterns (e.g., *ough* and *ille* at the end of a word are unique to English and French, respectively, while *ame* is common to both). The authors explained these findings in terms of relative degree of print exposure; clearly, the children could be expected to encounter language-shared patterns more often than language-specific patterns. Second, scores were similar in the French and English versions of the task, despite the absence of direct instruction in English, suggesting that both explicit and implicit exposure may support the development of orthographic sensitivity. Finally, transfer at the sub-lexical level was restricted to orthographic units that were shared between English and French. It would appear then that cross-language transfer of orthographic processing is dependent on amount of print exposure at least to some extent.

To summarize, while research reveals cross-language transfer of orthographic processing to word reading in languages that share the same script, there is little evidence of cross-language relationships between orthographic processing and word reading in learners of languages represented by different scripts (e.g., Abu-Rabia, 2001; Gottardo et al., 2001; Wang, Park, et al., 2006). Thus, the overall pattern of findings related to orthographic processing suggests that, contrary to previously held beliefs, transfer of orthographic processing across languages is not entirely language-specific. It is, however, highly constrained, probably occurring only in cases where children are learning to read in two languages represented by the same script.

Cognate awareness

Cognates are word pairs in different languages that share common historical roots. They have the same meaning and similar, if not identical, spellings (e.g., the English and French words *train*). Cognate awareness is recognition of the relation between cognates in two languages (Malabonga, Kenyon, Carlo, August, & Louguit, 2008). Cognate awareness is a component of metalinguistic awareness that is available uniquely to bilinguals whose two languages are etymologically related. Its status as a metalinguistic skill derives from the fact that the ability to recognize words as cognates requires one to reflect on the relationship between lexical items in two languages (Chen, Ramírez, Luo, Geva, & Ku, 2012). Cognate awareness has been shown to exert influence on word reading (e.g., Duyk, Van Assche, Drieghe, & Hartsuiker, 2007; Lemhöfer & Dijkstra, 2004; Schwartz, Kroll, & Diaz, 2007; van Hell & de Groot, 2008) and on vocabulary (Hancin-Bhatt & Nagy, 1994). Furthermore, cognate awareness is related to reading comprehension (e.g., Jiménez et al., 1995, 1996; Nagy, García, Durgunoğlu, & Hancin-Bhatt, 1993; Ramírez et al., 2013). This finding is not surprising, given the demonstrated effects of cognate awareness on word reading and vocabulary, which in turn are determinants of reading comprehension outcomes (Gough & Tumner, 1986).

Few studies have explored cognate awareness from the perspective of between-group comparisons of performance, and those that have revealed mixed results, perhaps due to differences in methodologies (Cunningham & Graham, 2000). Two studies examining cognate awareness among English-French bilinguals and English monolinguals have been reported, one examining its facilitative effect on word learning, the second on word choice in written language production. Harley, Hart, and Lapkin (1986) found that native English-speaking students in Grade 6 who were educated in French performed no better than English monolinguals on the cognate items of an English vocabulary test, suggesting an absence of cognate facilitation in word learning. Conversely, Harley and King (1989) found evidence to suggest that EL1 French immersion students benefit from awareness of English-French cognate relationships. The authors analyzed sixth-grade written compositions for French verb use and found that students used more lower-frequency verbs in French (L2) that had an English (L1) cognate (e.g., *alarmer*) than lower-frequency verbs without an English cognate. The authors interpreted their findings as indicating that recognition of cognate relationships enhances vocabulary acquisition in an additional language.

Three studies involving speakers of English and Spanish also attest to the facilitative effect of cognate awareness in promoting word learning. Proctor and Mo (2009) compared the performance of bilingual and monolingual fourth graders identified as struggling readers on a vocabulary task developed by Malabonga et al. (2008). This task required children to choose the synonym of a target word from among four options. Target words were low-frequency English words, half of which had a high-frequency Spanish cognate. All study participants were recipients of a 4-week intervention designed to promote vocabulary knowledge and reading comprehension that included explicit instruction in cognate awareness. While total scores showed no significant differences between groups, the proportion of cognates correctly identified was found to be significantly higher among the bilingual children, suggesting that the presence of cognates positively influenced the overall performance of these students.

Similarly, Dressler, Carlo, Snow, August, and White (2011) reported that fourth- and fifth-grade Spanish-English bilinguals significantly outperformed their monolingual English peers on the cognate items of the cognate task devised by Malabonga et al. (2008). All children had participated in an intervention in which explicit strategies for inferring the meanings of unknown words, including using cognates, were explicitly taught. Taken together, the studies by Proctor and Mo (2009) and Dressler et al. provide convincing evidence that awareness of cognate relationships supports the cross-language transfer of semantic knowledge from the L1 to the L2, thereby promoting L2 vocabulary development.

Finally, in a study examining reverse transfer (i.e., transfer from the L2 to the L1) of cognate awareness to word knowledge, Cunningham and Graham (2000) tested Grades 5 and 6 Anglophone children in Spanish immersion to English monolinguals matched on a number of relevant variables on a subset of items from a standardized English vocabulary test. In addition, the participants were tested in English on an experimental measure of vocabulary made up of high-frequency Spanish words with corresponding low-frequency English cognates. Overall the two groups performed equally well on the vocabulary measure; however, when performance on the cognate items of the test was compared, differences in favour of the English-Spanish bilinguals were found. In addition, the bilingual children knew the meaning of significantly more words on the cognate task than their monolingual counterparts. Based on these findings, the authors concluded that semantic knowledge acquired in the L2 facilitated L1 word learning.

Most studies examining cognates are situated within the third empirical perspective, that of assessing their effect on skill in L2 word-level reading (Duyk et al., 2007; Lemhöfer & Dijkstra, 2004; Schwartz et al., 2007; van Hell

& de Groot, 2008) and reading comprehension (Jiménez et al., 1995, 1996; Nagy et al., 1993; Ramírez et al., 2013). The bulk of evidence relating cognate knowledge and word reading was derived under strictly controlled experimental conditions, using tasks that required participants to respond to words presented in isolation or in sentence contexts. For the most part, these studies employed a priming, lexical decision, or lexical naming paradigm, with response latency and/or accuracy as dependent variables. In addition, they involved adult learners as subjects. For example, Duyk et al. (2007) found that the lexical decision times of Dutch-English adult bilinguals were significantly faster in response to cognates than to non-cognate control words presented in the L2, whether they appeared in isolation or in the final word position of sentences. Cognate facilitation is generally attributed to simultaneous activation of L1 and L2 lexical representations in response to L2 stimuli, and is cited as evidence that access to lexical representations among bilinguals is language-independent. Elsewhere, a study by Schwartz et al. (2007) found that students' ability to recognize and utilize cognate relationships to facilitate L2 word reading is impeded as the semantic, phonological, and orthographic overlap between cognate pairs is reduced.

Cognate awareness has also been shown to exert an influence on reading comprehension in a limited number of studies. The bulk of the evidence comes from studies investigating Spanish-speaking ELLs' use of cognates in their L1 to promote L2 (English) skills in the middle to late elementary school years (e.g., Jiménez et al., 1995, 1996; Nagy et al., 1993; Ramírez et al., 2013). Using think-aloud protocols, Jiménez et al. (1996) determined that students who were relatively proficient readers in English in Grades 6 and 7 relied on an array of strategies to resolve comprehension difficulties, including the use of cognates to infer the meanings of unfamiliar English words. Nagy et al. (1993) reported a strong relationship between the ability to recognize cognates and English (L2) reading comprehension in 74 Spanish-English students in Grades 4 to 6. The relationship remained significant after controlling for Spanish and English vocabulary. The authors reported that students were most successful at identifying cognates that had a high degree of orthographic overlap. Finally, Ramírez et al. (2013) found that performance on the Spanish-English cognate items of a standardized test of English receptive vocabulary explained unique variance in English reading comprehension outcomes among fourth- and seventh-grade Spanish-English bilinguals. Taken together, these studies provide convincing evidence that awareness of cognate relationships transfers across languages and impacts on reading comprehension.

Thus research evidence appears to suggest that cognate awareness supports the cross-language transfer of vocabulary knowledge, thereby facilitating word reading and reading comprehension among bilingual speakers of two etymologically related languages. However, it would appear that cognate awareness is at least partly constrained by features of the cognates themselves, these being the degree of semantic, phonological, and orthographic overlap that characterizes them.

Working memory

Verbal working memory refers to the component of the human information processing system where auditory information is temporarily stored and actively processed (Baddeley, 1986). Working memory has a limited capacity, although the capacity appears to improve developmentally as a function of increasing automaticity (Huttenlocher & Burke, 1976). Generally speaking, developmental reading studies have focused on two related but slightly different verbal working memory processes. Short-term or static memory emphasizes the temporary storage function of the memory system and is often measured with digit (forward) span or pseudo-word repetition tasks (e.g., Geva & Ryan, 1993; Wagner, Torgesen, & Rashotte, 1999). Working memory, on the other hand, highlights the processing rather than the storage function of the memory system. Different measures have been created to capture this construct, such as digit (backward) span, sentence completion (e.g., Abu-Rabia, 1997), and opposites tasks (e.g., Gholamain & Geva, 1999). Verbal working memory is expected to play an important role in reading development because linguistic operations such as decoding, search for word meaning, and text comprehension pose heavy memory demands, especially in the child's L2 (Geva & Ryan, 1993).

Only a small number of developmental studies have explored the relationship between working memory in the L1 and L2. Geva and colleagues (Geva & Ryan, 1993; Geva & Siegel, 2000) observed moderate to high correlations between various memory tasks across Hebrew (L2) and English (L1) in school-age children. The strong cross-language association at the construct level suggests that there may exist a common underlying memory construct. However, the studies also found that L1 and L2 memory measures cannot be used interchangeably in predicting L2 reading comprehension. For example, in Geva and Ryan (1993), only Hebrew memory measures predicted unique variance in Hebrew reading comprehension after controlling for intelligence and other reading-related measures. English memory measures, by contrast, were not unique predictors of Hebrew reading comprehension. These results point to language-specific underpinnings of the memory construct. Apparently, storage and processing capacity in the L2 is influenced by children's proficiency in the language, whereas proficiency may be less of a factor in the performance on L1 memory measures.

Interestingly, findings of the developmental studies are largely congruent with those yielded by an extensive body of research examining bilingual memory in adults. Adopting experimental paradigms that measure reaction times (e.g., interference and priming tasks), the adult studies have produced a broad class of three-node hierarchical bilingual memory models that consist of a common conceptual store across the L1 and L2, but two separate lexical stores for the two languages (see French & Jacquet, 2004, for a review). Although the two lexicons can interact to varying degrees, they nevertheless remain separate. Whether a link exists between the two lexical stores, as well as the strength of the link, is determined by a number of factors, including L2 proficiency, age of acquisition, and the type of word being processed. Taken together, both developmental and experimental studies suggest that there is considerable overlap between memory in the L1 and L2, but at the same time there are also language-specific features influenced by L2 proficiency and experience.

Reading fluency

Reading fluency can be measured at both the word and text levels. Fluent word reading is characterized by rapid, automatic word recognition (Kuhn, Schwanenflugel, & Meisinger, 2010; Samuels, 2006). In young children who are not able to read connected text, reading fluency is often assessed by the rate and accuracy of reading lists of isolated words or pseudo-words aloud (Torgesen, Wagner, & Rashotte, 1999). Text reading fluency is "the oral trans- lation of text with speed and accuracy" (Fuchs, Fuchs, Hosp, & Jenkins, 2001, p. 239). A typical text reading fluency measure requires children to read a simple passage within a specified time, and their performance is evaluated on the basis of speed, accuracy, prosody, and comprehension (Jenkins, Fuchs, van den Broek, Espin, & Deno, 2003). Although word and text fluency are seemingly simple constructs, they are both multi-dimensional in nature. According to Hudson, Pullen, Lane, and Torgesen (2009), word reading flu- ency may implicate sight word automaticity, decoding fluency, orthographic knowledge, and integration of multiple cues, whereas text reading fluency additionally implicates comprehension, context, vocabulary, and metacognition.

Both word reading fluency and text reading fluency are important for children's reading development. This is because reading comprehension demands substantial cognitive resources. Increased efficiency at the word reading level releases attentional resources that extend the limited capacity of working memory, and the additional resources can be allocated to text-level processing (e.g., meaning construction) (Perfetti, 1985). Text reading fluency further contributes to reading comprehension because both involve meaning- related processes (Hudson et al., 2009). Research has shown that word reading fluency is an effective screening measure for determining at-risk status among beginning readers (Clemens, Shapiro, & Thoemmes, 2011; Compton et al., 2010; Compton, Fuchs, Fuchs, & Bryant, 2006; see also Fraser, Massey-Garrison, & Geva, this volume). Word reading fluency measured at an early age is also a strong predictor of later text reading fluency (Geva & Farnia, 2012; Good, Simmons, & Kame'enui, 2001; Jenkins et al., 2003) and reading comprehension (Aaron, Joshi, & Williams, 1999; Fuchs, Fuchs, & Maxwell, 1988; Joshi & Aaron, 2000). Moreover, there is strong and consistent evidence that text reading fluency is an important predictor of reading comprehension (Geva & Farnia, 2012; Jenkins et al., 2003).

To date, only a couple of studies have examined cross-language transfer of reading fluency. Pasquarella, Chen, Gottardo, and Geva (2015) compared transfer of word reading accuracy and word reading fluency in Spanish-English and Chinese-English bilinguals in Grade 2. The study reported moderate to high correlations between word reading fluency in the L1 and L2 in both groups. Regression analyses demonstrated that L1 word reading accuracy predicted English word reading accuracy for the Spanish-English group only after controlling for nonverbal reasoning and English rapid naming and phonological awareness. By contrast, in both groups, L1 word reading fluency was a significant predictor of L2 word reading fluency, and likewise, L2 word reading fluency was a significant predictor of L1 word reading fluency, after controlling for nonverbal reasoning and rapid naming and phonological awareness in the language of the predicted variable. These findings offer preliminary evidence that word reading fluency may be a common underlying process that is language-universal. On the other hand, transfer of reading fluency also exhibited language-specific influence, as the crossover effect was stronger in the Spanish-English group than the Chinese-English group in some instances.

Lee (2014) conducted a series of three studies to examine cross-language transfer of reading fluency at the construct level in English (L1)-French bilinguals over a 1-year period, starting when the participants were in Grade 2. In Study 1, the researcher found that Grade 2 English word reading fluency was a significant predictor of Grade 3 French word reading fluency, after controlling for nonverbal reasoning and French rapid naming, phonological awareness, and word reading fluency in Grade 2. Grade 2 French word reading was also a significant predictor of Grade 3 English word reading fluency, after accounting for the effects of nonverbal reasoning and within-language controls in Grade 2. Study 2 reported a similar pattern of bidirectional transfer for text reading fluency across English and French. Study 3 examined cross-language transfer from word reading fluency to text reading fluency. Grade 2 French word reading fluency predicted unique variance in Grade 3 English text reading fluency. However, Grade 2 English word reading fluency was not a significant predictor of Grade 3 French text reading fluency. Despite the non-significant prediction, commonality analysis showed that English and French word reading fluency shared a total of 33% variance in predicting French text reading fluency. Lee's findings provide further support for the notion that both word reading fluency and text reading fluency may be language-universal constructs.

THEORETICAL AND EDUCATIONAL IMPLICATIONS

To summarize, this chapter presents a comprehensive review of the theoretical frameworks and empirical evidence for cross-language transfer of metalinguistic and cognitive skills. The earlier frameworks, such as the contrastive framework and the interdependence hypothesis, laid the foundation for transfer theory but at the same time suffered serious limitations. As mentioned earlier, while the contrastive framework is useful for pinpointing the strengths and weaknesses of L2 learners, it fails to account for transfer effects from metalinguistic skills to literacy outcomes. Broadened in scope, the interdependence hypothesis integrates the influences of various linguistic, cognitive, and socio-cultural factors in cross-language transfer. However, the framework, symbolic and metaphoric in nature, remains largely a hypothesis and cannot be used to delineate the transfer pattern for any specific construct. Recent frameworks, such as Geva's common underlying cognitive processes and Koda's transfer facilitation model, provide more accurate accounts of cross-language transfer. These recent frameworks consider the effects of many key underlying factors in transfer, including the language-specific/language-general nature of the construct under study, distance between the L1 and L2, and cross-language interactions, and specify the nature of transfer, thus providing useful guidelines for identifying transfer patterns of linguistic and cognitive constructs.

We adopted three empirical perspectives in reviewing a relatively extensive body of research concerning cross-language transfer. The first perspective focuses on comparisons of performance across L1 groups on various metalinguistic and cognitive constructs. The second perspective considers transfer at the construct level, whereas the third perspective examines the crossover effect of a skill acquired in one language on reading outcomes in another language. Across the three different perspectives, it is clear that "transferability" of a construct is conditioned by the structural features of the languages involved, learner characteristics such as L1/L2 proficiency levels, and contextual and instructional factors, including the amount of oral and print exposure a child receives and access to explicit instruction in particular constructs (Saiegh-Haddad & Geva, 2010). The results of the empirical studies are further complicated by issues pertinent to research design, including representativeness of L1 and L2 samples, reliability and validity of measurement tools, and features of experimental design (e.g., cross-sectional vs. longitudinal), and therefore must be interpreted with great caution.

Perhaps a straightforward, albeit controversial, way to integrate the empirical findings presented in this chapter is to arrange the constructs along the continuum of transferability from most language-universal to most language-specific. Among the different constructs, phonological awareness appears to be a common underlying competence that transfers across any pair of L1 and L2, including distantly related languages, such as Chinese and English. Of course, this is not to say that there are no language-specific influences in the development of phonological awareness, as ample studies have documented such influences (e.g., Caravolas & Bruck, 1993). Rather, transfer from phonological awareness to reading is universal in the sense that a child's phonological awareness in the L1 facilitates reading development in the L2, regardless of L1-L2 distance. Similarly, reading fluency also appears to be underlain by language-general processes. Evidence for transfer of reading fluency is reported between Spanish and English as well as Chinese and English, supporting the language-general nature of the construct (Pasquarella et al., 2015). However, reading fluency can be achieved only once a threshold of accuracy is reached. Word-level reading is contingent upon language structures; it centers on decoding in reading alphabetic languages but visual-orthographic learning in reading Chinese characters and Japanese kanji. Consequently, transfer of reading fluency also reflects language-specific reading skills.

Comparatively speaking, morphological awareness appears to be a more language-specific construct. The aspect of morphological awareness that transfers between L1 and L2 is jointly determined by the morphological structures of the two languages. For example, compound awareness has been found to transfer between Chinese and English, due to the fact that both languages contain a large number of compounds, whereas inflectional awareness and derivational awareness have been found to transfer between alphabetic languages, such as French and English, again due to overlap in inflectional and derivational systems. In the same vein, memory processes also have both language-general and language-specific underpinnings. While working memory and short-term memory may operate in the same way across L1 and L2, storage and processing capacity in L2 is undoubtedly affected by proficiency in the language. Another issue that needs to be considered is that memory measures typically conflate language-specific and language-general cognitive processing in non-trivial ways. At the language-specific end of the continuum are orthographic processing and cognate awareness, which seem to transfer only between typologically close languages that have common orthographic regularities and vocabulary items. Conversely, no evidence of transfer has been reported between typologically different languages for these constructs. However, it must be pointed out that aside from phonological awareness, all the constructs presented in this chapter have been investigated only by a relatively small number of studies. Therefore, the results must be interpreted with great caution, especially considering the multi-dimensional nature of the constructs.

In addition to its theoretical implications, the empirical evidence related to transfer of metalinguistic and cognitive skills has practical implications. Notably, the extensive body of work examining the crossover effects of phonological awareness clearly indicates that it is a language-universal construct. The importance of this finding for educational and clinical practice cannot be overstated. From the perspective of instruction, decades of accumulated research support the practice of explicitly teaching phonological awareness (in addition to letter-sound knowledge) to foster understanding of the alphabetic principle and optimize student success in acquiring initial word reading skill (Adams, 1990). This evidence, in conjunction with that of studies examining cross-language transfer of phonological awareness, suggests that activities targeting word, syllable, onset-rime, and phoneme awareness should feature prominently in a balanced emergent literacy program targeting all children, including children for whom English is an additional language. Moreover, the evidence base indicates that assessment of English phonological awareness in limited-proficiency ELL children is a potentially valid means of identifying ELL learners at risk for reading difficulties since skills acquired in the L1 can reasonably be expected to facilitate L2 phonological awareness development. Conversely, in schools where there is a high concentration of ELL children from a particular L1 background, phonological awareness assessment can be conducted in the L1 to predict reading success in the L2.

As with phonological awareness, the research evidence related to cognate awareness highlights the benefits of instructional practices that explicitly teach students to attend to cognate relationships between words in their two languages. The cognate strategy has the potential to support children in their efforts to derive meaning from unfamiliar words encountered in text, thereby supporting vocabulary learning, word reading, and ultimately text comprehension. For example, Spanish and English share thousands of cognates. Moreover, it is frequently the case that cognate pairs in these languages are made up of low-frequency, academic English words (*rapid*) with high-frequency Spanish counterparts (*rápido*) (Ramirez et al., 2013). Teaching children to recognize the relationship between cognate words in these two languages may be beneficial in helping to reduce the gap between Spanish-speaking ELLs and English L1 children in English vocabulary and reading comprehension. It should be noted, however, that this type of instruction requires knowledge of children's L1 and may not be feasible for teachers who lack such knowledge or in diverse classrooms where the cognate strategy benefits only a small number of children. Alternatively, teachers can encourage subgroups of children to reflect on their L1 in the L2 vocabulary learning and their parents to adopt home literacy practices that highlight the L1 and L2 connections.

The research findings related to transfer of morphological awareness and orthographic processing are more nuanced. With respect to morphologic awareness, the overall pattern of results suggests that cross-language transfer is largely contingent on the presence of shared structural features between the source and target language. These findings have implications in the context of immersion programs, such as French immersion in Canada and English or Spanish immersion in the United States. They suggest that teaching children to attend to similarities in morphological structure between their common L1 and the language of instruction (the children's L2) may promote L2 morphological awareness, which may in turn have a positive impact on L2 reading outcomes. Similarly, instruction in French and Spanish immersion classrooms can draw attention to orthographic structures that are both common and particular to the children's L1 and L2, as a means of supporting the development of skill in word reading in each of their languages. On the other hand, acquiring morphological and orthographic skills may be more challenging for L2 learners whose L1 does not overlap in these areas. Teachers need to be aware of these challenges and adjust their instruction to make sure that all children can succeed regardless of their L1 backgrounds.

FUTURE DIRECTIONS

Research in the past few decades has greatly increased our understanding of cross-language transfer. At the same time, this body of research highlights the complexity in conceptualization and operation of transfer as it involves many componential skills of reading acquisition and is influenced by not only linguistic and cognitive processes but also socio-cultural experience (e.g., immigration, school instruction). Despite recent advances, there are a number of unresolved issues that require further investigation. First, the extant transfer frameworks cannot accurately predict the direction of transfer. While the majority of the studies have demonstrated transfer from the L1 to the L2, reverse transfer from the L2 to the L1 has also been observed, albeit by a smaller number of studies. Relatedly, it is not clear how transfer is affected by proficiency levels in the L1 and L2. Cummins (2000) postulated that transfer is likely to occur among balanced bilinguals whose L2 proficiency has reached a certain threshold level. However, there is substantial evidence supporting transfer from the L1 to the L2 in emergent bilinguals who are in the early stages of L2 learning. On the other hand, studies have also demonstrated transfer from the L2 to the L1, despite the lower level of proficiency in the L2. Koda (personal communication) argues that a threshold of language proficiency may be required for transfer of skills that support reading comprehension, such as morphological awareness, vocabulary, and cognates. On the other hand, transfer of skills that are essential for word reading, such as phonological awareness and orthographic processing, can occur in emergent bilinguals with low levels of L2 proficiency. Finally, the majority of the studies to date have adopted a cross-sectional design. Longitudinal and intervention studies are needed to examine causal relationships in cross-language transfer, and to evaluate the impact of instruction on the degree and direction of transfer.

NOTE

1   Due to large numbers of loanwords in unrelated languages – for example, Hungarian *tranzakció* and Catalan *transacció* – cognate facilitation also occurs between unrelated languages. This type of facilitation, however, is beyond the scope of our chapter.

REFERENCES

Aaron, P.G., Joshi, M., & Williams, K.A. (1999). Not all reading disabilities are alike. *Journal of Learning Disabilities, 32*(2), 120–137.

Abu-Rabia, S. (1997). Verbal and working memory skills of bilingual Hebrew-English speaking children. *International Journal of Psycholinguistics, 13*(1), 25–40.

Abu-Rabia, S. (2001). Testing the interdependence hypothesis among native adult bilingual Russian-English students. *Journal of Psycholinguistic Research, 30*(4), 437–455.

Adams, M. (1990). *Beginning to read.* Cambridge, MA: MIT Press.

Arab-Moghaddam, N., & Sénéchal, M. (2001). Orthographic and phonological processing skills in reading and spelling in Persian/English bilinguals. *International Journal of Behavioral Development, 25*(2), 140–147.

Baddeley, A. D. (1986). *Working memory.* Oxford: Oxford University Press.

Bailey, N., Madden, C., & Krashen, S. D. (1974). Is there a natural sequence in adult second language learning? *Language Learning, 24*(2), 235–243.

Barker, T. A., Torgesen, J. K., & Wagner, R. K. (1992). The role of orthographic processing skills on five different reading tasks. *Reading Research Quarterly, 27*, 334–345.

Berninger, V.B., Nagy, W.E., Carlisle, J.F., Thomson, J., Hoffer, D., Abbott, S., & Aylward, E. (2003). Effective treatment for children with dyslexia in grades 4–6: Behavioral and brain evidence. In B. Foorman (Ed.), *Preventing and remediating reading difficulties: Bringing science to scale* (pp. 381–347). Baltimore, MD: York Press.

Bialystok, E., McBride-Chang, C., & Luk, G. (2005). Bilingualism, language proficiency, and learning to read in two writing systems. *Journal of Educational Psychology, 97*(4), 580–590.

Bradley, L., & Bryant, P.E. (1983). Categorizing sounds and learning to read: A causal connection. *Nature, 301*, 419–421.

Bransford, J.D., Brown, A.L., & Cocking, R.R. (1999). *How people learn: Brain, mind, experience, and school.* Washington, DC: National Academy Press.

Bruck, M., & Genesee, F. (1995). Phonological awareness in young second language learners. *Journal of Child Language, 22*(2), 307–324.

Burt, J. S. (2006). What is orthographic processing skill and how does it relate to word identification in reading? *Journal of Research in Reading, 29*(4), 400–417.

Caravolas, M., & Bruck, M. (1993). The effect of oral and written language input on children's phonological awareness: A cross-linguistic study. *Journal of Experimental Child Psychology, 55*(1), 1–30.

Cárdenas-Hagan, E., Carlson, C. D., & Pollard-Durodola, S. D. (2007). The cross-linguistic transfer of early literacy skills: The role of initial L1 and L2 skills and language of instruction. *Language, Speech, and Hearing Services in Schools, 38*(3), 249–259.

Carlisle, J. F. (1995). Morphological awareness and early reading achievement. In L. B. Feldman (Ed.), *Morphological aspects of language processing* (pp. 189–209). Hillsdale, NJ: Erlbaum.

Carlisle, J. F. (2000). Awareness of the structure and meaning of morphologically complex words: Impact on reading. *Reading and Writing, 12*(3), 169–190.

Chen, X., Ramírez, G., Luo, Y. C., Geva, E., & Ku, Y-M. (2012). Comparing vocabulary development in Spanish- and Chinese-speaking ELLs: The effects of metalinguistic and sociocultural factors. *Reading and Writing, 25*(8), 1991–2020.

Chen, X., Xu, F., Nguyen, T.-K., Hong, G., & Wang, Y. (2010). Effects of cross language transfer on first-language phonological awareness and literacy skills in Chinese children receiving English instruction. *Journal of Educational Psychology, 102*(3), 712–728.

Cheung, H., Chung, K.K.H., Wong, S.W.L., McBride-Chang, C., Penney, T. B., & Ho, C.S.-H. (2010). Speech perception, metalinguistic awareness, reading, and vocabulary in Chinese-English bilingual children. *Journal of Educational Psychology, 102*(2), 367–380.

Chomsky, N., & Halle, M. (1968). *The sound pattern of English*. New York: Harper & Row.

Chow, B., McBride-Chang, C., & Burgess, S. (2005). Phonological processing skills and early reading abilities in Hong Kong Chinese kindergarteners learning to read English as a second language. *Journal of Educational Psychology, 97*(1), 81–87.

Chung, K.K.H., & Ho, C.S.-H. (2010). Second language learning difficulties in Chinese children with dyslexia: What are the reading-related cognitive skills that contribute to English and Chinese word reading? *Journal of Learning Disabilities, 43*(3), 195–211.

Cisero, C. A., & Royer, J. M. (1995). The development and cross-language transfer of phonological awareness. *Contemporary Educational Psychology, 20*(3), 275–303.

Clemens, N. H., Shapiro, E. S., & Thoemmes, F. (2011). Improving the efficacy of first grade reading screening: An investigation of word identification fluency with other early literacy indicators. *School Psychology Quarterly, 26*(3), 231–244.

Comeau, L., Cormier, P., Grandmaison, É., & Lacroix, D. (1999). A longitudinal study of phonological processing skills in children learning to read in a second language. *Journal of Educational Psychology, 91*(1), 29–43.

Commissaire, E., Duncan, L.G., & Casalis, S. (2011). Cross-language transfer of orthographic processing skills: A study of French children who learn English at school. *Journal of Research in Reading, 34*(1), 59–76.

Commissaire, E., Pasquarella, A., Chen, X., & Deacon, S.H. (2014). The development of orthographic processing skills in children in early French immersion programs. *Written Language & Literacy, 17*(1), 16–39.

Compton, D. L., Fuchs, D., Fuchs, L. S., Bouton, B., Gilbert, J. K., Barquero, L. A., … Crouch, R. C. (2010). Selecting at-risk first-grade readers for early intervention: Eliminating false positives and exploring the promise of a two-stage gated screening process. *Journal of Educational Psychology, 102*(2), 327–340.

Compton, D. L., Fuchs, D., Fuchs, L. S., & Bryant, J. D. (2006). Selecting at-risk readers in first grade for early intervention: A two-year longitudinal study of decision rules and procedures. *Journal of Educational Psychology, 98*(2), 394–409.

Cummins, J. (1979). Linguistic interdependence and the educational development of bilingual children. *Review of Educational Research, 49*(2), 222–251.

Cummins, J. (Ed.) (1981). The role of primary language development in promoting educational success for language minority students. In California Office of Bilingual Bicultural Education, *Schooling and language minority students: A theoretical framework* (pp. 3–49). Sacramento: California Department of Education.

Cummins, J. (2000). *Language, power, and pedagogy: Bilingual children in the crossfire* (Vol. 23). Clevedon: Multilingual Matters.

Cunningham, T. H., & Graham, C. R. (2000). Increasing native English vocabulary recognition through Spanish immersion: Cognate transfer from foreign to first language. *Journal of Educational Psychology, 92*(1), 37–49.

Deacon, S. H. (2012). Sounds, letters, and meanings: The independent influences of phonological, morphological and orthographic skills on early word reading accuracy. *Journal of Research in Reading, 35*(4), 456–475.

Deacon, S. H., Benere, J., & Castles, A. (2012). Chicken or egg? Untangling the relationship between orthographic processing skill and reading accuracy. *Cognition, 122*(1), 110–117.

Deacon, S. H., Chen, X., Luo, Y. C., & Ramírez, G. (2013). Beyond language borders: Orthographic processing and word reading in Spanish-English bilinguals. *Journal of Research in Reading, 36*(1), 58–74.

Deacon, S. H., Commissaire, E., Chen, X., & Pasquarella, A. (2013). Learning about print: The development of orthographic processing and its relationship to word reading in first grade children in French immersion. *Reading and Writing: An Interdisciplinary Journal, 26*(7), 1087–1109.

Deacon, S. H., Wade-Woolley, L., & Kirby, J. R. (2007). Crossover: The role of morphological awareness and in French immersion children's reading. *Developmental Psychology, 43*(3), 732–746.

Deacon, S. H., Wade-Woolley, L., & Kirby, J. R. (2009). Flexibility in young second-language learners: Examining the language specificity of orthographic processing. *Journal of Research in Reading, 32*(2), 215–229.

Dickinson, D. K., McCabe, A., Clark-Chiarelli, N., & Wolf, A. (2004). Cross-language transfer of phonological awareness in low-income Spanish and English bilingual preschool children. *Applied Psycholinguistics, 25*(3), 323–348.

Dressler, C., Carlo, M. S., Snow, C. E., August, D., & White, C. E. (2011). Spanish-speaking students' use of cognate knowledge to infer the meaning of English words. *Bilingualism: Language and Cognition, 14*(2), 243–255.

Durgunoğlu, A. Y., Nagy W. E., & Hancin-Bhatt, B. J. (1993). Cross-language transfer of phonological awareness. *Journal of Educational Psychology, 85*(3), 453–465.

Duyck, W., Van Assche, E., Drieghe, D., & Hartsuiker, R. J. (2007). Visual word recognition by bilinguals in a sentence context: Evidence for nonselective lexical access. *Journal of Experimental Psychology: Learning, Memory, and Cognition, 33*(4), 663–679.

Ferretti, G., Mazzotti, S., & Brizzolara, D. (2008). Visual scanning and reading ability in normal and dyslexic children. *Behavioural Neurology, 19*(1), 87–92.

French, R. M., & Jacquet, M. (2004). Understanding bilingual memory: Models and data. *Trends in Cognitive Sciences, 8*(2), 87–93.

Fries, C. (1945). *Teaching and learning English as a foreign language.* Ann Arbor: University of Michigan Press.

Fuchs, L. S., Fuchs, D., Hosp, M. K., & Jenkins, J. R. (2001). Oral reading fluency as an indicator of reading competence: A theoretical, empirical and historical analysis. *Scientific Studies of Reading, 5*(3), 239–256.

Fuchs, L. S., Fuchs, D., & Maxwell, L. (1988). The validity of informal reading comprehension measures. *Remedial and Special Education, 9*(2), 20–28.

Genesee, F., Geva, E., Dressler, D., & Kamil, M. (2006). Cross-linguistic relationships. In D. August & T. Shanahan (Eds.), *Developing literacy in second-language learners: Report of the National Literacy Panel on language-minority children and youth* (pp. 153–174). Mahwah, NJ: Erlbaum.

Geva, E. (2014). The cross-language transfer journey – a guide to the perplexed. *Written Language & Literacy, 17*(1), 1–15.

Geva, E., & Farnia, F. (2012). Developmental changes in the nature of language proficiency and reading fluency paint a more complex view of reading comprehension in ELL and EL1. *Reading and Writing, 25*(8), 1819–1845.

Geva, E., & Ryan, E. B. (1993). Linguistic and cognitive correlates of academic skills in first and second languages. *Language Learning, 43*(1), 5–42.

Geva, E., & Siegel, L. (2000). Orthographic and cognitive factors in the concurrent development of basic reading skills in two languages. *Reading and Writing, 12*(1–2), 1–30.

Geva, E., Wade-Woolley, L., & Shany, M. (1997). Development of reading efficiency in first and second language. *Scientific Studies of Reading, 1*(2), 119–144.

Gholamain, M., & Geva, E. (1999). Orthographic and cognitive factors in the concurrent development of basic reading skills in English and Persian. *Language Learning, 49*(2), 183–217.

Good, R. H., Simmons, D. C., & Kame'enui, E. J. (2001). The importance and decision-making utility of a continuum of fluency-based indicators of foundational reading skills for third-grade high-stakes outcomes. *Scientific Studies of Reading, 5*(3), 257–288.

Goswami, U. (1999). Phonological representations, reading development and dyslexia: Towards a cross-linguistic theoretical framework. *Dyslexia, 6*(2), 133–151.

Gottardo, A., Chiappe, P., Yan, B., Siegel, L., & Gu, Y. (2006). Relationships between first and second phonological processing skills and reading in Chinese-English speakers living in English-speaking contexts. *Educational Psychology, 26*(3), 367–393.

Gottardo, A., Yan, B., Siegel, L., & Wade-Woolley, L. (2001). Factors related to English reading performance in children with Chinese as a first language: More evidence of cross-language transfer of phonological processing. *Journal of Educational Psychology, 93*(3), 530–542.

Gough, P. B., & Tumner, W. E. (1986). Decoding, reading, and reading ability. *Remedial & Special Education, 7*(1), 6–10.

Haigh, C. A., Savage, R., Erdos, C., & Genesee, F. (2011). The role of phoneme and onset-rime awareness in second language reading acquisition. *Journal of Research in Reading, 34*(1), 94–113.

Hancin-Bhatt, B., & Nagy, W. (1994). Lexical transfer and second language morphological development. *Applied Psycholinguistics, 15*(3), 289–310.

Harley, B., Hart, D., & Lapkin, S. (1986). The effects of early bilingual schooling on first language skills. *Applied Psycholinguistics, 7*(4), 295–322.

Harley, B., & King, M. L. (1989). Verb lexis in the written compositions of young L2 learners. *Studies in Second Language Acquisition, 11*(4), 415–439.

Hipfner-Boucher, K., Lam, K., & Chen, X. (2014). The effects of bilingual education on the English language and literacy outcomes of Chinese-speaking children. *Written Language & Literacy, 17*(1), 116–138.

Hudson, R. F., Pullen, P. C., Lane, H. B., & Torgesen, J. K. (2009). The complex nature of reading fluency: A multidimensional view. *Reading & Writing Quarterly, 25*(1), 4–32.

Huttenlocher, J., & Burke, D. (1976). Why does memory span increase with age? *Cognitive Psychology, 8*(1), 1–31.

Jared, D., Cormier, P., Levy, B. A., & Wade-Woolley, L. (2012). Cross-language activation of phonology in young bilingual readers. *Reading and Writing, 25*(6), 1327–1343.

Jenkins, J. R., Fuchs, L. S., van den Broek, P., Espin, C., & Deno, S. L. (2003). Sources of individual differences in reading comprehension and reading fluency. *Journal of Educational Psychology, 95*(4), 719–729.

Jiménez, R. T., García, G., & Pearson, D. (1995). Three children, two languages, and strategic reading: Case studies in bilingual/monolingual reading. *American Educational Research Journal, 32*(1), 67–97.

Jiménez, R. T., García, G., & Pearson, D. (1996). The reading strategies of bilingual Latina/o students who are successful English readers: Opportunities and obstacles. *Reading Research Quarterly, 31*(1), 90–112.

Joshi, R. M., & Aaron, P. G. (2000). The component model of reading: Simple view of reading made a little more complex. *Reading Psychology, 21*(2), 85–97.

Katz, L., & Frost, R. (1992). The reading process is different for different orthographies: The orthographic depth hypothesis. In R. Frost & L. Katz (Eds.), *Advances in Psychology: Vol. 94. Orthography, phonology, morphology, and meaning* (pp. 67–84). Amsterdam: Elsevier North-Holland.

Keung, Y. C., & Ho, C. S.-H. (2009). Transfer of reading-related cognitive skills in learning to read Chinese (L1) and English (L2) among Chinese elementary school children. *Contemporary Educational Psychology, 34*(2), 103–112.

Kieffer, M. J., & Lesaux, N. K. (2012). Direct and indirect roles of morphological awareness in the English reading comprehension of native English, Spanish, Filipino, and Vietnamese speakers. *Language Learning, 62*(4), 1170–1204.

Kirby, J. R., Parilla, R. K., & Pfeiffer, S. L. (2003). Naming speed and phonological awareness as predictors of reading development. *Journal of Educational Psychology, 95*(3), 453–464.

Koda, K. (2000). Cross-linguistic variations in L2 morphological awareness. *Applied Psycholinguistics, 21*(3), 297–320.

Koda, K. (2005). *Insights into second language reading.* New York: Cambridge University Press.

Koda, K. (2007). Reading and language learning: Cross linguistic constraints on second language reading development. *Language Learning, 57*(S1), 1–44.

Koda, K. (2008). Impacts of prior literacy experience on second language learning to read. In K. Koda & A. M. Zehler (Eds.), *Learning to read across languages: Cross-linguistic relationships in first and second-language literacy development* (pp. 68–96). New York: Routledge.

Koda, K., & Zehler, A. M. (2008). *Learning to read across languages: Cross-linguistic relationships in first- and second-language literacy development.* Mahwah, NJ: Routledge.

Kuhn, M. R., Schwanenflugel, P. J., & Meisinger, E. B. (2010). Aligning theory and assessment of reading fluency: Automaticity, prosody, and definitions of fluency. *Reading Research Quarterly, 45*(2), 230–251.

Kuo, L.-J., & Anderson, R. C. (2006). Morphological awareness and learning to read: A cross-language perspective. *Educational Psychologist, 41*(3), 161–180.

Lado, R. (1957). *Linguistics across cultures: Applied linguistics for language teachers.* Ann Arbor: University of Michigan Press.

Lafrance, A., & Gottardo, A. (2005). A longitudinal study of phonological processing skills and reading in bilingual children. *Applied Psycholinguistics, 26*(4), 559–578.

Lee, K. (2014). *Development and cross-language transfer of oral reading fluency using longitudinal and concurrent predictors among Canadian French immersion primary-level children* (Unpublished master's thesis). University of Toronto, Canada.

Lemhöfer, K., & Dijkstra, T. (2004). Recognizing cognates and interlingual homographs: Effects of code similarity in language-specific and generalized lexical decision. *Memory & Cognition, 32*(4), 533–550.

Lindsey, K. A., Manis, F. R., & Bailey, C. E. (2003). Predictions of first-grade reading in Spanish-speaking English language learners. *Journal of Educational Psychology, 95*(3), 482–494.

Liu, P. D., Chen, X., Chung, K. K.-H., & Wang, Y. (in press). The role of visual-spatial attention in Chinese children's reading abilities. *Scientific Studies of Reading.*

Lonigan, C. J., Burgess, S. R., Anthony, J. L., & Baker, T. A. (1998). Development of phonological sensitivity in 2- to 5-year-old children. *Journal of Educational Psychology, 90*(2), 294–311.

Luk, Z. P., & Shirai, Y. (2009). Is the acquisition order of grammatical morphemes impervious to L1 knowledge? Evidence from the acquisition of plural-s, articles, and possessive 's. *Language Learning, 59*, 721–754.

Luo, Y. C., Chen, X., & Geva, E. (2014). Concurrent and longitudinal cross-linguistic transfer of phonological awareness and morphological awareness in Chinese-English bilingual children. *Written Language & Literacy, 17*(1), 89–115.

MacCoubrey, S. J., Wade-Woolley, L., Klinger, D., & Kirby, J. R. (2004). Early identification of at-risk L2 readers. *Canadian Modern Language Review/La Revue canadienne des langues vivantes, 61*(1), 11–29.

Malabonga, V., Kenyon, D. M., Carlo, M. S., August, D., & Louguit, M. (2008). Development of a cognate awareness measure for Spanish-speaking English language learners. *Language Testing, 25*(4), 495–519.

Manis, F.R., Lindsey, K.A., & Bailey, C.E. (2004). Development of reading in grades K-2 Spanish-speaking English-language learners. *Learning Disabilities Research & Practice, 19*(4), 214–224.

Marinova-Todd, S.H., Zhao, J., & Bernhardt, M. (2010). Phonological awareness skills in the two languages of Mandarin- English bilingual children. *Clinical Linguistics & Phonetics, 24*(4–5), 387–400.

Nagy, W.E., & Anderson, R.C. (1995). *Metalinguistic awareness and literacy acquisition in different languages* (Technical Report No. 618). Urbana-Champaign: University of Illinois at Urbana-Champaign.

Nagy, W.E., & Anderson, R.C. (1999). Metalinguistic awareness and literacy acquisition in different languages. In D. Wagner, R. Venezky, & B. Street (Eds.), *Literacy: An international handbook* (pp. 155–160). New York: Garland.

Nagy, W.E., García, G., Durgunoğlu, A.Y., & Hancin-Bhatt, B. (1993). Spanish-English bilingual students' use of cognates in English reading. *Journal of Reading Behavior, 25*(3), 241–259.

Odlin, T. (1990). *Language transfer: Cross-linguistic influence in language learning.* Cambridge: Cambridge University Press.

Pasquarella, A., Chen, X., Gottardo, A., & Geva, E. (2015). Common and language-specific processes in word reading accuracy and fluency: Comparing cross-language transfer between Spanish-English and Chinese-English bilinguals. *Journal of Educational Psychology, 107*(1), 96–110.

Pasquarella, A., Chen, X., Lam, K., Luo, Y.C., & Ramírez, G. (2011). Cross-language transfer of morphological awareness in Chinese-English bilinguals. *Journal of Research in Reading, 34*(1), 23–42.

Perfetti, C.A. (1985). *Reading ability.* New York: Oxford University Press.

Perfetti, C.A., Beck, L., Bell, L., & Hughes, C. (1982). Phonemic knowledge and learning to read are reciprocal: A longitudinal study of first grade children. *Merrill-Palmer Quarterly, 33*, 283–319.

Proctor, C.P., & Mo, E. (2009). The relationship between cognate awareness and English comprehension among Spanish – English bilingual fourth grade students. *TESOL Quarterly, 43*(1), 126–136.

Quiroga, T., Lemos-Britton, Z., Mostafapour, E., Abbott, R.D., & Berninger, V.W. (2002). Phonological awareness and beginning reading in Spanish-speaking ESL first graders: Research into practice. *Journal of School Psychology, 40*(1), 85–111.

Ramírez, G., Chen, X., Geva, E., & Keifer, H. (2010). Morphological awareness in Spanish-speaking English language learners: Within and cross-language effects on word reading. *Reading and Writing, 23*(3–4), 337–358.

Ramírez, G., Chen, X., Geva, E., & Luo, Y. (2011). Morphological awareness and word reading in English language learners: Evidence from Spanish- and Chinese-speaking children. *Applied Psycholinguistics, 32*(3), 601–618.

Ramírez, G., Chen, X., & Pasquarella, A. (2013). Cross-linguistic transfer of morphological awareness in Spanish-speaking English-language learners: The facilitating effect of cognate knowledge. *Topics in Language Disorders, 33*(1), 73–92.

Ringbom, H. (1987). *The role of first language in foreign language learning.* Clevedon: Multilingual Matters.

Roberts, T., & Corbett, C. (1997). *Efficacy of explicit English instruction in phonemic awareness and the alphabetic principle for English learners and English proficient kindergarten 34 children in relationship to oral language proficiency, primary language and verbal memory* (No. ED 417 403). Retrieved from ERIC database.

Roman, A.A., Kirby, J.R., Parrila, R.K., Wade-Woolley, L., & Deacon, S.H. (2009). Toward a comprehensive view of the skills involved in word reading in Grades 4, 6, and 8. *Journal of Experimental Child Psychology, 102*(1), 96–113.

Saiegh-Haddad, E., & Geva, E. (2008). Morphological awareness, phonological awareness, and reading in English-Arabic bilingual children. *Reading and Writing: An Interdisciplinary Journal, 21*(5), 481–504.

Saiegh-Haddad, E., & Geva, E. (2010). Acquiring reading in two languages: An introduction to the special issue. *Reading and Writing, 23*(3–4), 263–267.

Samuels, S.J. (2006). Reading fluency: Its past, present, and future. *Fluency Instruction: Research-Based Best Practices, 2*, 3–16.

Schiff, R., & Calif, S. (2007). Role of phonological awareness and morphological awareness in L2 oral word reading. *Language Learning, 57*(2), 271–298.

Schuele, C.M., & Boudreau, D. (2008). Phonological awareness intervention: Beyond the basics. *Language, Speech & Hearing Services in Schools, 39*(1), 3–20.

Schwartz, A.I., Kroll, J.F., & Diaz, M. (2007). Reading words in Spanish and English: Mapping orthography to phonology in two languages. *Language and Cognitive Processes, 22*(1), 106–129.

Stanovich, K.E., Cunningham, A.E., & Feeman, D.J. (1984). Intelligence, cognitive skills, and early reading progress. *Reading Research Quarterly, 19*, 120–139.

Stanovich, K.E., West, R.F., & Cunningham, A.E. (1991). Beyond phonological processes: Print exposure and orthographic processing. In S.A. Brady & D.P. Shankweiler (Eds.), *Phonological processes in literacy: A tribute to Isabelle Y. Liberman* (pp. 219–235). Hillsdale, NJ: Erlbaum.

Sun-Alperin, K., & Wang, M. (2011). Cross-language transfer of phonological and orthographic processing skills from Spanish L1 to English L2. *Reading and Writing, 24*(5), 591–614.

Tong, X., & McBride-Chang, C. (2010). Chinese-English biscriptal reading: Cognitive component skills across orthographies. *Reading and Writing, 23*(3–4), 293–310.

Torgesen, J.K., Wagner, R.K., & Rashotte, C.A. (1999). *TOWRE: Test of Word Reading Efficiency*. Austin, TX: PRO-ED.

van Hell, J.G., & de Groot, A.M.B. (2008). Sentence context modulates visual word recognition and translation in bilinguals. *Acta Psychologica, 128*(3), 431–451.

Vidyasagar, T.R., & Pammer, K. (2010). Dyslexia: A deficit in visuo-spatial attention, not in phonological processing. *Trends in Cognitive Sciences, 14*(2), 57–63.

Wade-Woolley, L., & Geva, E. (2000). Processing novel phonemic contrasts in the acquisition of L2 word reading. *Scientific Studies of Reading, 4*(4), 295–311.

Wagner, R.K., & Barker, T. (1994). The development of orthographic processing ability. In V. Berninger (Ed.), *Varieties of orthographic knowledge: Theoretical and developmental issues* (pp. 243–276). Dordrecht, the Netherlands: Kluwer.

Wagner, R.K., & Torgesen, J.K. (1987). The nature of phonological processing and its causal role in the acquisition of reading skills. *Psychological Bulletin, 101*(2), 192–212.

Wagner, R. K., Torgesen, J. K., & Rashotte, C. A. (1994). Development of reading-related phonological processing abilities: New evidence of bidirectional causality from a latent variable longitudinal study. *Developmental Psychology, 30*(1), 73–87.

Wagner, R. K., Torgesen, J. K., & Rashotte, C. A. (1999). *Comprehensive test of phonological processing.* Austin, TX: PRO-ED.

Wang, M., Cheng, C., & Chen, S.-W. (2006). Contribution of morphological awareness to Chinese-English biliteracy acquisition. *Journal of Educational Psychology, 98*(3), 542–553.

Wang, M., Ko, I.Y., & Choi, J. (2009). The importance of morphological awareness in Korean-English biliteracy acquisition. *Contemporary Educational Psychology, 34*(2), 132–142.

Wang, M., Park, Y., & Lee, K.R. (2006). Korean-English biliteracy acquisition: Cross language and orthography transfer. *Journal of Educational Psychology, 98*(1), 148–158.

Wang, M., Perfetti, C.A., & Liu, Y. (2005). Chinese-English biliteracy acquisition: Cross-language and writing system transfer. *Cognition, 97*(1), 67–88.

Wang, M., Yang, C., & Cheng, C. (2009). The contributions of phonology, orthography, and morphology in Chinese-English biliteracy acquisition. *Applied Psycholinguistics, 30*(2), 291–314.

Weinreich, U. (1953). *Languages in contact: Findings and problems.* New York: Linguistic Circle of New York.

Zhang, D., & Koda, K. (2012). Contribution of morphological awareness and lexical inferencing ability to L2 vocabulary knowledge and reading comprehension: Testing direct and indirect effects. *Reading and Writing: An Interdisciplinary Journal, 25*(5), 1195–1215.

Zhang, J., Anderson, R.C., Li, H., Dong, Q., Wu, X., & Zhang, Y. (2010). Cross-language transfer of insight into the structure of compound words. *Reading and Writing: An Interdisciplinary Journal, 23*, 311–336.

Ziegler, J.C., & Goswami, U. (2005). Reading acquisition, developmental dyslexia, and skilled reading across languages: A psycholinguistic grain size theory. *Psychological Bulletin, 131*(1), 3–29.

5

The role of lexical knowledge in second language reading

Brent Wolter and Rena Helms-Park

1. INTRODUCTION

This chapter focuses on the interaction between lexical knowledge and reading ability, as evaluated through visual word recognition during the emergent stages of literacy and the comprehension of texts when reading becomes fluent. The chapter draws on theoretical issues and empirical findings in not only second language (L2) reading but also germane areas of research, notably first language (L1) reading, L2 acquisition, and the organization and functioning of the bilingual lexicon. Such an approach seems especially necessary in those cases where L2 language and literacy acquisition takes place in elementary school, and the boundaries between language acquisition and literacy acquisition are blurred as are the divisions between L1 and L2 lexical acquisition.

The chapter begins by examining lexical issues relevant to both L1 and L2 reading. Section 2 focuses on L2 reading, emphasizing the special lexical challenges faced by L2 readers. Section 3 takes the discussion to classroom situations, which regularly call for special vocabulary-enhancing instruction. Section 4 addresses some of the limitations of vocabulary testing and factors that hamper the comparability of studies on the role of the lexicon in reading. In terms of terminology, we have attempted to use "lexical" when discussing theoretical or psycholinguistic issues (as in "lexical links" in the mental lexicon or "lexical transfer") and "vocabulary" in pedagogical or evaluation contexts (as in "vocabulary teaching" or "vocabulary testing").

In an L1 context, *lexical knowledge* acquired through oral interaction with caregivers, siblings, and peers during the early pre-literacy years constitutes a necessary, but not sufficient, condition for comprehension of oral language. In a typical interactive activation model, other necessary conditions for listening comprehension are *general knowledge* and *linguistic knowledge* (Perfetti, 1999; Perfetti, Landi, & Oakhill, 2005), both of which can be viewed as being inextricably linked to lexical knowledge, as will be elucidated later. A commonly accepted view is that in a typical L1 situation, reading comprehension is built on the foundation provided by comprehension of oral language ensuing from interaction with caregivers, peers, and members of the child's community. Comprehension of oral language is a complex process that begins with fine-tuning phoneme perception (in syllabic units) to match the L1 phonemic repertoire and using phrasal boundaries (with acoustic correlates) to arrive at typical phonological forms of words (obeying L1 phonotactics) before the age of 1 (Jusczyk, 2000; Werker & Tees, 1984). Following this are the pre-kindergarten years of tremendous lexical growth, where meaning is mapped onto phonological forms through numerous intersecting influences, such as social interaction with caregivers, bootstrapping via the linguistic system itself, cognitive development, and a growing knowledge of the world (Clark, 1995; Tomasello, 2003). During these stages, it also believed that children undergo a process called lexical restructuring (Metsala, 1997a, 1997b), which describes how a more refined and segmented understanding of the phonological structure of words develops as new, often phonologically similar words are added to their lexicon.

An additional condition that needs to be met for reading comprehension, however, is visual word recognition, which engages the visual and the phonological systems during sublexical decoding through grapheme-phoneme correspondences and, among skilled readers, large-scale visuo-phonological word recognition, distinct from the less efficient grapho-semantic sight-word reading processes prevalent during emergent literacy (Ehri, 2005). The mapping of meaning onto decoded visual forms is facilitated by previously known lexical items because without prior knowledge of word meaning, decoding would simply provide the child with a word's phonological form. In short, oral knowledge of words allows meaning to be mapped upon word form, and further, recognition and reading comprehension when the orthographic form of a word is encountered. This is one reason why it is thought that listening to stories by pre-readers or emergent readers is important since they can neither read efficiently enough to learn vocabulary through reading nor do they benefit much from explicit vocabulary teaching (Robbins & Ehri, 1994). Such word-by-word deciphering allows the child to arrive at a sentence-level or surface representation, a process that does not include the type of inferencing required to capture propositional meaning (Kintsch, 1998; Perfetti, Landi, & Oakhill, 2005).

As has been reiterated in the L1 reading literature, when decoding during word recognition is laborious or when word recognition needs to be facilitated by top-down processes, word identification alone expends much of the reader's cognitive resources, with little left for comprehension. In short, bottom-up word recognition needs to be automated in order for "processing space" to be freed up for comprehension, particularly for longer texts (Stanovich, 2000; Verhoeven & Perfetti, 2008; see also Chapter 2, this volume). For such automatization to take place, the lexical entry needs to be well-established, allowing for knowledge of the orthographic form, pronunciation, and meaning of the word to be tightly integrated and available instantaneously to the reader (Ehri, 2005). Moreover, efficient and effective reading requires prior knowledge of a large proportion of the words in a text without relying on the context since context is often unhelpful (Beck, McKeown, & Kucan, 2013) or can assist comprehension only when a vast majority of surrounding words are known (Laufer, 1997; Nagy & Scott, 2000); since inferencing ability is correlated with working memory (Daneman, 1988), guessing the meanings of unknown words might be especially challenging for readers with deficits in this area.

In the case of a subset of the words encountered in a text, lexical knowledge also needs to be "deep", allowing the reader to understand extended meanings of polysemous words as well as their connotations and associations, as will be elaborated upon below. In light of the commonly accepted view that comprehension of speech is the platform on which reading comprehension develops in an L1, Bowey (2005) points out that when visual word recognition begins to become automated (generally during or after Grade 3), the correlation between reading comprehension and listening comprehension begins to rise. Automated visual word recognition of a large repertoire of words paves the way for the child being able to function at what is termed the "propositional level" of meaning representation, or, in other words, parsing syntax in order to determine what the grammatical relationships are between words whose meanings are known (Kintsch, 1998; Perfetti et al., 2005). It is worth noting, however, that there are disorders which can either impede syntactic processing or prevent the reader from gleaning propositional meaning from a correctly parsed sentence (Caplan & Waters, 1999; Gathercole, 2007).

With further reading practice, general knowledge, and an expanding lexicon after Grade 3, children can progress to processing longer and more complex texts, requiring connections to be made between various parts of the text as well as sophisticated inferencing beyond the sentence level (see Chapter 7 for more on the topic of higher-level processing). We should also note that between Grades 3 and 5, there is evidence of an acceleration in the rate of lexical growth (Anglin, 1993), often through encountering words incidentally while reading.

There are noteworthy parallels between the place of the lexicon in reading in an L1 and in an L2. In both areas of research, findings highlight the mutually supportive roles of lexical knowledge and reading success. In L1 research, lexical knowledge and reading comprehension are said to work reciprocally in the early grades, with incremental growth in each in the higher grades (Joshi, 2005; Luyten & ten Bruggencate, 2011; Stanovich, 1986). In fact, lexical knowledge is touted as the *strongest* predictor of reading ability in some circles (e.g., Bradley & Bryant, 1985; Freebody & Anderson, 1983). (There are, however, a small number of studies that find weak connections between reading skills and lexis – e.g., Wagner, Torgesen, & Rashotte, 1994, or Johnson & Goswami, 2010, where the participants were children with cochlear implants.) In both L1 and L2 reading circles, a major concern is how the gap between poor and good readers can be bridged expeditiously in the early grades – for example, through explicit vocabulary instruction or proficiency-appropriate extensive reading – in order to forestall the "Matthew effect". (Christened by Merton, 1968, the Matthew effect in a school system refers to the advantage of those with greater resources to gain even more, while those with few resources experience growing deficits.)

Accounting for the connections between lexical knowledge and reading comprehension in an L2, however, is complicated by a variety of factors related to the organization and functioning of the L2 lexicon. In consecutive child L2 acquisition, the L2 lexicon emerges after the fundamentals of the L1 linguistic system have been acquired and usually after the child has achieved some level of literacy in the L1 script. When the L1 is a heritage (minority) language that is not spoken much in the larger community and the L2 is a mainstream language in school and probably the language of future employment, it is inevitable that a sizeable number of concepts, especially those frequent in textbooks and classroom discourse, will be learned through the L2 and not the L1 (Sherkina-Lieber & Helms-Park, 2014). Here L2 lexical items are being acquired simultaneously with exposure to written language; typically such children are not literate in their L1. In contexts where the L1 is maintained through regular interaction within a large minority language group, as is typical in Hispanic communities in large urban centers in the United States, a problem can arise when children are introduced to literacy in a mainstream language they are not proficient in (Lesaux & Geva, 2006).

Irrespective of the types of L1 and L2 patterns of acquisition, the fact remains that the L2 lexicon interacts with the L1 lexicon in ways that are both helpful and unhelpful, and at various levels of representation (Jarvis, 2009; Jiang, 2000; Pavlenko, 2009; Wolter, 2006). For example, concepts attached to L1 and L2 words, especially those with concrete referents, are frequently identical or near-identical (De Groot & Keijzer, 2000), allowing for positive bidirectional transfer of conceptual knowledge. However, discrepancies between L1 and L2 concepts are ubiquitous, often even when associated with concrete items (e.g., cups and bowls, as illustrated by Labov's 1973 study), but regularly when referents are abstract (e.g., "democracy", "honesty"), rendering supposed translation equivalents potentially misleading (Pavlenko, 2009). As for the outcome of L2 lexical learning, there is some consensus that L2 word knowledge is both qualitatively and quantitatively different from L1 word knowledge, an issue that will be raised later. In addition, L2 word recognition is often made more laborious by L1-L2 differences in writing systems, scripts, or orthographies; in fact, automaticity of word recognition might be delayed or never on a par with L1 skilled word recognition.

Given these complexities and difficulties, it is not surprising that L2 reading comprehension is said to rely more heavily on lexical knowledge than is the case with L1 comprehension (Lervåg & Aukrust, 2010; Verhoeven, 2000). Further evidence for L2 learners' dependence on lexical knowledge during real-time processing is provided by the "shallow structure hypothesis" (Clahsen & Felser, 2006b). (As noted in Clahsen & Felser, 2006a, this hypothesis needs further testing with early bilinguals.) Based on L1 and L2 speakers' online sentence processing, Clahsen and Felser propose that L2 learners exclude morphosyntactic detail while parsing (e.g., filler-gap processing in *wh*-questions) and rely more heavily on basic lexico-semantic information (e.g., argument structure of verbs) irrespective of even when the L1 structures could be potentially facilitative. Thus, in L2 reading pedagogy, and most especially among novice readers, an even stronger argument can be made for eschewing the "psycholinguistic guessing game" model (Goodman, 1967), which had overtaken L2 reading pedagogy in the 1970s and 1980s. Publications on L2 reading in recent decades have taken pains to highlight lexical thresholds that need to be crossed before various types of L2 texts become comprehensible to readers (Cobb, 2007; Laufer, 1997; Schmitt, Jiang, & Grabe, 2011).

2.   THE LEXICON AND L2 READING

2.1   Visual word recognition in L1 and L2 readers

Basic word recognition, like reading itself, is a complex and multifaceted skill. It has been linked to a number of underlying skills, all of which seem to contribute to one's ability to recognize written words. These include oral language competence, listening comprehension skills, phonological awareness, orthographic awareness, and, of course, lexical knowledge (defined in this context as the ability to match forms with meanings). When beginning to explore possible differences regarding the acquisition of reading skills in an L1 versus an L2, it is important to bear in mind the fact that the basic task and the skills that underpin the task are believed to be more or less the same. As Koda (2013, p. 1) points out in her discussion of "The Universal Grammar of Reading" (Perfetti, 2003), "Reading … is the dynamic pursuit embedded in two interrelated systems – a language and its writing system – and its acquisition requires making links between the two systems." Similarly, in respect to skills, Proctor, Carl, August, and Snow (2005, p. 247) contend that "there appear to be more similarities than differences between [native speakers and non-native speakers] in the arena of component skills' contribution to reading achievement".

This does not mean, of course, that L1 and L2 speakers develop reading skills in the same way. There are at least a couple of factors that make the L2 learner's experience unique. One is the development of not one but two systems. Although L1 children of early school age are still very much entrenched in the process of learning their native tongue, their reading tasks will mostly be limited to forming the links between language they have already acquired to a reasonable extent and the writing system for that language. L2 children, on the other hand, often find themselves attempting to acquire both systems simultaneously. Not surprisingly, this poses a challenge since the process is not simply one of mapping written forms to words that are already known orally. In many cases, all aspects of word knowledge will be acquired simultaneously, including the word's phonology, orthography, and meaning, as well as the many other potentially salient aspects of a word, such as morphology, word class, and so on. Furthermore, there is no guarantee that children raised in bilingual scenarios will acquire the same lexical items in *their* L1 and L2. If the two lexicons are employed for different purposes in the bilingual child's life, as they often are, it can give rise to diglossia (Fishman, 1967), which, in turn, influences what types of texts are comprehensible in each of the two languages.

Another factor that makes L2 learners' experience distinct is what they bring with them from their L1 that can either enhance or interfere with the task of acquiring the underlying skills required for proficient reading. Though some L2 learners will come to the task of learning to read in the L2 lacking functional literacy in their L1, many will have both an established base of L1 knowledge and age-appropriate literacy skills. If a child's L1 has many features in common with the L2, such as shared or similar orthographies, phonologies, and/or morphologies, this can serve to boost his or her progression toward successful L2 reading (Bialystok, 2001; Grabe, 2009). In cases where there is a mismatch, proficient L2 reading will likely not take place until sufficient mastery for these L2 skills has been obtained. In respect to orthographic systems, for instance, Coulmas (2003) identifies three main classifications among the world's languages: phonological, syllabic, and morphosyllabic. In phonological languages, there is a grapheme for each phoneme. In syllabic languages, graphemes are associated with syllables, and in morphosyllabic languages the characters "indicate both a meaning component and a phonological, or syllabic, component" (Grabe, 2009, p. 112). And, of course, there are several languages that share not only the same orthographic type but also the same alphabetic system (e.g., the many European languages that use the Roman alphabet, or Japanese, which uses two syllabic scripts unique to Japanese as well as a logographic script borrowed from Chinese). Where there is such obvious overlap, the task of word recognition will typically be more straightforward.

Nonetheless, there may be other factors that can further affect the development of proficient L2 word recognition. One such factor is the extent to which there is consistent *grapheme-phoneme* correspondence, an idea that is captured in the orthographic depth hypothesis (Katz & Frost, 1992; for in-depth discussions see Chapter 3, this volume). The hypothesis describes languages with consistent and regular correspondence in phoneme-grapheme representations as transparent, and languages with less regular correspondence as opaque. Perhaps not surprisingly, decoding skills appear to be acquired faster for languages with transparent orthographies versus opaque orthographies (e.g., Lervåg & Aukrust, 2010). This means that even in situations where an L2 learner is approaching L2 reading with the same type of orthography, or even the same alphabetic system, like a Spanish speaker learning English, L1-based knowledge will be only partly helpful. In fact, research investigating the effects of transfer comparing learners with similar versus dissimilar orthographic systems has revealed that transfer effects, though existent, may not be as extensive as was once believed (see Koda, 2013, for an overview). Nonetheless, there still do seem to be advantages gained for L2 learners who can draw on their L1 orthographic knowledge in helping them to recognize words in the L2.

Clearly orthography is only one of the systems that is acquired in the L1 and can either assist or interfere with the task of L2 reading. Languages can also vary considerably in terms of their *phonological and morphological* systems, although these will intersect with the orthography, and there is evidence to suggest that transfer occurs in these realms as well. Furthermore, it is largely believed that this sort of transfer, particularly after L1 reading has become fairly proficient and automatized, is ballistic; an L2 learner is incapable of switching it off (e.g., Cook, 1992). Even advanced L2 readers have been shown to rely on information, knowledge, and strategies they initially obtained in their L1 (Upton & Lee-Thompson, 2001). On top of these issues of orthography, morphology, and phonology, there is the more centrally lexical issue of word meaning. Not surprisingly, this can also be subject to transfer effects. There is sufficient evidence to suggest that L1-L2 cognates, with some notable exceptions, are both visually/phonologically recognized more automatically (Peeters, Dijkstra, & Grainger, 2013; van Hell & De Groot, 1998) and acquired more easily (De Groot & Keijzer, 2000; Helms-Park & Dronjic, in press) than non-cognates (see Chapter 4, this volume, for a more detailed account of transfer involving cognates). Finally, this L1 influence seems to manifest at grain sizes larger than the word level as well. Studies investigating the processing of congruent collocations (i.e., those with a word-for-word translation in the L1 and L2) and incongruent collocations (i.e., those that are acceptable in the L2 but do not translate word-for-word into the L1) have uniformly shown a processing advantage for congruent over incongruent collocations (Wolter & Gyllstad, 2011; 2013; Yamashita & Jiang, 2010).

The impact an L2 word's orthography has on recognition has been depicted in the bilingual interactive activation (BIA) model and its revised version, the BIA+ model. The BIA posits four nodes involved in visual word recognition: a features node, a letter node, a word node, and a language node. The BIA conceptualizes word recognition as an initially bottom-up process that is instigated by visual input of a word form and that moves from feature to letter to word. The model assumes shared storage and non-selectivity for the L1 and L2, meaning that either L1 or L2 words can (and likely will) be activated through the visual input. The early stages of word recognition are characterized by patterns of activation and inhibition within and across the nodes until a particular word form is chosen and linked to its meaning. However, the model also requires a mechanism by which words can be further identified as either L1 or L2. This is achieved through the language node that feeds back to the word node and suppresses the non-selected language in cases of conflicts (e.g., cognates and false friends). Nonetheless, this feedback mechanism can be activated only after words in both languages have been selected as candidates; no early suppression of words in either language is possible, which essentially means there will be competition between words in both languages until a candidate word has been identified and competitors eliminated.

The BIA+ model extends and alters the BIA in a number of ways. Perhaps most importantly, it adds a phonological component to the model to account for sound-based similarities, and a semantic node to accommodate semantic overlap. Finally, the BIA+ adds a non-linguistic task/decision system that incorporates other factors that might have a bearing on how a word is identified and selected (e.g., a participant's expectancies in the task). In addition to creating a model that more closely aligns with empirical findings regarding the importance of phonological processes for reading, the phonological component also allows the model to explain possible L1 influences for readers with a distinct L1 orthography (e.g., an L1 Chinese speaker learning English). Both of these models have been used to simulate empirical findings from a range of studies with reasonably good success, suggesting that the L1 influence might be related to simultaneous stimulation of similar orthographic and/or phonological forms.

2.2 Lexical knowledge and reading comprehension

As noted earlier, skillful word recognition is almost certainly a necessary component of proficient reading. It is, however, not a sufficient condition for reading comprehension. Several empirical studies have been conducted with the aim of determining what factors seem to best predict reading comprehension in both L1 and L2 children.

Generally speaking, these studies have employed research designs that took into account a number of possible predictor variables and correlated these with reading comprehension measures. In most cases, it has been found that lexical knowledge is a key, if not the key, predictor for successful text comprehension. Proctor, Carlo, August, and Snow (2005) used structural equation modeling to investigate the factors that predicted reading comprehension for English L1-speaking and English L2-speaking (L1 Spanish) fourth-grade students in the United States. The predictor variables included measures of L2 alphabetic knowledge, L2 decoding fluency, L2 vocabulary knowledge, and L2 listening comprehension. They found that "positive changes in vocabulary knowledge had direct effects on reading comprehension but also on listening comprehension, through which reading comprehension was further affected" (p. 253), and concluded that "L2 vocabulary knowledge is crucial for improved English reading comprehension outcomes for Spanish-speaking ELLs" (p. 246).

Another study that highlighted the importance of lexical knowledge for reading comprehension was conducted by Verhoeven (2000). Verhoeven used componential analysis to explore the factors underlying reading comprehension in first- and second-grade L1 and L2 Dutch-speaking children. He found that "for reading comprehension, vocabulary knowledge was found to have more of an impact on the L2 learners than on the L1 learners" and goes on to suggest that "children learning to read in an L2 should be helped to build their lexical knowledge" (p. 313). Similarly, Lervåg and Aukrust (2010) developed latent-growth word models to assess the longitudinal impact of decoding skills and vocabulary skills on reading comprehension for L1- and L2-speaking second graders learning to read in Norwegian. Their results also indicated the important role of vocabulary, especially for long-term gains in reading comprehension. They found that "individual differences in decoding and vocabulary predicted initial reading comprehension skills, but only vocabulary predicted the subsequent growth of reading comprehension skills" (p. 612). Furthermore, they claim that vocabulary was a stronger predictor for L2 than L1 learners, and suggest that "the limitations in vocabulary skills in the L2 learners seemed sufficient to explain their lag in developing reading comprehension skills" (p. 612).

A final study that merits mention here is Rydland, Aukrust, and Fulland (2012). Once again, the authors administered a battery of word recognition and vocabulary knowledge measures, this time to fifth-grade L2 Norwegian-speaking students. However, the comprehension tests were based on two sets of readings: one set on a topic that was unfamiliar to the participants and one set that it was assumed students would have varying levels of knowledge about prior to encountering the texts. Multiple regression analyses revealed that vocabulary was a more important factor for predicting the unfamiliar texts than it was for the familiar texts, with prior topic knowledge being the strongest predictor for the familiar texts.

Collectively, these studies support the position that both word decoding skills and vocabulary knowledge are important for successful reading comprehension in L2. However, their comparative influence may not be maintained as the novice reader in the early grades transitions into later grades. Perhaps not surprisingly, word decoding seems particularly important at novice levels. Once word decoding skills have been acquired to the point of fluency, however, it is vocabulary knowledge that becomes increasingly important to text comprehension (Chall, Jacobs, & Baldwin, 1990; Madden, Slavin, Karweit, Dolan, & Wasik, 1993; Pinnell, Lyons, Deford, Bryk, & Seltzer, 1994; Proctor, Carlo, August, & Snow, 2005). Indeed, it is widely believed that the importance of vocabulary for text comprehension continues to increase as students move into higher grade levels (for both L1 and L2). Nonetheless, as indicated by the results of Ryland, Auktrust, and Fulland (2012), prior topic knowledge appears to also play a role in comprehension in the sense that it seems it can make up for some gaps in a learner's L2 vocabulary. (The difficulty involved in separating lexical knowledge from general or topic knowledge is discussed in Section 4.2.)

As with word recognition, a number of models have been proposed to describe the nature of the connections between L1 word forms, L2 word forms, and the underlying concepts that are linked to these word forms. Tokowicz and Tuninetti (2013) describe these models as memory representation models (which they contrast with word recognition models). Among the most well-known is Kroll and Stewart's (1994) revised hierarchical model (RHM). The RHM assumes separate lexicons for L1 and L2 words, but a shared underlying conceptual system. The RHM is also dynamic in the sense that the connection between L2 words and concepts and L2 words and L1 words can change with gains in proficiency. Kroll and Stewart argue that L2 words can develop a direct link to their underlying concepts, and L1 words can develop bidirectional links to their L2 translations.

Another memory representation model is the distributed feature model (De Groot, 1992). The distributed feature model is similar to the RHM in that it assumes separate lexical stores for L1 and L2 words. It is different, however, in how it deals with underlying concepts. While the RHM assumes a unified conceptual underpinning for L1 and L2 words, the distributed feature model suggests there is only partial overlap at the conceptual level. That is, although translation equivalents in two languages are likely to share some essential semantic features, there will almost always be some differences as well. Furthermore, these differences will be more pronounced when the words are abstract rather than concrete. The distributed feature model, therefore, argues that translation "equivalents" are never really equivalent at all on the conceptual level. Instead they are semantic approximations.

An additional model that might also be considered a memory representation model is Jiang's (2000) model of L2 lexical development. The model provides a framework for describing the development of knowledge for individual words. Jiang's starting point is Levelt's (1989) model of the lexical entry. Levelt's model posits a distinction between knowledge at the lemma level and the lexeme level. Lemma-level knowledge includes information about a word's syntactic and semantic properties, while lexeme-level knowledge contains information about a word's morphological and phonological/orthographic properties. Jiang assumes a similar structure for L2 lexical entries, but he asserts that L2 lexical acquisition follows a unique trajectory that often results in an L2 lexical entry for a particular word that is qualitatively different from an L1 speaker's entry for the same word. In brief, Jiang argues that the L2 learner will often retain L1-based information in the lexical entries at the lemma level. This means that the learner will have a large number of lexical entries that are not quite aligned with native speakers, particularly in terms of their semantic and syntactic information. Furthermore, as this misalignment is generally unlikely to result in any noticeable breakdowns in communication, L2 learners will usually not notice the discrepancy and therefore will not be motivated (consciously or unconsciously) to alter their understanding of these words.

An important implication of these memory representation models is that L2 lexical knowledge is influenced by L1 knowledge in a way that colours the L2 learner's understanding. Although the RHM provides for the possibility of direct access, the other two models suggest that L2 lexical knowledge will likely not be qualitatively the same as an L1 speaker's. This can have implications for how an L2 learner interprets written texts. And indeed, research into gesture usage by L2 speakers indicates that advanced learners maintain an L1-like understanding for even basic words like verbs of placement (e.g., *put*; see Gullberg, 2009).

3.   IMPROVING L2 VOCABULARY

Regardless of whether a learner can ever obtain native-like lexical knowledge in an L2, it stands to reason that teachers should endeavor to improve vocabulary knowledge at all levels of education. This may be particularly true for disadvantaged children in the earliest years of their schooling. This is because richness of vocabulary at the point of entry into the school system has been correlated with socio-economic class in numerous contexts globally (as is also the case with other predictors of reading ability – e.g., phonological awareness; see Luyten et al., 2003; Walberg & Tsai, 1983). Those with poor vocabulary are disadvantaged readers, and disadvantaged readers tend to pick up less vocabulary from reading activities because not only do they read less but also what they do read is read less efficiently. Cain and Oakhill (2011), for example, found that readers with poor reading comprehension abilities also demonstrated slower rates of vocabulary acquisition. Similarly, Biemiller and Slonim (2001) found that as early as Grade 2, students with poor vocabulary found it hard to catch up with average readers. Further, Cunningham and Stanovich (1997), in a longitudinal study, found that vocabulary knowledge in first grade accounted for more than 30% of the variance in reading comprehension in eleventh grade, the most variance contributed by a single variable in their study. Finally, studies by Dickinson and Tabors (2001), Hart and Rinsley (1995), and White, Graves, and Slater (1990) demonstrated that poor vocabulary development in children's early years negatively affects their reading comprehension in later years.

All of these studies point to the Matthew effect, described earlier. Not surprisingly, it is not only reading comprehension that suffers when a student lacks a sufficiently rich vocabulary. It also limits access to essential knowledge and concepts, since so much knowledge is gained through written texts in an academic setting. In fact, even a slight disadvantage in vocabulary size can result in a considerable cost in terms of reading comprehension. In a recent large-scale study investigating the link between coverage and comprehension, Schmitt, Jiang, and Grabe (2011) found that 90% coverage for vocabulary in a text translated to around only 50% comprehension, while 100% coverage led to, on average, around 75% comprehension. Furthermore, the authors found that the relationship between gains in coverage and gains in comprehension was, more or less, linear above the 90% mark, with a gain of 1% coverage linked to an average improvement of around 2.3% on comprehension tests. This means modest gains in size can lead to fairly sizeable gains in comprehension, which, again, can provide better access to key ideas and concepts.

Findings like these have led researchers to call for a proactive approach to vocabulary development from the early years of schooling (e.g., Joshi, 2005). The question that arises here is what should be done to improve L2 vocabulary skills and, in doing so, improve one's ability to read effectively in the L2. If it is indeed correct to assume that better vocabulary knowledge leads to better reading ability, then it stands to reason that focused study on vocabulary will likely be of use. Much has been written on vocabulary learning strategies

(VLS) that learners can employ to improve their vocabulary knowledge. Schmitt (1999) argues that strategies can be bifurcated to reflect two broad aims: (1) discovering a word's meaning, and (2) consolidating a word once it has been encountered.

Strategies for discovering a word's meaning include some very traditional practices, like memorizing L2 words from a word list, making vocabulary flash cards, looking up the meaning of a new word in the dictionary, or learning common affixes and roots found in English words. Strategies for consolidating a word include many of the same practices, along with many other strategies designed to integrate a given word into networks for semantically or syntactically related words. The one thing that underpins all of these strategies, however, is that there is an overt focus on learning vocabulary for the sake of learning vocabulary. The underpinning assumption, however, is obviously that knowing a large number of words (and the words these words associate with) is essential to general performance in an L2. And although these practices have fallen from favour in some circles lately due to their decontextualized nature (see ahead), as Nation (2001) points out there is overwhelming evidence to suggest that direct vocabulary learning has numerous benefits and should therefore be actively encouraged, even if it is not itself sufficient for mastery of words in an L2.

At the other extreme is the viewpoint that most (if not all) vocabulary learning should take place in the context of some form of comprehensible input through activities like extensive reading (e.g., Cho & Krashen, 1994; Dupuy & Krashen, 1993; Krashen, 1989). Underlying this view is often the observation that L1 speakers assemble impressively large vocabularies mostly through input alone, coupled with the assumption that direct strategies are too inefficient to be of practical use. Additionally, proponents of contextualized acquisition through extensive reading point to the belief that learning new words in a rich context provides L2 speakers with a much deeper and more pragmatic understanding of words, an understanding that would not always be accessible through direct strategies (e.g. knowledge of connotations, collocational patterns, register). This argument is clearly justified to some extent. As with grammatical knowledge, vocabulary knowledge can probably never be sufficiently acquired without the benefits that come from extensive and varied input. Furthermore, there is empirical evidence that suggests that extensive reading has benefits for not only language proficiency in general but also vocabulary development. In particular, the research that exists indicates that extensive reading programs can result in faster word recognition for known words (Segalowitz, Watson, & Segalowitz, 1995; Snelling, van Gelderen, & De Glopper, 2002; van Gelderen et al., 2004) and improvements in vocabulary size (Grabe & Stoller, 1997; Horst, 2005, 2009; Lao & Krashen, 2000; Pigada & Schmitt, 2006; Poulshock, 2010).

Nonetheless, there are some criticisms against this perspective as well, especially for learners who have achieved anything less than a native-like or near native-like mastery of the L2. Laufer (2003, p. 568) in particular has criticized what she describes as the "vocabulary through reading hypothesis". Laufer believes that this view is predicated on four basic assumptions, none of which, she argues, is supported by empirical evidence. The assumptions are: (1) the noticing assumption, (2) the guessing ability assumption, (3) the guessing-retention link assumption, and (4) the cumulative gain assumption. Laufer's argument against the first assumption is that learners do not regularly recognize unfamiliar words as unfamiliar (i.e., a learner might confuse a word with another word with a similar form). Her contention with the second assumption is that contexts are often either insufficient for successful guessing to take place or misleading as to the actual meaning of a word. In respect to the third assumption, Laufer reiterates her stance that incorrect guessing does not count as learning. She also points to studies (Haastrup, 1991; Mondria & Wit de Boer, 1991) that indicate that easy and successful guessing can actually lead to lower retention of a word's meaning, owing to the fact that learning with difficulty enhances memory traces whereas learning with ease does not. Finally, Laufer questions the fourth assumption on the basis of practical restraints. She acknowledges that repeated exposures to words in texts can lead to vocabulary gains, but she questions whether this is actually a more efficient approach to vocabulary learning given the fact that repeated exposures are needed and words will sometimes appear sparingly in a given text. Laufer concludes her paper by presenting the results of a number of empirical studies comparing incidental vocabulary acquisition through reading alone with more explicitly focused vocabulary study (either "reading supplemented with a language focused task" or "word-focused tasks without reading"). The studies uniformly confirmed the notion that retention is improved through explicit study.

In summarizing the main ideas from these opposing perspectives, it should be self-evident that what is needed for successful L2 vocabulary development is an approach that promotes both direct strategies and extensive reading. As Grabe (2009, p. 273) points out, "Both paths to vocabulary learning are needed and they support each other in complementary ways." Direct strategies are useful for the development of a sufficiently large vocabulary and also for helping learners focus their attention on important words that they are likely to encounter time and time again. Extensive reading, on the other hand, is likely essential for the refinement and enhancement of vocabulary knowledge, as well as for the exposure it provides to new vocabulary, which may eventually be acquired through exposure alone or else coupled with more direct means of instruction. The link between vocabulary and reading is cyclical and undeniable. Reading builds vocabulary and better vocabulary leads to more effective reading. Furthermore, L2 learners have been shown to find reading to be a rewarding and pleasurable experience, which can also help to propel the cycle (Yamashita, 2013). As such, reading needs to feature prominently in any L2 learner's studies.

Finally, we would argue that any approach to L2 vocabulary teaching should incorporate instruction not only on single words but also on larger stretches of language that are mapped to single meanings (the so-called formulaic language described earlier). Though there is considerable debate in the field regarding whether L2 adult learners can store and process formulaic language in the same way as L1 speakers (see Wray, 2002, 2008, and Boers & Lindstromberg, 2012, or Durrant & Schmitt, 2010, for opposing views), there seems to be broad agreement that L2 children make extensive use of formulaic language in the early stages of language acquisition. Even Wray, who argues strongly for an L1-L2 distinction in terms of storage and processing of formulaic language in post-childhood learners, suggests that L2 children can acquire a store of formulaic language that is on a par with their L1 counterparts. But even if older learners are less capable of storing and processing language formulaically, this does not mean that formulaic language should be given short shrift in vocabulary teaching practices. Many tasks can be incorporated into teaching to raise learners' awareness of items like collocations, fixed phrases, idioms, and so forth (see Nation, 2001, for specific pedagogical techniques).

4. COMPARABILITY OF STUDIES ON LEXICAL KNOWLEDGE AND READING: CAVEATS AND POSSIBLE REMEDIES

This section singles out a few issues that we have found to be problematic in the research literature on the interaction of lexical knowledge and reading, irrespective of whether the language in question is a primary or non-primary one. The first centers on what type of structural unit constitutes a "word" and a general tendency in empirical research to test only single words rather than multi-word units. Furthermore, tests generally highlight vocabulary size rather than depth but assess size in a variety of formats. The remaining issue centers on the link between lexical knowledge and the two other conditions that need to be fulfilled to facilitate reading comprehension, possibly inextricably: knowledge of the linguistic code and general (world) knowledge (Perfetti et al., 2005).

4.1 Vocabulary tests: choice of test items and quality of knowledge

It has long been observed that there is no stable cross-linguistic definition of a word based on factors such as visual representation, meaning unit, stress unit, or autonomy (Carter, 1998). As for word meaning, while a small number of words can be defined unambiguously or viewed as simply a sum of semantic components (e.g., a chemical compound such as *carbon dioxide* or a geometrical shape such as a *square*), the same is not true of cases of polysemy (Aitchison, 2012; Kellerman, 1979). *Square*, for example, encompasses not only its literal meaning but also the extended meaning of "a straight-laced, uninventive, and probably boring person". In the same way, words with "fuzzy boundaries" are prone to being interpreted subjectively (Aitchison, 2012), as in the case of *bachelor*, whose traditional components (+male, +adult, and +single) ignore socio-historic, culture-specific issues related to convivial cohabitation, orientation, and so on.

For those investigating the relationship between lexical knowledge and reading comprehension, the issues then are (a) when a learner's vocabulary size is being assessed, whether polysemes constitute multiple or unified lexical entries, and (b) in the case of polysemes and words with fuzzy boundaries, how comprehensive the knowledge of these words needs to be for text comprehension. Equally controversial is whether derived forms sharing a root constitute discrete or unitary entries in the mental lexicon. For example, if we take a derived word, such as "reactivation" [re[[[[act]ive]at]ion]], do all of the forms appear under "act"? Or are "act", "active", "activate", and "activation" separated in some fashion? (For lexical testing purposes, a deciding factor could be how transparent the meaning of the derived form is, as seen in the close connection between the root and the affixed form in *puzzlement* but not in *department*).

In addition, languages have a large number of multi-word items that are governed by the principles of non-compositionality, fixedness, and institutionalization, each to a greater or lesser extent (Sinclair, 1991). Moon's (1997) taxonomy includes compound words (e.g., "butter tart"), phrasal verbs (e.g., "look down on"), idioms (e.g., "to not touch someone with a ten-foot pole"), fixed phrases, such as greetings and similes, and prefabricated "gambits" (e.g., "as a matter of fact"). However, in spite of the frequency of multi-word items in both oral and written discourse, these are greatly underrepresented in lexical tests.

A related and more consequential source of variation among lexical tests (and, therefore, differing accounts of the impact of lexical knowledge on reading) is that tests differ in whether they are assessing vocabulary size (or breadth) or quality (or depth), and if the latter, which aspects of quality are being tapped. Most current L1 tests assess only size (e.g., Dunn & Dunn's Peabody Picture Vocabulary Test, 2007, which is also used with L2 children), but a variety of other formats are employed in L2 contexts (e.g., Schmitt, 2000). Nation (2001), however, identifies nine receptive aspects of word knowledge. Six of these nine aspects reflect quality/depth of word knowledge. Under the heading of "meaning", Nation identifies three elements: (1) form and meaning (What meaning does this word form represent?), (2) concept and referents (What is included in the concept?), and (3) associations (What other words does this word make us think of?). Under the heading of "use", Nation identifies an additional three receptive aspects: (1) grammatical functions (In what patterns does the word occur?), (2) collocations (What words or types of words occur with this one?), and (3) constraints on use (Where, when, and how often would we expect to meet this word?). Other processing-related aspects of word knowledge that could also be considered in the realm of vocabulary depth are speed of recognition, speed of semantic access, automaticity, ballisticity, and strength of semantic priming (see, e.g., Favreau & Segalowitz, 1983; Magiste, 1986; Neely, 1977; Phillips, Segalowitz, O'Briend, & Yamasaki, 2004; Tzelgov, Henik, Sneg, & Baruch, 1996). The issue of breadth versus depth cannot be solved by deciding to test one at the expense of the other since each type of lexical knowledge has an impact on reading comprehension, usually depending on the nature of the text. In *To Kill a Mockingbird*, for instance, words such as *coloured* (in combination with *folk, church,* or *balcony*) or *lynch mob*, being directly relevant to the plot and the core themes of the book, require depth of knowledge, while *truant lady* or *trotlines* make a minor contribution to the novel's small-town setting but are peripheral to its plot or themes and therefore can be dealt with cursorily.

The lack of consensus regarding the definition of a word and the variety of vocabulary size tests constitutes one reason for the wide range of findings related to the role of vocabulary in reading (National Reading Council, 2000). The problem is exacerbated when lexis is being examined in languages other than English or in bilingual situations where lexical knowledge in two or more languages is being compared (e.g., an inflectional language versus a polysynthetic or analytic one). The use of single-word test items at the expense of multi-word ones could be tackled by invoking the concept of the "lexical unit" (whether a single-word or a multi-word item) in which all the inflectional forms of an entry cluster together, or the concept of "word families", which encompass derived forms as well (Bauer & Nation, 1993). Similarly, despite the lack of suitable vocabulary depth tests (see Dronjic & Helms-Park, 2014, for some problems with current depth tests), instruments that test knowledge of polysemy might prove to be valuable to reading comprehension since comprehension frequently relies on the reader's ability to choose a relevant meaning of a polysemous word.

4.2   Interfaces between lexico-semantic knowledge, syntactic knowledge, and topic/general knowledge

It is reasonable to think of *linguistic knowledge* as including syntactic knowledge since reading comprehension relies heavily on the parsing of sentences.

Separating the roles of lexical and (morpho) syntactic knowledge might be justifiable during early childhood, when L1 children produce one-word to two-word utterances, the latter probably constituting a "semantic grammar" (Bloom, 1970; Pinker, 1984). Later, during their preschool years, children arrive at an adult-like syntactic grammar. Thus, claims made by Share, Jorm, Maclean, and Matthews (1984), based on a large-scale study, that grammatical development at the outset of kindergarten accounted for 17% of the variance in reading achievement at the end of Grade 1 seem reasonable, at least at first glance.

In both L1 and L2 reading research, there are undoubtedly syntactic effects on reading, as when syntactically ambiguous or "garden path" constructions lead to parsing difficulties even among skilled readers (Grabe, 2009). In fact, a small number of studies propose that syntax trumps vocabulary in their relative contributions to reading comprehension (e.g., Shiotsu & Weir, 2007, but see Floyd & Carrell, 1987, among others, for an opposite perspective). In a similar vein, Grabe (2009, p. 63) lists paying explicit attention to syntactic structure as one of the routes a reader can use to comprehend difficult texts. Yet, there are theoretical and empirical grounds for considering lexical and syntactic knowledge to be interwoven in such complex ways that dissociating the influence of one from the other is difficult in most textual contexts. A traditional view of a lexical entry in the mental lexicon, for example, is that it consists of (a) a lexeme or word form (phonological or orthographic), and (b) a lemma, containing both meaning and word class, or in other words a semantic structure that parallels syntactic structure (Jarvis, 2009; Kempen & Huijbers, 1983; Levelt, 1989; but see also Caramazza & Miozzo, 1998, for an alternative view); furthermore, syntactic structure can be viewed as being driven by the lexicon in certain frameworks (e.g., Pustejovsky, 1995). Non-generative lexical approaches to grammar through "patterns" derived via corpus analysis also view vocabulary and grammar (syntax) as inseparable (Hunston & Francis, 2000).

A further complication with the notion that grammar and lexis can be neatly separated is that terms such as "grammatical knowledge" or "grammar" are used variously in the research literature. Various aspects of the linguistic code are investigated under these umbrella terms: word order alone (syntax); both word order and morphology (inextricably linked to syntax in most generative models); explicit knowledge or use of the linguistic code; implicit knowledge and use; and so on. Much of what is referred to as "syntactic knowledge" has consisted of metalinguistic tasks, such as sentence rearrangement (e.g., Bryant, MacLean, & Bradley, 1990), thereby confounding syntactic abilities with semantic processing and verbal working memory (Bowey, 2005). In light of these views, it is not surprising that Bowey comes to the conclusion that, during the years of emergent literacy in the L1 it is not clear … to what extent different facets of oral language develop-ment (including vocabulary, grammatical, and phonological skills) can be meaningfully separated and how best to conceptualize the underlying causal relationships between different constructs in this domain.

(2005, p. 158)

In L2 reading research as well, in the majority of cases where a correlation between "grammatical proficiency" and reading ability has been examined – for example, in Alderson's (1993) examination of IELTS results – there has been a similar overlap between grammatical proficiency and semantic pro-cessing (including lexical knowledge).

Similarly, *general knowledge*, which is considered to be a major contributor to listening comprehension (as mentioned earlier), not only interacts with lexico-semantic knowledge but also is probably inextricable from it. In early L2 reading research, Carrell (1982) cogently reinterpreted Haliday and Hasan's (1976) concept of "lexical cohesion" as the domain of "coherence" created not by the text but by the reader's prior knowledge of lexical items in schemata (Rumelhart, 1980). Thus, *puck, dead puck, carom, cross-checking, flat pass, penalty killer*, and *ragging* would cohere for most Canadians reading about ice hockey but might not for those unfamiliar with the game. The existence of vocabulary peculiar to "scripts", "frames", "semantic fields", or topics has been confirmed by psycholinguistic research involving priming, word associations, speech errors, and so on, conducted with healthy and aphasic participants (Aitchison, 2012). Thus, it is not surprising that vocabulary can be a "proxy" for the general knowledge needed for the comprehension of sentences and larger pieces of text during the reading process (Perfetti, 1998; Verhoeven, 2000).

These ambiguities between lexical and linguistic (including syntactic) knowledge and between lexical and general knowledge highlight the method-ological difficulty of examining the full reach of vocabulary knowledge in the reading process. Together with variation in the definition of words and word knowledge, these discrepancies explain why the role of vocabulary knowledge in reading is reported as merely one of the factors contributing to successful reading in some research while being treated as the near-perfect correlate of reading prowess in other studies (Carver, 2003). The issue is particularly thorny when non-English-type languages are considered, where a word is frequently a single morpheme (e.g., analytic languages) or multi-morphemic, as in a polysynthetic language, like Labrador Inuttitut, where there is a high correla-tion between receptive lexical and grammatical knowledge (Lieber-Sherkina et al., 2015). One viable solution would be to acknowledge that what is called lexical knowledge overlaps with both linguistic knowledge and general knowl-edge. In short, lexical knowledge could be characterized as knowledge that transcends not only single words but also the linguistic code.

5. CONCLUSION

In this chapter, we have looked at a number of issues central to lexical knowledge and reading. Although there are clearly many factors involved in effective reading in an L2 (or an L1 for that matter), there seems to be broad agreement that lexis plays an essential role in the efficient and successful processing of written texts. However, as we discussed in the previous section, much work remains to be done if researchers hope to disambiguate the influence of lexis from other interwoven and interrelated aspects of linguistic and general (world) knowledge. In this respect, there is a need for research designed to investigate the connections between reading and lexical knowledge in various school subjects, genres, semantic fields, and the like. Furthermore, future research could examine the connections between lexis and other aspects of a grammar in not only relatively well-researched languages, like English, French, and Spanish, but also other second languages, such as Mandarin, Japanese, and Tamil. This would allow us to come up with better operational definitions for variables that frequently appear in empirical studies aimed at uncovering factors underlying reading comprehension. Perhaps most importantly, broader definitions of lexis would encourage researchers to incorporate items beyond single words, such as multi-word units and polysemous words, into test instruments that measure both breadth and depth of vocabulary.

REFERENCES

Aitchison, J. (2012). *Words in the mind: An introduction to the mental lexicon*. Malden, MA, Wiley.

Alderson, J. (1993). The relationship between grammar and reading in an English for academic purposes test battery. In D. Douglas & C. Chapelle (Eds.), *A new decade of language testing research: selected papers from the 1990 language testing research colloquium* (pp. 203–219). Alexandria, VA: Teachers of English to Speakers of Other Languages.

Anglin J.M. (1993). Vocabulary development: A morphological analysis. *Monographs of the Society for Research in Child Development, 58*(10), Serial #238.

Bauer, L., & Nation, I.S.P. (1993). Word families. *International Journal of Lexicography, 6*(4), 253–279.

Beck, I., McKeown, M. , & Kucan, L. (2013). Bringing words to life: Robust vocabulary instruction (second edition). New York, NY, Guilford Press.

Bialystok, E. (2001). *Bilingualism in development: Language, literacy, & cognition*. New York: Cambridge University Press.

Biemiller, A., & Slonim, N. (2001). Estimating root word vocabulary growth in normative and advantaged populations: Evidence for a common sequence of vocabulary acquisition. *Journal of Educational Psychology, 93*(3), 498–520.

Bloom, L. (1970). *Language development: Form and function in emerging grammars*. Cambridge, MA: MIT Press.

Boers, F., & Lindstromberg, S. (2012). Experimental and intervention studies on formulaic sequences in a second language. *Annual Review of Applied Linguistics, 32*, 83–110.

Bowey, J.A. (2005). Predicting individual differences in learning to read. In M. Snowling & C. Hulme (Eds.), *The science of reading* (pp. 155–172). Malden: Blackwell.

Bradley, L., & Bryant, P. (1985). *International Academy for Research in Learning Disabilities: Vol. 1. Rhyme and reason in reading and spelling*. Ann Arbor: University of Michigan Press.

Bryant, P.E., MacLean, M., & Bradley, L.L. (1990). Rhyme, language, and children's reading. *Applied Psycholinguistics, 11*, 237–252.

Cain, K., & Oakhill, J. (2011). Matthew effects in young readers: Reading comprehension and reading experience aid vocabulary development. *Journal of Learning Disabilities, 44*(5), 431–443.

Caplan, D., & Waters, G.S. (1999). Verbal working memory and sentence comprehension. *Behavioural and Brain Sciences, 22*, 77–126.

Caramazza, A., & Miozzo, M. (1998). More is not always better: A response to Roelofs, Meyer, and Levelt. *Cognition, 69*(2), 231–241.

Carrell, P.L. (1982). Cohesion is not coherence. *TESOL Quarterly, 16*(4), 479–488.

Carter, R. (1998). *Vocabulary: Applied linguistic perspectives*. London: Routledge.

Carver, R.P. (2003). The highly lawful relationships among pseudoword decoding, word identification, spelling, listening, and reading. *Scientific Studies of Reading, 7*(2), 127–154.

Chall, J.S., Jacobs, V. A., & Baldwin, L. E. (1993). *The reading crisis: Why poor children fall behind*. Cambridge, MA: Harvard University Press.

Cho, K.S. and Krashen, S. (1994). Acquisition of vocabulary from the Sweet Valley Kids series : adult ESL acquisition. *The Journal of Reading, 37*: 662–667.

Clahsen, H., & Felser, C. (2006a). Continuity and shallow structures in language processing. *Applied Psycholinguistics, 27*(1), 107–126.

Clahsen, H., & Felser, C. (2006b). Grammatical processing in language learners. *Applied Psycholinguistics, 27*(1), 3–42.

Clark, E.V. (1995). *Cambridge Studies in Linguistics: Vol. 65. The lexicon in acquisition*. Cambridge, UK: Cambridge University Press.

Cobb, T. (2007). Computing the vocabulary demands of L2 reading. *Language Learning & Technology, 11*(3), 38–63.

Cook, V.J. (1992). Evidence for multicompetence. *Language Learning, 42*, 557–591.

Coulmas, F. (2003). *Writing systems*. New York: Cambridge University Press.

Cunningham, A. E., & Stanovich, K. E. (1997). Early reading acquisition and its relation to reading experience and ability 10 years later. *Developmental Psychology, 33*, 934–945.

Daneman, M. (1988). Word knowledge and reading skill. In M. Daneman, G. MacKinnon, & T. G. Waller (Eds.), *Reading research: Advances in theory and practice* (Vol. 6, pp. 145–175). San Diego, CA: Academic.

De Groot. A. M. B. (1992). Determinant of word translation. *Journal of Experimental Psychology: Learning, Memory, and Cognition, 18*, 1001–1018.

De Groot, A., & Keijzer, R. (2000). What is hard to learn is easy to forget: The roles of word concreteness, cognate status, and word frequency in foreign-language vocabulary learning and forgetting. *Language Learning, 50*, 1–56.

Dickinson, D., & Tabors, P. (Eds.). (2001). *Beginning literacy with language*. Baltimore, MD: Brookes.

Dronjic, V., & Helms-Park, R. (2014). Fixed-choice word-association tasks as second-language lexical tests: What native-speaker performance reveals about their potential weaknesses. *Applied Psycholinguistics, 35*(1), 193–221.

Dunn, L.M., & Dunn, D.M. (2007). *PPVT-4: Peabody picture vocabulary test*. San Antonio, TX: Pearson Assessments.

Dupuy, B., & Krashen, S. (1993). Incidental vocabulary acquisition of French as a foreign language. *Applied Language Learning*, 4, 55–63.

Durrant, P., & Schmitt, N. (2010). Adult learners' retention of collocations from exposure. *Second Language Research, 26*(2), 163–188.

Ehri, L.C. (2005). Development of sight word reading: Phases and findings. In M. Snowling & C. Hulme (Eds.), *The science of reading* (pp. 135–154). Malden: Blackwell.

Favreau, M., & Segalowitz, N.S. (1983). Automatic and controlled processes in the first- and second-language reading of fluent bilinguals. *Memory and Cognition, 11*, 565–574.

Fishman, J.A. (1967). Bilingualism with and without diglossia; diglossia with and without bilingualism. *Journal of Social Issues, 23*(2), 29–38.

Floyd, P., & Carrell, P.L. (1987). Effects on ESL reading of teaching cultural content schemata. *Language Learning, 37*(1), 89–108.

Freebody, P., & Anderson, R. (1983). Effects of vocabulary difficulty, text cohesion and schema availability on reading comprehension. *Reading Research Quarterly, 18*(3), 277–294.

Gathercole, S.E. (2007). Working memory and language. In G. Gaskell (Ed.), *Oxford handbook of psycholinguistics* (pp. 761–769). Oxford: Oxford University Press.

Goodman, K.S. (1967). Reading: A psycholinguistic guessing game. *Journal of the Reading Specialist, 6*, 126–135.

Grabe, W. (2009). *Reading in a second language: Moving from theory to practice*. Cambridge, UK: Cambridge University Press.

Grabe, W., & Stoller, F. (1997). Reading and vocabulary development in a second language: A case study. In J. Coady & T. Huckin (Eds.), *Second language vocabulary acquisition* (pp. 98–122). Cambridge, UK: Cambridge University Press.

Gullberg, M. (2009). Gestures and the development of semantic representations in first and second language acquisition. *Acquisition et Interaction en Langue Etrangère: Languages, Interaction, and Acquisition* (former AILE), *1*, 117–139.

Haastrup, K. (1991). *Lexical inferencing procedures or talking about words*. Tubingen, Germany: Gunter Narr.

Halliday, M.A.K., & Hasan, R. (1976). *Cohesion in English*. London: Longman.

Helms-Park, R., & Dronjic, V. (in press). Crosslinguistic lexical influence: Cognate facilitation. In R. Alonso (Ed.), *Crosslinguistic influence*. Multilingual Matters.

Horst, M. (2005). Learning L2 vocabulary through extensive reading: A measurement study. *The Canadian Modern Language Review, 61*, 355–382.

Horst, M. (2009). Developing definitional vocabulary knowledge and lexical access speed through extensive reading. In Z. Han & N. Anderson (Eds.), *Second language reading: Research and instruction* (pp. 40–64). Ann Arbor: University of Michigan Press.

Hunston, S., & Francis, G. (2000). *Pattern grammar: A corpus-driven approach to the lexical grammar of English*. Amsterdam: Benjamins.

Jarvis, S. (2009). Lexical transfer. In A. Pavlenko (Ed.), *The bilingual mental lexicon: Interdisciplinary approaches* (pp. 99–124). Bristol, UK: Multilingual Matters.

Jiang, N. (2000). Lexical representation and development in a second language. *Applied Linguistics, 21*, 47–77.

Johnson, C., & Goswami, U. (2010). Phonological awareness, vocabulary, and reading in deaf children with cochlear implants. *Journal of Speech, Language, and Hearing Research, 53*(2), 237–261.

Joshi, R. (2005). Vocabulary: A critical component of comprehension. *Reading & Writing Quarterly, 21*(3), 209–219.

Jusczyk, P. W. (2000). *The discovery of spoken language.* Cambridge, MA: MIT Press.

Katz, L., & Frost, R. (1992). The reading process is different for different orthographies: The orthographic depth hypothesis. In R. Frost & L. Katz (Eds.), *Orthography, phonology, morphology, and meaning* (pp. 45–66). Amsterdam: Elsevier.

Krashen, S. (1989). We acquire vocabulary and spelling by reading: additional evidence for the input hypothesis. *Modern Language Journal, 73,* 440–464.

Kellerman, E. (1979). Transfer and non-transfer: Where we are now. *Studies in Second Language Acquisition, 2*(1), 37–57.

Kempen, G., & Huijbers, P. (1983). The lexicalization process in sentence production and naming: Indirect election of words. *Cognition, 14*(2), 185–209.

Kintsch, W. (1998). *Comprehension: A paradigm for cognition.* Cambridge, UK: Cambridge University Press.

Koda, K. (2013). Second language reading, scripts, and orthographies. In C. Chapelle (Ed.), *The encyclopedia of applied linguistics* (pp. 1–7). Boston: Blackwell.

Kroll, J. F., & Stewart, E. (1994). Category interference in translation and picture naming: Evidence for asymmetric connections between bilingual memory representations. *Journal of Memory and Language, 33,* 149–174.

Labov, W. (1973). The boundaries of words and their meanings. In C.-J. Bailey & R. Shuy (Eds.), *New ways of analyzing variation in English* (pp. 340–373). Washington, DC: Georgetown University Press.

Lao, C.Y., & Krashen, S. (2000). The impact of popular literature study on literacy development in EFL: More evidence of the power of reading. *System, 28,* 261–270.

Laufer, B. (1997). The lexical plight in second language reading. In J. Coady & T. Huckin (Eds.), *Second language vocabulary acquisition: A rationale for pedagogy* (pp. 20–34). Cambridge, UK: Cambridge University Press.

Laufer, B. (2003). Vocabulary acquisition in a second language: Do learners really acquire most vocabulary by reading? Some empirical evidence. *The Canadian Modern Language Review, 59*(4), 567–587.

Lervåg, A., & Aukrust, V.G. (2010). Vocabulary knowledge is a critical determinant of the difference in reading comprehension growth between first and second language learners. *Journal of Child Psychology and Psychiatry, 51*(5), 612–620.

Lesaux, N.K., & Geva, E. (2006). Synthesis: Development of literacy in language-minority students. In D. August & T. Shanahan (Eds.) (pp. 53–74), *Developing literacy in second-language learners.* Mahwah, NJ: Erlbaum.

Levelt, W. (1989). *Speaking: From intention to articulation.* Cambridge, MA: MIT Press.

Luyten, H., Creemers-van Wees, L.M.C.M., & Bosker, R.J. (2003). The Matthew effect in Dutch primary education: Differences between schools, cohorts and pupils. *Research Papers in Education, 18,* 167–195.

Luyten, H., & ten Bruggencate, G. (2011). The presence of Matthew effects in Dutch primary education, development of language skills over a six-year period. *Journal of Learning Disabilities, 44,* 444–458.

Madden, N.A., Slavin, R.E., Karweit, N.L., Dolan, L.J., & Wasik, B.A. (1991). Success for all: Ending reading failure from the beginning. *Language Arts, 68,* 47–52.

Magiste, E. (1986). Selected issues in second and third language learning. In J. Vaid (Ed.), *Language processing in bilinguals: Psycholinguistic and neuropsychological perspectives* (pp. 97–122). Hillsdale, NJ: Erlbaum.

Merton, R.K. (1968). The Matthew effect in science. *Science, 159*(3810), 56–63.

Metsala, J.L. (1997a). An examination of word frequency and neighborhood density in the development of spoken-word recognition. *Memory & Cognition, 25,* 47–56.

Metsala, J.L. (1997b). Spoken word recognition in reading disabled children. *Journal of Educational Psychology, 89,* 159–169.

Milton, J., & Fitzpatrick, T. (2013). *Dimensions of vocabulary knowledge.* London: Palgrave Macmillan.

Mondria, J.-A., & Wit-de Boer, M. (1991). The effects of contextual richness on the guessability and the retention of words in a foreign language. *Applied Linguistics, 12,* 249–267.

Moon, R. (1997). Vocabulary connections: Multi-word items in English. In Schmitt, N. and McCarthy, M. (eds.), *Vocabulary: Description, Acquisition and Pedagogy* (pp. 40–63). Cambridge: Cambridge University Press.

Nagy, W.E., & Scott, J.A. (2000). Vocabulary processes. In M. Kamil, P. Mosenthal, P. Pearson, & R. Barr (Eds.), *Handbook of reading research* (Vol. 3, pp. 269–284). Mahwah, NJ: Erlbaum.

Nation, I.S.P. (2001). *Learning vocabulary in another language.* New York: Cambridge University Press.

National Reading Panel. (2000). *Teaching children to read: An evidence-based assessment of the scientific research literature on reading and its implications for reading instruction* (NIH Publication No. 00–4769). Washington, DC: U.S. Government Printing Office.

Neely, J.H. (1977). Semantic priming and retrieval from lexical memory: Roles of inhibitionless spreading activation and limited-capacity attention. *Journal of Experimental Psychology: General, 106,* 226–254.

Pavlenko, A. (2009). Conceptual representation in the bilingual lexicon and second language vocabulary learning. In A. Pavlenko (Ed.), *The bilingual mental lexicon: Interdisciplinary approaches* (pp. 125–160). Bristol, UK: Multilingual Matters.

Peeters, D., Dijkstra, T., & Grainger, J. (2013). The representation and processing of identical cognates by late bilinguals: RT and ERP effects. *Journal of Memory and Language, 68,* 315–332.

Perfetti, C.A. (1998). Two basic questions about reading and learning to read. In P. Reitsma & L. Verhoeven (Eds.), *Problems and interventions in literacy development* (pp. 15–47). Dordrecht, the Netherlands: Springer.

Perfetti, C.A. (1999). Comprehending written language: A blueprint of the reader. In C. Brown & P. Hagoort (Eds.), *The neurocognition of language* (pp. 167–208). Oxford: Oxford University Press.

Perfetti, C.A. (2003). The universal grammar of reading. *Scientific Studies of Reading, 7*(1), 3–24.

Perfetti, C.A., Landi, N., & Oakhill, J. (2005). The acquisition of reading comprehension skill. In M. Snowling & C. Hulme (Eds.), *The science of reading* (pp. 227–247). Malden: Blackwell.

Phillips, N., Segalowitz, N., O'Briend, I., & Yamasaki, N. (2004). Semantic priming in a first and second language: Evidence from reaction time variability and event-related brain potentials. *Journal of Neurolinguistics, 17,* 237–262.

Pigada, M., & Schmitt, N. (2006). Vocabulary acquisition from extensive reading: A case study. *Reading in a Foreign Language, 18*, 1–28.

Pinker, S. (1984). *Language learnability and language development.* Cambridge, MA: Harvard University Press.

Pinnell, G. S., Lyons, C. A., DeFord, D. E., Bryk, A. S., & Seltzer, M. (1994). Comparing instructional models for the literacy education of high-risk first graders. *Reading Research Quarterly, 29*, 9–38.

Poulshock, J. (2010). Extensive graded reading in the liberal arts and sciences. *Reading in a Foreign Language, 22*, 304–322.

Proctor, C. P., Carlo, M., August, D., & Snow, C. (2005). Native Spanish-speaking children reading in English: Toward a model of comprehension. *Journal of Educational Psychology, 97*, 246–256.

Pustejovsky, J. (1995). *The generative lexicon.* Cambridge, MA: MIT Press.

Reichle, E. D., Pollatsek, A., Fisher, D. L., & Rayner, K. (1998). Towards a model of eye movement control in reading. *Psychological Review, 105*, 125–157.

Robbins, C., & Ehri, L. C. (1994). Reading storybooks to kindergartners helps them learn new vocabulary words. *Journal of Educational Psychology, 86*(1), 54.

Rumelhart, D. E. (1980). Schemata: The building blocks of cognition. In R. J. Spiro, B. C. Bruce, & W. F. Brewer (Eds.), *Theoretical issues in reading comprehension* (pp. 33–58). Hillsdale, NJ: Erlbaum.

Rydland, V., Aukrust, V. G., & Fulland, H. (2012). How word decoding, vocabulary and prior topic knowledge predict reading comprehension. A study of language-minority students in Norwegian fifth grade classrooms. *Reading and Writing, 25*(2), 465–482.

Schmitt, N. (2000). *Vocabulary in language teaching.* Stuttgart, Germany: Ernst Klett Sprachen.

Schmitt, N., Jiang, X., & Grabe, W. (2011). The percentage of words known in a text and reading comprehension. *The Modern Language Journal, 95*(1), 26–43.

Segalowitz, N., Watson, V., & Segalowitz, S. (1995). Vocabulary skill: Single-case assessment of automaticity of word recognition in a timed lexical decision task. *Second Language Research, 11*, 121–136.

Share, D. L., Jorm, A. F., Maclean, R., & Matthews, R. (1984). Sources of individual differences in reading acquisition. *Journal of Educational Psychology, 76*(6), 1309.

Sherkina-Lieber, M. & Helms-Park, R. (prepublished). A prototype of a receptive lexical test for a polysynthetic heritage language: The case of Inuttitut in Labrador. *Language Testing.* Prepublished 15/15/2014, DOI: 10.1177/0265532214560799

Shiotsu, T., & Weir, C. J. (2007). The relative significance of syntactic knowledge and vocabulary breadth in the prediction of reading comprehension test performance. *Language Testing, 24*, 99–128.

Sinclair, J. (1991). *Describing English Language: Vol. 1. Corpus, concordance, collocation.* Oxford: Oxford University Press.

Snellings, P., van Gelderen, A., & De Glopper, K. (2002). Lexical retrieval: An aspect of fluent second language production that can be enhanced. *Language Learning, 52*(4), 723–754.

Stanovich, K. E. (1986). Matthew effects in reading: Some consequences of individual differences in the acquisition of literacy. *Reading Research Quarterly, 21*, 360–407.

Stanovich, K. E. (2000). *Progress in understanding reading: Scientific foundations and new frontiers.* New York: Guilford Press.

Tokowicz, N., & Tuninetti, A. (2013). Formal models of bilingual lexicons. In C. Chapelle (Ed.), *The encyclopedia of applied linguistics* (pp. 1–7). Boston: Blackwell.

Tomasello, M. (2003). *Constructing a language.* Cambridge, MA: Harvard University Press.

Tzelgov, J., Henik, A., Sneg, R., & Baruch, O. (1996). Unintentional word reading via the phonological route: The Stroop effect with cross-script homophones. *Journal of Experimental Psychology: Learning, Memory, and Cognition, 22,* 336–349.

Upton, T. A., & Lee-Thompson, L. (2001). The role of the first language in second language reading. *Studies in Second Language Acquisition, 23,* 469–495.

Van Gelderen, A., Schoonen, R., De Glopper, K., Hulstijn, J., Simis, A., Snellings, P., & Stevenson, M. (2004). Linguistic knowledge, processing speed, and metacognitive knowledge in first- and second-language reading comprehension: A componential analysis. *Journal of Educational Psychology, 96,* 19–30.

Van Hell, J. G., & De Groot, A. M. B. (1998). Conceptual representation in bilingual memory: Effects of concreteness and cognate status in word association. *Bilingualism: Language and Cognition, 1,* 193–211

Verhoeven, L. (2000). Components in early second language reading and spelling. *Scientific Studies of Reading, 4*(4), 313–330.

Verhoeven, L., & Perfetti, C. A. (2008). Introduction: Advances in text comprehension: Model, process and development. *Applied Cognitive Psychology, 22,* 293–301.

Wagner, R. K., Torgesen, J. K., & Rashotte, C. A. (1994). Development of reading-related phonological processing abilities: New evidence of bidirectional causality from a latent variable longitudinal study. *Developmental Psychology, 30*(1), 73.

Walberg, H. J., & Tsai, S. L. (1983). Matthew effects in education. *American Educational Research Journal, 20,* 359–373.

Werker, J., & Tees, R. (1984). Cross-language speech perception: Evidence for perceptual reorganization during the first year of life. *Infant Behavior and Development, 7*(1), 49–63.

Wolter, B. (2006). Lexical network structures and L2 vocabulary acquisition: The role of L1 lexical/conceptual knowledge. *Applied Linguistics, 27,* 741–747.

Wolter, B., & Gyllstad, H. (2011). Collocational links in the L2 mental lexicon and the influence of L1 intralexical knowledge. *Applied Linguistics, 32*(4), 430–449.

Wolter, B., & Gyllstad, H. (2013). Frequency of input and L2 collocational processing: A comparison of congruent and incongruent collocations. *Studies in Second Language Acquisition, 35*(3), 451–482.

Wray, A. (2002). *Formulaic language and the lexicon.* Cambridge, UK: Cambridge University Press.

Wray, A. (2008). *Formulaic language: Pushing the boundaries.* Oxford: Oxford University Press.

Yamashita, J. (2013). Effects of extensive reading on reading attitudes in a foreign language. *Reading in a Foreign Language, 25,* 248–263.

Yamashita, J., & Jiang, N. (2010). L1 influence on the acquisition of L2 collocations: Japanese ESL users and EFL learners acquiring English collocations. *TESOL Quarterly, 44*(4), 647–668.

6

Higher-level processes in second language reading comprehension

Miao Li and Nadia D'Angelo

INTRODUCTION

Considered the ultimate goal of reading, comprehension is a highly complicated task that involves the ability to integrate various sources of information in order to construct a meaning-based representation of text. Proficient readers draw on many different linguistic and cognitive skills to integrate information at the word, sentence, and text levels (Cain & Oakhill, 2006; Nation & Snowling, 2000). These skills involve lower-level processes, such as phonological awareness, word recognition, and vocabulary knowledge, and higher-level processes, such as inference-making, working memory, and background knowledge (e.g., Cain & Oakhill, 2006; National Reading Panel, 2000; Oakhill, Cain, & Bryant, 2003). Higher-level skills are associated with reading comprehension because they facilitate the application of background knowledge and integrate semantic relations among words and sentences, enabling the reader to process and interpret text. However, efficient lower-level skills are also needed for reading comprehension to make more resources available for higher-level processing (Koda, 2005; Perfetti & Hart, 2001). The skills that influence higher-level processing in children's reading comprehension have been well documented in the L1 literature. Less is known, however, about the higher-level processes of second language learners, who, by definition, have limited language proficiency.

This chapter aims to review the research base on higher-level processes in reading comprehension and explore its implications for L2 reading. It begins with an overview of higher-level processes in reading with a focus on the building of text and situational models (i.e., mental representations of text). In order to understand how learning a language impacts the process of reading, one must consider how text itself influences comprehension (e.g., text structure and the organization of memory for specific text). Particular attention is given to higher-level skills that have shown to affect first (L1) and second (L2) reading comprehension, including working memory, background knowledge, inference-making, and textual coherence and cohesion. Differences and similarities between L1 and L2 reading are examined in order to ascertain a model of L2 reading comprehension. Toward the end of this chapter, implications of higher-level processing for L2 pedagogy and assessment are considered.

BUILDING A MODEL OF TEXT COMPREHENSION

Theories of text comprehension view reading as an incremental process involving the integration of information from various levels of text and from the reader's prior knowledge. These views articulate how text information is integrated in memory (e.g., Craik & Lockhart, 1972; Kintsch, 1998). For example, Craik and Lockhart (1972) proposed a continuum of reading processes from shallow to deep, leading to better memory recall (Craik, 2002). According to this model, memory and learning are dependent on the depth of processing. When readers comprehend text, they progress from shallow to deep levels of processing. Shallow processing, such as visual word processing, is carried out on the surface of text, while deep, semantic processing involves enriched thought about the meaning of words and their associations. Deep processing leads to higher levels of retention and learning from text (Kirby, Cain, & White, 2012).

Another prominent theory views reading as an interactive process involving both bottom-up and top-down processing (Carrell & Eisterhold, 1983). In bottom-up processing, learning to read progresses from acquiring the skills needed to decipher printed words to understanding the meaning of words. In top-down processing, the purpose of reading is to understand the main ideas of the text by using prior knowledge and context cues to make predictions about the meaning of text. As an example, consider the following sentence: "Jane took her _____ for a walk." A reader can complete this statement based on previous experiences that guide the comprehension of the text (i.e., Jane is most likely taking her *dog* for a walk). Top-down processing is conceptually driven and involves reader-based variables, such as background knowledge and strategy use (Graesser, Singer, & Trabasso, 1994), whereas bottom-up processing emphasizes text-based variables, such as decoding and vocabulary knowledge (Perfetti, 1985). In the interactive view of reading comprehension, bottom-up processing and top-down processing complement one another and function interactively as a process between the reader and text.

Finally, one of the most influential theories of text processing is the construction-integration (CI) model proposed by van Dijk and Kintsch (1983) and Kintsch (1998). In brief, this model assumes that there are three distinct levels of memory representations formed during reading comprehension: the surface form, the textbase, and the situational model. The surface form consists of a literal representation of text constructed directly from words and phrases in the text. In contrast, the textbase depicts the semantic propositions in a text and the relationships between them. The textbase involves deeper processing than the surface form because it represents ideas conveyed by the text and preserves meaning rather than exact wording. The third level, known as the situational model, is an integration of the constructed textbase and a reader's prior knowledge to form a coherent mental representation of the text. The situation model involves even deeper processing than the textbase because it incorporates information from long-term memory (prior knowledge) to make sense of the text (Fletcher, 1994; Kintsch, 1988; Kintsch, Welsch, Schmalhofer, & Zimny, 1990). The basic assumption of the CI model is that a reader's mental representation of text goes beyond the literal meaning of words; instead, it captures a reader's ability to integrate information based on prior knowledge.

These three related theoretical frameworks, although differing in details, share many common features in illustrating how a reader constructs a mental representation of text. In particular, these explanations of text processing assume that a reader creates hierarchical representations of information in which reading skills are subdivided into lower- and higher-level skills. Lower-level skills (bottom-up processing) facilitate word reading, such as phonological awareness, decoding, fluency, and vocabulary knowledge (National Reading Panel, 2000). Higher-level skills (top-down processing) aid in the construction of a meaning-based representation of text and include inference-making skills, comprehension monitoring, and integration of text information (Oakhill et al., 2003; Snow, 2002; van den Broek, Lorch, Linderholm, & Gustafson, 2001). Resourceful functioning of lower-level information allows higher-level processing to function more efficiently (Perfetti, 1985). Thus, it is the interaction between lower- and higher-level processes that is necessary for effective reading comprehension (Stanovich, 1980, 1984). Interactive models of reading comprehension take into account individual differences during reading and propose that deficits in one level of processing can be compensated by strengths in another level (e.g., Rumelhart, 1977; Stanovich, 1980). With this in mind, the following section reviews the literature on higher-level processes and reading comprehension in L1 and L2 learners, while considering differences in lower-level processes that may influence a reader's interpretation of text.

HIGHER-LEVEL PROCESSES IN L1
AND L2 READING COMPREHENSION

Working memory

To construct, maintain, and interpret text in a meaningful way, a reader must draw on a range of cognitive mechanisms to remember what is read and concurrently process relevant information and background knowledge. Working memory is considered the workspace where the reader can store, manipulate, and integrate information (Baddeley, 1986, 1998, 2003; Kintsch, 1998). It serves as a buffer for recently read text, enabling the reader to make meaningful connections within and between sentences, while retrieving information from long-term memory to facilitate comprehension through the integration of background knowledge (Daneman & Carpenter, 1980, 1983; Ericsson & Kintsch, 1995; Graesser et al., 1994).

The original working memory model proposed by Baddeley and Hitch (1974; Baddeley, 1986, 1996) is a useful framework for understanding the relationship between memory and reading comprehension and has been widely used in reading research. In this model, working memory is conceptualized as a processing resource of limited capacity, made up of three components: the central executive, the phonological loop, and the visuo-spatial sketchpad. The central executive controls the flow and processing of incoming information. The other two components are temporary storage systems that hold verbal (phonological loop) and visual and spatial information (visuo-spatial sketchpad) respectively for a short period of time. The episodic buffer was added to the revised model to account for the influence of background knowledge (or long-term memory) on working memory (Baddeley, 2000). Thus, the episodic buffer serves as a link to long-term memory, integrates information from the other systems, and stores various types of information temporarily. Figure 6.1 illustrates the revised working memory model. The shaded area at the bottom of the model represents long-term memory storage, into which information from all other components is integrated.

The phonological loop is the most extensively studied component of Baddeley's model and is made up of two subsystems: a phonological store that holds representations of speech-based information for one to two seconds and an articulatory rehearsal process that rehearses and refreshes verbal information into phonological form for storage (Baddeley, 2000). Phonological loop capacity is associated with phonological short-term memory and plays an important role in reading comprehension and language acquisition (Baddeley, 2003). In contrast to the phonological loop, the visuo-spatial sketchpad has been less studied, but is believed to function similarly,

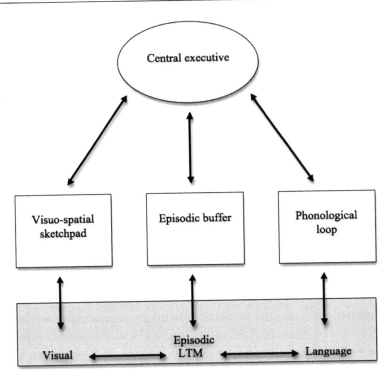

FIGURE 6.1 The revised working memory model.

maintaining representations of visual and spatial information for storage, rehearsal, and retrieval (Grabe, 2009).

Phonological short-term memory (STM) capacity is commonly measured through tests of non-word repetition, word span, and forward digit span (van den Noort, Bosch, & Hugdahl, 2006). These tasks consider only storage capacity and involve recalling sets of unrelated words or digits of increasing length, in the order in which they were presented (e.g., *shoe-bear-apple, clock-tiger-sand-water*). Conversely, the reading, counting, and listening span and the backward digit span task measure the capacity of complex verbal working memory (not just phonological STM), because they place simultaneous demands on both storage and processing to assess functioning of the central executive (Daneman & Carpenter, 1980; Kormos & Safar, 2008; Stothard & Hulme, 1992). In the reading and listening span tasks, participants read or hear sentences that are presented in sets of increasing length. Participants are asked to decide whether the sentences are grammatically correct (the processing component) and are then required to recall the last word of each sentence (the storage component) in a set (Daneman & Carpenter, 1980; van den Noort et al., 2006). Similarly, in the backward digit span task participants are required to recall a sequence of random digits in the *reverse* order in which they were presented (Kormos & Safar, 2008). Unlike reading span tasks, the backward digit span task is not dependent on general reading ability, and therefore helps to distinguish the relative contributions of working memory processes and word reading ability to comprehension skills (Seigneuric, Ehrlich, Oakhill, & Yuill, 2000). Measures of working memory capacity are significantly correlated with higher-level reading skills important to text processing, such as language comprehension, comprehension monitoring, and inference-making skills (Daneman & Green, 1986; Daneman & Merikle, 1996; de Beni, Palladino, Pazzaglia, & Cornoldi, 1998; Seigneuric et al., 2000; Yuill, Oakhill, & Parkin, 1989).

Working memory and L1 reading comprehension

A number of studies examining children's L1 reading comprehension have included measures of both phonological STM and working memory to determine the relative contribution of each construct to the different stages of reading development. This research has demonstrated that tests assessing phonological STM capacity and working memory capacity are significantly correlated, in that they tap a common underlying construct and are both related to children's reading ability (Engle, Tuholski, Laughlin, & Conway, 1999). However, phonological STM, although necessary for word recognition, plays a minimal role in reading comprehension, whereas the relationship between working memory and reading comprehension is much stronger (Daneman & Blennerhassett, 1984; de Jong, 2006; Leather & Henry, 1994; Seigneuric & Ehrlich, 2005; Swanson & Berninger, 1995; Swanson & Howell, 2001). In a study of the relative contributions of phonological STM (word span) and working memory (listening span and counting span) to the early reading skills of 7-year-old children, Leather and Henry (1994) found that phonological STM accounted for only 5% of the variance in children's reading comprehension scores, whereas working memory explained an additional 33% of the variance. Swanson and Howell (2001) reported similar findings in a cross-sectional study that explored the contribution of phonological STM and working memory to reading performance in older children, aged 9 years and 14 years. They found that working memory capacity explained a significant portion of variance in children's reading comprehension over and above the contribution of phonological STM. In addition to this finding, the researchers demonstrated that phonological STM and working memory are important predictors of developmental changes in reading. As the processing demands of text increase as children progress through school, working memory becomes an important determinant of reading comprehension, beyond the influence of phonological STM (Daneman & Carpenter, 1980; Seigneuric & Ehrlich, 2005; Swanson & Howell, 2001).

In order to determine the specific relationship between working memory capacity and reading comprehension, several studies have compared children with good and poor comprehension skills matched on word recognition and vocabulary knowledge. These studies suggest that phonological STM does not differentiate between good and poor comprehenders (Cain & Oakhill, 1999; Oakhill, Yuill, & Parkin, 1986; Stothard & Hulme, 1992; Swanson & Berninger, 1995). However, investigations of working memory capacity in children with comprehension difficulties have found that poor comprehenders perform less well than control groups, confirming that there is a relationship between verbal working memory, but not visual-spatial working memory (i.e., the storage and manipulation of shapes and patterns), and comprehension skills in children (Cain, 2006; Nation, Adams, Bowyer-Crane, & Snowling, 1999; Yuill et al., 1989). For example, in a study examining working memory deficits in poor comprehenders, Nation et al. (1999) found no differences between 10-year-old poor comprehenders and a control group on measures of spatial memory span that did not require linguistic or numerical resources. Instead, they found that the relation between working memory and reading comprehension was determined by verbal and semantic abilities, as measured by a listening span task and children's recall of abstract words. Nation et al. argued that poor comprehenders have specific semantic weaknesses in the domain of language comprehension; that is, they do not understand sentences as well as typical readers and this lack of understanding restricts their ability to store and process verbal information.

The studies described earlier suggest that working memory capacity is heavily dependent on verbal ability and vocabulary knowledge since the working memory tasks they used tap into verbal resources (Nation et al., 1999; Stothard & Hulme, 1992). To test this claim, Cain, Oakhill, and Bryant (2004) investigated the association between working memory and reading comprehension in children aged 7, 8, and 10 years after accounting for word reading, vocabulary knowledge, and verbal ability. Working memory capacity was measured by a composite task of numerical working memory (Yuill et al., 1989), in which children read groups of three random digits and were asked to recall the two final digits of each group, and sentence span, in which children were asked to fill in the final word of a short sentence and remember the word for later recall (Cain et al., 2004). At each of the three time points, working memory and components of text processing (inference making and comprehension monitoring) made a significant and unique contribution to reading comprehension after word-level skills and verbal ability were partialled out. These findings lead to the conclusion that verbal skills alone cannot account for the association between working memory and reading comprehension. Unlike Nation et al. (1999), who proposed that the relationship between working memory tasks and reading comprehension is heavily dependent on children's language abilities, Cain et al. suggest that it is a combination of processing skills (lower- and higher-level skills) and processing capacity (working memory) that influences reading comprehension ability and development.

In summary, the literature investigating the relationship between working memory and reading comprehension skills in L1 readers demonstrates similar findings for children with typical comprehension skills and those with comprehension difficulties. Although there is evidence that both phonological STM and working memory capacity are related to reading ability, it appears that working memory has a direct relationship with reading comprehension beyond STM, word reading ability, and vocabulary knowledge. Moreover, it appears that individual differences in working memory capacity influence reading comprehension outcomes. Thus, working memory not only is an important determinant of children's L1 reading comprehension but also accounts for how children vary in their reading abilities.

Working memory and L2 reading comprehension

Over the past two decades, research has demonstrated that individual differences in working memory account for significant variation in L2 reading (Leeser, 2007; Walter, 2006). Given that working memory capacity is an important aspect of language comprehension, it is not surprising that it contributes unique variance to L1 and L2 language and reading acquisition (e.g., Geva & Siegel, 2000; Swanson, Orosco, Lussier, Gerber, & Guzman-Orth, 2011). Similar to the L1 research, L2 studies have examined the relative contribution of phonological STM and working memory capacity to L2 reading comprehension. Some studies show that measures of phonological STM play an important role in aspects of L2 reading, including word recognition, vocabulary knowledge, and grammar (Daneman & Case, 1981; Ellis & Sinclair, 1996; Service, 1992; Service & Kohonen, 1995). Other studies demonstrate that working memory capacity contributes unique variance to L2 reading, beyond STM (e.g., Engle, Tuholski, Laughlin, & Conway, 1999; Harrington & Sawyer, 1992; Leeser, 2007; Swanson, Saez, & Gerber, 2006). For example, Geva and Ryan (1993) examined the contribution of working memory to L2 reading comprehension in a sample of Grade 5 to 7 English-Hebrew bilinguals. They found that working memory, measured in Hebrew as an L2, explained significant and unique variance in children's L2 reading comprehension after controlling for age, oral language proficiency, and intelligence, whereas L2 STM did not. These findings were explained by the limited capacity working memory model. According to this model, reading in L2 places greater demands on the analysis and processing of verbal information than does reading in L1 because children's language knowledge is more automated in L1 than L2.

The finding that working memory capacity is a unique predictor of L2 reading comprehension is supported by the literature on L2 reading difficulties. Consistent with the L1 research (e.g., Cain et al., 2004; Oakhill, Hartt, & Samols, 2005), L2 studies of typical and poor readers have demonstrated that L2 children with reading difficulties tend to perform less well on working memory tasks than L2 children with typically developing reading skills (e.g., Da Fontoura & Siegel, 1995; Swanson et al., 2006). In a longitudinal study following Spanish-English bilinguals from Grades 1 to 3, Swanson et al. (2006) found that L2 children who were identified as at risk for reading difficulties had significantly lower growth scores on measures of English (L2) and Spanish (L1) WM and Spanish STM compared to L2 children who were not at risk. Moreover, Spanish working memory growth contributed 12% of unique variance to English word reading even after accounting for the influence of Spanish STM. In a more recent study, Lipka and Siegel (2012) examined working memory performance in a sample of Grade 7 English L1 and L2 children with reading comprehension difficulties. Children identified as good comprehenders (good word reading and comprehension skills) outperformed children who were poor comprehenders (average word reading skills and poor comprehension skills) on measures of working memory capacity in both the L1 and L2 groups. Taken together, these findings suggest a generalized deficit in working memory capacity for children with reading comprehension difficulties, regardless of language proficiency.

In sum, the studies reviewed here provide empirical support for the relationship between working memory capacity and L2 reading comprehension. Similar to the L1 research, studies have shown that working memory is a significant predictor of L2 reading comprehension above and beyond the effects of phonological STM. Furthermore, working memory capacity accounts for individual differences in children's L2 reading comprehension. However, in contrast to the L1 research, L2 research on working memory and reading comprehension in children is relatively minimal. Clearly, there is a need for further research to determine the precise nature of the relationship between working memory capacity and L2 reading comprehension.

Background knowledge

Interactive models of reading comprehension draw on schema theory. Schema theory seeks to explain the configuration of information in memory and relationships between the text and the reader's background knowledge (Anderson & Pearson, 1984). According to this theory, text does not provide all the necessary information for the construction of meaning. Instead, it presents new information for readers to integrate into existing knowledge (or schemata) about a topic (Pearson-Casanave, 1984). In general, schemata represent knowledge about the world. They are stored in a reader's memory and provide clues for remembering ideas, comprehending text, and acquiring new knowledge. The schema or background knowledge stored in a reader's memory affects the way information is interpreted. As a result, it influences reading comprehension processes (Kendeou, Rapp, & van den Broek, 2003). Consider the following example: Within the schema for a cat, there is general knowledge about cats (they have paws, fur, and whiskers), specific knowledge about cats (there are different breeds of cats – e.g., Siamese and Maine Coon), and knowledge about cats within a broader context (they are mammals who are warm-blooded, eat, breathe, and sleep). Depending on a reader's personal experience, the knowledge of a cat as a domesticated and loyal pet or a pesky animal that hisses and scratches will be part of their schema. Thus, new experiences and information become incorporated in a reader's schema and determine what information is extracted from text and how that information is to be interpreted.

Background knowledge and L1 reading comprehension

A large body of research has established that schema or background knowledge plays a significant role in reading comprehension among English L1 school-age children (e.g., Adams & Bruce, 1982; Cromley & Azevedo, 2007; Spires & Donley, 1998; Stein, 1978). For example, to demonstrate the effect of background knowledge on reading comprehension, Dole, Valencia, Greer, and Wardrop (1991) provided an experimental group of Grade 5 children with direct instruction on background knowledge. The researchers found that the experimental group performed significantly higher on post-test reading comprehension measures compared to the children in the control group, who did not receive background knowledge instruction. Studies such as these provide support for background knowledge as a strong basis of L1 reading comprehension.

There are some studies that suggest the relationship between background knowledge and children's reading comprehension is much more complex. In a sample of adolescents, McNamara, Kintsch, Songer, and Kintsch (1996) found that readers who had limited domain (specific) background knowledge of a text performed better on cohesive texts, whereas readers who had high domain knowledge of a text benefited more from less cohesive texts. The researchers interpreted these findings by suggesting that the low-cohesion texts required high domain knowledge readers to integrate their background knowledge with the text to enhance comprehension. By contrast, readers with low domain knowledge gained more from greater text cohesion because they lacked the prior knowledge needed to generate meaning from text. Subsequent studies have demonstrated that this effect is moderated by inference-making skills, where only less skilled, high domain knowledge readers benefit from low-cohesion texts (e.g., O'Reilly & McNamara, 2007). Thus, it appears that the relationship between background knowledge and children's L1 reading comprehension is influenced by other higher-level processing skills, including inference-making ability and text cohesion.

Background knowledge and L2 reading comprehension

Numerous studies have also demonstrated that schema or background knowledge facilitates L2 reading comprehension (e.g., Bernhardt, 1991; Carrell, 1991; Carrell & Wise, 1998; Johnson, 1981; Steffenson, Joag-Dev, & Anderson, 1979; Yuet Hung Chang, 2003). The research has operationalized background knowledge in various ways (McNeil, 2011). Some studies have explored background knowledge in terms of the culture represented by text and found that readers who were familiar with the culture had a better understanding of the text (e.g., Alptekin, 2006; Johnson, 1981; Lee, 2007; Steffensen et al., 1979). For instance, Steffenson et al. (1979) examined the comprehension skills of American and Indian students by asking them to read and recall a passage about a traditional wedding in each culture. The results showed that when reading a passage that most closely matched their cultural background, participants read faster and were able to recall more information. However, when reading passages that were not from their own cultural background, participants took longer to read and made culturally inappropriate distortions of the text. A number of studies have generated similar findings (Johnson, 1981; Reynolds, Taylor, Steffensen, Shirey, & Anderson, 1982). Other studies have explored the effects of background knowledge on reading comprehension for more general topics, such as movies and weather (Al-Shumaimeri, 2006), gender (Bugel & Buunk, 1996), and sports (Levine & Hause, 1985). These findings support the view that background knowledge has robust effects on reading comprehension.

A limitation of the aforementioned studies is that they do not account for the effects of L2 language proficiency. Clapham (1996) attempted to solve this problem by dividing a sample of English L2 students into three groups based on L2 language proficiency (score thresholds of 60% and 80% on an English grammar test). Results demonstrated that the reading performance of students in the lower (below 60%) and upper threshold (80%) groups of L2 language proficiency did not benefit from background knowledge, whereas the reading performance of students with medium proficiency was affected by background knowledge. These findings provide evidence in support of a "language threshold effect" (Clapham, 2000; Wolter & Helms-Park, this volume), which suggests that L2 readers with lower levels of language proficiency must meet a minimum threshold of L2 vocabulary knowledge to access background knowledge (Cummins, 1976; Stahl, Jacobson, Davis, & Davis, 1989). Likewise, Clapham (2000) argues that there is a maximum threshold of L2 vocabulary knowledge. Advanced L2 readers may be able to compensate for a lack of background knowledge because of adequate vocabulary knowledge, and therefore may not have to rely on background knowledge (Carrell, 1983, 1991). Further research is needed to support this hypothesis.

Additional evidence supports the view that a certain level of language proficiency is needed to activate relevant background knowledge. A recent study conducted by Burgoyne, Whiteley, and Hutchinson (2013) showed that Grade 3 children learning English as an L2 with low vocabulary knowledge performed significantly lower than English L1 children on literal comprehension questions and questions that relied heavily on vocabulary knowledge, even when relevant background knowledge was taught before the administration of reading comprehension assessments. In this study, lower language proficiency acted as a bottleneck, causing inefficiency in lower-level text processing, which placed excessive demands on children's limited cognitive resources, preventing the activation of background knowledge necessary to comprehend text.

In sum, the review of studies examining the role of background knowledge in reading comprehension suggests that L1 and L2 readers' background knowledge and familiarity with topics have a profound effect on reading comprehension. Moreover, background knowledge affects reading comprehension in different ways for readers with different levels of L2 language proficiency.

Inference-making

Inference-making involves integrating and connecting background knowledge with text information (Anderson & Pearson, 1984). Inferencing skills are necessary for reading comprehension as readers rely on inferences to fill in ideas and details that are not explicitly stated in the text in order to develop an accurate and coherent situation model (e.g., Cain & Oakhill, 1999; Graesser, Singer, & Trabasso, 1994; McNamara, Kintsch, Songer, & Kintsch, 1996; van den Broek, Risden, & Husebye-Hartman, 1995). Many studies have suggested that readers must engage in extensive inferential processing to achieve skilled reading comprehension (Barnes, Denis, & Haefele-Kalvaitis, 1996; Cain & Oakhill, 1999; Cain, Oakhill, & Bryant, 2004; Clarke & Silberstein, 1977; Coady, 1979; van den Broek et al., 1995).

Broadly speaking, inferences can be categorized into two types: coherence inferences and elaborative or extending inferences. Coherence inferences refer to meaningful connections of information in a text, and can be further classified into cohesive devices and knowledge-based inferences. Cohesive devices are commonly used to maintain textual coherence and will be discussed in greater detail later in the chapter. Knowledge-based inferences form a link between explicit and implicit ideas to maintain textual coherence both locally (across sentences within a passage) and globally (across the passage as a whole). Similarly, elaborative inferences are generally knowledge-based inferences that are not necessary for textual coherence; rather, elaborative inferences serve to enrich and extend the mental representation of text by connecting information to the reader's background knowledge. By way of illustration, consider the following example: "She mixed the perfect colour for her painting of lemons." Here, the reader can assume that the colour mixed by the painter is yellow, based on prior knowledge about lemons. This information is not needed in the text in order to maintain coherence. While relevant background knowledge is a strong predictor of children's ability to generate inferences from text, studies have shown that background knowledge alone is not sufficient for inference-making skills (Barnes, Dennis, & Haefele-Kalvaitis, 1996; Cain, Oakhill, Barnes, & Bryant, 2001).

Given that inference generation is an internal activity, it is often difficult to recognize and assess. Children's inferencing skills are commonly measured with written or oral recall and think-aloud tasks. In a recall task, children write down or say what they can remember about a passage after reading it. Recall tasks have been extensively used in L1 and L2 reading studies (e.g., Barry & Lazarte, 1998; Hammadou, 1991; Horiba, 1993, 1996). This approach is considered to be *offline* because data is collected after comprehension as opposed to during comprehension. Offline tasks are useful for assessing how readers use inferential information to update and develop a coherent representation of text (van den Broek, Tzeng, Risden, Trabasso, & Basche, 2001). In contrast, think-aloud tasks are *online* tasks that measure how readers use inferential information to maintain coherence during reading. In a think-aloud task, participants are asked to read a passage out loud, one sentence at a time, discussing what comes to mind after they read each sentence. Online tasks are considered to be more advantageous because these tasks do not impose a memory load on the reader, whereas offline tasks (e.g., recall) heavily depend on working memory. In spite of this, online tasks have been mainly used in studies with older children and adults based on the assumption that younger readers are unable to produce accurate think-alouds because of underdeveloped metacognitive awareness or the ability to understand, control, and manipulate cognitive processes while reading (Afflerbach & Johnston, 1984; Laing & Kamhi, 2002).

Inference-making and L1 reading comprehension

Several studies have demonstrated that children's inference-making ability is closely related to their L1 reading comprehension (e.g., Cain & Oakhill, 1999; van den Broek et al., 2001). These studies indicate that children as young as 4-years-old have the ability to generate inferences from narrative texts (Kendeou, Bohn-Gettler, White, & van den Broek, 2008; Lynch et al., 2008; Lynch & van den Broek, 2007; Tompkins, Guo, & Justice, 2013; Wenner, 2004). However, younger children are less likely than older children to spontaneously make inferences without prompting or questioning (e.g., Casteel & Simpson, 1991).

In order to examine the direction of the relationship between inference making and reading comprehension, Cain and Oakhill (1999) identified three groups of 6- to 8-year-old children on the basis of reading comprehension performance: skilled and less skilled comprehenders matched for chronological age, vocabulary, and word reading accuracy, and a comprehension-age match group (i.e., younger readers with comprehension levels equivalent to the less skilled comprehenders). Children read five narrative texts and were asked six questions about each text, probing literal information, text-connecting inferences (coherence), and gap-filling inferences (elaborative). Skilled comprehenders and the comprehension-age match group answered more coherence inferences correctly than did the less skilled comprehenders. The finding that the comprehension-age match group outperformed the less skilled comprehenders on coherence inferences despite equivalent comprehension levels suggests that the capacity to make inferences is not a consequence of comprehension ability; rather poor inference-making skills are a plausible cause of poor reading comprehension. This study also indicated that less skilled comprehenders were more capable of making coherence inferences than elaborative inferences when the text was available as a resource during questioning. A possible explanation for this finding is that children with poor comprehension skills may not know when it is appropriate to relate prior knowledge to text in order to extend the meaning base of information (Cain et al., 2001; Cain & Oakhill, 1999; Yuill & Oakhill, 1991).

Inference-making and L2 reading comprehension

Most of the existing L2 research on the relationship between inference making and reading comprehension is limited to adult readers. This body of research suggests that L2 learners use inference-making skills to infer new word meanings from context (Nassaji, 2003; Paribakht & Wesche, 1999; Pulido, 2007). Horiba (1993, 1996) examined the number of inferences constructed by English-speaking adult learners of Japanese (L2) in reading Japanese text. The results demonstrated that the adult learners with higher L2 proficiency produced inferences more frequently than learners with lower L2 proficiency. These findings were confirmed by subsequent studies (Muramoto, 2000; Shimizu, 2005). Furthermore, Yoshida (2003) reported that Japanese (L1) university students with higher English (L2) proficiency produced more elaborative inferences than coherence inferences compared to learners with lower English proficiency while reading English text. Together, these studies suggest that the effects of inference-making skills on L2 reading comprehension may be influenced by L2 language proficiency.

Thus far, only a few empirical studies have examined whether children generate inferences during L2 reading and how these skills contribute to L2 reading comprehension. In a recent study, Li and Kirby (2014) investigated the effects of inference-making skills on L2 reading comprehension among Grade 8 students learning English as an L2 in China. The students were classified as good comprehenders, average comprehenders, and poor comprehenders on the basis of their English reading comprehension scores. Significant differences were found between average comprehenders and good comprehenders on inference-making skills, but not between average comprehenders

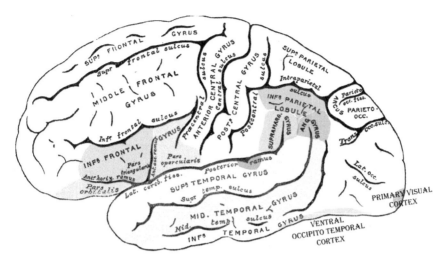

PLATE 1 The main cortical regions involved in reading in the left hemisphere. Adapted from *Anatomy of the Human Body* (20th ed.), by H. Gray, 1918, Philadelphia: Lea & Febiger.

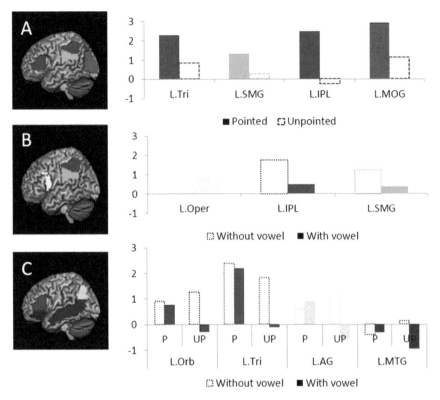

PLATE 2 Effects of orthographic transparency and familiarity in reading Hebrew. (A) Regions showing effects of diacritic marks, (B) regions showing effect of vowel letters, (C) regions showing an interaction between diacritic marks and vowel letters. L.Tri (left IFG pars Triangularis), L.Oper (left IFG pars Opercularis), L.Orb (left IFG pars Orbitalis), L.SMG (left Supramarginal Gyrus), L.IPL (left Inferior Parietal Lobule), L.AG (left Angular Gyrus), L.MTG (left Middle Temporal Gyrus) and L.MOG. Adapted from Many Ways to Read Your Vowels – Neural Processing of Diacritics and Vowel Letters in Hebrew, by Y. Weiss, T. Katzir, and T. Bitan, *NeuroImage*, 121 pp. 10–19.

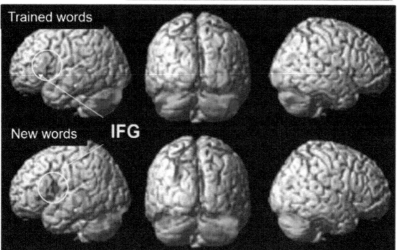

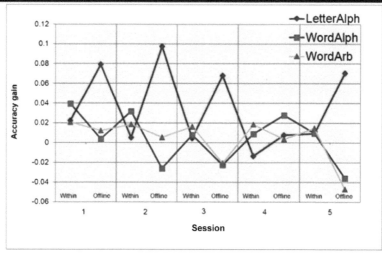

PLATE 3 Upper panel: artificial script learned in alphabetical and non-alphabetical training conditions. Middle panel: activation map in three training conditions. Adapted from "Effects of Alphabeticality, Practice and Type of Instruction on Reading an Artificial Script: An fMRI Study," by T. Bitan, D. Manor, I. A. Morocz, and A. Karni, 2005, *Cognitive Brain Research*, 25(1), pp. 90–106. Lower panel: performance gains within and between sessions. Adapted from "Offline Improvement in Learning to Read a Novel Orthography Depends on Direct Letter Instruction," by T. Bitan and J. R. Booth, 2012, *Cognitive Science, 36*(5), pp. 896–918.

and poor comprehenders. The researchers suggest that the good inference-making skills may be a defining characteristic of good comprehenders, who have general cognitive and word reading abilities that exceed typical development. Furthermore, they hypothesize that inference-making skills contribute effectively to L2 reading comprehension only when a certain level of L2 language proficiency has been reached. However, these conclusions are speculative. Further research is needed exploring the relationship between inference-making skills and reading comprehension for children learning in L2.

In summary, young readers are less likely to generate inferences than older children (Casteel & Simpson, 1991), less skilled comprehenders draw fewer inferences than skilled comprehenders (Cain & Oakhill, 1999; Long, Oppy, & Seely, 1997; Oakhill, 1982, 1984), and less proficient L2 learners tend to infer much less than more proficient L2 learners (Li & Kirby, 2014; Muramoto, 2000; Shimizu, 2005). Hence, the studies reviewed here suggest that the contribution of inference-making skills to children's reading comprehension develops as a function of age and language proficiency, and poor inference-making ability may be a cause of comprehension difficulties. However, very limited research has been conducted to explore the role of children's inference-making in L2 reading comprehension, and one can only infer from the L1 reading research how inference-making skills influence children's reading comprehension in an L2. Clearly, future research is needed to investigate if and how different types of inference skills lead to substantial reading benefits for L2 children and adolescents.

Textual cohesion and coherence

To fully understand text, readers must acquire and coordinate knowledge about events to construct content, knowledge about text structure to create coherence, and knowledge about linguistic devices (e.g., conjunctions and connectives) to establish cohesion (Shapiro & Hudson, 1991, 1997). While coherence and cohesion are related concepts, they are distinct aspects of text organization and should be considered separately when evaluating text comprehension skills. Coherence in text is realized by organizing content into a defined sequence, achieved by using cues to connect characters, settings, and events in a logical manner – for example, following a beginning, middle, and end (Cain, 2003; Ehrlich, 1988; Gernsbacher, 1997; Shapiro & Hudson, 1991, 1997). Cohesion is realized through the use of linguistic devices, such as temporal and causal connectives, that indicate the semantic relationships between different sentences or clauses (Halliday & Hasan, 1976; Shapiro & Hudson, 1991). It is possible for a text to have coherence but lack linguistic cohesion because a reader's background knowledge helps provide information for sufficient interpretation (Geva, 1992; Morgan & Sellner, 1980; Tierney &

Mosenthal, 1983). To illustrate this point, consider the following example: "The Maple Leafs scored a goal. The crowd goes wild." This text can be considered coherent even though there are no words to describe how the first and second sentences are related. It is cultural knowledge of hockey games that helps to construct a coherent representation of the text.

Textual coherence and L1 reading comprehension

Research on the relationship between coherence and L1 reading comprehension has focused on structure in narratives and expository texts (Cain, 2003; Cain & Oakhill, 1996; Sanders, Spooren, & Noordman, 1992). These studies have found that differences in the sensitivity to text coherence can lead to differences in text comprehension. As demonstrated by Cain and Oakhill (1996), children with weak comprehension skills produce less structurally coherent stories than skilled comprehenders and comprehension-age match children when provided with story title prompts (e.g., "Pirates"). Moreover, poor comprehenders are less explicitly aware of story features that can bolster the interpretation of story events than skilled comprehenders. For instance, when compared to skilled comprehenders, poor comprehenders demonstrate less knowledge that the beginning of a story provides information about the story's characters and setting (Cain, 2003; Cain & Oakhill, 1996). In another study, Cain (2003) demonstrated that the story production of poor comprehenders improved with more informative story prompts. Studies such as these suggest that children's understanding of story production and their ability to produce coherent representations are facilitated by knowledge of story structure and familiarity with certain event topics, such as birthday parties or animated characters (Trabasso & Nickels, 1992). Thus, the ability to produce a well-structured and coherent story influences children's reading comprehension skills.

Textual coherence and L2 reading comprehension

Although L2 reading research has explored the ability of L2 learners to produce coherent discourse in spoken and written form (Abeywickrama, 2007; Canale & Swain, 1980; Connor, 1984; Geva, 1992; Goldman & Murray, 1992), most studies have focused on adult learners, framing textual coherence in terms of *text structure*, which is the organization of text information (Aebersold & Field, 1997; Carrell, 1987; Meyer, 1985). For example, in a pioneering study, Carrell (1987) examined the effect of text structure on English L2 students' reading comprehension by administering two recall tasks to an experimental group (who received coherent and culturally familiar text) and a control group (who received less coherent and culturally unfamiliar text). Immediately after reading two passages, participants were asked to answer a series of multiple-choice comprehension questions for each passage and recall the text in writing. The findings of this study showed that L2 learners who read coherent and culturally familiar content performed better on reading comprehension and recalled more text information than L2 learners in the control group. These findings suggest that text with familiar text structure and culturally specific content is easier to read and comprehend for L2 learners than text with unfamiliar structure and content. In a similar study, Horiba (1993) compared the recall of text information in Japanese L1 and L2 learners. Participants were asked to read text of varying degrees of coherence. The study indicated that L2 learners had more difficulty recalling high-coherence texts compared to L1 learners, but their ability to recall text information improved with repeated exposure to the text.

There is little research on the relationship between coherence and L2 reading comprehension in children. Of the few existing studies, Verhoeven (1990) conducted a longitudinal investigation of reading processes, following Dutch and Turkish children from Grades 1 to 2 as they learned to read in Dutch. In a coherence task, children were asked to point to the first and last sentence of a story, which was made up of sentences presented in an illogical sequence. Findings demonstrated that, although the Dutch L1 children had higher scores than the Turkish L2 children, there were no significant differences between the two groups at the end of Grade 2. In fact, results showed that both groups of children had more difficulty searching for the last sentence of the text than the first sentence. This is because children had to read the whole text in order to process and recognize the last sentence of the story. The researchers concluded that it is primarily the structure of the target language being acquired that accounts for L2 comprehension difficulties, not the structure of a reader's native language. However, recent research persuades us that it is most likely the linguistic similarities and structural distance of an L1 and L2 that influence L2 textual coherence (Grabe, 2009; Koda, 2005).

In sum, while the research literature on children's textual coherence in L2 reading comprehension is underdeveloped, the aforementioned studies provide evidence for a possible relationship between text structure and children's L2 reading comprehension. It seems plausible that the familiarity of text and knowledge of L2 text structure contribute to textual coherence in children's L2 reading comprehension.

Textual cohesion and L1 reading comprehension

Cohesion enables the process of integrating ideas and information across a text by explicitly signaling how text ideas relate to one another. According to Halliday and Hasan (1976), there are five types of cohesion: reference (used to indicate that information is to be retrieved from elsewhere), substitution (e.g., substitution of a word), ellipsis (e.g., omission of a word), connective (e.g., *so, like, and, but, yet*), and lexical cohesion (e.g., repeated occurrences of the same or related vocabulary items). Connectives (or conjunctions) are the most widely researched cohesive device in the reading literature. They mark semantic relations between different words, sentences, and clauses (Halliday & Hasan, 1976). For example, a causal relation is signaled by the connectives *so* or *because*: "Mary was tired, *so* she took a nap." Other types of connectives signal additive (*and, in addition*), contrastive (*whereas*), temporal (*before, after*), or adversative (*but, although*) relations. Connectives explicitly signal how two clauses are related – for example, "Adam lost his wallet *before* he went shopping." The temporal connective *before* directs the sequence of events: Adam lost his wallet and then went shopping. In this way, connectives provide readers with cues to guide the integration of information and interpretation of text.

Children begin to acquire and use connectives to express semantic relations as young as 5-years-old (Kail & Weissenborn, 1991; Spooren & Sanders, 2008). Generally speaking, additives (*and*) are acquired first, followed by temporal, causal, and adversative connectives (Bloom, Lahey, Hood, Lifter, & Fiess, 1980). Although young children have the ability to produce connectives appropriately in their speech, studies suggest that children's understanding of the semantic relations expressed by connectives continues to develop for several years after initial production (Cain, Patson, & Andrews, 2005; McClure & Geva, 1983). For example, in a study of Grades 4, 6, and 8 students, McClure and Geva (1983) examined the extent to which readers of different age levels understood the adversative connective terms *but* and *although*. They found that children had mastered the ability to produce adversative connectives by Grade 4, but they still had difficulties in understanding when to correctly use coordinating (*but*) and subordinating (*although*) adversative terms even in Grade 8. In a more recent study, Cain et al. (2005) demonstrated that younger children were less likely to choose the correct temporal, causal, and adversative terms to fill in the blanks left when connectives had been deleted from a story.

There is ample research evidence to suggest that the use of connectives aids in children's reading comprehension. Cain and Nash (2011) compared the understanding and processing of temporal, causal, and adversative connectives between 8- and 10-year-olds using online and offline tasks. The findings indicate that the presence of an appropriate connective resulted in faster text processing for both groups, relative to when an inappropriate connective or no connective was present. Similarly, studies have shown that when children are directed to focus on appropriate connectives, they become more efficient readers (e.g., Cain, 2003; Geva & Ryan, 1985). Indeed, children who were less skilled at reading improved their ability to structure cohesive and coherent stories when they were provided with more informative prompts, including story titles that provide a direction for the sequence of events (e.g., "How the pirates lost their treasure") and title and picture sequences made up of six pictures that illustrate an outcome as the consequence of a previous action (Cain, 2003). Thus, the presence of appropriate connectives can aid children's ability to construct a coherent and meaningful representation of text.

Further evidence demonstrates that children classified as poor comprehenders are less likely to select the correct connective terms as compared to children with age-appropriate comprehension skills. Cain (2003) demonstrated that children with poor reading comprehension included fewer causal relations (*because, so*) between events when narrating a made-up story. These findings indicate that reading comprehension skills affect children's ability to make use of connectives. Less skilled readers may not be familiar with the function and precise meaning expressed by some connectives and, as a result, fail to be guided by connective devices when reading. Therefore, a lack of understanding of connectives may be a source of difficulty that hinders text comprehension.

In short, research on the effectiveness of cohesive devices, specifically connectives, on L1 reading comprehension presents two somewhat contrasting views: (1) connectives may hinder text comprehension in readers who have not yet fully developed an understanding of semantic relations; and (2) the presence of appropriate connectives may help readers to understand the relation between ideas and events, aiding in children's comprehension and learning.

Textual cohesion and L2 reading comprehension

Until now, only a small number of studies have examined the relationship between cohesion and reading comprehension among L2 children. These studies suggest that L2 learners have more difficulty than L1 learners in understanding and identifying the semantic relations expressed by connectives in text (Crosson & Lesaux, 2013; Crosson, Lesaux, & Martiniello, 2008; Droop & Verhoeven, 2003). This may be due to variations across different languages. For example, the adversative connective *but* (in English) can be translated to *aber* or *sondern* in German (Oakhill, Cain, & Elbro, 2015). While *aber* can be used as a connective (*but, however*) after a positive clause, *sondern* can be used only after a negative clause to express a contradiction (*but rather, on the contrary*). It is likely that children who have a limited understanding of connectives in their L2 are less likely to recognize that connective words signal relationships between text propositions.

In order to explore the factors that influence L2 learners' difficulty in understanding connectives, Crosson et al. (2008) conducted a study with Grade 4 Spanish-speaking children who were learning English as an L2. They found that children's understanding of connectives in L2 English was influenced by their L2 vocabulary and listening comprehension skills. In particular, the L2 learners struggled with the vocabulary of certain connective terms, such as temporal, causal, and adversative relations, that were more complex. Thus, the results of this study suggest that L2 learners' understanding of connectives and their functions is influenced by language proficiency. In a subsequent study, Crosson and Lesaux (2013) examined whether knowledge of connectives played a unique role in the reading comprehension of Grade 5 L1 and L2 learners of English. They found that knowledge of connectives was a significant predictor of reading comprehension beyond vocabulary and word reading fluency for both L1 and L2 learners. Although L2 children had relatively strong knowledge of connectives, they were less likely than L1 children to use knowledge of connectives to support their comprehension. The researchers concluded that despite knowledge of connectives, the presence of unknown vocabulary words in text reduced the effect of connectives in reading comprehension for L2 learners.

Taken together, these studies suggest that L2 children experience more difficulties in understanding relations expressed by connective terms than L1 children. It appears that whether L2 readers use their knowledge of connectives to facilitate comprehension depends on L2 language proficiency – specifically, their familiarity with the words linked by connectives.

UNDERSTANDING THE RELATIONSHIP BETWEEN L1 AND L2 READING COMPREHENSION

Generally speaking, the higher-level component skills used to comprehend text in L1 and L2 are remarkably similar. Moreover, the underlying processes involved in learning to read are essentially the same, where readers construct a mental representation of text through the interaction between lower- and higher-level skills. Finally, as demonstrated in the earlier review, L1 and L2 learners store and process information and use their background knowledge and various reading strategies, such as inference-making, to interpret and comprehend text in a comparable manner.

At the same time, given that L2 learners are typically less proficient in the language they are acquiring, there are several ways in which L2 reading can differ from L1 reading. First, due to a lack of L2 language exposure at home, and simply less practice in L2 reading, L2 learners begin school with a much more limited vocabulary knowledge than L1 learners. This gap in language knowledge has been reflected in a number of studies which demonstrate that L2 learners often lag behind their L1 counterparts in reading comprehension and vocabulary knowledge, even after many years of schooling in L2 (Carlisle, Beeman, Davis, & Spharim, 1999; Farnia & Geva, 2011; Jean & Geva, 2009; Lesaux, Geva, Koda, Siegel, & Shanahan, 2008). Second, L2 learners rely on linguistic similarities across languages (e.g., English and Spanish) to facilitate the L2 reading process. Therefore, the extent of linguistic differences between the learner's L1 and L2 (e.g., Chinese and English) will have an impact on L2 reading (Grabe, 2009; Koda, 2005). Finally, because readers draw upon background knowledge to comprehend text, L2 learners may experience difficulties in reading L2 text that vary from their own socio-cultural experiences and assumptions (Grabe, 2009).

IMPLICATIONS FOR L2 PEDAGOGY AND ASSESSMENT

Several implications can be drawn from the earlier review. First, higher-level reading skills can promote efficient reading comprehension for L2 children. Second, because of L2 learners' limited language proficiency and background knowledge, instructional approaches should be aimed at the development of these reading abilities. The following section discusses the various reading strategies that teachers can use to aid L2 children's comprehension prior to reading, during reading, and post-reading.

Pre-reading instruction

As illustrated in this chapter, a reader's background knowledge is crucial for constructing a coherent representation of L2 text. Therefore, teachers should assess and activate students' background knowledge of a topic before they begin to read (Peregoy & Boyle, 2000). This *pre-reading activity* allows teachers to find out what children already know so they can adapt their instruction to fill in gaps in knowledge or address misconceptions held by children. Such activities can take place in small groups, where the teacher introduces a concept by choosing a phrase or word that represents the key ideas from the reading and asks students to share what comes to mind when they think of the word or phrase. The teacher then asks the students to share what made them think of their response. This gives students the opportunity to make connections between their background knowledge and the material to be taught. The ultimate goal of pre-reading activities is to prepare students for what they are about to read, have students approach reading tasks with expectations about the information they are about to process, and help students build schemata that are culturally appropriate.

An effective pre-reading strategy for less proficient L2 learners is one that combines content learning with language learning. Research supports a number of vocabulary learning strategies, such as extensive reading and learning words from context (Beck, McKeown, & Kucan, 2002). However, these strategies are often not enough to acquire precise meanings of specific words necessary for comprehension. The information needed to support a word meaning may not be available in the immediate context, resulting in the reader making guesses at word meaning from context (Grabe, 2009; National Reading Panel, 2000). In some instances, the guessed meaning of a word may be accurate. More often than not, though, poor guesses made from context misdirect L2 learners' understanding of word meanings and disrupt text comprehension (Beck et al., 2002). As such, many researchers argue that learning words from context is not an efficient way to support vocabulary learning for better reading comprehension in L2 learners and recommend that teachers emphasize direct and systematic vocabulary instruction (Beck et al., 2002; Graves, 2000; National Reading Panel, 2000). Systematic instruction emphasizes key words that relate semantically and thematically to other words and provides a foundation for the acquisition of new words in different contexts (Grabe, 2009). Likewise, cognate instruction (teaching children to use word knowledge acquired in their L1 to infer the meaning of unfamiliar words they encounter in L2 text) is a useful strategy for reviewing L2 learners' understanding of new words. Recent research has shown that children can be taught to recognize cognates and that cognate instruction has a positive influence on children's L2 reading comprehension (Hipfner-Boucher, Chen, Pasquarella, & Deacon, 2014).

To sum, L2 children's background knowledge should be assessed prior to reading. Pre-reading activities, such as small group discussions and vocabulary instruction, can promote word learning and text comprehension. Notably, unfamiliar key words should be taught to children prior to reading, through systematic vocabulary or cognate instruction, to integrate new words into children's background knowledge and enrich L2 reading comprehension.

Strategic reading

To effectively comprehend text, a strategic reader determines a purpose for reading and adjusts his or her reading for each purpose (National Reading Panel, 2000). For example, reading for the purpose of extracting main ideas and writing a summary requires a different set of strategies than leisure reading. By applying appropriate strategies before, during, and after reading, L2 children can learn to read purposefully and selectively, while actively building meaning from text.

The National Reading Panel (2000) recommends several strategies for teaching children to read with a purpose that have been shown to improve reading comprehension, including student-teacher question answering and feedback, student question generation about what is read, and student summarization of text information. A common, yet effective, strategy is *reciprocal teaching*. Reciprocal teaching is a shared reading technique that actively involves the reader in a dialogue about what is being read. It is based on the notion of gradual release of responsibility from teacher to student. It has been shown to be particularly effective in supporting language development (Hargrave & Sénéchal, 2000). In reciprocal teaching, teachers or peers can generate questions about the text that are culturally relevant to L2 learners, starting a conversation about the text. According to Palinscar and Brown (1984), reciprocal teaching involves the use of four strategies that can help to enhance children's reading comprehension:

1   Summarizing: Summarizing involves identifying and integrating relevant information across sentences, paragraphs, and the text as a whole. This strategy develops over time and should be taught differently for narrative and expository texts. In narrative texts, summarizing includes elements of story grammar (e.g., characters, setting, plot), whereas in expository texts, summarizing involves identifying main ideas (Baumann, 1986).
2   Question generation: This strategy involves reviewing and refining background knowledge. Students generate their own questions to be answered as they read. Generating questions requires students to focus on the main ideas of the text, while activating background knowledge. Research suggests that question generation helps to monitor comprehension of text (Palinscar & Brown, 1984).
3   Monitoring: Comprehension monitoring, a metacognitive skill, is a reader's ability to recognize that what they are reading does not make sense, often applying a strategy to clarify their understanding (Oakhill et al., 2005). While the research on comprehension monitoring in L2 learners is limited, it is plausible that monitoring can help L2 students improve their ability to construct meaning from text. By monitoring their understanding of what they have read, L2 learners can identify reasons for a breakdown in comprehension, such as unfamiliar vocabulary, as well as learn strategies for constructing or repairing meaning (e.g., rereading text).
4   Predicting: Predicting involves the activation of relevant background knowledge about a topic to confirm or disprove a hypothesis about what will happen next in the text. The predicting strategy provides students with an opportunity to connect new knowledge they encounter in the text with their existing background knowledge. It also facilitates use of text structure as students learn how cohesive devices can be used as a way of anticipating what might occur next (Beers & Howell, 2003).

In addition to these strategies, reciprocal teaching can be used to encourage L2 learners to make inferences during and after reading. Literal questions often involve having students answer what they already know, whereas inferential questions challenge children to think and build their knowledge and critical thinking skills. Teachers can engage L2 students in inference making through questions about the text, such as: *Who? What? Where? When? What happened next? Why?* and *How?* Among them, *Why?* questions can improve L2 learners' inference-making skills, as well as their performance on understanding the literal meaning of related parts in a text. *How?* questions can draw inferences about subordinate goals actions (e.g., "The boy picked up the pencil from the floor to finish writing his test." Inferential question: How did the boy finish his test?), and *What happened next?* questions can draw inferences about causal consequences (Graesser et al., 1994). As different questions can activate different types of inferences, classroom teachers should keep in mind that there are connections between question type and inference type.

It is important to note that when attempting to foster inferential language skills, literal questions should also be asked. This holds true for several reasons. First, engaging in inference-making requires that children have a basic literal understanding of text (Perfetti, Marron, & Foltz, 1996). Second, telling adults what they already know is an important aspect of classroom discourse or "school talk" that many children get little experience with in their homes (see van Kleeck, 2006). Furthermore, when classroom teachers give a set of inferential questions to their students, they should be aware of the order of question difficulty due to L2 learners' limited L2 proficiency and cognitive load. For example, it can be less demanding if the questions asking for details come before those requiring a main theme of a passage. This sequence of questioning also seems to be particularly effective for L2 poor readers (Shimizu, 2005).

Taken together, the implications for strategic reading involve reciprocal teaching, where children are taught to summarize, generate questions, monitor comprehension, and predict outcomes during reading. Inferential and literal questioning is particularly important for engaging L2 learners in inference-making.

Building text structure awareness

The strategies for effective reading comprehension reviewed here have focused on reciprocal teaching of text (content) information in order to create a coherent representation and understanding of what is read. An additional strategy for the facilitation of reading comprehension among L2 learners is *text structure awareness*. Text or discourse structure aids readers in the organization of information (e.g., description, sequence) and therefore facilitates the process of constructing meaning from text (Dymock & Nicholson, 2007). As discussed earlier, a reader's lack of text structure awareness can lead to comprehension difficulties.

Several studies have shown that both L1 and L2 students comprehend and recall information much better when they can see how text is organized (Carrell, 1992; Jiang & Grabe, 2007; Lukica, 2011; Meyer & Poon, 2001). These studies suggest that teachers can effectively communicate text structure awareness in their classrooms by implementing the following strategies (Grabe, 2009). The first recommendation emphasizes direct text structure instruction. The goal is to raise children's awareness of text structure through explicit instruction of structural features in a written text, such as topic sentences, cohesive devices (e.g., *and, but, so*), and anaphoric references. An anaphoric reference is a word that relates back to previous information in the text for its meaning. For example, "I did not go shopping with Mary yesterday. She was sick." One can infer that *she* refers to Mary. Accordingly, children's ability to recognize these text structures influences their interpretation and understanding of text.

In the same way, teachers are encouraged to teach the function of specific text substructures. There are five common substructures that appear in most expository texts (Dymock & Nicholson, 2007):

1 Description: The description of a text provides details, characteristics, features, and examples of objects, ideas, topics, persons, places, or events. Signal words include: *such as, for example, consists of.*
2 Compare/Contrast: This structure explains how two or more objects, ideas, and so forth are related and/or differ. Signal words include: *although, however, on the other hand.*
3 Sequence: The sequence of a text organizes items or events in steps or in a chronological or procedural process. Signal words include: *first, finally, lastly, next.*
4 Cause-Effect: This structure presents a resulting event (consequence) and the reasons for its occurrence. Signal words include: *consequently, as a result, because.*
5 Problem-Solution: The problem-solution structure outlines or analyzes one or more solutions to an identified problem. Signal words include: *this leads to, therefore, thus.*

In another line of research, teaching implications for students' text structure awareness include the use of visual representations, such as graphic organizers, tree diagrams, semantic maps, and hierarchical summaries (Alvermann, 1986; Taylor, 1992; Taylor & Beach, 1984; Trabasso & Bouchard, 2002; Vacca, 2002; Vacca & Vacca, 1999). These studies demonstrate that students comprehend text better when they are provided with a visual framework of how text information is organized and are directed to the relationship between the visual information and the text structure. Therefore, teachers are encouraged to instruct students on how to use visual representations to organize information and ideas in texts.

CONCLUSION

This chapter reviews the primary higher-level skills and processes that contribute to children's L2 reading comprehension, including working memory, background knowledge, inference-making, and the understanding of textual cohesion and coherence. The processes involved in building a mental representation of text are first reviewed, highlighting an interactive model of reading between a reader and text. Next, an overview of the literature on higher-level processes in children's L1 and L2 reading comprehension is presented. This review demonstrates that, while there are differences in L1 and L2 reading processes that involve higher-level skills, there are also many overlapping features. It appears that working memory, background knowledge, inference-making, and textual cohesion and coherence are important for the development of reading comprehension in L2 learners. However, because of limited language proficiency and background knowledge, L2 children may experience difficulties accessing the higher-level skills needed to construct and convey meaning from text. Implications for effective reading strategies and instructional practices in L2 education are discussed.

REFERENCES

Abeywickrama, P. S. (2007). *Measuring the knowledge of textual cohesion and coherence in learners of English as a Second Language (ESL)* (Unpublished doctoral dissertation). University of California at Los Angeles.

Adams, M. J., & Bruce, B. (1982). Background knowledge and reading comprehension. In J. A. Langer & M. T. Smith-Burke (Eds.), *Reader meets author: Bridging the gap* (pp. 2–25). Newark, DE: International Reading Association.

Aebersold, J. A., & Field, M. L. (1997). *From reader to reading teacher: Issues and strategies for second language classrooms.* Cambridge, UK: Cambridge University Press.

Afflerbach P., & Johnston P. (1984). On the use of verbal reports in reading research. *Journal of Reading Behavior, 16*, 307–322.

Alptekin, C. (2006). Cultural familiarity in inferential and literal comprehension in L2 reading. *System, 34*, 494–508.

Al-Shumaimeri, Y. (2006). The effects of content familiarity and language ability on reading comprehension performance of low- and high-ability Saudi tertiary students studying English as a foreign language. *Education Science and Islamic Studies, 18*, 1–19.

Alvermann, D. (1986). Graphic organizers: Cuing devices for comprehending and remembering main ideas. In J. Baumann (Ed.), *Teaching main idea comprehension* (pp. 210–238). Newark, DE: IRA.

Anderson, R. C., & Pearson, P. D. (1984). A schema-theoretic view of basic processes in reading comprehension. In P. D. Pearson, R. Barr, M. L. Kamil, & P. Mosenthal (Eds.), *The handbook of reading research* (pp. 255–292). New York: Longman.

Baddeley, A. D. (1986). *Working memory.* Oxford: Oxford University Press.

Baddeley, A. D. (1996). Exploring the central executive. *Quarterly Journal of Experimental Psychology, 49A*, 5–28.

Baddeley, A. D. (1998). Recent developments in working memory. *Current Opinion in Neurobiology, 8*, 234–238.

Baddeley, A. D. (2000). The episodic buffer: A new component of working memory? *Trends in Cognitive Science, 4,* 417–423.

Baddeley, A. D. (2003). Working memory and language: An overview. *Journal of Communication Disorders, 36,* 189–208.

Baddeley, A. D., & Hitch, G. (1974). Working memory. In G. H. Bower (Ed.), *Recent advances in learning and motivation* (pp. 47–89). New York: Academic Press.

Barnes, M. A., Dennis, M., & Haefele-Kalvaitis, J. (1996). The effects of knowledge availability and knowledge accessibility on coherence and elaborative inferencing in children from six to fifteen years of age. *Journal of Experimental Child Psychology, 61,* 216–241.

Barry, S., & Lazarte, A. (1995). Embedded clause effects on recall: Does high prior knowledge of content domain overcome syntactic complexity in students of Spanish? *The Modern Language Journal, 79,* 491–504.

Barry, S., & Lazarte, A. (1998). Evidence for mental models: How do prior knowledge, syntactic complexity, and reading topic affect inference generation in a recall task for nonnative readers of Spanish? *The Modern Language Journal, 82,* 176–193.

Baumann, J. F. (1986). *Teaching main idea comprehension.* Newark, DE: International Reading Association.

Beck, I. L., McKeown, M. G., & Kucan, L. (2002). *Bringing words to life: Robust vocabulary instruction.* New York: Guilford Press.

Beers, S., & Howell, L. (2003). *Reading strategies for the content areas.* Alexandria, VA: Association for Supervision and Curriculum Development.

Bernhardt, E. B. (1991). *Reading development in a second language.* Norwood, NJ: Ablex.

Berquist, B. (1998, March). *Individual differences in working memory span and L2 proficiency: Capacity or processing efficiency?* Paper presented at the American Association for Applied Linguistics 1998 Annual Conference, Seattle, WA.

Bloom, L., Lahey, M., Hood, L., Lifter, K., & Fiess, K. (1980). Complex sentences: Acquisition of syntactic connectives and the semantic relations they encode. *Journal of Child Language, 7,* 235–261.

Bugel, K., & Buunk, B. (1996). Sex differences in foreign language text comprehension: The role of interests and prior knowledge. *The Modern Language Journal, 80,* 15–31.

Burgoyne, K., Whiteley, H. E., & Hutchinson, J. M. (2013). The role of background knowledge in text comprehension for children learning English as an additional language. *Journal of Research in Reading, 36,* 132–148.

Cain, K. (2003). Text comprehension and its relation to coherence and cohesion in children's fictional narratives. *British Journal of Developmental Psychology, 21,* 335–351.

Cain, K. (2006). Individual differences in children's memory and reading comprehension: An investigation of semantic and inhibitory deficits. *Memory, 14,* 553–569.

Cain, K., & Nash, H. M. (2011). The influence of connectives on young readers' processing and comprehension of text. *Journal of Educational Psychology, 103,* 429–441.

Cain, K., & Oakhill, J. V. (1996). The nature of the relationship between comprehension skill and the ability to tell a story. *British Journal of Developmental Psychology, 14,* 187–201.

Cain, K., & Oakhill, J. V. (1999). Inference making ability and its relation to comprehension failure in young children. *Reading and Writing: An Interdisciplinary Journal, 11,* 489–503.

Cain, K., & Oakhill, J.V. (2006). Profiles of children with specific reading comprehension difficulties. *British Journal of Educational Psychology, 76*, 683–696.

Cain, K., Oakhill, J.V., Barnes, M.A., & Bryant, P.E. (2001). Comprehension skill, inference-making ability, and their relation to knowledge. *Memory and Cognition, 29*, 850–859.

Cain, K., Oakhill, J., & Bryant, P. (2004). Children's reading comprehension ability: Concurrent prediction by working memory, verbal ability, and component skills. *Journal of Educational Psychology, 96*, 31–42.

Cain, K., Patson, N., & Andrews, L. (2005). Age- and ability-related differences in young readers' use of conjunctions. *Journal of Child Language, 32*, 877–892.

Canale, M., & Swain, M. (1980). Theoretical bases of communicative approaches to second language teaching and testing. *Applied Linguistics, 1*, 1–47.

Carlisle, J.F., Beeman, M., Davis, L.H., & Spharim, G. (1999). Relationship of metalinguistic capabilities and reading achievement for children who are becoming bilingual. *Applied Psycholinguistics, 20*, 459–478.

Carrell, P.L. (1983). Three components of background knowledge in reading comprehension. *Language Learning, 33*, 183–207.

Carrell, P.L. (1987). Text as interaction: Some implications of text analysis and reading research for ESL composition. In R.B. Kaplan (Ed.), *Writing across languages: Analysis of L2 text* (pp. 47–56). Reading, MA: Addison-Wesley.

Carrell, P.L. (1991). Second language reading: Reading ability or language proficiency? *Applied Linguistics, 12*, 159–179.

Carrell, P. (1992). Awareness of text structure: Effects on recall. *Language Learning, 42*, 1–20.

Carrell, P.L., & Eisterhold, J.C. (1983). Schema theory and ESL reading pedagogy. *TESOL Quarterly, 17*, 553–573.

Carrell, P.L., & Wise, T.E. (1998). The relationship between prior knowledge and topic interest in second language reading. *Studies in Second Language Acquisition, 20*, 285–309.

Casteel, M.A., & Simpson, G.B. (1991). Textual coherence and the development of inferential generation skills. *Journal of Research in Reading, 14*, 116–129.

Clapham, C. (1996). *The development of IELTS: A study of the effect of background knowledge on reading comprehension*. Cambridge, UK: Cambridge University Press.

Clapham, C. (2000). Assessment for academic purposes: Where next? *System, 28*, 511–521.

Clarke, M.A., & Silberstein, S. (1977). Toward a realization of psycholinguistic principles in the ESL reading class. *Language Learning, 27*, 135–154.

Coady, J. (1979). A psycholinguistic model of the ESL reader. In R. Mackay, B. Barkman, & R.R. Jordan (Eds.), *Reading in a second language* (pp. 5–12). Rowley, MA: Newbury House.

Connor, U. (1984). A study of cohesion and coherence in English as a second language students' writing. *Papers in Linguistics, 17*, 301–316.

Craik, F.I.M. (2002). Levels of processing: Past, present … and future? *Memory, 10*, 305–318.

Craik, F.I.M., & Lockhart, R.S. (1972). Levels of processing: A framework for memory research. *Journal of Verbal Learning and Verbal Behavior, 11*, 671–684.

Cromley, J.G., & Azevedo, R. (2007). Testing and refining the direct and inferential mediation model of reading comprehension. *Journal of Educational Psychology, 99*, 311–325.

Crosson, A.C., & Lesaux, N.K. (2013). Does knowledge of connectives play a unique role in the reading comprehension of English learners and English-only students? *Journal of Research in Reading, 36*, 241–260.

Crosson, A.C., Lesaux, N.K., & Martiniello, M. (2008). Factors that influence comprehension of connectives among language minority children from Spanish-speaking backgrounds. *Applied Psycholinguistics, 29*, 603–625.

Cummins, J. (1976). The influence of bilingualism on cognitive growth: A synthesis of research findings and explanatory hypotheses. *Working Papers in Bilingualism, 9*, 1–43.

Da Fontoura, H.A., & Siegel, L.S. (1995). Reading, syntactic, and working memory skills of bilingual Portuguese-English Canadian children. *Reading and Writing: An Interdisciplinary Journal, 7*, 139–153.

Daneman, M., & Blennerhassett, A. (1984). How to assess the listening comprehension skills of prereaders. *Journal of Educational Psychology, 76*, 1372–1381.

Daneman, M., & Carpenter, P.A. (1980). Individual differences in working memory and reading. *Journal of Verbal Learning and Verbal Behavior, 19*, 450–466.

Daneman, M., & Carpenter, P.A. (1983). Individual differences in integrating information between and within sentences. *Journal of Experimental Psychology: Learning Memory and Cognition, 9*, 561–584.

Daneman, M., & Case, R. (1981). Syntactic form, semantic complexity, and short-term memory: Influences on children's acquisition of new linguistic structures. *Developmental Psychology, 17*, 367–378.

Daneman, M., & Green, I. (1986). Individual differences in comprehending and producing words in context. *Journal of Memory and Language, 25*, 1–18.

Daneman, M., & Merikle, P.M. (1996). Working memory and language comprehension: A meta-analysis. *Psychonomic Bulletin & Review, 3*, 422–433.

de Beni, R., Palladino, P., Pazzaglia, F., & Cornoldi, C. (1998). Increases in intrusion errors and working memory deficit of poor comprehenders. *Quarterly Journal of Experimental Psychology: Human Experimental Psychology, 51A*, 305–320.

de Jong, P. (2006). Understanding normal and impaired reading development: A working memory perspective. In S. Pickering (Ed.), *Working memory and education* (pp. 33–60). London: Academic Press.

Dole, J.A., Valencia, S.W., Greer, E.A., & Wardrop, J.L. (1991). Effects of two types of prereading instruction on the comprehension of narrative and expository text. *Reading Research Quarterly, 26*, 142–159.

Droop, M., & Verhoeven, L. (2003). Language proficiency and reading ability in first- and second-language learners. *Reading Research Quarterly, 38*, 78–103.

Dymock, S., & Nicholson, T. (2007). *Teaching text structures: A key to nonfiction reading success.* New York: Scholastic.

Ehrlich, S. (1988). Cohesive devices and discourse competence. *World Englishes, 7*, 111–118.

Ellis, N.C., & Sinclair, S.G. (1996). Working memory in the acquisition of vocabulary and syntax: Putting language in good order. *Quarterly Journal of Experimental Psychology, 49*, 234–250.

Engle, R.W., Tuholski, S.W., Laughlin, J.E., & Conway, A.R. (1999). Working memory, short-term memory, and general fluid intelligence: A latent variable approach. *Journal of Experimental Psychology: General, 128*, 309–331.

Ericsson, K.A., & Kintsch, W. (1995). Long-term working memory. *Psychological Review, 102*, 211–245.

Farnia, F., & Geva, E. (2011). Cognitive correlates of vocabulary growth in English language learners. *Applied Psycholinguistics, 32*, 711–738.

Fletcher, C. R. (1994). Levels of representation in memory for discourse. In M. A. Gernsbacher (Ed.), *Handbook of psycholinguistics* (pp. 589–607). San Diego: Academic Press.

Gernsbacher, M.A. (1997). Coherence cues mapping during comprehension. In J. Costermans & M. Fayol (Eds.), *Processing interclausal relationships in the production and comprehension of text* (pp. 3–21). Mahwah, NJ: Erlbaum.

Geva, E. (1992). The role of conjunctions in L2 text comprehension. *TESOL Quarterly, 26*, 731–747.

Geva, E., & Ryan, E.B. (1985). Use of conjunctions in expository texts by skilled and less skilled readers. *Journal of Reading Behaviour, 17*, 331–46.

Geva, E., & Ryan, E. (1993). Linguistic and cognitive correlates of academic skills in first and second languages. *Language Learning, 43*, 5–42.

Geva, E., & Siegel, L. (2000). Orthographic and cognitive factors in the concurrent development of basic reading skills in two languages. *Reading and Writing, 12*, 1–30.

Goldman, S. R., & Murray, J. D. (1992). Knowledge of connectors as cohesion devices in text: A comparative study of native-English and English-as-a-second-language speakers. *Journal of Educational Psychology, 84*, 504–519.

Grabe, W. (2009). *Reading in a second language: Moving from theory to practice.* New York: Cambridge University Press.

Graesser, A.C., Singer, M., & Trabasso, T. (1994). Constructing inferences during narrative text comprehension. *Psychological Review, 101*, 371–395.

Graves, M. (2000). A vocabulary program to complement and bolster a middle-grade comprehension program. In B. Taylor, M. Graves, & P. van den Broek (Eds.), *Reading for meaning: Fostering comprehension in the middle grades* (pp. 116–135). Newark, DE: International Reading Association.

Halliday, M.A.K., & Hasan, R. (1976). *Cohesion in English.* London: Longman.

Hammadou, J. (1991). Interrelationships among prior knowledge, inference, and language reading. *The Modern Language Journal, 75*, 27–38.

Hargrave, A.C., & Sénéchal, M. (2000). A book reading intervention with preschool children who have limited vocabularies: The benefits of regular reading and dialogic reading. *Early Childhood Research Quarterly, 15*, 75–90.

Harrington, M. (1992). Fostering critical reflection through technology: Preparing prospective teachers for a changing society. *Journal of Information Technology, 1*, 67–82.

Harrington, M., & Sawyer, M. (1992). L2 working memory capacity and L2 reading skill. *Studies in Second Language Acquisition, 14*, 25–38.

Hipfner-Boucher, K., Chen, X, Pasquarella, A., & Deacon, S. H. (2014, April). *The contribution of cognate awareness to French reading comprehension in French immersion children.* Paper presented at the American Educational Research Association Annual Meeting, Philadelphia, PA.

Horiba, Y. (1993). The role of causal reasoning and language competence in narrative comprehension. *Studies in Second Language Acquisition, 15*, 49–81.

Horiba, Y. (1996). Comprehension processes in L2 reading. *Studies in Second Language Acquisition, 18*, 433–473.

Jean, M., & Geva, E. (2009). The development of vocabulary in English as a second language children and its role in word recognition ability. *Applied Psycholinguistics, 30*, 153–185.

Jiang, X., & Grabe, W. (2007). Graphic organizers in reading instruction: Research findings and issues. *Reading in a Foreign Language, 19*, 34–55.

Johnson, P. (1981). Effects on reading comprehension of language complexity and cultural background of a text. *TESOL Quarterly, 15*, 169–181.

Kail, M., & Weissenborn, J. (1991). Connectives: Developmental issues. In G. Pie´raut-le-Bonniec & M. Dolitsky (Eds.), *Language bases . . . Discourse bases: Some aspects of contemporary French-language psycholinguistics research* (pp. 125–142). Amsterdam: Benjamins.

Kendeou, P., Bohn-Gettler, C., White, M. J., & van den Broek, P. (2008). Children's inference generation across different media. *Journal of Research in Reading, 31*, 259–272.

Kendeou, P., Rapp, D.N., & van den Broek, P. (2003). The influence of readers' prior knowledge on text comprehension and learning from text. In R. Nata (Ed.), *Progress in education* (pp. 189–209). New York: Nova Science.

Kintsch, W. (1988). The use of knowledge in discourse processing: A construction-integration model. *Psychological Review, 95*, 163–182.

Kintsch, W. (1998). *Comprehension: A paradigm for cognition.* Cambridge, UK: Cambridge University Press.

Kintsch, W., Welsch, D. M., Schmalhofer, F., & Zimny, S. (1990). Sentence memory: A theoretical analysis. *Journal of Memory and Language, 29*, 133–159.

Kirby, J.R., Cain, K., & White, B. (2012). Deeper learning in reading comprehension. In J.R. Kirby & M.J. Lawson (Eds.), *Enhancing the quality of learning: Dispositions, instruction, and learning processes* (pp. 315–338). New York: Cambridge University Press.

Koda, K. (2005). *Insights into second language reading: A cross-linguistic approach.* New York: Cambridge University Press.

Kormos, J., & Safar, A. (2008). Phonological short-term memory, working memory and foreign language performance in intensive language learning. *Bilingualism: Language and Cognition, 11*, 261–271.

Laing, S.P., & Kamhi, A.G. (2002). The use of think-aloud protocols to compare inferencing abilities in average and below-average readers. *Journal of Learning Disabilities, 35*, 436–447.

Leather, C.V., & Henry, L.A. (1994). Working memory span and phonological awareness tasks as predictors of early reading ability. *Journal of Experimental Child Psychology, 58*, 88–111.

Lee, S.K. (2007). Effects of textual enhancement and topic familiarity on Korean EFL students' reading comprehension and learning of passive form. *Language Learning, 57*, 87–118.

Leeser, M.J. (2007). Learner-based factors in L2 reading comprehension and processing grammatical form: Topic familiarity and working memory. *Language Learning, 57*, 229–270.

Lesaux, N. K., Geva, E., Koda, K., Siegel, L. S., & Shanahan, T. (2008). Development of literacy in second-language learners. In D. August & T. Shanahan (Eds.), *Developing reading and writing in second-language learners: Lessons from the Report of the National Literacy Panel on Language-Minority Children and Youth* (pp. 27–59). New York: Routledge.

Levine, M. G., & Hause, G. J. (1985). The effect of background knowledge on the reading comprehension of second language learners. *Foreign Language Annals, 18,* 391–397.

Li, M., & Kirby, J. K. (2014). Unexpected poor comprehenders among adolescent ESL students. *Scientific Studies of Reading, 18,* 75–93.

Lipka, O., & Siegel, L. (2012). The development of reading comprehension skills in children learning English as a second language. *Reading and Writing, 25,* 1873–1898.

Long, D. L., Oppy, B. J., & Seely, M. R. (1997). Individual differences in readers' sentence and text-level representations. *Journal of Memory and Language, 36,* 129–145.

Lukica, I. (2011). Building awareness of discourse structure through teaching reading strategies in English for legal purposes class. *Proceeding of 1st International Conference on Foreign Language Teaching and Applied Linguistics, Sarajevo,* pp. 643–647.

Lynch, J. S., & van den Broek, P. (2007). Understanding the glue of narrative structure: Children's on and off-line inferences about characters' goals. *Cognitive Development, 22,* 323–340.

Lynch, J. S., van den Broek, P., Kremer, K. E., Kendeou, P., White, M. J., & Lorch, E. P. (2008). The development of narrative comprehension and its relation to other early reading skills. *Reading Psychology, 29,* 327–365.

McClure, E., & Geva, E. (1983). The development of the cohesive use of adversative conjunctions in discourse. *Discourse Processes, 6,* 411–432.

McNamara, D. S., Kintsch, E., Songer, N. B., & Kintsch, W. (1996). Are good texts always better? Interactions of text coherence, background knowledge, and levels of understanding in learning from text. *Cognition and Instruction, 14,* 1–43.

McNeil, L. (2011). Investigating the contributions of background knowledge and reading comprehension strategies to L2 reading comprehension: An exploratory study. *Reading and Writing, 24,* 883–902.

Meyer, B. J. F. (1985). Prose analysis: Purposes, procedures and problems. In B. K. Britton & J. B. Black (Eds.), *Understanding expository text* (pp. 269–304). Hillsdale, NJ: Erlbaum.

Meyer, B. J. F., & Poon, L. W. (2001). Effects of the structure strategy and signaling on recall of text. *Journal of Educational Psychology, 93,* 141–159.

Miyake, A., & Friedman, N. P. (1998). Individual differences in second language proficiency: Working memory as language aptitude. In A. Healy & L. Bourne (Eds.), *Foreign language learning: Psycholinguistics studies on training and retention* (pp. 339–364). Mahwah, NJ: Erlbaum.

Morgan, R. L., & Sellner, T. S. (1980). Discourse and linguistic theory. In R. J. Spiro, B. C. Bertram, & W. F. Brewer (Eds.), *Theoretical issues in reading comprehension* (pp. 165–200). Hillsdale, NJ: Erlbaum.

Muramoto, T. (2000). Daini gengo no bunsho rikai katei ni oyobosu shujukudo no eikyo [The effects of second-language proficiency on text comprehension]. *Science of Reading, 44,* 43–50.

Nassaji, H. (2003). Higher-level and lower-level text processing skills in advanced ESL reading comprehension. *The Modern Language Journal, 87*, 261–276.

Nation, K., Adams, J.W., Bowyer-Crane, C.A., & Snowling, M.J. (1999). Working memory deficits in poor comprehenders reflect underlying language impairments. *Journal of Experimental Child Psychology, 73*, 139–158.

Nation, K., & Snowling, M.J. (2000). Factors influencing syntactic awareness in normal readers and poor comprehenders. *Applied Psycholinguistics, 21*, 229–241.

National Reading Panel. (2000). *Teaching children to read: An evidence-based assessment of the scientific literature on reading and its implications for reading instruction* (NIH Pub. No. 00–4754). Washington, DC: National Institutes of Health.

Oakhill, J.V. (1982). Constructive processes in skilled and less-skilled comprehenders' memory for sentences. *British Journal of Psychology, 73*, 13–20.

Oakhill, J.V. (1984). Inferential and memory skills in children's comprehension of stories. *British Journal of Educational Psychology, 54*, 31–39.

Oakhill, J.V., Cain, K., & Bryant, P.E. (2003). The dissociation of single-word reading and text comprehension: Evidence from component skills. *Language and Cognitive Processes, 18*, 443–468.

Oakhill, J.V., Cain, K., & Elbro, C. (2015). *Understanding and teaching reading comprehension: A handbook*. Abington, UK: Routledge.

Oakhill, J.V., Hartt, J., & Samols, D. (2005). Levels of comprehension monitoring and working memory in good and poor comprehenders. *Reading and Writing, 18*, 657–686.

Oakhill, J., Yuill, N., & Parkin, A. (1986). On the nature of the difference between skilled and less-skilled comprehenders. *Journal of Research in Reading, 9*, 80–91.

O'Reilly, T., & McNamara, D. S. (2007). Reversing the reverse cohesion effect: Good texts can be better for strategic, high-knowledge readers. *Discourse Processes, 43*, 121–152.

Palinscar, A.S., & Brown, A.L. (1984). Reciprocal teaching of comprehension-fostering and comprehension-monitoring activities. *Cognition and Instruction, 1*, 117–175.

Paribakht, T.S., & Wesche, M. (1999). Reading and "incidental" L2 vocabulary acquisition: An introspective study of lexical inferencing. *Studies in Second Language Acquisition, 21*, 195–224.

Pearson-Casanave, C.R. (1984). Communicative pre-reading activities: Schema theory in action. *TESOL Quarterly, 18*, 334–336.

Peregoy, S.F., & Boyle, O.F. (2000). English learners reading English: What we know, what we need to know. *Theory Into Practice, 39*, 237–247.

Perfetti, C.A. (1985). *Reading ability*. New York: Oxford University Press.

Perfetti, C.A., & Hart, L. (2001). The lexical quality hypothesis. In L. Vehoeven, C. Elbro, & P. Reitsma (Eds.), *Precursors of functional literacy* (pp. 189–214). Amsterdam: Benjamins.

Perfetti, C.A., Marron, M.A., & Foltz, P.W. (1996). Sources of comprehension failure: Theoretical perspectives and case studies. In C. Cornoldi & J.V. Oakhill (Eds.), *Reading comprehension difficulties: Processes and remediation* (pp. 137–165). Mahwah, NJ: Erlbaum.

Pulido, D. (2007). The effects of topic familiarity and passage sight vocabulary on L2 lexical inferencing and retention through reading. *Applied Linguistics, 26*, 66–86.

Reynolds, R.E., Taylor, M.A., Steffensen, M.S., Shirey, L.L., & Anderson, R.C. (1982). Cultural schemata and reading comprehension. *Reading Research Quarterly, 17*, 353–366.

Rodriguez, G.A. (2008). *Second language sentence processing: Is it fundamentally different?* (Unpublished doctoral thesis). University of Pittsburgh, PA.

Rumelhart, D.E. (1977). Toward an interactive model of reading. In S. Dornic (Ed.), *Attention and performance VI* (pp. 265–303). Hillsdale, NJ: Erlbaum.

Sanders, T.J.M., Spooren, W.P.M., & Noordman, L.G.M. (1992). Toward a taxonomy of coherence relations. *Discourse Processes, 15*, 1–35.

Seigneuric, A., & Ehrlich, M.-F. (2005). Contribution of working memory capacity to children's reading comprehension: A longitudinal investigation. *Reading and Writing, 18*, 617–656.

Seigneuric, A., Ehrlich, M.-F., Oakhill, J.V., & Yuill, N.M. (2000). Working memory resources and children's reading comprehension. *Reading and Writing, 13*, 81–103.

Service, E. (1992). Phonology, working memory, and foreign-language learning. *Quarterly Journal of Experimental Psychology, 45*, 21–50.

Service, E., & Kohonen, V. (1995). Is the relation between phonological memory and foreign language learning accounted for by vocabulary acquisition? *Applied Psycholinguistics, 16*, 155–172.

Shapiro, L.R., & Hudson, J.A. (1991). Tell me a make-believe story: Coherence and cohesion in young children's picture-elicited narratives. *Developmental Psychology, 27*, 960–974.

Shapiro, L.R., & Hudson, J.A. (1997). Coherence and cohesion in children's stories. In J. Costermans & M. Fayol (Eds.), *Processing interclausal relationships: Studies in the production and comprehension of text* (pp. 23–48). Mahwah, NJ: Erlbaum.

Shimizu, M. (2005). *Inference generation processes of Japanese EFL learners: Effects of questioning on their reading comprehension* (Unpublished doctoral dissertation). University of Tsukuba, Japan.

Snow, C. (2002). *Reading for understanding: Toward and R & D program in reading comprehension*. Santa Monica, CA: RAND.

Spires, H.A., & Donley, J. (1998). Prior knowledge activation: Inducing engagement with informational texts. *Journal of Educational Psychology, 90*, 249–260.

Spooren, W., & Sanders, T. (2008). The acquisition order of coherence relations: On cognitive complexity in discourse. *Journal of Pragmatics, 40*, 2003–2026.

Stahl, S.A., Jacobson, M.G., Davis, C.E., & Davis, R.L. (1989). Prior knowledge and difficult vocabulary in the comprehension of unfamiliar text. *Reading Research Quarterly, 24*, 27–43.

Stanovich, K.E. (1980). Toward an interactive-compensatory model of individual differences in the development of reading fluency. *Reading Research Quarterly, 16*, 32–71.

Stanovich, K.E. (1984). The interactive-compensatory model of reading: A confluence of developmental, experimental, and educational psychology. *Remedial and Special Education, 5*, 11–19.

Steffensen, M.S., Joag-Dev, C., & Anderson, R.C. (1979). A cross-cultural perspective on reading comprehension. *Reading Research Quarterly, 15*, 10–29.

Stein, N.L. (1978). *How children understand stories: a developmental analysis* (Technical Report No. 69). Champaign-Urbana: Center for the Study of Reading, University of Illinois.

Stothard, S.E., & Hulme, C. (1992). Reading comprehension difficulties in children: The role of language comprehension and working memory skills. *Reading and Writing, 4,* 245–256.

Swanson, H.L., & Berninger, V. (1995). The role of working memory in skilled and less skilled readers' comprehension. *Intelligence, 21,* 83–108.

Swanson, H.L., & Howell, M. (2001). Working memory, short-term memory, and speech rate as predictors of children's reading performance at different ages. *Journal of Educational Psychology, 93,* 720–734.

Swanson, H.L., Orosco, M.J., Lussier, C.M., Gerber, M.M., & Guzman-Orth, D.A. (2011). The influence of working memory and phonological processing on English language learner children's bilingual reading and language acquisition. *Journal of Educational Psychology, 103,* 838–856.

Swanson, H.L., Saez, L., & Gerber, M. (2006). Growth in literacy and cognition in bilingual children at risk or not at risk for reading disabilities. *Journal of Educational Psychology, 98,* 247–264.

Taylor, B. (1992). Text structure, comprehension, and recall. In S. Samuels & A. Farstrup (Eds.), *What research has to say about reading instruction* (2nd ed., pp. 220–235). Newark, DE: IRA.

Taylor, B., & Beach, R. (1984). The effect of text structure instruction on middle grade students' comprehension and production of expository prose. *Reading Research Quarterly, 19,* 134–146.

Tierney R., & Mosenthal, J. (1983). Cohesion and textual coherence. *Research in the Teaching of English, 17,* 215–229.

Tompkins, V., Guo, Y., & Justice, L.M. (2013). Inference generation, story comprehension, and language skills in the preschool years. *Reading and Writing, 26,* 403–429.

Trabasso, T., & Bouchard, E. (2002). Teaching readers how to comprehend text strategically. In C. Collins & M. Pressley (Eds.), *Comprehension instruction: Research-based best practices* (pp. 176–200). New York: Guilford Press.

Trabasso, T., & Nickels, M. (1992). The development of goal plans of action in the narration of a picture story. *Discourse Processes, 15,* 249–275.

Vacca, R. (2002). Making a difference in adolescent school lives: Visible and invisible aspects of content area reading. In A. Farstrup & S.J. Samuels (Eds.), *What research has to say about reading instruction* (3rd ed., pp. 124–139). Newark, DE: International Reading Association.

Vacca, R., & Vacca, J. (1999). *Content area reading: Literacy and learning across the curriculum* (6th ed.). New York: Addison Wesley Longman.

van den Broek, P., Lorch, R.F., Jr., Linderholm, T., & Gustafson, M. (2001). The effects of readers' goals on inference generation and memory for texts. *Memory & Cognition, 29,* 1081–1087.

van den Broek, P., Risden, K., & Husebye-Hartman, E. (1995). The role of readers' standards for coherence in the generation of inferences during reading. In R.F. Lorch, Jr., & E.J. O'Brien (Eds.), *Sources of coherence in text comprehension* (pp. 353–373). Hillsdale, NJ: Erlbaum.

van den Broek, P., Tzeng, Y., Risden, K., Trabasso, T., & Basche, P. (2001). Inferential questioning: Effects on comprehension of narrative texts as a function of grade and timing. *Journal of Educational Psychology, 93,* 521–529.

van den Noort, M.W.M.L., Bosch, P., & Hugdahl, K. (2006). Foreign language proficiency and working memory capacity. *European Psychologist, 11*, 289–296.

van Dijk, T.A., & Kintsch, W. (1983). *Strategies of discourse comprehension.* New York: Academic Press.

van Kleeck, A. (2006). Cultural issues in promoting interactive book sharing in the families of preschoolers. In A. van Kleeck (Ed.), *Sharing books and stories to promote language and literacy* (pp. 179–230). San Diego: Plural.

Verhoeven, L. (1990). Acquisition of reading in a second language. *Reading Research Quarterly, 25*, 90–114.

Walter, C. (2006). Transfer of reading comprehension skills to L2 is linked to mental representations of text and to L2 working memory. *Applied Linguistics, 25*, 315–339.

Wenner, J.A. (2004). Preschoolers' comprehension of goal structure in narratives. *Memory, 12*, 193–202.

Yoshida, M. (2003). Working memory capacity and use of inference in L2. *JACET Bulletin, 36*, 1–17.

Yuet Hung Chang, C. (2003). Cultural content and reading proficiency: A comparison of mainland Chinese and Hong Kong learners of English. *Language Culture and Curriculum, 16*, 60–69.

Yuill, N., & Oakhill, J. (1991). *Children's problems in text comprehension: An experimental investigation.* Cambridge, UK: Cambridge University Press.

Yuill, N.M., Oakhill, J.V., & Parkin, A.J. (1989). Working memory, comprehension skill and the resolution of text anomaly. *British Journal of Psychology, 80*, 351–361.

7

The social context of second language literacy and biliteracy

Mila Schwartz and Liubov Baladzhaeva

INTRODUCTION

The chapter consists of seven sections. Sections 1 and 2 present a brief overview of prominent theoretical frameworks examining home and community settings in second language literacy acquisition. Section 3 includes a brief description of the language and literacy policies in North America. Section 4 addresses home literacy practices and parental attitudes and beliefs toward first and second language literacy. Section 5 explores community-based literacy development practices and community support for biliteracy. Section 6 describes the relationships between home and community literacy practices, language and literacy educational policies, and the mainstream schooling of minority language students in the North American context. Research on bilingual programs in a number of contexts is reviewed, and the impact of such programs on literacy is discussed. The last section examines the magnitude of the effects of immigration status, socio-economic status, parental education, the child's gender, heritage country, and length of residence in the host country on children's achievements in L2 literacy.

In terms of methodological approach to exploring the role of a social context in the L2 literacy acquisition, in this chapter we focus on triangulation – that is, "using different measures or research methods to investigate a particular phenomenon" (Mackey & Gass, 2005, p. 181).

The chapter presents the challenges and conflicts between children's own culture and identity and the culture of the second language community on the second language reading development. The chapter is concluded by describing the teaching implications for addressing home and community-based literacy and biliteracy practices, cultural background, and socio-economic status of the English language learners in the L2 literacy practices in the school context.

In every society, literacy has a powerful status and is acknowledged as a way to provide a window of economic, social, and political opportunities for an individual (Baker, 2001; Datta, 2000). Alongside the research examining the cognitive, linguistic, and metalinguistic bases for reading ability in L1 or L2 among language minority children, the development of reading ability cannot be considered without the wider societal and cultural context. This context consists of the family and ethno-linguistic communities, particularly in educational settings.

Numerous studies have shown that the acquisition of literacy in minority languages within a home or community setting may serve as a springboard for the acquisition of literacy in the second language (e.g., Dressler & Kamil, 2006). Still, in North America, where English is the dominant language, there is relatively little opportunity for language minority children to acquire literacy skills in such languages as Mandarin, Punjabi, or Spanish. Family and community make an effort to provide such an opportunity; however, cultures differ in the ways they support children's literacy development.

Recent studies have addressed the need for negotiation between home and community-based literacy practices, parental attitudes toward L1 and L2 literacy acquisition, and mainstream literacy acquisition (e.g., Li, 2006; Schwarzer, 2001). Nevertheless, these negotiation practices are relatively rare, and the language minority child's "funds of knowledge" tend to be neglected by mainstream educators and policy-makers (Shohamy, 2006). Children coming from a minority language background may even be treated as an at-risk group, as in the case of the No Child Left Behind policy (Caldas, 2013).

There is growing research on the roles of the following factors in the acquisition of second language literacy: immigration status, socio-economic status, parental education, the child's gender, length of family residence in the host country, and heritage country and culture. Maternal education and country of birth, for example, have been found to affect children's L2 literacy outcomes (Winsler et al., 2014). There are tendencies toward an "immigrant advantage" and an "immigrant disadvantage" in regards to literacy acquisition. The term "immigrant advantage" refers to the situation when children of first-generation immigrants surpass the children of U.S.-born parents on certain developmental and academic outcomes (Garcia Coll & Marks, 2012). This advantage usually diminishes with successive generations (De Feyter & Winsler, 2009). However, the hardships of immigration, lower SES, parents' insufficient L2 skills, and other factors may lead to an "immigrant disadvantage" when immigrant children perform worse than their non-immigrant counterparts (Winsler et al., 2014). The aim of this chapter is to provide a comprehensive overview of the current research on the socio-cultural context of the development of L2 literacy and biliteracy in childhood. It is important to note that a detailed and exhaustive meta-analysis of this research domain is beyond the scope of this chapter. Instead, we focus on the key research that contributes to our understanding of the socio-cultural factors affecting L2 literacy and biliteracy within the North American context.

The chapter consists of seven sections. Sections 1 and 2 present a brief overview of prominent theoretical frameworks that outline home and community settings in second language literacy acquisition. Section 3 includes a brief description of language and literacy policies in North America. Section 4 addresses home literacy practices and parental attitudes and beliefs toward first and second language literacy. Section 5 explores community-based literacy development practices and community support for biliteracy. Section 6 describes the relationships between home and community literacy practices, language and literacy educational policies, and the mainstream education of minority language students in a North American context. Research on bilingual programs in a number of contexts is reviewed, and the impact of such programs on literacy is discussed. The last section examines the magnitude of the effects of immigration status, socio-economic status, parental education, the child's gender, heritage country, and length of residence in the host country on children's achievements in L2 literacy.

In approaching such a complex research domain as the socio-cultural context of L2 and biliteracy, it is important to highlight that research in this area is interdisciplinary. More specifically, this research relates to a number of substantial research fields, such as bilingual child rearing and parenting, family language policies, language educational policies and planning, educational linguistics, and educational ethnography. The chapter presents the challenges and conflicts between a child's cultural identity and the culture of the second language community and, more specifically, how these conflicts influence L2 literacy development. We conclude the chapter with teaching implications. Also, directions for future research will be mapped, and resources will be provided for educators for further reading on the topic.

1.   SOCIETAL AND CULTURAL CONTEXT OF SECOND LANGUAGE LITERACY AND BILITERACY: A THEORETICAL BACKGROUND

Vygotsky's socio-cultural theory (1978)

Children acquire conventions of written language through assistance from others (family members, teachers and peers) in specific socio-cultural contexts. During this process the child's literacy skills further develop by using tools available in the child's environment, such as books, keyboard, and blessing cards. In this regard, two related notions, *zone of proximal development* and *scaffolding*, should be addressed. These notions were proposed by Vygotsky

(1978, 1986) and one of his followers, Bruner (1986). Vygotsky (1978, 1986) viewed the concept of scaffolding as synonymous with the process of adult-child interaction. This interaction occurs within the *zone of proximal development*, which is one of the central notions of his theory. Vygotsky (1978) defined the zone of proximal development as "the distance between the actual developmental level as determined by independent problem solving, and the level of potential development as determined by problem solving under adult guidance or in cooperation with the more capable peers" (p. 86). To advance children's developmental potential, experienced teachers provide them with *scaffolding* during social interaction. Bruner (1986) further defined scaffolding as the critical support provided to the learner by the learning context, teachers, competent peers, and experienced others. For example, scaffolding could be provided to the learner by simplifying the task as in breaking it down into smaller steps and modelling. In this chapter, we illustrate how, through home literacy practices, parents and other family members provide scaffolding for children's literacy acquisition in L2.

Family language policy

Family language policy is a useful concept for understanding parental attitudes toward diverse literacies, particularly home literacy activities that parents provide to support the biliteracy development of their children. Research on family language policy incorporates the analysis of language ideology, practice, and management, classified by Spolsky (2004) as components of a language policy model for an ethno-linguistic community (e.g., Kopeliovich, 2010; Schwartz, 2008). In adopting this model in order to explore the role of the home in L1 and L2 literacy development, we distinguish among three components: family beliefs about L1 and L2 literacy, family literacy practices, and efforts to modify or influence practices through intervention, planning, or management. Thus, this model enables us to explore parental beliefs about children's biliteracy development and their practices aimed at providing this development.

Funds of knowledge

Educators frequently lack the knowledge of minority language children's culturally specific ways of learning outside of school. Important questions arise when classroom teachers try to understand children from diverse cultural and linguistic backgrounds. What do home literacy environments look like and in what ways are L1 and L2 literacies supported at home? How do home literacy practices and experiences differ from school experiences? To seek answers to these questions we need to address the concept of *funds of knowledge*. This concept refers to "historically accumulated and culturally developed bodies of knowledge and skills essential for household or individual functioning and well-being" (Moll, Amanti, Neff, & Gonzalez, 1992, p. 133). In the context of this chapter, the notion of funds of knowledge refers to family and community literacy, and cultural practices which inevitably influence the child's L2 literacy acquisition. We will address research exploring the funds of knowledge of language minority homes in an attempt to understand children's home literacy practices in both L1 and L2. The following studies will be presented: De La Piedra (2011); Li (2006); Reyes (2006); Reyes and Azuara (2008); and Schwarzer (2001). All of these studies underscore the need for mainstream teachers to learn about the child's funds of knowledge as a potential way to enhance the child's success in school.

Ecological approach toward childhood second language literacy and biliteracy

Haugen (1972) defined language ecology as "the study of interactions between any given language and its environment" (p. 325). According to this definition, a language does not exist independently of its environment. As Creese and Martin (2003) noted, the research on language ecology includes "discussion related to cognitive development and human interaction, the maintenance and survival of languages, the promotion of linguistic diversity, and language policy and planning" (p. 2). Barton (1994) defined the ecological approach to literacy as an "interaction between individuals and their environments" (p. 29). Adopting this approach in the present chapter, we describe the interplay of different factors, such as characteristics of the child's close and extended family, the bicultural community she belongs to, and the nature of the connections and the processes taking place between home and school that shape her second language literacy and biliteracy development (Reyes & Azuara, 2008).

Deficit model

The deficit model, proposed by McCaleb (1997), states that culture and socioeconomic status determine whether parents can provide an environment that facilitates children's literacy development. According to this model, the linguistic capital of ethnic and language minority families cannot contribute to their children's literacy development in the L2. This theory is often perpetuated among educators and policy-makers, and even among minority language parents themselves (Stagg-Peterson & Heywood, 2007). For example, Stagg-Peterson and Heywood (2007) observed that school teachers and minority language parents both thought that parents were unable to help their children with schoolwork due to their lack of English knowledge. In order to solve this problem, ESL classes for parents were established in their children's schools.

Teachers in mainstream schools sometimes see language minority parents as uncooperative. Aside from the language barrier, participation in school life may not be common in parents' native cultures, and thus it is hard for them to adapt to a new model of parent-school interactions. Parents, however, are usually highly motivated to help their children with schoolwork because they see schooling as an opportunity for acculturation and upward mobility for their children (Stagg-Peterson & Heywood, 2007). Even parents with lower educational levels want to help their children with schoolwork (Caesar & Nelson, 2013). Therefore, it takes an additional effort on the part of the school to help parents be involved in school life.

There is some research evidence supporting the deficit model. Bilingual children sometimes have lower levels of achievement in verbal and literacy tests (Bialystok, 2009; Shany & Geva, 2012), especially when they are tested in their weaker language. At the same time, even children who display deficits in one area may perform better than monolinguals in other areas. For example, in a study by Calvo and Bialystok (2014), bilingual children scored lower than monolinguals on language tests, but outperformed them on executive functioning tests. While the deficit model encompasses many aspects of child development, in this chapter, only its sociolinguistic applications to biliteracy will be addressed. All in all, the balance of the available evidence suggests that, while immigrant children face many obstacles in acquisition of L2 literacy, their parents have resources and motivation to provide the necessary help and collaborate with mainstream schools.

2. METHODOLOGICAL APPROACHES TO EXPLORING THE IMPACT OF THE SOCIO-CULTURAL CONTEXT ON SECOND LANGUAGE LITERACY AND BILITERACY

Most research on home and community biliteracy practices presented and discussed in this chapter applied longitudinal ethnographic observation as the main methodological approach. As a method of social research, ethnography seeks to capture and understand the meanings and dynamics of human behaviour in particular socio-cultural settings which are impossible to observe by using quantitative methods (Hammersley & Atkinson, 1983). The ethnographic method focuses on observations of both the form and content of verbal and non-verbal interactions between individuals (teacher, parents and children, and peers) and their patterns of action (Gregory, 1998). In the case of home and community literacy practices, data collection includes various documents (e.g., self-made books, greeting cards, reading reports, shopping lists), drawings, in-depth interviews with participants (children, parents, teachers, and policy-makers) and their life histories.

During the last two decades, a new research methodology has emerged and developed. Linguistic ethnography is a combination of ethnographic (observations, field notes) and linguistic methods, such as the analysis of home literacy practices and scaffolding strategies (Creese, 2008; Rampton et al., 2004). This methodology permits researchers to address literacy practices at home and in the community, not as a separate discipline but as viewed from the natural socio-cultural context in which they take place. Reyes and Azuara (2008) highlighted that this natural context is critical to exploring the second language literacy and biliteracy acquisition. "The advantage of analyzing these data across multiple methods is that in naturalistic activities relevant to the children's daily lives, they are able to demonstrate knowledge that they cannot show in the more artificial setting of the reading assessment tasks" (Reyes & Azuara, 2008, p. 387). Kenner, Kress, Al-Khatib, Kam, and Tsai (2004) also stressed the limitation of the task-based experimental approach for examining language minority children's second language literacy and biliteracy. While "naturalistic observation may be more taxing to analyze", it "can potentially illuminate children's developmental pathways by showing how they make use of symbols in different kinds of texts within a variety of social interactions" (Kenner et al., 2004, p. 128).

Quantitative methods are employed less often in this field. It is difficult to quantify family language practices, policies, and attitudes because the use of structured questionnaires and scales often leads to the loss of fine distinctions. However, quantitative methods also have their strengths. Standardized tests can be administered to large samples, allowing researchers to perform statistical analysis and build quantitative models to reveal the impact of social factors on second language literacy and biliteracy. Quantitative studies usually collect information about social factors through questionnaires or structured interviews, while information about literacy development is usually collected through standardized tests.

To summarize, research on the social context of second language literacy and biliteracy employs both qualitative and quantitative methodology. Currently, linguistic ethnography is the leading approach to research literacy in bilingual children as it allows researchers to conduct observations in a naturalistic environment. Quantitative studies allow researchers to assess large samples, but are limited in the depth of sociolinguistic information they collect, and may be more suitable for minority languages with large numbers of speakers than those with small numbers.

3. NORTH AMERICAN CONTEXT – DIFFERENCES IN LANGUAGE AND LITERACY POLICY

Studying the social context of second language literacy and biliteracy is impossible without addressing state policies on bilingual and biliteracy education, which affect both school and family policies. While bilingual and biliterate children exist in every corner of the world, in each country they have unique experiences depending on the country's educational policy, the status of their language, and societal attitudes toward bilingualism. The United States and Canada have long traditions of immigration; however, there are still unresolved issues in the state policies and societal attitudes toward bilingual children in these North American countries. In this section, we present an overview of bilingual education policies in the United States and Canada. In addition, throughout the chapter we will address the interaction of the state policies and other factors in the societal context of biliteracy.

The number of children growing up bilingually in North America, especially in the United States, is steadily increasing, and this situation is expected to continue in the future (M. Suárez-Orozco & Páez, 2008). The bilingual population is very diverse. The majority are immigrants or children/grandchildren of immigrants; however, there are also children from minority communities that have lived in North America for a while (or since humans arrived in North America), such as the Amish or Hutterites, or children from Native American communities. Not surprisingly, there are different policies regarding heritage language education and L2 acquisition concerning different subpopulations of bilingual children. In addition, Canadian and American policies for bilingual education vary due to the different linguistic landscapes and histories in these countries.

The Canadian context

Canada, being officially bilingual, provides state support for education in both English and French. Although educational practices vary from province to province, full secondary education at public schools is available in English, French, or a combination of both. State-funded preschools can offer support for additional languages – for example, the Aboriginal Head Start program provides instruction in indigenous languages (HDRC, 2010). French is the native language of 21% of Canadians, an additional 20.6% speak a language other than English or French as their mother tongue, and the remainder are native English speakers (Statistics Canada, 2011). About 4% of the Canadian population are Native Americans (usually referred to as First Nations, Inuit, and Métis in Canadian discourse). However, only about 30% of them have some knowledge of an indigenous language, not necessarily at the native level

(Statistics Canada, 2011). Many language minorities are interested in preserving and promoting their languages; however, teaching these languages happens mostly through private and community institutions (Duff & Li, 2009). Some state schools offer instruction in minority languages. For example, schools in Nova Scotia offer classes in Scottish Gaelic, due to the presence of a Gaelic minority (Dunbar, 2008). Schools with large indigenous populations offer classes in the corresponding indigenous languages. First Nations (indigenous) communities enjoy growing control over the education of their children as almost all schools on the reserves are under band leadership. In these schools English is usually the official language of instruction, while indigenous languages are taught as subjects and used for school events and informal interactions (Bell, 2004). Public school boards also provide instruction in heritage languages (defined as languages other than English, French, Aboriginal, and sign languages) to students from minority language communities (Cummins, 2001).

Immigrant children in areas with big immigrant populations are provided with some help learning English in special classes (Burnaby, 2008). However, there are still relatively few bilingual programs for ESL learners. Throughout Canada, French immersion programs are provided for English speakers and other language minorities (Burnaby, 2008). Thus, Canada is both *de jure* and *de facto*, a multilingual country with two official languages in which schooling is available, and with multiple indigenous and minority languages having official status and state support within certain local communities. However, speakers of languages that do not have any official status in the country have limited state support for education in these languages.

The American context

American English is *de facto* the only official language of the United States at the federal level, although there is no law that would state so and no mention of it in the Constitution (Crawford, 2000). Individual states may pass legislation that gives an official status to other languages. For example, Hawaiian is the second official language of Hawaii; Alaska gives official status to its native languages; in Oklahoma the Cherokee language has official status within Cherokee territories; and New Mexico grants Spanish special status (Crawford, 2000). Several states have also passed bills that support the "English plus" policy in which English holds official status, but learning and maintenance of other languages are also encouraged (Crawford, 1992).

Individual states also have the power to implement programs that provide support to language minority children, including bilingual programs in the public school system. The majority of immigrants in the United States are from Latin America, and the majority of bilingual children speak Spanish as their first language (Hernandez, Macartney, & Denton, 2010). Accordingly, there are more services and programs for Spanish-English bilingual children than for other bilinguals.

The No Child Left Behind bill was authorized by the American government in 2001 (NCLB, 2001). It caused a massive change in how schools assess and educate bilinguals and English language learners (ELLs). It created a *de facto* official language policy for public schools, which might put ELL students at a disadvantage (Caldas, 2013). The idea behind the bill is to allow equal educational opportunities for all children in the United States. A significant portion of the bill is concerned with ELLs, who are defined as "limited English proficient" and "at risk" for not acquiring English at the same rate as native speakers of English. The bill does not address these children's funds of knowledge, and the focus of the policies following the bill is to increase the English proficiency of ELLs, not to promote their native languages. Several parts of the bill state that school programs may include materials in languages other than English and make instructional use of other languages. However, in order to receive funding, schools are pressured to focus on the acquisition of English in order for students to perform better on state-wide standardized tests (Caldas, 2013). Since knowledge of minority languages is not tested, it receives lower priority than knowledge of English. The issue with the bill, and the testing standards it requires, is that ELLs are not defined as bilinguals but as children with low scores on measures of English proficiency. As soon as their scores achieve the "proficient" level, students are no longer defined as ELLs and are put into the same category as native speakers of English (Caldas, 2013). Thus, the tests do not monitor the longitudinal progress of ELLs.

In summary, bilingualism and biliteracy in the United States are not an official priority, and the emphasis is on the acquisition of English literacy. In Canada, French-English bilingualism is actively supported by the government and significant efforts have been made with regard to producing relatively balanced bilinguals. Indigenous languages, after years of persecution, now enjoy many benefits in both the United States and Canada, and revitalization projects are underway in many indigenous communities (Reyhner & Lockard, 2009). However, English remains the dominant language of education for the indigenous peoples as well. In the United States, due to a large percentage of Spanish speakers in the population, Spanish has special status in the educational system. There are numerous Spanish-English bilingual and biliterate programs, although most exist at kindergarten and elementary levels. Children speaking other languages usually have rather limited options for developing language and literacy skills in their native languages in public schools.

4.   HOME LITERACY PRACTICES AND PARENTAL
ATTITUDES TOWARD L1 AND L2 LITERACY

There is increasing evidence from ethnographic studies that children growing up in multilingual or bilingual homes tend to have access to literacy practices in different languages (Dworin & Moll, 2006; Kenner & Gregory, 2012). These studies examine literacy acquisition in L1 and L2 as embedded in specific social contexts, such as the home, the community, or the classroom. What socio-cultural factors in a home context influence the development of biliteracy? How does the home environment contribute to children's literacy development and how do children transfer knowledge between their L1 and L2? In order to understand children's L2 literacy and biliteracy development, teachers and policy-makers need to explore the strategies that minority parents use at home to support their children's literacy development.

Home literacy practices

There is a wide range of home literacy practices. Some practices are universal, while others are culture-specific. A growing number of longitudinal ethnographic studies have shown that language minority children are likely to be engaged in diverse home literacy activities which enhance their emergent biliteracy skills (e.g., Kenner & Gregory, 2012; Schwarzer, 2001). These practices often start before children enter preschool and continue with school education. Home literacy practices have been found to be related to the family language and literacy policy and to fulfill social purposes, such as intergenerational transmission of funds of knowledge, communication with family members living abroad, and religious observance (Schwartz, 2010). In addition, drawing on Vygotsky's socio-cultural theory (1978), studies have found that biliteracy development scaffolds L2 literacy acquisition (Li, 2006; Reyes, 2006; Ruiz, 1984). Through biliterate practices at home, children begin to develop metalinguistic awareness, which is defined by psycholinguists as a person's explicit knowledge about language, knowledge that can be brought into awareness, verbally reported, and declaratively presented (Bialystok, 2001; Bruck & Genesee, 1995). Children begin to compare the prominent characteristics of their two languages and notice different aspects of oral language (e.g., phonemes, morphemes) and print (Kenner & Gregory, 2012). Metalinguistic awareness, in turn, enhances biliteracy development.

Notably, parental attitudes toward literacy practices are culture-dependent, as are their choices of literacy activities (Volk & de Acosta, 2001; Winsler et al., 2014). Educators need to keep in mind that all cultures with written traditions pay attention to literacy, but ways of literacy acquisition may differ from the mainstream culture of the host country (Schwarzer, 1996; Volk & de Acosta, 2001). This assumption will be addressed in detail in Section 6.

Home and community support of emergent biliteracy

Emergent literacy refers to skills, knowledge, and beliefs that develop before formal acquisition of reading and writing (Crone & Whitehurst, 1999; Sénéchal, LeFevre, Smith-Chant, & Colton, 2001). In alphabetic languages, emergent literacy consists of several components: print knowledge (e.g., how to hold a book and turn pages), letter knowledge, phonological awareness, grapheme-phoneme correspondence, and emergent writing (Whitehurst & Lonigan, 1998). In a longitudinal research project, Reyes (2006) examined emergent literacy practices at home among first-generation Mexican families living in Arizona. The study showed that four-year-old children in these families learned to represent ideas in writing in Spanish and English simultaneously.

According to Reyes (2006), "in a supportive environment, emergent literacy may be a 'natural' process, but it is not a simple one for any child, particularly one who is bilingual; emergent bilinguals need continuous support in both languages from parents and teachers" to become fully biliterate (p. 270). Longitudinal home observations conducted by Reyes revealed that, through participating in diverse literacy practices, family members supported not only the child but also each other in biliteracy development. This role was defined by Reyes as *bidirectional*. Thus, parents and older siblings served as experts and scaffolded L1 print knowledge, yet they became novice learners when they carried out English (L2) literacy practices together. This bidirectional literacy learning within the home context was illustrated by the following example, which shows how Katia's English typing and spelling were facilitated by her father and 10-year-old sister. To help Katia find English letters on the keyboard, the father pronounced them in Spanish. Katia repeated after her father, first in Spanish and then in English. Later her sister joined the activity and everyone spelled the word together in English. The mother also became interested and wanted to know what word they spelled together in English and what the word meant in Spanish. This observation demonstrates how the family members learned from each other in the process of emergent biliteracy development.

In addition, Reyes (2006) showed how home and community environments (supermarket, local library, tax office, clothing store) supported the development of the concept of print in different languages. Through their exposure to different prints, children developed theories about L1 and L2 scripts. For example, when Adam, a four-year-old child, was asked by the researcher to identify which words were written in Spanish, he explicitly noted the letter patterns used in Spanish but not in English, such as double *rr* in the word *perro* "dog" and Ñ as in the word *niña* "girl". Reyes concluded that the diverse literacy practices that took place at home and in the community enabled children to practice in their "zone of proximal development" and provided them with the "opportunity to transact with two overlapping and interactive literate worlds" (2006, p. 286).

The bidirectional nature of home literacy support was also observed by Gregory (2001, 2004), who examined the older sibling's role as a mediator of L2 (English) literacy. The studies focused on Bangladeshi and English children living in neighbouring communities in London's East End. Data were collected through observations of home literacy activities, semi-structured interviews with children, and literacy diaries recorded by older siblings. The older siblings were found to be engaged in a wide range of literacy activities, such as teaching the younger siblings English letters, performing quizzes and competitions, and visiting the library. The nature of the interaction between the older and younger siblings went beyond "scaffolding" or "collaborating learning" and was referred to by the researcher "as a *synergy*, a unique reciprocity whereby siblings act as adjuvants in each other's learning, i.e. older children 'teach' younger siblings and at the same time develop their own learning" (Gregory, 2001, p. 309).

Notably, home literacy practices are more important when it comes to L1 literacy than to L2 literacy. Since schools are not always willing or have resources to support L1 literacy, the responsibility falls on parents. Duursma et al. (2007) found that Hispanic children in bilingual programs were able to acquire English (L2) literacy solely through instruction at school, but they relied on home support for Spanish (L1) literacy. Schwarzer (2001) observed the literacy practices of a trilingual girl. The researcher reported that although the child was in a Spanish-English bilingual elementary program, writing and reading instruction at school was provided mostly in English, with only a few opportunities to practice Spanish. Her Hebrew literacy was supported only at home. Thus, family plays a key role in developing bi- and multiliteracy. Even if parents focus entirely on L1 literacy, this still may produce positive effects on L2 literacy acquisition (Hancock, 2002; L. Reese, Garnier, Gallimore, & Goldenberg, 2000) by increasing language awareness, providing necessary tools and skills for the acquisition of L2 literacy, and building the child's confidence in her abilities to learn.

To conclude, through diverse biliteracy experiences at home and in the community, minority language children acquire print knowledge and develop metalinguistic awareness in different scripts. Thus, home literacy practices facilitate biliteracy development.

Family literacy policy

Family literacy policies are affected by general language policies in particular families. Many immigrant and minority language parents feel strongly about teaching their children the heritage language and literacy as a way of transmitting their values and traditions, strengthening their ethnic identity, and keeping in touch with monolingual relatives (Schwartz, 2010).

Research has shown that limited proficiency in the L2 does not prevent parents from helping their children develop L2 literacy skills (Caesar & Nelson, 2013; Riches & Curdt-Christiansen, 2010; Volk & de Acosta, 2001). In a study of Chinese parents in Montreal, Riches and Curdt-Christiansen (2010) observed that participants helped their children with English homework and read books with them. They also purchased French reading materials and hired tutors to help their children learn French, although they did not speak French themselves. One father sat with two dictionaries for hours to help his daughter with French homework, and several mothers took French classes. While this study was conducted among middle-class, well-educated parents, it does not necessarily mean that parents with lower SES and education levels are not invested in their children's education. Several studies showed that Latino parents from lower SES backgrounds might be eager to be involved and help their children with homework (Anderson & Minke, 2007; Caesar & Nelson, 2013; Volk & de Acosta, 2001; Walker et al., 2013). However, minority parents, especially with lower SES, might experience difficulties in communicating with schools due to a lack of common language or cultural differences. When family literacy policies practices differ from those of the schools, teachers might subscribe to the deficit model and assume that parents are not willing or able to help their children, even more so if parents are uneducated or do not speak English (de Jong, Harper, & Harper, 2005). Minority parents who had negative experiences interacting with teachers and school administrators may become reluctant to communicate with the school. Schools need to encourage parental participation, and these encouragements have to be culturally sensitive (Hidalgo, 1993; Huntsinger & Jose, 2009; Walker et al., 2013).

Reyes and Azuara (2008) examined family literacy policy by taking a close look at three four-year-old children, Dariana, Frida, and Sercan, who lived with their families in an urban area in the U.S. Southwest. The parents of the children were Mexican immigrants with low SES. The parents were interviewed at the beginning of the study to understand their beliefs about home literacy practices and their influence on the children's biliteracy development. In addition, the children, their parents, and relatives were observed participating in diverse biliteracy activities at home. In all three cases the parents reported on the importance of promoting Spanish oral and literacy skills at home. The analysis of the longitudinal observations showed that these parental beliefs were consistent with the literacy practices they commonly conducted at home. The parents' literacy management strategies included involving the children in different literacy events, such as reading a label on yogurt packaging, writing in personal notebooks, or constructing a bilingual prayer book. All observed shared literacy activities were "embedded in meaningful contexts" (Reyes & Azuara, 2008, p. 392). Reyes and Azuara also observed how during shared literacy activities parents used scaffolding strategies to promote children's print knowledge and phonological awareness. In Spanish activities the family members helped the children to distinguish between phonemes and letters in L1 and L2. Thus, these activities facilitated letter–sound correspondence in both languages. In other words, basic literacy skills acquired in L1 were helpful for L2 acquisition.

Similarly, Li (2006) found a critical role of the home context in children's biliteracy development in Mandarin or Cantonese (L1) and English (L2). This one-year ethnographic study examined how family language policy, and in particular parents' attitudes toward biliteracy development, is related to practices at home. The study focused on three Chinese immigrant families with children studying in Grade 1/2 combined classes in Vancouver, an ideal location for biliteracy development due to the high density of Chinese immigrants and good economic prospects for bilinguals. Semi-structured interviews, however, revealed that the parents had different perceptions of literacy learning in L1 and L2. Thus, Alana's parents believed that literacy skills in Chinese would help her acquire English literacy. Their beliefs led to Alana's positive attitude toward biliteracy. The parents also reported teaching Alana oral and written Chinese at home. In the other two cases, the findings showed some discrepancy between the parents' overall positive view of biliteracy and their home practices. Although Anthony and Kevin regularly attended weekend heritage language schools, their parents had low expectations concerning their progress in Chinese. Furthermore, Anthony's parents believed that Chinese learning would be a barrier to his English development, whereas Kevin's parents did not believe that young children could acquire two languages and cultures at the same time. This diversity in the family literacy policy was attributed to intra-family factors, such as parents' perceptions of their minority status in the host society, proficiency levels in the two languages, and several school and societal factors, such as a lack of interest in children's linguistic resources, funds of knowledge among the mainstream teachers, and low quality of instruction in the heritage language schools (see Section 2 for details).

To summarize, the studies reported showed that emergent biliteracy is possible only when there are consistent family literacy practices in L1 or in both L1 and L2. In addition, proactive biliteracy management at home needs to be examined from the ecological perspective, taking into account different intra- and inter-family factors.

5. COMMUNITY-BASED LITERACY DEVELOPMENT PRACTICES AND A COMMUNITY SUPPORT FOR BILITERACY

Minority language parents, unless isolated from their community, do not work on L1 preservation alone. Usually, they have the help of community resources, such as heritage language schools, community centers, and churches. For example, L1 speech is heard at community gatherings, L1 texts are published in community newsletters, and L1 advertisements are posted on the walls of local stores and community centers. Exposure to L1 in the environment shows children that their heritage language is alive and useful in daily life.

Community-based school and biliteracy development

Some immigrant communities assign more value to learning a heritage language in a structured way and establish community schools for that purpose. For example, Chinese immigrant communities in North America usually have heritage language schools. Montreal, which has a large Chinese population, has several Chinese schools, with the largest of them educating over 1,000 students (Curdt-Christiansen, 2009). In a study by Riches and Curdt-Christiansen (2010), Canadian Chinese parents deemed Chinese schools extremely important for their children's development, because they believed in the advantages of bilingualism and biliteracy, and thought that knowledge of an additional language is beneficial. They also felt that only through learning to read in Chinese would the children be able to fully appreciate the rich Chinese culture (Riches & Curdt-Christiansen, 2010). Huang (2013) states that, in his Chinese community, attending Chinese school was almost like a religious practice to which the parents fervently adhered: "Chinese people would drive hours from every direction to take their kids to school. While the rest of America went to church, we learned how to read right to left" (Chapter 2).

However, children might be reluctant to attend heritage language schools for different reasons. In the study by Li (2006), two boys disliked the Chinese school for its rigid and authoritative instructional methods. The methods used in the school were traditional to the Chinese educational system, but the students, used to Canadian schools, found it boring and lacking in freedom and creativity for students. Also, the teachers in these schools are often parent volunteers who do not necessarily have the skills and knowledge to teach. As children grow up, heritage schools might interfere with other extracurricular activities and ultimately lose to cheerleading, football, or just socializing with friends. In order to become more attractive to children, heritage schools need to be attuned to children's interests and, perhaps, re-examine their curriculums and teaching methods.

Besides heritage schools, minority communities often have their own organizations, such as libraries, gyms, restaurants, and community centers. They might also have stores with traditional foods that primarily serve the community, although outsiders might come to shop there as well. Such places inevitably have print objects – signs, ads, price tags, newspapers. They may be only in the L1 or in both L1 and L2. Just by visiting these places and observing adults reading all these objects, children become aware of different scripts. In addition, parents, older siblings, and other community members may teach children to read these print objects, both just for the sake of learning and for practical purposes, such as being able to learn the price of an item.

Community religious practices

Many immigrant and minority communities have their own religious institutions. In these institutions, literacy in L1 is acquired through reading the sacred texts: The Bible, the Torah, and the Quran are the major examples of such texts. While these texts are certainly available in English, the community and family might prefer to read them in their native language. For example, in a study of literacy practices in Puerto Rican families in the United States, children participated in Bible readings in Spanish at home and attended Sunday school and services in Latino churches (Volk & de Acosta, 2001). They were expected by their families and communities to read the Bible in Spanish, not English. In the same vein, being also the hubs of communal gatherings, gossip, fundraisers, and so on, churches are instrumental in heritage language preservation through secular activities, as is the case of Korean immigrants in the United States and Canada (Min, 1992; Park & Sarkar, 2007). They are also seen as places where second-generation children can acquire knowledge of the Korean language and literacy and their Korean identity. International students from Korea also come to these churches in order to keep in touch with their culture while abroad. Thus, a younger generation in these churches can interact not only with adult immigrants but also with their peers, fresh from Korea (Park & Sarkar, 2007). Similar interactions happen in other communities since North America attracts large numbers of international students and expats. Schwarzer (2001) gives an account of the Jewish community in Tucson, Arizona, comprising both local Jewish families and Hebrew-speaking expats and students from Israel.

In addition, in Islam and Judaism, the sacred scripts in Classical Arabic and Hebrew are often used as decorative elements in temples and homes.

While children do not necessarily learn to read the scripts, they become aware of the existence of the scripts, which are different from English. Teachers may also use the alphabets of these scripts for art activities (Schwarzer, 2001). However, the significance assigned to these sacred scripts may actually have a negative effect on L1 maintenance. While for Arabic-speaking Muslims reading the Quran promotes their native language, Muslim children who speak languages other than Arabic, such as Urdu or Farsi, may not have a chance to acquire L1 literacy in community schools because they are taught to read the Quran in Classical Arabic. In a study by Zhang and Bano (2010), Pakistani parents complained that their children learned only Classical Arabic in Sunday school in the local mosques, while Urdu was not taught because it did not have religious significance. Russian- or French-speaking Jews, for example, may have a similar experience in American synagogues that teach only Hebrew in Sunday school.

Summary

Minority language communities have rich resources and practices that help develop L1 literacy and maintain the L1. Some communities may invest more into direct teaching of L1 literacy, such as language schools, while other communities prefer more meaning-focused activities, such as Bible-reading in the L1.

6.   THE INTERACTION BETWEEN HOME, COMMUNITY, AND MAINSTREAM SCHOOLING AND BILITERACY

This section of the chapter will present our analysis of complex relationships between home and community literacy practices and children's experience in mainstream classrooms. As was seen earlier, language minority children gain literacy knowledge not only in mainstream classrooms but also in their homes and communities. The main question is whether there is a continuity of literacy practices between these environments. Most research studies have reported a discontinuity of practices between home, community, and mainstream schools (Li, 2006; Reyes 2006; Reyes & Azuara, 2008; Schwarzer, 2001). One possible explanation for this disconnect is the well-known English-only policy, which might be attributed to policy-makers' and teachers' concerns that their bilingual pupils may become "confused" when dealing with different languages and scripts (Kenner et al., 2004). In such a case, home literacy practices in the L1 might be viewed as hampering the development of literacy in English. This misunderstanding is still frequent even though there are numerous psycholinguistic studies showing how bilingual and biliterate experiences may in fact strengthen metalinguistic awareness and literacy development in the L2 (for reviews see Bialystok, 2001; Dressler & Kamil, 2006; Chapter 4, this volume).

To examine the effect of combining L1 and L2 literacy practices at home and in the community, Kenner et al. (2004) focused on the question of whether the *simultaneous* acquisition of literacy skills in two rather different scripts, such as Chinese and English or Arabic and English, would result in "confusion" for six-year old children. The children received limited input in L1 literacy, Arabic, Chinese, or Spanish in the community schools, while at the same time they acquired literacy in English in mainstream classrooms in London. During a number of videotaped sessions, the children were encouraged by the researchers to teach primary school classmates how to write in their L1. These sessions showed that, even after limited input in L1 literacy, children were able to develop diverse hypotheses about how their writing system works and to draw comparisons between the L1 and L2 scripts. For example, the L1 Arabic-speaking girl, Tala, could stress such distinctive principles of Arabic orthography as the directionality of Arabic (writing from right to left) and in cursive form (letters within words are connected, except for four letters). The researchers also found that the children reinterpreted the differences between English and other writing systems and taught them to their peers in a very original and creative way. The ability to present their L1 orthographies in contrast to the English script was a reflection of metalinguistic awareness which developed as a result of the children's biliterate experience. The researchers concluded that the children were able to handle learning different writing systems at the same time quite well and were not "confused" by simultaneous input.

On the whole, it is important to highlight that there is little evidence that learning to read in the L1 is detrimental to literacy development in the L2. While investigating the influence of home literacy practices in L1 on L2 literacy acquisition, some studies found a positive effect (Hancock, 2002; L. Reese et al., 2000), while others did not find an effect (Howard et al., 2014; Pucci & Ulanoff, 1998). Initially, bilingual children might perform less well than their monolingual peers on L2 tests (e.g., vocabulary, spelling) due to less exposure; however, over time and *with proper schooling, growing input of L2, and a supporting home environment*, these differences lessen and disappear (Golberg, Paradis, & Crago, 2008; Schwartz & Katzir, 2012), while the cognitive and metalinguistic advantages of bilingualism persist for the lifetime.

Discontinuity of literacy practices between home, community, and mainstream school

In certain contexts mainstream teachers do not draw on the children's fund of knowledge as a potential resource for enhancing their success in L2 literacy acquisition and development in mainstream schools. A longitudinal observational study conducted by Reyes and Azuara (2008) showed that young Spanish-English bilingual children were not encouraged to display their knowledge of literacy in Spanish even when the Spanish language was used by bilingual mainstream teachers for clarification and discipline in the classroom. Reyes (2006) stressed that mainstream teachers need to provide academic and social support for emergent biliterate children at school. In addition, the researcher highlighted the need to "listen to the children's voices, to read their emergent biliteracy messages, and most of all, to learn critical lessons from them" (p. 288). It is important for mainstream teachers to understand that natural biliteracy practices at home contribute to children's intensive development of metalinguistic and meta-literacy awareness as well as meta-cognitive skills, as was illustrated earlier by the four-year-old children's ability to compare different scripts and to formulate their theories about L1 and L2 scripts (Kenner, 1999, 2000; Kenner & Gregory, 2012).

Li (2006) noted that even in a school in which 80% of the students were Chinese, no consideration was given to incorporating Chinese into the classroom. The school had only one Chinese employee, who was a teacher's aide and worked with special needs children. No Chinese courses were offered, and students with limited English proficiency were pulled out of classes to study ESL with English-speaking teachers. Even informal use of Chinese was discouraged in school contexts because the teachers believed that the use of Chinese negatively affected the acquisition of English (Li, 2006). Such attitudes toward students' L1 are in line with the deficit model of bilingualism and have many negative consequences, both for immediate success at school and for students' future. If teachers do not consider children's knowledge and skills in the L1, they might underestimate students' abilities and potential (Gathercole, 2013). Devaluing students' first language and literacy and enforcing an English-only policy can diminish students' confidence, lead them to internalize and develop negative attitudes toward their culture, and possibly result in identity problems and family conflicts (Li, 2002, 2006; Valdés, 2001).

Mainstream school teachers might subscribe to the deficit model, thinking that minority families do not practice literacy activities at home or spend only very limited time on literacy events. This may stem from ignorance about the minority culture or from a rigid definition of literacy activities. For example, teachers may think that reading children's books is the most important literacy activity, while parents may come from a culture that does not deem reading children's books important. However, these parents may practice literacy in different ways, such as reading the Bible, telling folk stories, learning to recite prayers and poems, and so on (Volk & de Acosta, 2001). Even when a teacher comes from the same culture as the parents, she may have internalized the deficit model to such an extent that she fails to recognize the valuable literacy practices of her own culture. For example, in Volk and de Acosta's study (2001), while the Latino kindergarten teacher thought that the parents did not conduct any literacy activities at home, leaving all the literacy teaching to the bilingual school, the researchers who closely studied three of the Latino families in question found a multitude of literacy activities both at home and in the community.

In another study by Zhang and Bano (2010), Chinese and Pakistani parents in Ontario complained that the schools did not make any effort to link the school and home literacy practices, and teachers had little idea of the nature of home literacy practices and policies. Current authors' view that it is extremely important for the school and for teachers to send the message to their students' parents that their involvement in school life is crucial. Even if parents have limited resources, they usually find ways to help when they feel that their child needs it and the teacher wants their involvement (Anderson & Minke, 2007).

How can monolingual mainstream teachers foster biliteracy development in linguistically diverse classrooms?

Monolingual teachers do not have to become fluent in their students' languages in order to acknowledge their cultures and to foster bi- and multiliteracy in the classroom (Schwarzer, 2001). Despite speaking only one language, they can still find ways to demonstrate the value and importance of diversity. Creating a multilingual environment is also beneficial for monolingual students because it raises their language awareness and helps them develop metalinguistic skills (Armand & Dagenais, 2005).

Taking time to know children's interests and connecting their home experience ("funds of knowledge") to their school experience may be very beneficial for their literacy acquisition. For example, Kenner (1999) observed that knowledge about the children's interests was helpful for creating meaningful and interesting literacy activities in the classroom. Using culturally familiar materials in the classroom motivates children to study and provides an additional context that facilitates their L2 literacy acquisition (Jiménez, 1997).

Schwarzer et al. (2003) offer multiple strategies for monolingual teachers to foster biliteracy in the mainstream classroom in the United States. According to them, while monolingual teachers may not be able to employ all the literacy resources available in specific languages without a working knowledge of the languages, there are still plenty of resources and strategies for them to use. They can create a multi-literate print environment in the classroom or encourage students to keep bilingual journals or address cards to the family in their native languages. Teachers can also enlist the help of parents, older siblings, and community members to create multilingual projects together with the students. These activities show that the school values children's languages and cultures and provides them with bi- and multilingual adult role models.

Home and mainstream school cooperation on literacy practices in the L2 at home and at school

Cummins (2001) believes that literacy in both L1 and L2 should be promoted simultaneously because the two languages "enrich each other rather than subtracting from each other" (p. 121). In some traditional cultures, mothers might not be able to help their children with studying because of their limited mobility; it might be culturally unacceptable for them to go to a library or an educational center without an adult male relative (Mahrous & Ahmed, 2010). One of the ways for schools to connect with parents is to organize English classes for them. Since mothers are most often the primary caregivers and the ones who stay at home with children, they may have limited knowledge of English and few resources for its acquisition. Immigrant mothers also usually have lower levels of education than immigrant fathers and fewer opportunities to acquire English prior to immigration (Mahrous & Ahmed, 2010). Thus, classes at school, especially during school hours, can give them an opportunity to learn English, which in turn provides them with tools to help their children with schoolwork (Stagg-Peterson & Heywood, 2007). Such classes can also help the school to learn more about parents and their students' cultures.

Intervention programs for minority language children and parents in L1 and L2

An example of a program that aims to involve minority parents in academics and other aspects of their child's life is the Head Start program in the United States. Head Start is a program of the United States Department of Health and Human Services that provides comprehensive early childhood education, health, nutrition, and parent involvement services to low-income children and their families. Although the program runs in all 50 states, several states also have other programs of early childhood education for low-income families. Federal regulations for Head Start programs require that "When a majority of children speak the same language, at least one classroom staff member or home visitor interacting regularly with the children must speak their language" (Human Resources Management, 2004). Furthermore, "Teachers must demonstrate an understanding of the child's family culture and, whenever possible, speak the child's language" (Education and Early Childhood Development, 2004).

Head Start and similar programs help minority children acquire literacy in the L2, and in some cases, when offered in the areas with large minority populations, in the L1. Bumgarner and Brooks-Gunn's (2015) study indicates that children in these programs score higher on English literacy assessments than children from similar backgrounds who stay in home care. Despite the fact that literacy instruction in both L1 and L2 is provided in the Head Start program, home literacy practices are still extremely important. For example, mothers' elaborating and story-reading significantly correlated with emergent literacy skills for children in Head Start (Sparks & Reese, 2012). Some researchers, though, have pointed out that participating in center-based care during infancy is detrimental to the development of L1 skills, especially in the case of underrepresented minorities because the chance of a caregiver speaking their L1 at the care center is practically non-existent (Bumgarner & Brooks-Gunn, 2015).

Summary

Schools, parents, and communities must work together to develop balanced biliteracy in language minority children and instil a sense of pride in their linguistic and cultural background. There are many strategies for fostering multiliteracy in the classroom that can be employed even by monolingual teachers. Existing programs that promote biliteracy in the mainstream classroom demonstrate that children are capable of developing literacy in both languages with proper support and biliteracy, in turn, increases their metalinguistic ability.

7. BIO-SOCIAL FACTORS AFFECTING CHILDREN'S ACHIEVEMENTS IN L2 LITERACY

This section examines the magnitude of bio-social factors, such as immigration status, socio-economic status, parental education, the child's gender, heritage country, and the length of family residence in the host country on children's achievements in L1 and L2 literacy.

Bio-social factors might play even more important roles than the knowledge of L1 in the child's second language literacy acquisition. Winsler et al. (2014), for example, found that demographic factors, such as SES, parental education, and immigration status, had more effect on literacy outcomes than language use at home. Unfortunately, the majority of existing studies on bilingual children in North America do not provide detailed information on the bio-social characteristics of the participants. The information that is typically provided is also problematic because often there are inconsistent criteria for identifying minority language status and few distinctions between different groups. For example, pan-group labels, such as "Latino" or "Asian", are frequently used (Winsler et al., 2014). Studies often do not report parents' age of arrival and lengths of residence and do not report and control for the child's proficiency in the L1, the order and age of acquisition, and the amount of exposure to each language (Castro, 2014). However, all of these factors affect the child's L2 literacy acquisition, and if not controlled for, make direct comparisons between children in one study and between different studies complicated. Ahead we provide a detailed explanation of how the bio-social factors can affect biliteracy acquisition.

Immigration status (parents' place of birth, parents' and children's age of arrival, length of residence, parents' language competence, generational factors)

As was stated earlier, minority language children might come from families where one or both parents were born outside the United States, or from minority communities in which parents were born in the United States, but use a language other than English at home. Immigrant parents can differ in their immigrant status, as some of them arrive in the United States as young children, some as adolescents, and some as adults. Parents' age at the time of arrival and their length of residence in the United States affect patterns of language use at home; those who arrived as children usually know English better and might prefer to use more English with their children, or even switch to English completely. In that case, children pick up their heritage language only from grandparents and other relatives, not from their parents (Winsler et al., 2014). Parents' age of arrival and length of residence in the host country also affect how assimilated they are in the new culture and how familiar they are with the local educational system. If they arrived in the United States at a young age, they would either experience U.S. education first-hand, or understand how to prepare their children for success at school, or else at least be able to internalize the literacy practices of the host community. In many studies of immigrant children, the parents' age of arrival is disregarded, but an immigrant mother who arrived in the United States as a young child would be more similar to second-generation immigrants and less so to those who arrived as adults (Winsler et al., 2014). U.S.- and Canada-born mothers also might have higher levels of education than immigrant mothers from the same language minority (Winsler et al., 2014).

Legal status of the parents in the host country is also important for the child's education. If parents are undocumented immigrants, this might severely affect their children's schooling. Parents without legal status might be reluctant to send their children to state-sponsored preschool programs, such as Head Start, and less willing to communicate with teachers at schools.

To our knowledge, this effect is not demonstrated in studies (Goldenberg, Rueda, & August, 2007). However, undocumented immigrants might also be reluctant to communicate with researchers, which makes them an extremely hard group to study.

The circumstances of immigration also need to be considered. These circumstances can be very traumatic, as is the case with refugees. It might lead parents to abandon their first language and literacy because of its association with traumatic events. This happened, for instance, to some Holocaust survivors from Germany who immigrated to the United States and Canada (Schmid, 2011) and intentionally switched to English. In such cases, parents might not only not be proficient enough in the L2 to help their children to acquire L2 literacy, but also not teach the L1 to their children because of the negative associations. Traumatic circumstances of immigration can also lead to a more painful adaptation process in the new country and to parents paying less attention to their children's education in the first years after immigration, when the traumatic experiences are still fresh in memory. Currently, it is still not clear how immigration circumstances and the adaptation process affect children's L2 literacy (Arzubiaga, Rueda, & Monzo, 2002; Monzo & Rueda, 2001).

Socio-economic status

Children from families with lower SES are known to have difficulties acquiring language and developing literacy, even when they are monolingual (Whitehurst & Lonigan, 1998). According to the parental investment model, parents with lower SES tend to invest less time and fewer resources in children's cognitive and linguistic development (Conger, Conger, & Martin, 2010). Lower SES might lead to fewer educational resources and activities inside and outside the home (Mistry & Wadsworth, 2011).

As a group, language minority children are more likely to have lower SES than the general population. Almost 70% of language minority children in the United States are considered low-income, and more than a third have parents with less than a high-school education, which also contributes to lower SES (Matthews & Ewen, 2010). Therefore, in many studies of bilingual children, it is very hard to distinguish between the influence of SES and bilingualism on academic outcomes (Castro, 2014). The notion that bilingualism puts children at risk for lower academic performance is mistaken because academic results are actually better predicted by SES (Halle et al., 2014; Winsler et al., 2014). Children with lower SES are more likely to live in poorer neighbourhoods and attend schools with more language minority students. They are also more likely to live in poverty and/or have learning disabilities. All of these factors affect the general standards of education at school (Aikens & Barbarin, 2008; Pianta et al., 2002; Xue & Meisels, 2004).

SES usually correlates highly with parents' educational level, and maternal education is sometimes used as an indicator of SES (Duncan & Magnuson, 2005). However, in immigrants, especially in the early years after immigration, there might be discrepancies between educational level and SES; educated immigrants are not necessarily able to find jobs that fit their qualifications, especially if their knowledge of the language of the host country is limited (e.g., Duursma et al., 2007; Schwartz, 2012).

Parents' education

Maternal education is positively associated with early vocabulary development (Richman, Miller, & LeVine, 1992; Rogoff, 2003), and this, in turn is a significant predictor of later reading comprehension (Rowe, Raudenbush, & Goldin-Meadow, 2012). For monolingual children, maternal education may be a stronger predictor of language acquisition than SES (Hoff, 2003, 2013). However, in immigrant populations, mothers might be less educated not due to their academic abilities but due to the fact that in their home country there were significantly fewer opportunities for women to receive education. Both parents' educational levels, therefore, need to be considered while studying literacy development of children from immigrant families. For instance, in a study by Winsler et al. (2014), parental education predicted literacy acquisition alongside other factors.

The child's gender

A child's gender is determined by far more than biological characteristics. Different cultures associate specific customs and practices with gender and have different expectations with respect to education for boys and girls. In more traditional cultures boys and girls may engage in radically different socialization practices (Qin, 2006). As a result, gender could affect children's academic performance in terms of grades. Immigrant girls in the United States mostly outperform boys academically, regardless of country of origin (Cammarota, 2004; Feliciano & Rumbaut, 2005; Rong & Brown, 2001; Qin, 2006). Research on the non-immigrant White population concludes that the female advantage, which also exists in the general monolingual population, might be due to a perception that girls are better suited for traditional school practices and that teachers favour girls (Connel, 2000). However, as will be discussed ahead, other factors might add to girls' success at school in the immigrant population.

While the difference in academic performance between immigrant boys and girls continues well into college (Qin, 2006), it starts as early as preschool, when girls outperform boys on L2 literacy and cognitive measures (Winsler et al., 2014). In middle and high school, immigrant girls continue to outperform boys on reading and other measures (Feliciano, 2012). The female advantage in the immigrant population is especially striking, since many of the immigrants come from countries in which females have limited educational opportunities and where schooling for girls is not encouraged. Mothers in immigrant families are typically less educated than fathers (Capps et al., 2005). However, just in one generation the situation turns around completely.

Several factors might explain the female advantage: stricter parental control, more positive school experiences and attitudes toward school, and perception of education as the ultimate opportunity for an independent future (Feliciano, 2012; Qin, 2006). Immigrant parents tend to monitor girls' behaviour and socialization practices much more strictly than those of boys (Lee, 2001; Qin, 2006; Sarroub, 2001). Girls might be given more domestic responsibilities than boys (Zhou & Bankstone, 2001), and fewer opportunities to spend time outside and apart from the family (Espiritu, 2001; Feliciano, 2012). This leads to more time being available for homework, and perhaps more identification with school, because in many cases school becomes the only activity not related to the family that girls are allowed to do (Lopez, 2003; Olsen, 1997). Girls might also view education as an opportunity for future emancipation and empowerment (Keaton, 1999).

SES may also contribute to the gender gap in educational achievements; lower SES seems to be much more detrimental to boys' performance, while in families with higher SES, the gap between the genders is very small (Feliciano, 2012). In general, school seems to be a more positive environment for immigrant girls than for boys. Research findings suggest that boys are more influenced by social pressure to engage in problematic behaviours at school, especially at schools with more disadvantaged populations (Peguero, 2009; Qin, 2003; Smith, 2002; Stanton-Salazar, 2001; C. Suárez-Orozco & Qin, 2006). Boys might feel less support from teachers and administrators, and more prejudices especially later on in middle and high schools, when immigrant boys of lower SES are "criminalized" by school staff (Cammarota, 2004; Lopez, 2003; Watkins & Melde, 2010). As a result, boys begin to care less about their studies and have lower expectations of and fewer positive attitudes toward education (Feliciano, 2012; Valenzuela, 1999).

Heritage country

The factor of the heritage country (country of origin) may have a smaller influence on literacy acquisition than socio-economic status, but this influence is still perceptible and significant (Winsler et al., 2014). Not all children of immigrant parents necessarily have difficulties in school. As presented earlier, children of highly educated immigrants from higher SES backgrounds, such as the children of immigrant university professors, may have an advantage over their monolingual peers. A difference in cultural practices may also contribute to school achievements; for example, Asian students are generally high-achieving because school, discipline, and rote learning are valued in the Asian culture (Jung, Fuller, & Galindo, 2012).

However, an overarching category such as "Asian" cannot possibly be homogeneous. The stereotype about high-achieving students, characterizing primarily the Chinese culture, is often attributed to all Asian students, even though they come from different countries and cultures. In reality, Chinese students tend to outperform Korean, Thai, and Vietnamese students academically (Lim & Lim, 2003; Winsler et al., 2014). In addition, even Chinese immigrants do not represent a homogeneous community. High-achieving students in the Chinese community usually come from middle-class families with educated parents, often university graduates and academics (Shah, 2011). Because of their achievements, the school system tends to overlook the needs of children from low-income Chinese families with less educated parents who speak limited English. Such children often experience difficulties in school but are not provided with the resources to solve these difficulties since they are expected to do well by educators and administrators (Derderian-Aghajanian & Cong, 2012; Shah, 2011).

The largest group of language minority children in the United States comes from Latin America. Latino students, as a group, have the lowest attainment and achievement rates of all ethnic groups in the United States (Duursma et al., 2007; Roderick, 2000). For example, the Latino-White achievement gaps are as large as 0.77 standard deviations in math and 0.52 standard deviations in reading in English in kindergarten. By first grade, this gap shrinks by about a third; however, it remains evident at least until the end of elementary school (Reardon & Galindo, 2009).

As with Chinese students, the Latino population is far from being homogenous. For instance, verbal development and school readiness have been found to vary according to heritage country in the Latino population (De Feyter & Winsler, 2009; Leventhal, Xue, & Brooks-Gunn, 2006). It might be that literacy skills in the Latino population also depend on heritage country, as there are variations in cultural practices. For instance, Dominican immigrant mothers tend to use more language with children than Mexican immigrant mothers, who rely more on gestures and gaze (Tamis-Lemonda et al., 2012). Even immigrants from one country can come from different cultural backgrounds. A significant number of immigrants from Latin America come from indigenous populations. As such, their native language might not be Spanish, and even when it is Spanish, their culture may differ from the mainstream culture of their country. However, most studies treat all Latino students as one homogenous group and overlook these differences. For example, Caesar and Nelson (2013), in a study of literacy development in children of Mexican origin enrolled in a Migrant Head Start program, reported that approximately 25% of their participants were families speaking one of the Mixtec languages, a group of indigenous languages spoken in Mexico. Nevertheless, all these families were simply included in the "Latino" group, and participated in a literacy intervention that promoted L1 Spanish literacy while it was not clear whether Spanish was the L1 of all the participating children. Including indigenous immigrants from Latin America into the Latino group prevents them from receiving support for their native languages, as all the additional support they can count on is given in Spanish.

To recapitulate, simply lumping immigrants together into larger umbrella categories, such as "Asian" or "Latino", or even "Chinese" and "Mexican", can lead to overlooking differences between distinct immigrant groups and cultures, which in turn may lead to overlooking the problems certain groups can have with literacy acquisition and not providing necessary services.

Summary

The effects of bio-social factors on literacy acquisition in language minority children are a complex and under-researched issue. Most of the studies on the issue in North America were conducted in the United States, and it is not clear whether the conclusions can be extrapolated to the Canadian context. More studies are needed that would specifically investigate the issue in Canada. It is also extremely difficult to disentangle the various factors since they are tightly interwoven. Some bio-social factors may lead to an immigrant advantage in the acquisition of the L2 literacy, while others can lead to an immigrant disadvantage. It is important to understand that children should be considered in the context of both their minority language community and their personal bio-social factors, such as their gender, SES, and country of origin. Researchers need to be extremely careful when making conclusions about different groups of language minority children, as sometimes these conclusions can suffer from overgeneralization and stigmatization.

SUMMARY OF THE MAIN POINTS

Research on the social context of L2 literacy and biliteracy is grounded within diverse theoretical perspectives, such as funds of knowledge, Vygotsky's sociocultural framework, family literacy policy, the deficit model, and the ecological approach toward L2 literacy and biliteracy. With regards to methodology, although research on the social context of L2 literacy and biliteracy employs diverse methodologies, linguistic ethnography is the leading approach to the study of literacy in bilingual children as it allows observing them in a naturalistic environment.

Children growing up in multilingual or bilingual homes tend to have access to a variety of texts and literacy practices involving different languages and scripts. This access is largely supported and frequently initiated by family members and relatives through scaffolding and bidirectional interactions. Minority language communities provide children with rich resources and practices for L1 literacy acquisition and development. Communities may value direct teaching of L1 literacy in language schools or prefer more meaning-focused activities, such as Bible-reading in the L1. In addition, collaborative interactions among families, communities, and mainstream schools are vital to the development of L2 literacy and biliteracy in language minority children and their cultural and linguistic identity.

Up until now, the effects of bio-social factors on literacy acquisition in language minority children have been an under-researched issue. The existing data on the link between bio-social factors and L2 literacy acquisition and development are not clear-cut and should be verified in longitudinal studies.

FURTHER RESEARCH DIRECTIONS

- There is a need for longitudinal research on the effect of the home language literacy and biliteracy practices on L2 literacy development.
- It is important to verify practical suggestions for fostering multilingual literacy awareness in the classroom (see Chapter 4), by means of intervention studies.
- Future investigation of the social context of L2 literacy and biliteracy in under-researched language minority communities will extend our understanding of the issue.
- It is necessary to construct culturally sensitive tools for examining family literacy beliefs and practices.
- With regards to methodology, more studies employing mixed methods are needed.
- In approaching current language and literacy policy within the North American context, it is important to take into consideration the differences between the US and Canadian linguistic landscapes.

SUGGESTIONS FOR FURTHER READING

García, O., Zakharia, Z., & Otcu, B. (Eds.). (2013). *Bilingual community education and multilingualism*. Bristol: Multilingual Matters.

Hornberger, N. (Ed.). (2003). *Continua of biliteracy*. Clevedon, UK: Multilingual Matters.

Kenner, C. (2000). *Home pages: Literacy links for bilingual children*. Stoke-on-Trent: Trentham Books.

Zentella, A. C. (Ed.). (2005). *Building on strength: Language and literacy in Latino families and communities*. New York: Teachers College Press.

RESOURCES FOR EDUCATORS

- Creating a multilingual print environment in the classroom helps children to utilize their native language for L2 learning and shows them that their language and culture are valued. In kindergarten and elementary school, teachers can make bilingual alphabet posters with pictures to display on classroom walls. There are also videos on YouTube with alphabet songs in different languages.

    Alphabets on Omniglot (http://www.omniglot.com/writing/alphabets. htm)

- Free online translators, such as Google Translate, can help translate basic words and expressions to use in the classroom. If one is unsure about pronunciation, one can check it on Forvo.com, which has pronunciations of millions of words from most major world languages. Google Translate provides translations in the target language script. If the script is not Latin, one can use My Languages (http://mylanguages.org/transliteration.php) to transliterate the words.

- Memrise, Quizlet, and Anki websites offer free language learning flashcard sets. The cards are organized according to language and topic. For example, one can find sets of cards for teaching the days of the week in English with translations to Spanish, Russian, Hindi, and many more languages. These flashcards can be used for activities in a computer classroom or for homework.

    Anki (http://ankisrs.net/index.html)
    Memrise (https://www.memrise.com)
    Quizlet (http://quizlet.com/)

- RhinoSpike offers audio in foreign languages on demand. Posted texts will be recorded by native speakers. https://rhinospike.com/

- Chilolla has English learning activities for children. http://www.chillola. com/index.html/

- International Children's Digital Library offers thousands of digital children's books in many languages. Books are searchable by language, country, genre, subject, and age of the audience. http://en.childrenslibrary. org/

- Mamalisa's World features children's songs and poetry in many languages. There are original lyrics, English translations, and recordings. http://www. mamalisa.com/
- ELODiL is a Canadian project aimed at raising language awareness in school students. The website has activities that help to develop metalinguistic skills in children of all school ages. http://www.elodil.com/

REFERENCES

Aikens, N.L., & Barbarin, O. (2008). Socioeconomic differences in reading trajectories: The contribution of family, neighborhood, and school contexts. *Journal of Educational Psychology, 100*(2), 235–251.

Anderson, K.J., & Minke, K.M. (2007). Parent involvement in education: Toward an understanding of parents' decision making. *Journal of Educational Research, 100*, 311–323.

Armand, F., & Dagenais, D. (2005). Languages and immigration: Raising awareness of language and linguistic diversity in schools. *Journal of the Canadian Studies Association* [Special issue], 99–102.

Arzubiaga, A., Rueda, R., & Monzo, L. (2002). *Family matters related to reading engagement of Latina/o children. CIERA REPORT #1–015.* Ann Arbor: Center for the Improvement of Early Reading Achievement, University of Michigan.

August, D., Carlo, M., Dressler, C., & Snow, C. (2005). The critical role of vocabulary development for English language learners. *Learning Disabilities Research & Practice, 20*(1), 50–57.

Baker, C. (2001). *Foundation of bilingual education and bilingualism* (3rd ed.). Boston, MA: Allyn and Bacon.

Barton, D. (1994). *Literacy: An introduction to the ecology of written language.* Oxford: Blackwell.

Bell, D. (2004). *Sharing our success: The case studies in Aboriginal schooling.* Kelowna, BC: Society for the Advancement of Excellence in Education. Retrieved from http://www. cla.sd57.bc.ca/fileadmin/sites/cla.sd57.bc.ca/SPSS/ab_ed/Sharing_our_Success.pdf

Berry, V. (2013). *English impact report: Investigating English language learning outcomes at the primary school level in rural India.* British Council. Retrieved from http://www. britishcouncil.in/sites/britishcouncil.in2/files/english_impact_report_2013.pdf

Bialystok, E. (2001). *Bilingualism in development.* Cambridge: Cambridge University Press.

Bialystok, E. (2009). Bilingualism: The good, the bad, and the indifferent. *Bilingualism, Language and Cognition, 12*, 3–11.

Bruck, M., & Genesee, F. (1995). Phonological awareness in young second language learners. *Journal of Child Language, 22*, 307–324.

Bruner, J. (1986). *Actual minds, possible worlds.* Cambridge, MA: Harvard University Press.

Bumgarner, E., & Brooks-Gunn, J. (2015). The association between early care arrangements, quality, and emergent bilingual Latino American children's math and literacy skills in English. *Early Childhood Research Quarterly, 30*, 32–44.

Burnaby, B. (2008). Language policy and education in Canada. In In S. May & N. H. Hornberger (Eds.), *Encyclopedia of Language and Education: Vol. 1. Language policy and political issues in education* (2nd ed., pp. 331–341). New York: Springer.

Caesar, L. G., & Nelson, N. W. (2013). Parental involvement in language and literacy acquisition: A bilingual journaling approach. *Child Language Teaching and Therapy, 30*(3), 317–336.

Caldas, S. J. (2013). Assessment of academic performance: The impact of No Child Left Behind policies on bilingual education: A ten year retrospective. In V. C. Mueller Gathercole (Ed.), *Issues in the assessment of bilinguals* (pp. 205–231). Bristol: Multilingual Matters.

Calvo, A., & Bialystok, E. (2014). Independent effects of bilingualism and socioeconomic status on language ability and executive functioning. *Cognition, 130*(3), 278–288.

Cammarota, J. (2004). The gendered and racialized pathways of Latina and Latino youth: Different struggles, different resistances in the urban context. *Anthropology and Education Quarterly, 35*(1), 53–74.

Capps, R., Fix, M. E., Murray, J., Ost, J., Passel, J. S., & Herwantoro Hernandez, S. (2005). *The new demography of America's schools: Immigration and the No Child Left Behind Act.* Washington, DC: Urban Institute.

Carlo, M., August, D., McLaughlin, B., Snow, C., Dressler, C., Lippman, D., . . . White, C. (2004). Closing the gap: Addressing the vocabulary needs of English language learners in bilingual and mainstream classrooms. *Reading Research Quarterly, 39*(2), 188–215.

Castro, D. C. (2014). The development and early care and education of dual language learners: Examining the state of knowledge. *Early Childhood Research Quarterly, 29*(4), 693–698.

Conger, R. D., Conger, K. J., & Martin, M. J. (2010). Socioeconomic status, family processes, and individual development. *Journal of Marriage and Family, 72*, 685–704.

Connell, R. W. (2000). *The men and the boys.* Berkeley: University of California Press.

Crawford, J. (1992). *Language loyalties: A source book on the official English controversy.* Chicago: University of Chicago Press.

Crawford, J. (2000). *At war with diversity: US language policy in an age of anxiety.* Clevedon, UK: Multilingual Matters.

Creese, A. (2008). Linguistic ethnography. In K. A. King & N. H. Hornberger (Eds.), *Encyclopedia of Language and Education: Vol. 10. Research methods in language and education* (2nd ed., pp. 229–241). New York: Springer.

Creese, A., & Martin, P. (Eds.). (2003). *Multilingual class room ecologies.* Clevedon, UK: Multilingual Matters.

Creese, A., & Martin P. (2008). Classroom ecologies: A case study from a Gujarati complementary school in England. In A. Creese, P. Martin, & N. H. Hornberger (Eds.), *Encyclopedia of Language and Education: Vol. 9. Ecology of language* (2nd ed., pp. 263–272). Boston: Springer Science + Business Media.

Crone, D. A., & Whitehurst, G. J. (1999). Age and schooling effects on emergent literacy and early reading skills. *Journal of Educational Psychology, 91*(4), 604.

Cummins, J. (2001). *Negotiating identities: Education for empowerment in a diverse society* (2nd ed.). Los Angeles: California Association for Bilingual Education.

Curdt-Christiansen, X. L. (2009). Invisible and visible language planning: Ideological factors in the family language policy of Chinese immigrant families in Quebec. *Language Policy, 8*(4), 351–375. doi:10.1007/s10993–009–9146–7

Datta, M. (2000). *Bilinguality and literacy: Principles and practice*. London: Continuum.

De Feyter, J., & Winsler, A. (2009). The early developmental competencies and school readiness of low-income, immigrant children: Influences of generation, race/ethnicity, and national origins. *Early Childhood Research Quarterly, 24*, 411–431.

De Jong, E. J., Harper, C. A., & Harper, A. (2005). Preparing mainstream teachers for English-language learners: Is being a good teacher good enough? *Teacher Education Quarterly, 32*(2), 101–124.

De La Piedra, M. T. (2011). "Tanto necesitamos de aqu´ı como necesitamos de all´a": *Leer juntas* among Mexican transnational mothers and daughters. *Language and Education, 25*(1), 65–78.

Derderian-Aghajanian, A., & Cong, W. C. (2012). How culture affects on English Language Learners' (ELLs') outcomes, with Chinese and Middle Eastern immigrant students. *International Journal of Business and Social Sciences, 3*(5), 172–180.

Dressler, C., & Kamil, M. (2006). Chapter 6 – First and second-language literacy. In D. August & T. Shanahan (Eds.), *Developing literacy in second-language learners: A report of the national literacy panel on language-minority children and youth* (pp. 197–238). Mahwah, NJ: Erlbaum.

Dworin, J., & Moll, L. (2006). Introduction to special issue on biliteracy. *Journal of Early Childhood Literacy, 6*(3), 293–322.

Duff, P. A., & Li, D. (2009). Indigenous, minority, and heritage language education in Canada: Policies, contexts, and issues. *Canadian Modern Language Review/ La Revue Canadienne Des Langues Vivantes, 66*(1), 1–8.

Dunbar, R. (2008, May). Minority language renewal: Gaelic in Nova Scotia, and lessons from abroad. *Reader in Celtic and Law*. Retrieved from https://gaelic.novascotia.ca/sites/default/files/files/MinorityLanguageRenewalGaelic-En.pdf

Duncan, G. J., & Magnuson, K. A. (2005). Can family socioeconomic resources account for racial and ethnic test score gaps? *The Future of Children, 15*, 35–54. http://dx.doi.org/10.1353/foc.2005.0004

Duursma, E., Romero-Contreras, S., Szuber, A., Proctor, P., Snow, C., August, D., & Calderón, M. (2007). The role of home literacy and language environment on bilinguals' English and Spanish vocabulary development. *Applied Psycholinguistics, 28*(1), 171–190.

Education and Early Childhood Development, 45C.F.R. § 1304. 21 (2004).

Espiritu, Y. L. (2001). "We don't sleep around like White girls do": Family, culture and gender in Filipina American lives. *Signs, 26*, 415–440.

Evans, M. A., & Saint-Aubin, J. (2005). What children are looking at during shared storybook reading. *Psychological Science, 16*, 913–920.

Feliciano, C. (2012). The female educational advantage among adolescent children of immigrants. *Youth & Society, 44*, 431–449.

Feliciano, C., & Rumbaut, R. G. (2005). Gendered paths: Educational and occupational expectations and outcomes among adult children of immigrants. *Ethnic and Racial Studies, 28*, 1087–1118.

Fuller, B., Bridges, M., Bein, E., Jang, H., Jung, S., Rabe-Hesketh, S., . . . Kuo, A. (2009). The health and cognitive growth of Latino toddlers: At risk or immigrant paradox? *Maternal and Child Health Journal, 13*, 755–768.

Garcia Coll, C., & Marks, A.K. (Eds.). (2012). *The immigrant paradox in children and adolescents: Is becoming American a developmental risk?* Washington, DC: American Psychological Association.

Gathercole, V.C.M. (2013). *Issues in the assessment of bilinguals.* Bristol: Multilingual Matters.

Golberg, H., Paradis, J., & Crago, M. (2008). Lexical acquisition over time in minority first language children learning English as a second language. *Applied Psycholinguistics, 29,* 1–25.

Goldenberg, C., Rueda, R. S., & August, D. (2007). *Sociocultural contexts and literacy development.* In D. August & T. Shanahan (Eds.), *Developing reading and writing in second-language learners: Lessons from the Report of the National Literacy Panel on Language-Minority Children and Youth* (pp. 95–130). Washington, DC: Center for Applied Linguistics; Newark, DE: International Reading Association.

Gormley, W.T., & Phillips, D. (2005). The effects of universal pre-kindergarten in Oklahoma: Research highlights and policy implications. *Policy Studies Journal, 33,* 65–82.

Gregory, E. (1998). Siblings as mediators of literacy in linguistic minority communities. *Language and Education, 1*(12), 33–55.

Gregory, E. (2001). Sisters and brothers as language and literacy teachers: Synergy between siblings playing and working together. *Journal of Early Childhood Literacy, 1,* 301–322.

Gregory, E. (2004). "Invisible" teachers of literacy: Collusion between siblings and teachers in creating classroom cultures. *Literacy, 38*(2), 97–105.

Halle, T., Whittaker, J.V., Zepeda, M., Rothenberg, L., Anderson, R., Daneri, P., . . . Buysse, V. (2014). The social-emotional development of dual language learners: Looking back at existing research and moving forward with purpose. *Early Childhood Research Quarterly, 29,* 734–739.

Hammersley, M., & Atkinson, P. (1983). *Ethnography: Principles in practice.* London: Routledge.

Hancock, D. R. (2002). The effects of native language books on the pre-literacy skill development of language minority kindergartners. *Journal of Research in Childhood Education, 17*(1), 62–68.

Haugen, E. (1972). *The ecology of language: Essays by Einar Haugen* (A. S. Dil, Ed.). Stanford, CA: Stanford University Press.

Hemphill, F. C., & Vanneman, A. (2011). *Achievement gaps: How Hispanic and White students in public schools perform in mathematics and reading on the National Assessment of Educational Progress* (NCES 2011–459). Washington, DC: National Center for Education Statistics, Institute of Education Sciences, U.S. Department of Education.

Hernandez, D., Macartney, S., & Denton, N.A. (2010). A demographic portrait of young English language learners. In E.E. Garcia & E.C. Frede (Eds.), *Young English language learners* (pp. 10–41). New York: Teachers College Press.

Hidalgo, N. (1993). Multicultural teacher introspection. In T. Perry & J. Fraser (Eds.), *Freedom's plow: Teaching in the multicultural classroom* (pp. 99–106). New York: Routledge.

Hoff, E. (2003). The specificity of environmental influence: Socioeconomic status affects early vocabulary development via maternal speech. *Child Development, 74,* 1368–1378.

Hoff, E. (2013). Interpreting the language trajectories of children from low-SES and language minority homes: Implications for closing achievement gaps. *Developmental Psychology, 49,* 4–14.

Howard, E.R., Páez, M.M., August, D.L., Barr, C.D., Kenyon, D., & Malabonga, V. (2014). The importance of SES, home and school language and literacy practices, and oral vocabulary in bilingual children's English reading development. *Bilingual Research Journal, 37*(2), 120–141.

HRDC. (2010). *Public investments in early childhood education and care in Canada.* Retrieved from http://www.ecd-elcc.ca/eng/ecd/ececc/early_childhood_education-eng.pdf

Huang, E. (2013). *Fresh off the boat: A memoir.* New York: Spiegel and Grau.

Human Resources Management, 45 C.F.R. § 1304. 52 (2004).

Huntsinger, C.S., & Jose, P.E. (2009). Parental involvement in children's schooling: Different meanings in different cultures. *Early Childhood Research Quarterly, 24,* 398–410.

Ima, K., & Rumbaut, R.G. (1989). Southeast Asian refugees in American schools: A comparison of fluent English-proficient and limited-English proficient students. *Topics in Language Disorders, 9*(3), 54–77.

Jiménez, R.T. (1997). The strategic reading abilities and potential of five low-literacy Latina/o readers in middle school. *Reading Research Quarterly, 32*(3), 224–243.

Jung, S., Fuller, B., & Galindo, C. (2012). Family functioning and early learning practices in immigrant homes. *Child Development, 83,* 1510–1526.

Keaton, T. (1999). Muslim girls and the "other France": An examination of identity construction. *Social Identities, 5*(1), 47–64.

Kenner, C. (1999). Children's understandings of text in a multilingual nursery. *Language and Education, 13*(1), 1–16.

Kenner, C. (2000). Biliteracy in a monolingual school system? English and Gujarati in South London. *Language, Culture and Curriculum, 13*(1), 13–30.

Kenner, C., & Gregory, E. (2012). Becoming biliterate. In J. Larson & J. Marsh (Eds.), *The SAGE handbook of early childhood literacy* (pp. 364–378). London: SAGE.

Kenner, C., Kress, G., Al-Khatib, H., Kam, R., & Tsai, K.C. (2004). Finding the keys to biliteracy: How young children interpret different writing systems. *Language and Education, 18*(2), 124–144.

Kopeliovich, S. (2010). Family language policy: From a case study of a Russian-Hebrew bilingual family towards a theoretical framework. *Diaspora, Indigenous, and Minority Education, 4*(3), 162–178.

Lee, S.J. (2001). Exploring and transforming the landscape of gender and sexuality: Hmong American teenaged girls. *Race, Gender & Class, 8*(1), 35–46.

LeFevre, J., Clarke, T., & Stringer, A.P. (2002). Influences of language and parental involvement on the development of counting skills: Comparisons of French- and English-speaking Canadian children. *Early Child Development and Care, 172,* 283–300.

Leventhal, T., Xue, Y., & Brooks-Gunn, J. (2006). Immigrant differences in school-age children's verbal trajectories: A look at four racial/ethnic groups. *Child Development, 77,* 1359–1374.

Leyva, D., Reese, E., & Wiser, M. (2012). Early understanding of the function of print: Parent-child interaction and preschoolers' notating skills. *First Language, 32,* 301–323.

Li, G. (2002). *"East is east, west is west"? Home literacy, culture, and schooling.* New York: Peter Lang.

Li, G. (2006). What do parents think? Middle-class Chinese immigrant parents' perspectives on literacy learning, homework, and school-home communication. *School Community Journal, 16*(2), 27–46.

Lim, S., & Lim, B. K. (2003). Parenting style and child outcomes in Chinese and immigrant Chinese families: Current findings and cross-cultural considerations in conceptualization and research. *Marriage & Family Review, 35*(3–4), 21–43.

Lopez, N. (2003). *Hopeful girls, troubled boys: Race and gender disparity in urban education.* New York: Routledge.

Mackey, A. & Gass, S. M. (2005). *Second language research: Methodology and design.* Mahwah, NJ: Erlbaum.

Mahrous, A. A., Ahmed, A. A. (2010). A cross-cultural investigation of students' perceptions of the effectiveness of pedagogical tools: The Middle East, the United Kingdom, and the United States. *Journal of Studies in International Education, 14*(3), 289–306.

Matthews, H., & Ewen, D. (2010). *Early education programs and children of immigrants: Learning each other's language.* Washington, DC: Urban Institute. Retrieved from http://www.urban.org/UploadedPDF/412205-early-education.pdf

McCaleb, S. P. (1997). *Building communities of learners: A collaboration among teachers, students, families and community.* Mahwah, NJ: Erlbaum.

Min, P. G. (1992). The structure and social functions of Korean immigrant churches in the United States. *International Migration Review, 26*(4), 1370–1394.

Mistry, R. S., & Wadsworth, M. E. (2011). Family functioning and child development in the context of poverty. *The Prevention Researcher, 18*, 11–15.

Moll, L., Amanti, C., Neff, D., & González, N. (1992). Funds of knowledge for teaching: A qualitative approach to developing strategic connections between homes and classrooms. *Theory into Practice, 31*, 132–141.

Monzo, L. D., & Rueda, R. (2001). *Sociocultural factors in social relationships: Examining Latino teachers' and paraeducators' interactions with Latino students. Research Report 9.* Santa Cruz, CA: Center for Research on Education, Diversity, and Excellence.

Neale, M. D. (1997). *Neale analysis of reading ability – revised: Manual for schools.* Windsor: NFER-Nelson.

No Child Left Behind (NCLB) Act of 2001, Pub. L. No. 107–110, § 115, Stat. 1425 (2002).

O'Grady, K., & Houme, K. (2013). PSAP 2013: *Report on the Pan-Canadian Assessment of Science, Reading, and Mathematics.* Toronto: Council of Ministers of Education Canada (CMEC).

Olsen, L. (1997). *Made in America: Immigrant students in our public schools.* New York: New Press.

Park, S. M., & Sarkar, M. (2007). Parents' attitudes toward heritage language maintenance for their children and their efforts to help their children maintain the heritage language: A case study of Korean-Canadian immigrants. *Language, Culture and Curriculum, 20*(3), 223–235.

Peguero, A. A. (2009). Victimizing the children of immigrants. *Youth & Society, 41*, 186.

Pianta, R. C., LaParo, K. M., Payne, C. C., Cox, M. J., & Bradley, R. H. (2002). The relation of kindergarten classroom environment to teacher, family, and school characteristics and child outcomes. *Elementary School Journal, 102*, 225–238.

Pucci, S. L., & Ulanoff, S. H. (1998). What predicts second language reading success? A study of home and school variables. *ITL, Review of Applied Linguistics, 121–122*, 1–18.

Qin, D. B. (2003). Gendered expectations and gendered experiences: Immigrant students' adaptation in school. *New Directions in Youth Development Special Issue: The Social Worlds of Immigrant Youth, 100*, 91–110.

Qin, D. B. (2006). The role of gender in immigrant children's educational adaptation. *Current Issues in Comparative Education, 9*(1), 8–19.

Raikes, H. H., Raikes, H. A., Pan, B. A., Luze, G., Tamis-LeMonda, C., Rodriguez, E. T., . . . Tarullo, L. B. (2006). Mother-child book reading in low-income families: Correlates and outcomes during the first three years of life. *Child Development, 77*, 924–953.

Rampton, B., Tusting, K., Maybin, J., Barwell, R., Creese, A., & Lytra, V. (2004). UK linguistic ethnography: A discussion paper. Retrieved from http://www.ling-ethnog.org.uk/documents/papers/ramptonetal

Reardon, S. F., & Galindo, C. (2009). The Hispanic-White achievement gap in math and reading in the elementary grades. *American Educational Research Journal, 46*(3), 853–891.

Reese, E. (1995). Predicting children's literacy from mother-child conversations. *Cognitive Development, 10*, 381–405.

Reese, L., Garnier, H., Gallimore, R., & Goldenberg, C. (2000). Longitudinal analysis of the antecedents of emergent Spanish literacy and middle-school English reading achievement of Spanish-speaking students. *American Educational Research Journal, 37*(3), 633–662.

Reyes, I. (2006). Exploring connections between emergent biliteracy and bilingualism. *Journal of Early Childhood Literacy, 6*, 267–292.

Reyes, I., & Azuara, P. (2008). Emergent biliteracy in young Mexican immigrant children. *Reading Research Quarterly, 43*(4), 374–398.

Reyhner, J., & Lockard, L. (2009). *Indigenous language revitalization: Encouragement, guidance, and lessons learned.* Flagstaff: Northern Arizona University.

Riches, C., & Curdt-Christiansen, X. L. (2010). A tale of two Montreal communities: Parents' perspectives on their children's language and literacy development in a multilingual context. *The Canadian Modern Language Review, 66*(4), 525–555.

Richman, A. L., Miller, P. M., & LeVine, R. A. (1992). Cultural and educational variations in maternal responsiveness. *Developmental Psychology, 28*, 614–621.

Roderick, M. (2000). Hispanics and education. In P.S.J. Cafferty & D. W. Engstrom (Eds.), *Hispanics in the United States* (pp. 123–174). New Brunswick, NJ: Transaction.

Rogoff, B. (2003). *The cultural nature of human development.* Oxford, UK: Oxford University Press.

Rong, X. L., & Brown, F. (2001). The effects of immigrant generation and ethnicity on educational attainment among young African and Caribbean Blacks in the United States. *Harvard Educational Review, 71*(3), 536–565.

Rowe, M. L., Raudenbush, S. W., & Goldin-Meadow, S. (2012). The pace of vocabulary growth helps predict later vocabulary skill. *Child Development, 83*, 508–525.

Ruiz, R. (1984). Orientations in language planning. *NABE Journal, 8*(2), 15–34.

Sarroub, L. K. (2001). The sojourner experience of Yemeni American high school students: An ethnographic portrait. *Harvard Educational Review, 71*(3), 390–415.

Scarborough, H.S., & Dobrich, W. (1994). On the efficacy of reading to preschoolers. *Developmental Review, 14*, 245–302.

Schmid, M.S. (2011). *Language attrition*. Cambridge: Cambridge University Press.

Schwartz, M. (2008). Exploring the relationship between family language policy and heritage language knowledge among second generation Russian-Jewish immigrants in Israel. *Journal of Multilingual and Multicultural Development, 29*(5), 400–418.

Schwartz, M. (2010). Family language policy: Core issues of an emerging field. *Applied Linguistics Review, 1*(1), 171–192.

Schwartz, M. (2012). Second generation immigrants: Towards a socio-linguistic approach to linguistic development. In M. Leikin, M. Schwartz, & Y. Tobin (Eds.), *Current issues in bilingualism: Cognitive and socio-linguistic perspectives* (pp. 119–135). Dordrecht, Netherlands: Springer.

Schwartz, M., & Katzir. T. (2012). Depth of lexical knowledge among bilingual children: The impact of schooling. *Reading and Writing, 25*(8), 1947–1971.

Schwarzer, D. (1996). *Parallel development of writing in Hebrew, Spanish and English in a multilingual child* (Unpublished doctoral dissertation). University of Arizona, Tucson, Arizona.

Schwarzer, D. (2001). *Noah's ark: One child's voyage into multiliteracy*. Portsmouth, NH: Heinemann.

Schwarzer, D., Haywood, A., & Lorenzen, C. (2003). Fostering multiliteracy in a linguistically diverse classroom. *Language Arts, 80*, 453–460.

Sénéchal, M. (2006). Testing the home literacy model: Parent involvement in kindergarten is differentially related to grade 4 reading comprehension, fluency, spelling, and reading for pleasure. *Scientific Studies of Reading, 10*, 59–87.

Sénéchal, M., & LeFevre, J. (2002). Parent involvement in the development of children's reading skill: A five-year longitudinal study. *Child Development, 73*, 445–460.

Sénéchal, M., LeFevre, J., Smith-Chant, B. L., & Colton, K. (2001). On refining theoretical models of emergent literacy: The role of empirical evidence. Journal of School Psychology, 39, 439–460.

Sénéchal, M., LeFevre, J., Thomas, E.M., & Daley, K.E. (1998). Differential effects of home literacy experiences on the development of oral and written language. *Reading Research Quarterly, 33*, 96–116.

Shah, P.G. (2011). *Asian Americans' achievement advantage: When and why does it emerge?* (Unpublished dissertation). Ohio State University, Columbus, Ohio.

Shany, M., & Geva, E. (2012). Cognitive, language, and literacy development in socio-culturally vulnerable school children – the case of Ethiopian Israeli children. In M. Leikin, M. Schwartz, & Y. Tobin (Eds.), *Literacy Studies: Vol. 5. Current issues in bilingualism* (pp. 77–117). Dordrecht, Netherlands: Springer.

Shohamy, E. (2006). *Language policy: Hidden agendas and new approaches*. London: Routledge.

Smith, R.C. (2002). Gender, ethnicity, and race in school and work outcomes of second-generation Mexican Americans. In M. Suarez-Orozco & M. Paez (Eds.), *Latinos remaking America* (pp. 110–125). Berkeley: University of California Press & DRCLAS.

Sparks, A., & Reese, E. (2012). From reminiscing to reading: Home contributions to children's developing language and literacy in low-income families. *First Language, 33*(1), 89–109.

Spolsky, B. (2004). *Language policy*. Cambridge: Cambridge University Press.

Stagg-Peterson, S., & Heywood, D. (2007). Contributions of families' linguistic, social, and cultural capital to minority-language children's literacy: Parents', teachers', and principals' perspectives. *The Canadian Modern Language Review, 63*(4), 517–538.

Stanton-Salazar, R.D. (2001). *Manufacturing hope and despair: The school and kin support networks of U.S.-Mexican youth*. New York: Teachers College Press.

Statistics Canada. (2011). *Linguistic characteristics of Canadians: Language, 2011 census of population*. Retrieved from http://www12.statcan.gc.ca/census-recensement/2011/as-sa/98–314-x/98–314-x2011001-eng.pdf

Suárez-Orozco, C., & Qin, D.B. (2006). Gendered perspectives in psychology: Immigrant origin youth. *International Migration Review, 40*, 165–198.

Suárez-Orozco, C., & Suárez-Orozco, M. (1995). *Transformations: Immigration, family life, and achievement motivation among Latino adolescents*. Palo Alto, CA: Stanford University Press.

Suárez-Orozco, M., & Páez, M. (Eds.). (2008). *Latinos: Remaking America*. Berkeley: University of California Press.

Tamis-Lemonda, C.S., Song, L., Leavell, A.S., Kahana-Kalman, R., & Yoshikawa, H. (2012). Ethnic differences in mother-infant language and gestural communications are associated with specific skills in infants. *Developmental Science, 15*, 384–397.

Valdés, G. (2001). *Learning and not learning English: Latino students in American schools*. Multicultural Education Series. New York: Teachers College Press.

Valenzuela, A. (1999). *Subtractive schooling: U.S.-Mexican youth and the politics of caring*. Albany: State University of New York Press.

Volk, D., & de Acosta, M. (2001). "Many differing ladders, many ways to climb . . .": Literacy events in the bilingual classroom, homes, and community of three Puerto Rican kindergartners. *Journal of Early Childhood Literacy, 1*, 193–224.

Vygotsky, L. S. (1978). *Mind in society: The development of higher psychological processes*. Cambridge, MA: Harvard University Press.

Vygotsky, L. S. (1986). *Thought and language* (A. Kozulin, Trans.). Cambridge, MA: MIT Press. (Original work published 1934)

Walker, J.M.T., Ice, C.L., Hoover-Dempsey, K. V., & Howard, M. (2013). Latino parents' motivations for involvement in their children's schooling: An exploratory study. *The Elementary School Journal, 111*(3), 409–429.

Watkins, A. M., & Melde, C. (2010). Latino and Asian students' perceptions of the quality of their educators: The role of generational status and language proficiency. *Youth & Society, 42*(1), 3.

Weiland, C., & Yoshikawa, H. (2013). Impacts of a prekindergarten program on children's mathematics, language, literacy, executive function, and emotional skills. *Child Development, 84*, 2112–2130.

Whitehurst, G.J., & Lonigan, C.J. (1998). Child development and emergent literacy. *Child Development, 69*, 848–872.

Winsler, A., Burchinal, M.R., Tien, H., Peisner-Feiberg, E., Espinosa, L., Castro, D.C., . . . De Feyter, J. (2014). Early development among dual language learners: The roles of language use at home, maternal immigration, country of origin, and socio-demographic variables. *Early Childhood Research Quarterly, 29*, 750–764.

Woodcock, R. W. (1991). *Woodcock Language Proficiency Battery-Revised.* Itasca, IL: Riverside.

Xue, Y., & Meisels, S. J. (2004). Early literacy instruction and learning to read in kindergarten. *American Educational Research Journal, 41,* 191–229.

Yarosz, D. J., & Barnett, W. S. (2001). Who reads to young children? Identifying predictors of family reading and activities. *Reading Psychology, 22,* 67–81.

Zhang, Z., & Bano, N. (2010). Multiple cultures, multiple literacies, and collective agencies: Chinese and Pakistani immigrants' perceptions of family literacy support. *Canadian and International Education, 39*(3), 81–100.

Zhou, M., & Bankston, C. L. (2001). Family pressure and the educational experience of the daughters of Vietnamese refugees. *International Migration, 39,* 133–151.

8

Problems with reading

*Christie Fraser, Angela Massey-Garrison,
and Esther Geva*

INTRODUCTION

This chapter is concerned with research on reading difficulties in second language (L2) learners. We therefore begin the chapter with a brief and general discussion concerning the definition of learning disabilities. An authoritative guide to the diagnosis of mental disorders used by both clinicians and researchers to provide a common language in studying disorders is the fifth edition of the *Diagnostic and Statistical Manual of Mental Disorders* (*DSM-5*). The *DSM-5* uses the term *specific learning disorder* as an umbrella term for reading, mathematics, and written expression disorders. When a reading disorder is present, it is referred to as a "specific learning disorder", and the diagnosis will specify the nature of the reading impairment (e.g., word reading, reading fluency, reading comprehension, or language impairment). In order to provide consistency and reflect the common usage found within the reading literature, in this chapter the term *reading disability* (RD) is used to refer to specific learning disorders related to reading.

One can find various similar definitions of learning disabilities provided by other organizations and diagnostic manuals, but they tend to be rather similar (it is beyond the scope of this chapter to compare the various definitions, and the details are not essential to the focus of this chapter). For example, the National Association of School Psychologists (NASP, 2007, p. 2) provides the following elaborations:

- Specific learning disabilities are endogenous in nature, and are characterized by neurologically-based deficits in cognitive processes;
- These deficits are specific, that is, they impact particular cognitive processes that interfere with the acquisition of formal learning skills;
- Specific learning disabilities are heterogeneous – there are various types of learning disabilities, and there is no single defining characteristic common to all learning disabilities;

- Specific learning disabilities may co-exist with other disabling conditions (e.g., sensory deficits, language impairment, behaviour problems), but are not due to these conditions;
- Of children identified as having specific learning disabilities, the great majority (over 80 percent) have a disability in the area of reading;
- The manifestation of a specific learning disability is contingent upon the type of instruction, supports, and accommodations provided, and the demands of the learning situation;
- Early intervention can reduce the impact of many learning difficulties;
- Specific learning disabilities vary in their degree of severity; and moderate to severe learning disabilities can be expected to impact performance throughout the lifespan.

It is important to recognize that L2 learners have generally lower academic vocabulary and reading comprehension skills in the L2 than their L1 counterparts (August & Shanahan, 2006; Droop & Verhoeven, 2003; Farnia & Geva, 2011; Hutchinson, Whitely, Smith, & Connors, 2003; Lam, Chen, Geva, Luo, & Li, 2012; Lesaux, Rupp, & Siegel, 2007; Proctor, Carlo, August, & Snow, 2005; Verhoeven, 2000). Yet, some L2 children and adolescents have persistent reading- or language-related difficulties of the kind defined earlier that cannot be attributed simply to their L2 status, and that may reflect a language disorder or a specific reading disorder (Geva & Herbert, 2012; Geva & Massey-Garrison, 2013; Paradis, Genesee, & Crago, 2011; Sparks, Patton, Ganschow, & Humbach, 2009). It is not easy to tease apart difficulties in L2 reading that reflect the typical course of L2 development from difficulties that reflect difficulties associated with having language impairment or a reading disability. One can find in the literature reports of issues related to overidentification of L2 speakers as having a learning disability when they do not (Cummins, 1984; Harry & Anderson, 1994; Larry P. v. Riles, 1972, 1974, 1979, 1984, 1986; Paton, 1998), and underidentification of L2 speakers who actually have a learning disability (Limbos & Geva, 2001; Solari, Petscher, & Folsom, 2012; U.S. Department of Education, 2003; Zehler, Fleischman, Hopstock, Pendzick, & Stephenson, 2003).

The overall goal of this chapter is to examine issues related to whether reading difficulties of L2 learners reflect inadequate proficiency in the societal language, or are due to a specific learning disorder. Because of heterogeneity in the nature of the L2 population, it is difficult to provide simple definitions of what is "normal" or "typical" L2 development (Klingner et al., 2006). In the past, the thinking was that this differentiation could not occur reliably until the L2 learner had sufficient opportunities to develop adequate levels of L2 proficiency (Cummins, 1984). The early identification of ELL children with reading difficulties is important as children who have a slow start in reading rarely catch up (Torgesen, 1998), leaving them at risk academically (Geva & Wiener, 2015). Their poor reading skills accumulate over time, leaving them more and more behind. In this chapter we discuss research on L2 children and adolescents who have persistent difficulties in reading or language skills that cannot be attributed simply to lack of opportunities to learn, to cultural differences, or to inadequate instruction.

The chapter begins with a brief overview of two relevant theoretical perspectives regarding L2 reading development; the simple view of reading framework and theories of cross-language transfer are discussed. Next, we summarize related developmental reading research findings about typical reading development in L2 learners. Our discussion includes topics such as the cognitive processes involved in word-level reading, the role of oral language, reading fluency, and reading comprehension. The chapter then turns to a discussion of the conceptual and assessment complexities involved in the identification of reading difficulties in L2 learners, and to a presentation of cognitive factors affecting reading difficulties. Noted are important risk factors for consideration in L2 populations. Research findings concerning categories of L2 learners with reading difficulties are reviewed: decoding (e.g., word-level) difficulties, poor reading fluency, poor comprehension, and language impairment. A discussion of research on assessment and intervention of reading difficulties and the outcomes of such interventions with L2 learners follows. The chapter closes with two case studies to facilitate deep thinking about the content of the chapter.

Guiding Questions

1   How do we know that the reading difficulty being experienced by the L2 learner is a real difficulty in reading and not due to developing language proficiency?
2   What additional risk factors should be considered in L2 learners who experience reading difficulties?
3   How can reading theory help us to better understand reading difficulties in L2 learners?
4   How similar are the cognitive and linguistic profiles of L1 and L2 learners experiencing reading difficulties?
5   Can reading difficulties in L2 learners be assessed and diagnosed using second language testing?
6   Do first language interventions work for L2 learners?

THEORETICAL PERSPECTIVES ON L2 READING DEVELOPMENT

The simple view of reading

The simple view of reading (SVR) framework helps to conceptualize subtypes of learners with reading difficulties. According to the SVR (Gough & Tunmer, 1986), reading comprehension depends on two interacting skill sets: decoding and language comprehension. Efficiency in both skill sets is necessary for effective reading comprehension; if there are deficits in either or both areas, reading comprehension will be negatively impacted. Decoding involves the visual and orthographic-phonological mapping skills needed to derive word meanings from print in an accurate and fluent manner (Wolf & Katzir-Cohen, 2001), while language comprehension involves a variety of language skills, including vocabulary, morphology, syntax, semantics, and pragmatics. The SVR model provides a general framework for explaining how different types of reading difficulties (e.g., poor decoding, poor comprehension) can occur as a result of the breakdown in the ability to decode, to comprehend language, or both. More recently, it has been suggested that the SVR framework should be augmented with other factors, such as fluency, working memory, and metacognitive strategies (Cain, Oakhill, & Bryant, 2004; Kirby & Savage, 2008). Later in this chapter we use this model in our discussion of types of reading difficulties: word-level difficulties (including problems with fluency), and poor comprehension and language impairment.

Much of the research supporting the SVR has been conducted with L1 learners. More recently however, attention has turned to the usefulness of the SVR in explaining reading comprehension in L2, and informing assessment and instruction for L2 learners. A review of this literature suggests that the SVR framework can be used to understand factors contributing to individual differences in L2 reading comprehension (e.g., Geva & Farnia, 2012; Gottardo & Mueller, 2009; Manis, Lindsey, & Bailey, 2004; Proctor et al., 2005; Yaghoub-Zadeh, Farnia, & Geva, 2012). In line with recent L1 findings, recent studies of L2 learners support the need to augment the SVR. To illustrate, Geva and Farnia (2012) conducted a longitudinal study with English L2 children of different linguistic backgrounds from Grades 2 to 5. They found that the SVR framework was helpful in understanding what factors distinguished the L2 learners with good English comprehension from those who struggled. They found that English word reading skills and English language skills – the two components of SVR – predicted L2 reading comprehension longitudinally and concurrently. In addition, word and text reading fluency assessed in Grade 5 predicted reading comprehension.

Support for the SVR in L2 reading comprehension is not limited to young children, or learners of English as an L2. For example, Prior, Goldina, Shany,

Geva, and Katzir (2014) found support for the SVR in understanding L2 reading comprehension in a study of L2 adolescents whose home language was Russian, and Hebrew was their L2. Verhoeven and van Leeuwe (2012) reported similar findings in a study targeting reading comprehension in Dutch L2 children whose home language was Turkish or Arabic. Noteworthy is a study by Pasquarella, Gottardo, and Grant (2012). These researchers found the SVR model effective in understanding how age of exposure to L2, in this case English, impacted the contributions of decoding and language comprehension to reading comprehension in adolescent L2 learners. They reported that when L2 learners began their L2 learning only in adolescence, both skill sets played an equally important role in their reading comprehension, even though typically one does not expect decoding skills to play a role in adolescence. Findings with young L2 children who began their L2 learning earlier (e.g., the primary grades) suggest that as with L1 learners, decoding may at first play a more important role. The influence of age of onset of L2 learning, and of having experience in learning to read in the L1, is important to consider, as is the importance of taking a developmental approach when considering L2 populations (Geva & Wiener, 2015).

As will be discussed in more detail to follow, the available L2 research suggests that the SVR framework is beneficial for clarifying the sources of difficulties of L2 learners who experience problems with reading. Geva and Massey-Garrison (2013) and Geva and Herbert (2012) used this model for conceptualizing poor readers (e.g., poor decoders, poor comprehenders) in their research exploring sources of reading difficulties in L2 learners. Fraser (2015) also used the SVR model to consider different types of poor comprehenders: those with only poor language comprehension and those with a compounded deficit in both language comprehension and decoding. On the whole, SVR appears to be a useful framework for understanding reading comprehension and sources of difficulties in reading comprehension for L1 and L2 learners, and the importance of augmenting it with factors such as reading fluency is widely accepted.

Cross-language transfer

To date, many studies have explored the notion of cross-language transfer – that is, the potential impact that a learner's L1 may have on the development of their L2, or how relevant skills correlate cross-linguistically. Three prevailing theoretical perspectives about cross-language transfer will be discussed here briefly: the interdependence perspective (Cummins, 1984), the underlying cognitive processes perspective (Geva & Ryan, 1993), and the contrastive or typological perspective (Lado, 1964). These perspectives are complementary and shed some light on the role that L1 language and reading skills play in facilitating or debilitating L2 reading development. Moreover, the topic of cross-linguistic transfer is important to consider because L2 learners commit errors that may reflect negative transfer from the L1 but also because it would be helpful to understand better how skills developed and taught in one language can "transfer" to the L2.

The interdependence perspective (Cummins, 1984) proposes that the acquisition of L1 and L2 skills is interdependent. Cummins (2000) suggests that L2 learners with developed L1 literacy will make stronger progress in their L2 literacy acquisition. This perspective speaks to "learned" skills that help in learning to read, versus the universal cognitive factors that are discussed in the underlying cognitive processes perspective. For example, conceptual understandings about oral language (e.g., conjunction knowledge) and strategies used to understand unfamiliar vocabulary (e.g., morphological skills) can promote acquisition of similar oral skills in the L2, which can in turn promote L2 literacy development (Cummins, 2012; Royer & Carlo, 1991). That said, not all aspects of L1 development are equally facilitative of L2 development; transfer of conceptual and strategic knowledge can be explained by Cummins's interdependence perspective, while components of development that are closely linked to language typology (see the following discussion on the contrastive perspective of cross-language transfer) are more contingent on orthographic and language structure similarities and differences between L1-L2.

The underlying cognitive processes perspective (Geva & Ryan, 1993; for a review see Genesee, Geva, Dressler, & Kamil, 2006) highlights the important role that common cognitive processes (i.e., universal cognitive factors) play in language development, regardless of the language under study. Examples of common cognitive processes include: phonological short-term memory, phonological awareness, and naming speed, as well as skills related to executive function, such as self-regulation and working memory. Individual differences in these skills can explain L1-L2 correlations found between similar reading and writing skills. They are also predictive of word reading, spelling, and word-level fluency in L1 and L2 for both typically developing L2 learners and L2 learners with reading difficulties (see Ndlovu & Geva, 2008, for a review). Because performance on these underlying cognitive processes does not require proficient levels of oral language or exposure to the L2, these skills can predict word-level reading skills cross-linguistically and are particularly useful in identifying children with reading difficulties at the word level. For example, research has shown that phonological awareness and rapid naming correlate with word reading not only when the L1 and L2 are orthographically similar (e.g., Durgunoglu, Nagy, & Hancin-Bhatt, 1993, for Spanish and English; Commeau, Cormier, Grandmaison, & Lacroix, 1999; Jared, Cormier, Levy, & Wade-Woolley, 2010, for French and English) but also when the two languages are orthographically more distant (e.g., Geva, Wade-Woolley, & Shany, 1993, for Hebrew and English; McBride-Chang & Ho, 2005, for Chinese and English).

The contrastive or typological perspective (Lado, 1964) focuses on typological similarities and differences between L1 and L2, and suggests that the level of similarity or difference between features of the written or spoken language (orthography) can help (positive transfer) or hinder (negative transfer) the development of specific features of the L2. Languages that are typologically similar (e.g., English and German) share similar orthographic features as well as many features of the spoken language. Languages that are typologically distant (e.g., English and Hebrew or Chinese) share fewer structures. When L1 and L2 are structurally similar, L2 learners are able to use what they know about the common structures to facilitate L2 development (i.e., positive transfer).

A good example of positive transfer is evidenced in findings from research about cognates; cognates are words that share common roots and spelling, sound, and meaning across languages or words in different languages that share a common root (e.g., *distance* in English and *distancia* in Spanish). Spanish children learning L2 English may be able to use their knowledge of Spanish-English cognates to aid in their English reading when encountering new and unfamiliar words in English (Ramirez, Chen, Geva, & Kiefer, 2010). When the L1 and L2 differ substantially, L2 learners may make errors during the development of their L2 proficiency (e.g., negative transfer). Wang and Geva (2003) found that Grade 1 Cantonese-speaking children learning L2 English had difficulty distinguishing between the phonemes /s/ and /θ/ in spelling because the phoneme /θ/ does not exist in Cantonese. An example of an error from this type of difficulty would be confusing *think* for *sink*. At the same time they found that by the end of Grade 2, these types of phonological errors disappeared as the children became more proficient in their L2. With respect to L2 learners with RD, it should be noted that although contrasts between L1 and L2 features may cause delays when L2 children and adolescents are first exposed to the L2, typological differences between the L1 and the L2 are not considered a risk factor and most typically developing children can acquire the features of the L2 that do not exist in their L1 as their language and literacy skills in the L2 develop (Wade-Woolley, 1999; Wang and Geva, 2003; see Geva & Wiener, 2015, for a review). At the same time, L2 learners with RD profiles are likely to perform similarly to L1 learners with RD regardless of typological differences between the L1 and L2 (Geva & Herbert, 2012; Geva & Massey-Garrison, 2013). For a further discussion of cross-language transfer, please see Chapter 4 of this book.

WORD-LEVEL READING DEVELOPMENT IN TYPICALLY
DEVELOPING L2 READERS

Overall, research findings reveal similarity between the development of L1 and L2 students' word-level reading skills, especially if they began their schooling in the L2 at a young age (Droop & Verhoeven, 2003; Geva, 2006; Geva, Yaghoub-Zadeh, & Schuster, 2000; Lesaux & Siegel, 2003; Wang & Geva, 2003). There have been fewer research studies examining word-level reading skills of children in higher elementary grades. Abu-Rabia and Siegel (2002) examined the word reading skills of Arabic-English (L2) learners and English (L1) learners in Grades 4 through 8. The findings indicated that L1 and L2 students performed similarly on word recognition and pseudoword decoding tasks. Other studies involving L1 and L2 learners in the middle grades of elementary school have also found similar results with various language groups (e.g., Da Fontoura & Siegel, 1995). There is less research on older L2 learners, especially those who began learning English as adolescents. As discussed earlier, Pasquarella et al. (2012) compared the performance of L2 students in Grades 9 and 10 who had arrived in Canada 2 to 3 years earlier to that of their English L1 peers. The L2 learners' performance on word reading skills was significantly below that of their L1 counterparts, highlighting the need for more research with that particular age group. The following section reviews literature about the cognitive processes involved in L2 word-level reading (e.g., phonological awareness, rapid naming, working memory skills), and relatedly, cross-language transfer of cognitive and word-level skills.

Cognitive processes involved in L2 word-level reading

Research has demonstrated that phonological processing skills are not strongly related to oral language proficiency in the L2 and that specifically phonological awareness assessed in the L2 predicts basic word reading skills in young L2 learners both concurrently and longitudinally (Chiappe & Siegel, 1999; Commeau, Cormier, Grandmaison, & Lacroix, 1999; Durgunoglu et al., 1993; Geva et al., 1993; Geva & Farnia, 2012; Gholamain & Geva, 1999; Gottardo, Yan, Siegel, & Wade-Woolley, 2001). Therefore, provided that L2 children have attended school on a regular basis, and have been exposed to appropriate literacy instruction in their L2, they should be able to perform phonological awareness tasks (e.g., identifying the onset and rime of words, blending sounds) without much difficulty even though their L2 language skills are still developing. Persistent difficulties in developing basic decoding and word recognition skills in the L2 in spite of good instruction cannot be attributed solely to students' L2 oral language proficiency even if those skills are not on par with their L1 peers (Geva & Herbert, 2012; Geva & Wiener, 2015).

Several underlying processes or subskills are needed for efficient word reading. These include phonological awareness, rapid naming, and working memory (see Wagner & Torgesen, 1987, for review). Phonological awareness is the ability to recognize and manipulate the sounds in a language (Goswami & Bryant, 1990). Research suggests that phonological awareness has influences on the acquisition of decoding skills and subsequent comprehension in L1 and L2 students (Yaghoub-Zadeh, Farnia, & Geva, 2012). Phonological awareness is one of the best predictors of word reading skills within the first years of school for L1 and L2 learners (Gottardo, Collins, Baciu, & Gebotys, 2008; Jared et al., 2010; Manis, Lindsey, & Bailey, 2004; Wagner, Torgesen, & Rashotte, 1994). Research findings have shown that phonological awareness skills assessed in the L2 can accurately predict L2 word reading skills even if the oral language proficiency of the L2 learner is not fully developed (Farnia & Geva, 2011; Geva & Yaghoub Zadeh, 2006; Lesaux, Rupp, & Siegel, 2007). For example, Geva and Yaghoub Zadeh (2006) investigated the oral language proficiency, reading skills, and underlying cognitive processes – including phonological awareness – of Grade 2 L1 and L2 students. Despite the oral language advantage of English in the L1 group, L2 phonological awareness was one of the significant predictors of L2 word-level reading performance and overall reading fluency. Additionally, in a longitudinal study with Canadian French immersion students who were followed between Grades 1 and 3, Jared et al. (2010) found that English phonological awareness was a significant predictor of French word identification. This type of cross-language transfer holds true even after controlling for receptive vocabulary, intelligence, memory, and social class in L1 students (Anthony & Ionigan, 2004; Wagner et al., 1994; Whitehurst & Lonigan, 1998), and has implications for the assessment of L2 learners who may have a reading disability.

Rapid automatized naming is the ability to name quickly and accurately familiar stimuli, such as objects, colours, digits, or letters. It is considered a cognitive index of speed of access to the representations of verbal information in memory; rapid naming tasks assess how quickly and effectively one can retrieve information from long-term memory. L2 learners tend to perform equally or sometimes even better than L1 learners on rapid naming tasks in the early stages of reading acquisition despite lower performance on tasks measuring skill in language and reading comprehension (Chiappe & Siegel, 1999; Chiappe, Siegel, & Gottardo, 2002; Chiappe, Siegel, & Wade-Woolley, 2002; Lesaux & Siegel, 2003). Although some studies show L2 learners to be slower at naming than their L1 peers, their naming speed improves and catches up with their L1 peers for typically developing children (Geva et al., 2000). Importantly, similar to rapid naming in L1 learners, individual differences in L2 rapid naming appear to be predictive of reading development in L2 for diverse language groups (Chung & Ho, 2010; Commeau et al., 1999; Geva & Farnia, 2012; Gholamin & Geva, 1999; Kirby et al., 2003).

Working memory and short-term memory can be differentiated by the fact that working memory involves storage and processing of information, whereas short-term memory involves only information storage (Baddeley, 2000). Working memory demands active manipulation of the information presented while simultaneously holding the information in short-term memory. In early reading development much effort is devoted to actively decoding the printed word, and working memory is critical for analyzing and recalling the grapheme-phoneme unit for each segment of the word and holding that information in memory until the whole word has been decoded (Verhoeven, Reitsma, & Siegel, 2011). Some studies suggest that working memory may be related to weaker word reading for English L2 learners measured in the L2 in the early grades; however, these differences decrease over time as the L2 learners become more proficient in the L2 (Chiappe, Siegel, & Wade-Woolley, 2002; D'Angiulli, Siegel, & Serra, 2001; Jongejan, Verhoeven, & Siegel, 2007; Lesaux & Siegel, 2003).

In general, language and literacy research with L2 learners has found that underlying processing skills, such as phonological awareness, rapid automatized naming, and working memory, better predict accurate word reading and explain more individual differences than aspects of English oral language proficiency, such as vocabulary and grammatical skills (Da Fontoura & Siegel, 1995; Gottardo et al., 2001; see Geva, 2006, for review). Moreover, children who receive adequate exposure and instruction to language and literacy in the L2 can obtain accurate word reading skills that are similar to their L1 peers (Lesaux & Siegel, 2003). Likewise, studies based on L2 learners from multiple language groups (e.g., Punjabi, Urdu, Portuguese, Spanish, Italian, Chinese) have also consistently demonstrated developmental trajectories associated with accuracy in word reading and pseudoword decoding skills that did not differ from L1 learners (e.g., Geva, Yaghoub-Zadeh, & Schuster, 2000). To sum, the better the ability the L2 learner has in these basic cognitive processes, the better the word reading skills in the L2, even when L2 proficiency is still developing. This conclusion has important implications for the feasibility of assessing L2 learners as having RD.

Cross-language transfer of cognitive and word-level skills

Languages vary in how phoneme-grapheme (sound-letter) relationships follow consistent and predictable patterns (Katz & Frost, 1992). Shallow or more transparent orthographies (e.g., Finnish, Spanish, Italian) should be easier to decode because the phoneme-grapheme relationships are regular and consistent. In contrast, deep or opaque orthographies (e.g., English, French) pose more reading challenges because one cannot rely consistently on phoneme-grapheme relationships when assembling the phonemes for decoding due to irregularity and inconsistency of spelling patterns. Instead, the reader must rely more on the word's visual orthographic structure and determine meaning through whole-word recognition (Katz & Frost, 1992).

The degree of transparency or consistency of the orthography plays a role in how long it takes for children to acquire literacy skills. Research has demonstrated that it is easier to develop accurate word reading skills in transparent, consistent orthographies than in opaque orthographies (Caravolas, Lervag, Defior, Seidlova Malkova, & Hulme, 2013; Geva & Siegel, 2000; Seymour, Aro, & Erskine, 2003). The degree of association between L1 and L2 reading skills is also related to how closely the L1 and L2 are typologically related to each other. It should be noted that the transparency or consistency of the orthography plays a role in how long it takes for children to acquire literacy skills and how highly parallel measures correlate cross-linguistically (Share, 2008). L1 and L2 decoding skills typically correlate positively with each other (Da Fontoura & Siegel, 1995; Genesee et al., 2006; Gholamain & Geva, 1999). These correlations tend to be stronger when the L1 and L2 share similar language structures or typologies (Shakkour, 2014). Phonological awareness has been examined extensively as an underlying cognitive skill that is important for word decoding, that displays cross-linguistic transfer between L1 and L2 word reading skills, and that serves as a predictor of reading ability in both the L1 and L2, including both alphabetic and logographic languages (Abu-Rabia & Shakkour, 2014; De Jong & Van der Leij, 1999; Durgunoglu & Oney, 1999; Gottardo et al., 2001; Jared et al., 2010; Keung & Ho, 2009; Laurent & Martinot, 2010; Wang et al., 2005; Yeung, Siegel, & Chan, 2013).

A review of studies by Shakkour (2014) concluded that phonological awareness in alphabetic (L1) scripts predicts English L2 word reading skills independent of the orthographic depth of the L1. To illustrate, Durgunoglu et al. (1993) demonstrated that Spanish L1 children who performed well on phonological awareness tasks in Spanish were more likely to perform well on English L2 word and pseudoword reading tasks. Abu-Rabia and Shakkour (2014) found a similar relationship with older Grade 11 Hebrew L1 learners, in which a positive correlation was demonstrated between Hebrew phonological awareness and English L2 text reading and pseudoword reading. Chung, Lo, Ho, Xiao, and Chan (2014) found that Chinese phonological awareness skills were associated with English L2 word reading skills among Chinese L1 children learning English. In addition, rapid naming and working memory are important cognitive factors whose cross-linguistic contributions need to be considered. Research has found that performance on rapid naming tasks is similar in L1 and L2 children with persistent decoding and fluency difficulties in the L2 (Geva & Yaghoub-Zadeh, 2006; Keung & Ho, 2009;

McBride-Chang, Liu, Wong, Wong, & Shu, 2012). Similarly, whether working memory skills are measured in the children's L1 or L2, these processes have been shown to be sources of individual differences in the development of L2 word-level reading skills across different language groups (DaFontoura & Siegel, 1995; Gholamain & Geva, 1999). For a further discussion of writing systems and cross-language transfer, please see Chapters 1 and 4 (this volume), respectively.

L2 ORAL LANGUAGE PROFICIENCY AND ITS ROLE IN READING COMPREHENSION

Perfetti and Adlof (2012, p. 3) provide the following definition of reading comprehension, which is also applicable to L2 readers:

> Reading comprehension is widely agreed to be not one, but many things. At the least, it is agreed to entail cognitive processes that operate on many different kinds of knowledge to achieve many different kinds of reading tasks. Comprehension occurs as the reader builds one or more mental representations of a text message (e.g., Kintsch & Rawson, 2005). Among these representations, an accurate model of the situation described by the text (Van Dijk & Kintsch, 1983) is the product of successful deep comprehension. The comprehension processes that bring about these mental representations occur at multiple levels across units of language: word-level, sentence-level, and text-level. Across these levels, processes of word identification, parsing, referential mapping, and inference all contribute, interacting with the reader's conceptual knowledge.

Skilled reading comprehension is made up of an intricate interaction between various aspects of oral language proficiency, word decoding, reading fluency, higher-order language comprehension, inferencing skills, familiarity with various text structures, cultural and background knowledge, and the ability to apply various metacognitive comprehension strategies. Children with deficits in one or more of these areas may face difficulties in the texts they read (Stanovich & Siegel, 1994).

Oral language skills provide the foundation for learning to read and are thus crucial to literacy development (Chall, 1996). Thus, language proficiency and reading comprehension are highly correlated in both L1 and L2 learners. Listening comprehension, syntactic knowledge, morphological skills, and, perhaps most importantly, vocabulary knowledge are components of L2 proficiency that are associated with reading comprehension in L2 children (e.g., August & Shanahan, 2006; Babayiğit, 2014; Droop & Verhoeven, 2003; Farnia & Geva, 2011; Geva, 2006; Hutchinson, Whitely, Smith, & Connors,

2003; Lam, Chen, Geva, Luo, & Li, 2012; Lesaux, Rupp, & Siegel, 2007; Proctor et al., 2005; Verhoeven, 2000). For example, in their study with monolingual and bilingual English children in Grade 5, Babayiğit (2014) found that oral language was the most powerful predictor of reading and listening comprehension. In their 6-year longitudinal study, Farnia and Geva (2011) found that the vocabulary skills of L2 English learners continued to significantly lag behind their L1 peers despite 6 years of schooling in English from Grade 1 to Grade 6. Likewise, Hutchinson et al. (2003) found that L2 learners had lower levels of receptive and expressive vocabulary when tested in Grades 2, 3, and 4, and that, relatedly, participants had lower levels of reading comprehension.

There is a dearth of research on L2 oral skill development in adolescent L2 students (August & Shanahan, 2006), and in particular in those who immigrate as adolescents. It is likely that these latecomers face more significant and acute challenges concerning their academic achievement and the pressure to develop their L2 language skills than L2 learners who began schooling in the L2 earlier (Geva & Wiener, 2015). In their study of adolescent newcomer L2 learners, Pasquerella et al. (2012) found that both L2 decoding and L2 vocabulary knowledge predicted reading comprehension in this group of L2 learners. These students were challenged because neither their word reading skills nor their command of English vocabulary was sufficiently developed, leaving them with the compounded task of struggling with decoding, language comprehension, and the comprehension of the texts, and, as might be expected, their performance on vocabulary, decoding, and reading comprehension was well below grade level. To date, very little is known about latecomers who may also have learning disabilities.

L2 READING FLUENCY AND READING COMPREHENSION

Reading fluency and its role in reading comprehension are topics that have been addressed from various theoretical and applied perspectives. The National Reading Panel (2000) concluded that reading fluency involves efficient (e.g., accurate and automatic) word recognition as well as "the ability to group words appropriately into meaningful grammatical units for interpretation" (p. 3–6). Relatedly, Wolf and Katzir-Cohen (2001) explain that text reading fluency involves "that level of reading competence at which textual material can be effortlessly, smoothly, and automatically understood" (p. 177).

Oral reading fluency develops gradually over the elementary school years (e.g., Biemiller, 1977/78; Fuchs & Deno, 1991). Both L1 and L2 learners in the early stages of reading development develop decoding skills and gradually learn to "unglue from print" (Chall, 1996). One expects to observe a gradual improvement in their ability to read isolated words with accuracy and fluency, to recognize high-frequency words with more fluency (even when their spelling is irregular), and to read grade-appropriate texts with more fluency (Nakamoto, Lindsey, & Manis, 2007). Typically, at this stage L2 children read with similar fluency words in isolation or in context (Biemiller 1977/78). Gradually their reading becomes less "choppy", and when they read texts that are at their level, there is an increasing match between sentence structure and the intonation contours and prosodic features used by the reader.

According to automaticity theory (LaBerge & Samuels, 1974) and verbal efficiency theory (Perfetti, 1985), the links between reading fluency and reading comprehension can be attributed to faster, consistent, and reliable word recognition processes which enable fluent readers to allocate their attentional resources to meaning and comprehension of the text (Perfetti, 1985). Word reading fluency is an essential skill that bridges accurate word recognition with reading comprehension (NICHD, 2000). Having fluent – automatic and efficient – word reading reduces processing demands and frees up mental capacity needed for text comprehension. Indeed, Fuchs, Fuchs, Hosp, and Jenkins (2001) argued that oral reading fluency can be considered a valid indicator of overall reading ability. A further discussion of word recognition, including accuracy and fluency, can be found in Chapter 3 (this volume).

There is evidence that reading fluency and reading comprehension share some common prerequisite skills, including phonological awareness and naming speed. Like reading comprehension, text-level reading fluency is associated with the key components of the SVR; reading fluency is related to language skills (e.g., Cohen-Mimran, 2009; Cutting, Materek, Cole, Levine, & Mahone, 2009; Puranik, Pletscher, Al Otaiba, Catts, & Lonigan, 2008) and decoding skills (Biemiller, 1999; Carver & David, 2001; Wolf & Katzir-Cohen, 2001). As is the case with L1 children, reading fluency plays a significant role in reading comprehension of L2 children, in addition to the two components of the SVR (i.e., decoding and language comprehension) (Azimi, Geva, & Gottardo, 2015; Geva & Farnia, 2012; Geva, Wade-Woolley, & Shany, 1997; Yaghoub-Zadeh, Farnia, & Geva, 2012).

Around Grade 4 the nature of reading undergoes additional qualitative changes. Some children may be able to read single words or text involving high-frequency words with fluency, and some children read texts with more fluency than words in isolation (Jackson & Donaldson, 1989) but experience difficulty with reading expository texts fluently, because the texts become more demanding linguistically, the content is novel and more dense (Oakhill & Cain, 2012), and one needs to attend to macro-level aspects of the texts one reads (Afflerbach, Pearson, & Paris, 2008). L1 and L2 research suggests that reading fluency at this point draws more heavily on language comprehension components, as well as "top-down" processes (e.g., context, world knowledge, pragmatics). As basic word reading skills become more fluent, reading comprehension skills become more closely aligned with language comprehension.

It is important to consider some recent refinements to the construct of reading fluency that are especially relevant to an understanding of L2 reading in typically developing children and those with reading difficulties. In the primary grades, L2 children read lists of familiar words and connected text with similar fluency (Geva et al., 1997; Geva & Farnia, 2012). This trend may reflect the fact that in the primary grades the materials children read include high-frequency words and that, regardless of whether they read texts or words in isolation, what develops are their fluent word reading skills. In higher grades, children have better word recognition and decoding skills and can take advantage of various top-down processes, such as topic familiarity and context, and they are able to anticipate words on the basis of syntactic and collocational information. As a result of this facilitation, they can read texts with more fluency than isolated words. To note, in some languages context is absolutely essential for reading (e.g., Hebrew, Arabic, Farsi, Urdu, Pashto) because vowels are missing from most texts.

The ability to read isolated words with fluency may not be strongly related to having well-developed L2 oral proficiency. In spite of the fact that L2 learners have a lower command of the L2 than their L1 peers, typically developing L2 learners often have word reading accuracy and fluency scores that are similar to their L1 peers (e.g., Geva et al., 1997; Geva & Yaghoub-Zadeh, 2006; Lesaux & Siegel, 2003). However, the fluent reading of texts is more closely aligned with L2 proficiency (e.g., Al Otaiba et al., 2009; Crosson & Lesaux, 2010; Geva & Farnia, 2012; Nakamoto et al., 2007). This means that typically developing L2 readers whose L2 language skills are better developed can read L2 texts with more fluency than their peers whose L2 language skills are less well developed. It also means that when the reading of L2 children and adolescents is consistently dysfluent (in comparison with L2 children coming from a similar background) the sources of this dysfluency need to be carefully analyzed; it is possible that the source of their difficulty in reading texts fluently cannot be attributed simply to lack of L2 proficiency, and that instead it may point to having word decoding difficulties, persistent difficulties in developing language skills that may be associated with a language impairment, a slow but accurate reading profile, or a combination of these factors (Geva & Farnia, 2012; Yaghoub-Zadeh et al., 2012). It follows that the impact of having poorly developed language skills will be evident on text reading fluency and reading comprehension tasks. Yet, these difficulties may not be as evident in early stages of reading development, when the focus of reading development is on learning to decode words with accuracy and fluency.

ISSUES IN IDENTIFICATION OF L2 WITH
READING DIFFICULTIES

Educators in multilingual settings are faced with the difficult task of differentiating L2 learners who struggle with reading because their developing English proficiency is not sufficient to read or comprehend what they read, and those who also struggle because of a more pervasive reading difficulty. Differentiation is further complicated by additional risk factors experienced by some subgroups of L2 learners, particularly immigrants and certain linguistic and culturally marginalized groups (e.g., lack of schooling or interrupted schooling resulting in underdeveloped L1 language and literacy skills, acculturation stress). As noted earlier, by definition, L2 learners are less proficient in their L2 than their monolingual peers. Thus, the task of distinguishing typically developing L2 learners from L2 learners with reading difficulties is complex because it is often unclear whether poor reading skills can be attributed to their developing language skills or to a genuine problem in reading (Geva, 2000).

As was highlighted earlier in this chapter, historically L2 children and adolescents with reading difficulties have been either overrepresented among those assessed as having a learning disability (LD) due to their developing language proficiency (Cummins, 1984) or under-represented due to a tendency to attribute their poor reading skills to poor language proficiency in the L2 and their L2 status (Limbos & Geva, 2001). These misrepresentations, coupled with a widespread belief that reading difficulties in children learning an L2 may not be reliably assessed until adequate command of the L2 has been attained, have led to bias and inaccurate identification (Fraser, Adelson, & Geva, 2014).

Research about the accurate identification of L2 learners with reading difficulties is an emerging area of focus due to increased sensitivity to the need to avoid bias and provide fair and equitable educational opportunities. For example, Statistics Canada reported that over 3 million children living in Canada speak a language other than English as their first language, and this number is growing (Statistics Canada, 2006). In the province of Ontario, 20% of the school-age children speak a home language that is not English or French (People for Education, 2013). Conversely, 17% of elementary students and 23% of secondary students across Ontario are identified as having learning difficulties and in need of special education support (People for Education, 2013). The number of students who both are L2 learners and have difficulties in learning is not known, but from these statistics it is clear that the number is not negligible. L2 children and adolescents are as likely as monolingual speakers to have RD (Lesaux & Kieffer, 2010). In the general population, roughly 10% of children have a diagnosed RD (Snowling, 2000). This should be the rate irrespective of the language or languages they speak. However, the same percentage of L2 learners is not necessarily *identified* as having a reading disability (Hamayan, Marler, Sanchez-Lopez, & Damino, 2007).

Biased assessment assumptions and processes have been associated with overidentification (Cummins, 1984). With increased awareness of the perils of overidentification, the pendulum has swung to the opposite extreme. Underidentification has emerged as a serious problem, associated with a simplistic attribution of learning difficulties to a lack of proficiency in the L2 and to cultural differences (Klingner, Artiles, & Mendez Barletta, 2006; Limbos & Geva, 2001). In many jurisdictions precautions related to a commitment to minimize bias in assessment and to provide learners with sufficient opportunities to improve their L2 proficiency have led to delays in the assessment, identification, and treatment of L2 children who were struggling academically as they were learning to develop their L2.

The need to address the identification and intervention provided to L2 children and adolescents who have learning difficulties is underscored by the findings of a recent study by Solari et al. (2012). Solari et al. examined growth in literacy skills of a large sample of children attending Grades 3 through 10. They compared developmental trajectories of typically developing children with three high-risk subgroups that were part of the sample: English L2, children with a specific LD, and children identified as being both LD and English L2. Analyses indicated that in all three high-risk groups, children began the year at substantially lower levels than their non-risk peers. Moreover, children who were LD and English L2 speakers had the lowest scores at the onset. In addition, students who were in any of the high-risk subgroups and came from low socio-economic status (SES) backgrounds performed worse than their peers in similar risk status groups who did not come from extremely poor backgrounds. In other words, there was a significant cumulative impact of membership in a risk group coupled with low SES on academic outcomes.

Interestingly, some studies suggest that L2 learners may be underrepresented in special education programs geared toward children with learning disabilities in the early elementary school grades but may be overrepresented in such programs after Grade 5 (Artiles, Rueda, Salazar, & Higareda, 2002). Striving toward timely, reliable, and unbiased assessment and intervention of L2 learners who may also have an LD is a complex and sensitive problem, and the sources of bias and delays should be better understood and addressed in terms of research, policy, accessibility, and professional training.

It is also important to be mindful of the heterogeneous nature of L2 learners, which means, for example, that what is "normal" L2 development in children of immigrants who have attended ESL programs since kindergarten may not be generalizable to youth who arrived in their new country as young adolescents and may have also experienced interrupted schooling. Recent years have witnessed a steady increase in systematic research that aims to clarify the learning and cognitive profiles of L2 learners who are typically developing and those who demonstrate difficulties (e.g., Geva & Herbert, 2012; Geva & Massey-Garrison, 2013). Findings have refined our understanding of aspects of reading development and cognitive processes that are closely tied to having adequate levels of L2 proficiency, and those aspects that are less tied to well-developed L2 proficiency. This nascent research has drawn attention to a number of issues, including characteristics of typical and atypical L2 language and literacy development; a better understanding of the relationships between L2 proficiency and reading and cognitive processing components; and refinement in approaches to assessment, such as response to intervention (RTI), which are more dynamic and carefully tailored to different groups of learners (Fuchs & Fuchs, 2006; Geva & Wiener, 2015).

Multiple risk factors

In addition to cognitive factors, a number of contextual risk factors may potentially impact reading development in second language learners, making them even more vulnerable to academic failure (Geva & Wiener, 2015). These include age at immigration (e.g., older students are more at risk), extent and quality of exposure to L2 language of instruction, level of L1 literacy, parental education, physical or mental health problems or disability, low SES, living in segregated communities or ghettos, mental distress or post-traumatic stress disorder caused by experiences of violence in home country, separation from parents or family unit, cultural changes due to immigration, conflict between generations, acculturation stress and the pressure to adjust to the new country, negative stereotypes and discrimination, and the nature of attributions to learning disabilities (see Geva & Wiener, 2015, for review).

L2 learners constitute a diverse group of students, with the only similarity between them being that their L1 is something other than the majority language. L2 learners may come from a wide variety of countries, but many were also born in their country of residence. Those who were born outside the country of residence may immigrate for many different reasons, such as following job or education opportunities or fleeing disaster and violence in their home country. L2 voluntary immigrants who have formal education from their home country will likely do better than L2 refugee immigrants who may have experienced trauma, relocation, or lack of formal schooling, or non-refugees who have little formal schooling (Geva & Wiener, 2015).

Research findings have shown that the older students are when they arrive in a new country, the weaker their reading performance is when assessed at age 15 or higher (PISA, 2012). This may be attributed to a combination of factors, such as the amount of time spent learning in the L1 in the home country and the type of instruction or schooling that students were exposed to prior to immigration. Older students may have the added challenge of learning a new language and acclimatizing to new instructional techniques and school expectations at the same time. In general, educational risks for L2 learners are associated with a mixture of factors, as mentioned earlier. The more risk factors the L2 student is exposed to, the greater the likelihood the student will do poorly in the school environment.

Risk factors such as those discussed here create a compounding negative impact for children experiencing reading difficulties. Fortunately, there are protective factors that have a supporting effect in the intervention and remediation of children and adolescents with reading difficulties. Protective factors can be internal and external (see Geva & Wiener, 2015, for further discussion). Internal protective factors include effective and efficient cognitive skills, good temperament, coping skills, and interpersonal skills. External factors include a supporting home literacy environment, prior literacy experience, prior intervention, and additional support networks (e.g., teachers, tutoring programs, community).

The amount of support L2 learners receive in the home environment and community is critical to developing language and literacy skills. Positive home experiences that promote print knowledge, language, and other literacy-related activities are important for all learners regardless of first language background (Cummins, 2012; Paradis et al., 2011). Furthermore, social support available to students and their families is also important. Immigrants who are part of a supportive community tend to demonstrate more resilience to the challenges associated with immigration (Beiser et al., 2011). Social support can give families practical, emotional, and social assistance, and can be provided by individuals, groups, and organizations (e.g., other family members, friends, neighbours, religious affiliations, settlement organizations, schools).

It is important to remember that despite the extra challenges that L2 learners face, the contextual risk factors associated with being an L2 learner do not cause reading disabilities. That said, they will likely exacerbate the difficulties experienced by the L2 student in developing proficient L2 language and literacy skills if a reading disability does in fact exist.

SPECIFIC READING DIFFICULTIES IN AN L2

Before we begin the discussion of specific reading difficulties, it is important to emphasize that reading and language components are dimensional in nature. Only those who perform below a certain cut-off qualify for a diagnosis. That is, children or adolescents who perform at a level "substantially and quantifiably" below age expectations on standardized measures as part of the clinical assessment qualify for a diagnosis of a *specific learning disorder*. Yet, children and adolescents may display *difficulties* in these domains even when these difficulties are not severe enough to merit a formal diagnosis.

In line with conceptualizations of specific learning disorders in the domain of reading and language (e.g., *DSM-5*; NASP, 2007), we discuss separately research pertaining to the following three subtypes: difficulties in *decoding* (also referred to as *dyslexia*), difficulties in reading *fluency*, and difficulties in reading *comprehension* (including *language impairment*). It should be emphasized that some individuals may qualify for a diagnosis of a specific learning disorder in more than one domain (in which case their problems will be more severe). In addition, we also describe research on children who may have a language disorder. In this chapter we use the broader term *language impairment* to describe children who are struggling with language difficulties (e.g., vocabulary, comprehension, morphological and syntactic difficulties, sentence structure). This term also encompasses those children who have met the criteria for a diagnosis of language disorder. We address some common overlapping deficit areas associated with children and adolescents who have language impairment and those that have either decoding or comprehension-based difficulties.

Decoding difficulties

Research findings consistently reveal that similar underlying cognitive processes – for example, phonological awareness and rapid naming skills – are associated with decoding difficulties (Geva et al., 2000; Lesaux & Geva, 2006; Lipka & Siegel, 2012; McBride-Chang et al., 2012; Ndlovu, 2010) and spelling difficulties (Fender, 2008; Geva & Lafrance, 2011; Khan-Horwitz, Sparks, & Goldstein, 2012) in L1 and L2 learners. Studies suggest that children who have decoding problems (i.e., word-level difficulties) in one language will also demonstrate decoding problems in their other language (Da Fontoura & Siegel, 1995; Lesaux & Geva, 2006). These studies suggest that even though L2 learners as a group have lower proficiency in the target language, one can expect similarities in the cognitive profiles of L1 and L2 students who have word reading difficulties. Thus, it is possible to predict word reading skills in one language from phonological awareness skills in another language (Commeau et al., 1999; Erdos, Genesee, Savage, & Haigh, 2014; Jared, Cormier, Levy, & Wade-Woolley, 2010; Saiegh-Haddad & Geva, 2010).

Rapid naming skills can also be used to predict word reading skills across languages. For example, McBride-Chang et al. (2012) looked at the longitudinal cognitive profiles of three groups of Chinese L1 children who had reading difficulties in Chinese, English, or both languages. Their findings demonstrated that rapid naming was significantly slower in the group of children who had reading difficulties associated with both English and Chinese in comparison to the other groups.

Research from a Canadian longitudinal study tracking L1 and English L2 learners throughout Grades 1 to 6 demonstrated that children with decoding difficulties can be reliably identified regardless of home language (Geva & Massey-Garrison, 2013; Ndlovu, 2010). These researchers used a cut-off point of the 30th percentile on a standardized test of word reading and demonstrated that L1 and L2 learners with severe decoding difficulties were proportionally represented. That is, the L2 learners were not over or under-identified as being poor decoders. The profiles of L2 and L1 learners who were identified with decoding difficulties were characterized by phonologically based difficulties, weaknesses in working memory, and more limited oral language skills (e.g., vocabulary, syntactic skills, listening comprehension). Additionally, the L1 and L2 learners with decoding difficulties had significant delays in literacy development, showing weaknesses in both word- and text-level reading and writing.

Children who have persistent poor decoding skills in spite of quality teaching constitute a group of students with an impairment in word reading accuracy often referred to as *dyslexia*. Research has consistently demonstrated that children with dyslexia have difficulties with phonological awareness, rapid naming, and phonological short-term memory skills. These cognitive processes play a direct role in their reading difficulties, especially the acquisition of word reading skills (Ramus, Marshall, Rosen, & van der Lely, 2013; Shaywitz & Shaywitz, 2005; Wolf & Bowers, 1999), and this is also the case with L2 learners with dyslexia (Chung et al., 2014; Chung & Ho, 2010; Geva & Herbert, 2012; Verhoeven et al., 2011). The "double deficit" hypothesis states that combined significant difficulties on both phonological awareness and rapid naming account for the most severe reading difficulties, while the reading difficulties of those with a deficit in only one domain are less severe (Wolf & Bowers, 1999). Studies have supported the double deficit hypothesis, indicating that children can be poor readers due to deficits in either phonological awareness or rapid naming skills; however, the most severe reading difficulties result when deficits in both of these aspects of phonological cognitive processing exist (Steacy, Kirby, Parrila, & Compton, 2014; Wolf & Bowers, 1999). Stated differently, the most severe reading difficulties result from an overload of cognitive deficits in more than one area.

Reading fluency and decoding difficulties

To read texts with fluency, readers need to have accurate and fluent decoding skills and have language skills that enable them to benefit from top-down processes. In reality, one can identify subtypes of L1 or L2 readers who may have an LD and face difficulties in developing accurate decoding skills, and L1 and L2 readers who are accurate but slow readers, regardless of their language skills. Some evidence for difficulties in developing fluent reading skills is available in studies of children learning to read in their L1, their L2, or concurrently in both their L1 and L2 (e.g., Geva et al., 1997; Quiroga, Lemos-Britton, Mostafapour, Abbott, & Berninger, 2002). For example, Geva and Yaghoub-Zadeh (2006) described the cognitive and literacy profiles of three distinct subgroups of English L1 and English L2 primary school children. The profiles of the L1 and L2 children who had *accurate and fluent* word reading skills were very similar to each other on reading comprehension and on cognitive measures, such as phonological awareness and rapid automatized naming. The L1 and L2 subgroup described as *accurate but slow* decoders performed more poorly on the cognitive and reading comprehension measures than children in the accurate and fluent L1 and L2 group, and the profiles of L1 and L2 children who were accurate but slow were highly similar. Finally, the L1 and L2 children with *severe decoding* problems had a very slow reading rate. Their performance on the cognitive measures was lower than that of the other two groups, and both L1 and L2 learners with severe decoding problems were unable to complete the text fluency tasks because reading was so onerous for them.

A handful of studies involving primary-level children attending bilingual programs have shown that poor decoders were less fluent than good decoders in reading texts in English, their home language, and in French (Geva & Clifton, 1994) or Hebrew (Geva et al., 1997). Geva et al. (1997) reported that performance on accuracy and speed of L1 word reading (English) and L2 word reading (Hebrew) was very similar. This finding is consistent with the observation that oral language proficiency does not make a unique contribution to word recognition in young L2 children (see Geva, 2006, for review). Additionally, in a result replicating Jackson and Donaldson (1989), Geva et al. found that in the L1 (English), children's text reading time was faster than reading the same words presented in isolation. Further, reading words in context was facilitated in L1 English, but no top-down facilitation was noted in their L2 Hebrew, as their Hebrew proficiency was minimal. It should be noted that this study used a pointed Hebrew measure (i.e., Hebrew with vowels indicated); the outcome of this study using an unpointed Hebrew task (i.e., no vowels) would likely be different as the reader would then need to draw on context, syntax, and morphological knowledge in his or her decoding to know what word is being referred to.

The studies reviewed in this section have implications for working with subgroups of poor readers. When L2 children experience difficulties in developing accurate and fluent reading even when they read simple materials that do not put heavy demands on their language comprehension, attribution to lack of adequate oral language proficiency is not warranted. This may be the case especially when L2 children and adolescents are enrolled in high-quality instructional programs. This logic applies especially when other children from similar backgrounds and educational histories show progress. The culprit in this case may be inaccurate and dysfluent word recognition skills and deficits in the underlying cognitive-linguistic processes that are needed for word recognition. These children may benefit from instruction that focuses on the development of efficient word recognition skills (Gersten & Baker, 2003; Gersten & Geva, 2003; Quiroga et al., 2002).

Comprehension difficulties

Within the reading research literature, poor comprehenders are referred to as late-emerging poor comprehenders (in L1 literature, e.g., Catts, Adlof, & Ellis-Weismer, 2006), and "unexpected" poor comprehenders (in L2 literature, Li & Kirby, 2014). The research related to poor comprehenders and poor readers more broadly supports the notion that different types of poor readers may emerge at different times in reading development (Catts et al., 2006). Phonological processing skills (e.g., word decoding, phonological awareness) form the foundation of word reading and thus are highly predictive of reading ability in the primary grades (Adams, 1990). Thus, readers with word-level difficulties and some children with language impairment who also experience phonological deficits will show difficulties in reading at this time (Bishop & Snowling, 2004). Some children with word-level difficulties may demonstrate good reading comprehension skills because they are able to rely on higher-level language, cognitive, and metacognitive skills that are crucial for text comprehension. However, late-emerging poor comprehenders begin to demonstrate reading difficulties in the middle school grades when the reading tasks shift to what Chall (1996) referred to as "reading to learn". For these late-emerging poor readers, deficits in higher-level skills, such as vocabulary, syntactic skills, and the ability to make inferences, begin to have a devastating impact on their reading performance (Cain & Oakhill, 2006; Geva & Massey-Garrison, 2013).

The body of research related to poor comprehenders in L2 is small but growing. L2 poor comprehenders have intact phonological skills and thus good word reading ability, but by definition are below other L2 children from similar backgrounds who have average reading comprehension – that is, even when their L2 status is taken into account (Geva & Herbert, 2012; Geva & Massey-Garrison, 2013; Li & Kirby, 2014; Ndlovu, 2010). The research thus far suggests that poor oral language proficiency results in persistent difficulties in reading comprehension. Research has demonstrated deficits in vocabulary breadth and depth, morphology, syntactic awareness, working memory, listening comprehension (Fraser, 2015; Geva & Massey-Garrison, 2013; Lesaux & Kieffer, 2010; Lesaux, Lipka, & Siegel, 2006; Li & Kirby, 2014), and higher-order skills, such as inferencing and conjunction knowledge (Fraser, Geva, Pasquarella, Gottardo, & Biemiller, 2015; Geva & Massey-Garrison, 2013; Li & Kirby, 2014).

Several studies have explored characteristics of L2 poor comprehenders. Geva and Massey-Garrison (2013) focused on Grade 5 English L2 learners from various home language backgrounds and a comparison group of L1 learners. They identified in relation to their reference group (L1 or L2) three subgroups: normal readers (intact decoding and comprehension), poor decoders (with typical comprehension), and poor comprehenders (with no decoding problems). The researchers found distinct cognitive and linguistic profiles for each of the three groups (regardless of whether they were L1 or L2 speakers). Of relevance here is the finding that L1 and L2 poor comprehenders had similar deficits with their oral language. Specifically the L2 English poor comprehenders had difficulties in producing more complex sentences, comprehending and making inferences when listening to stories, and with higher-level aspects of language, such as inferencing. Furthermore, in line with what has been found with typically developing L2 learners and their typically developing monolingual counterparts, the vocabulary skills of the L2 poor comprehenders lagged behind the vocabulary skills of the L1 poor comprehenders.

Lesaux, Lipka, and Siegel (2006) found in their study that the Grade 4 L2 poor comprehenders had deficits in vocabulary, as well as in verbal working memory, even though they did not have word reading difficulties when compared with L1 poor comprehenders. Lesaux and Kieffer (2010) reported similar findings in their study of Grade 6 English L2 learners of varying home backgrounds. Their poor comprehenders had low levels of vocabulary knowledge despite word-level reading accuracy and fluency. Li and Kirby (2014) explored potential sources of "unexpected" poor comprehenders in their study with Grade 8 English L2 students in China. Their poor comprehenders had difficulty with a wide range of oral language skills, such as inferencing, listening comprehension, and morphological awareness. They concluded that poor vocabulary (both breadth and depth) was the key source of reading comprehension difficulty for the poor comprehenders. To sum, these studies suggest that L2 poor comprehenders have difficulties with a range of skills, including oral language and specifically vocabulary, syntax, working memory, and higher-order comprehension skills.

Two studies have explored the relationship between poor reading comprehension and writing skill development. Ndlovu (2010) found that, as expected, the L2 poor comprehenders who had difficulty with vocabulary and listening comprehension also had difficulties in story writing, the mechanics of writing, sentence structure, and overall story organization. Li and Kirby (2014) found that their L2 poor comprehenders also had difficulties with summary writing (e.g., writing details and main ideas). These studies demonstrate the potentially far-reaching impact that poor reading comprehension can have on academic success among L2 learners. They also underscore the pervasiveness of poor oral language in reading comprehension. To date "unexpected" poor comprehenders are not as well understood as poor decoders. More research is needed to investigate the sources of this subtype of poor readers and best intervention techniques.

Language impairment

The extent to which L2 children and adolescents with language impairment are impacted in their reading is not well researched so far. We therefore turn to L1 research to gain some understanding. L1 literature suggests that some children have language impairment in the absence of word reading deficits, making their reading difficulties similar to those of poor comprehenders – that is, they have good decoding ability but poor language skills, leaving them with poor reading comprehension (Cain, 2013). But most children with language impairment have both phonological processing and other language deficits. That is, they have difficulties with phonology as well as with semantics, morphology, syntax, and discourse, and this "double whammy" has a serious impact on their reading. They have both weak decoding skills and weak language skills, causing overall difficulties in reading comprehension, reading fluency, and related higher-order skills (Cain, 2013). One ongoing point of discussion in the L1 literature is the distinction between dyslexia and language impairment, and the continuity between the two (Bishop & Snowling, 2004; Cain, 2013). As noted earlier, it is important to bear in mind that the underlying causes of reading difficulties experienced by children who have a language and reading impairment are dimensional and that there are some commonalities in their potentially poor phonological skills. We know more about predictors and profiles of poor decoders and poor comprehenders in L2 populations than about those who may have both decoding and language impairment. While only a couple of studies have examined reading comprehension in L2 learners with language impairment (e.g., Farnia & Geva, 2012; Petersen & Gillam, 2013), we expect, based on what has been observed in L1 research as well as the scant research with L2 poor comprehenders and poor decoders, that language impairment would also be related to reading comprehension difficulties.

Farnia and Geva (2012) examined a model for identifying early and later-emerging language impairment in 402 English L2 and 149 English L1 speakers in relation to the means of each reference group (i.e., separately for English

L2 and English L1). They identified similar percentages of early-emerging (Grade 1) and later-emerging (Grade 3) language impairment in English L2 and English monolingual students. The accuracy of classification of later-emerging LI cases was estimated as 93% and 95% for ELLs and EL1s, respectively. Of the Grade 1 (early predictor) variables, working memory and speed of processing reliably distinguished the groups with and without later-emerging language impairment. These findings indicate that regardless of L1-L2 status, it is possible to identify children at risk for developing later-emerging LI as early as Grade 1. Of the Grade 3 (late predictor) variables, phonological short-term memory and vocabulary reliably distinguished between the groups with and without later-emerging LI. These findings indicate that it is possible to predict indicators of later-emerging LI rather early in L1 and L2, and that the nature of the predictors is developmental and changes over time. In their study with Latino English L2 learners at risk for language impairment, Petersen and Gillam (2013) found that Spanish L1 measures in kindergarten did not predict children with reading difficulties in Grade 1 over and above the English L2 measures. They also found that oral language skills predicted unique variance in reading comprehension in Grade 1. Differences between those with poor reading comprehension (e.g., poor comprehenders) and those defined as language-impaired (e.g., also having word-level difficulties) were not specifically explored.

Taken together, these studies suggest that the profiles of language-impaired monolingual and L2 learners may be similar, with L2 learners having more severe deficits in their oral language skills than L1 learners possibly due to a combined impact of their L2 status and language impairment. Importantly, it appears that L2 measures can be used to predict L2 reading comprehension and language difficulties, at least where English is the L2. However, one should be cautious about using published test norms developed for L1 learners. To enhance validity it is good practice to interpret performance in relation to a reference group of L2 speakers coming from similar linguistic and educational backgrounds. Systematic developmental and intervention studies involving L2 children and adolescents who may have language impairment are needed.

ASSESSMENT OF READING DIFFICULTIES

Persistent difficulties in acquiring word reading skills despite effective intervention strategies may signify a reading disability in the L2 learner, just as they do for L1 learners. There are two main research findings that guide the conditions for valid assessment and diagnosis of L2 learners (Geva & Wiener, 2015). The first pertains to the role of L2 language proficiency. It appears that word-level reading and the cognitive processes that underlie word reading (e.g., phonological awareness, rapid naming) are not as closely tied to oral language as previously believed. Therefore, there is no need to wait until oral language proficiency is on par with L1 peers in order to provide reliable assessment of persistent difficulties of L2 learners in developing L2 word reading skills (Geva, 2006; Geva & Herbert, 2012; Geva & Wade-Woolley, 2004). Second, it is helpful to consider individual differences in the development of basic reading skills and language skills within similar groups of L2 learners. This allows the clinician to make an accurate diagnosis of a reading disability by making comparisons with typically developing L2 learners coming from similar backgrounds. This is particularly important when assessing L2 language skills, such as vocabulary knowledge or syntactic skills, since research demonstrates a persistent lag in this area when compared with typically developing L1 learners. When it becomes obvious that an L2 learner is not making the expected progress in basic reading skills compared to other students of similar background and receiving similar instruction, further assessment and intervention are required.

Good indicators of an underlying reading disability in L2 learners are weaknesses in decoding and cognitive skills, such as phonological awareness, rapid naming, and verbal working memory. Research has shown that performance on these measures is similar regardless of whether the student is assessed in the L1 or L2 (Lesaux & Geva, 2006). Furthermore, these skills are less dependent on language proficiency than other skills (e.g., vocabulary), which makes it possible to gain reliable information on L2 reading difficulties regardless of language proficiency. This is likely the case with older L2 learners as well, but at this point the research for this age group is lacking. Tests designed to measure word-level reading skills and related cognitive skills in L1 learners can, therefore, also be used to diagnose reading disabilities in L2 learners (Gersten et al., 2007; Geva & Farnia, 2012). The research also suggests that reading fluency exerts its influence on word reading skills in a similar manner between L1 and L2 learners, which further highlights the fact that the underlying cognitive and linguistic processes involved in L1 and L2 reading follow similar developmental paths (Geva & Farnia, 2012; Lipka & Siegel, 2012). This suggests the applicability of word-level reading fluency measures (e.g., word list reading) when assessing L2 learners with reading disabilities or suspected reading disabilities.

Research findings provide valuable empirical support to counteract the historically cautious belief that L2 learners should not be assessed until their oral language proficiency skills are on par with their L1 peers. It is well understood in the L1 literature that the earlier reading difficulties can be identified, the earlier intervention strategies can be put in place to mitigate the associated challenges for the struggling reader (Catts, 1991; Torgesen, 1998). The same can be said with confidence for struggling L2 readers. Nevertheless, less is known about the assessment and diagnosis of poor comprehension and language impairment in L2 learners. That said, some of the basic principles used for assessing and diagnosing difficulties at the word level can also be applied for evaluating difficulties in comprehension and language impairment. That is, (1) considerations are made with respect to other L2 learners from similar educational backgrounds, and not L1 learners and published test norms, and (2) there is a lack of development in comprehension and language when compared to other L2 learners of similar age and background.

TREATMENT AND INTERVENTION

Although limited, research findings examining the effectiveness of interventions with L2 learners with reading difficulties indicate that L2 learners benefit from the same types of instruction as struggling L1 learners (Geva & Herbert, 2012). Research has demonstrated that five components of reading instruction – phonics, phonemic awareness, reading fluency, vocabulary, and reading comprehension – benefit both L1 and L2 struggling learners, although instruction should be adjusted to meet the specific needs of L2 learners (August & Shanahan, 2006).

Intervention research suggests that L2 learners who struggle with reading difficulties respond well to interventions that work for L1 struggling readers (Cirino et al., 2009; Lovett et al., 2008; Wise & Chen, 2010). Specifically, interventions that target phonological awareness through activities that involve counting, segmenting, and blending syllables, phonemes, and words, comparing and matching phonemes, and identifying sounds with letters assist both L1 and L2 learner with decoding difficulties. Lovett et al. (2008) compared the effect of a phonologically based reading intervention program (PHAST) to that of a special education program. Both programs involved struggling readers ranging between Grades 2 and 8 who met criteria for a reading disability in both L1 and L2. The results from the study revealed that both L1 and L2 learners with a reading disability demonstrated significant improvement on measures of word identification and decoding skills in comparison to their L1 and L2 peers in the special education control group. Given that L2 learners may not understand the vocabulary used in the various phonological awareness activities, it is also helpful to teach the meaning of the words and draw attention to phonemes that do not exist in their L1 (Linan-Thompson & Hickman-Davis, 2002; Wang & Geva, 2003).

Morphology instruction is another effective strategy for teaching L2 learners with reading disabilities. Some sample strategies include teaching common affixes and using them in speeded drills and word building exercises, and using word sorting activities to help students discriminate words based on morphological features (Goodwin & Ahn, 2010; Lovett et al., 2008). Based on their meta-analysis of morphology-based reading interventions, Goodwin and Ahn (2010) concluded that morphological instruction can improve both phonological and morphological awareness. Considering that children with decoding difficulties and some children with language impairment tend to struggle on phonological awareness tasks, morphological instruction is potentially another avenue to employ to help strengthen that area. That said, morphological awareness instruction helps primarily with vocabulary (McBride-Chang, Wagner, Muse, Chow, & Shu, 2005).

Remediation for comprehension difficulties

There is a great deal of L2 research available on how to intervene and support children who have decoding difficulties. However, very little research is available on how to best intervene with L2 students who have comprehension difficulties. The available research suggests that explicit and intensive vocabulary instruction enhances L2 reading comprehension skills (Carlo et al., 2004; Shanahan & Beck, 2006; also see Chapter 5, this volume). These findings demonstrate similarities to intervention methods that have also been shown to be helpful for L1 students struggling with reading comprehension (Graves, August, & Mancilla-Martinez, 2013). Graves et al. (2013) suggest that best practices for effective vocabulary instruction include: dedicating a portion of the regular classroom lesson to explicit vocabulary instruction, using repeated exposure to new words in multiple contexts, providing various opportunities to practice the use of the new vocabulary in a variety of contexts and activities, and providing students with strategies to help with independent learning (e.g., morphological awareness strategies, such as word families and knowledge of affixes).

Focused instruction in higher-order reading comprehension skills, such as inferencing and conjunction knowledge, is also warranted. For example, a recent study by Fraser et al. (2015) found that the relationship between conjunction knowledge (i.e., using cohesive devices) and reading comprehension was partially mediated by vocabulary. They concluded that conjunctions play a unique and important role in reading comprehension for L2 learners. Conjunctions are complex words that serve at least two central functions. They are vocabulary items, and it is essential for readers to be familiar with their basic meaning. But conjunctions also signal abstract relationships, such as causality (e.g., *because*), adversity (e.g., *although*), and additively (e.g., *moreover*), that exist between idea units in text. The authors suggested that helping students to acknowledge their inferencing techniques by drawing their attention to the logical relationships between ideas in text that are signalled by conjunctions would be important for instruction, as would focused vocabulary instruction about conjunction words. Improving reading comprehension through focused vocabulary and higher-order reading skill instruction would be especially beneficial for L2 learners who are poor comprehenders or language-impaired.

Approaches to improving reading fluency

To help students improve their reading fluency, teaching is required that targets pivotal components of word reading, such as the graphophonic foundations for word reading fluency, expanding vocabulary and other oral language skills, providing opportunities for recognizing high-frequency words with automaticity, teaching common word parts and spelling patterns, teaching, modeling, and providing practice in the application of decoding strategies, selecting texts that enhance the use of reading strategies, using repeated reading procedures for struggling readers, and providing additional practice through independent reading of materials that are neither too easy nor too difficult in terms of the vocabulary. It is also important to monitor reading fluency development through appropriate assessment procedures (National Reading Panel, 2000; Pikulski & Chard, 2005) – for example, informal reading inventories (IRI), the Gray Oral Reading Test (GORT; Wiederholt & Bryant, 1992), or the Test of Word Reading Efficiency (TOWRE; Torgesen, Wagner, & Rashotte, 1999).

Response to intervention

There is strong evidence to suggest that RTI can lead to positive reading outcomes for L2 learners (Cirino et al., 2009; Gersten et al., 2007; Lovett et al., 2008). RTI is a three-tiered prevention model that focuses on early identification and uses evidence-based instruction (Fuchs & Fuchs, 2006). The tiered approach is a model for ongoing assessment, monitoring, and preventative intervention for students. Through this model, students are provided with intervention as soon as the need for support is evident, and without having to wait for a formal assessment. The approach is based on high-quality, evidence-based assessment and instructional methods, and intervention is systematic and sequential. How students respond to the intervention provided in each tier guides future decisions about the need to provide more or less support, or to use different approaches and teaching methods. In Tier 1, effective, evidence-based instruction is given to all students. Ongoing assessment and progress monitoring are provided by the teacher to note any students who are experiencing difficulty. In Tier 2, intervention is given to students in small groups who are not making adequate progress in a particular area. Progress is monitored, and instruction is adjusted as needed. In Tier 3, intervention is given to the small percentage of students identified as needing more intensive, specific, and individualized support.

Progress monitoring is an essential component of the RTI model. With progress monitoring, a student's academic performance is assessed frequently, using brief and easily administered measures. Curriculum-based measurement (CBM; Deno, 1985; Deno & Fuchs, 1987) is one example of progress monitoring that has been receiving increasing attention over the years. With CBM, benchmarks are used for screening and "slopes" (i.e., graphical representations of a student's change in performance over time) are used to confirm or disconfirm student risk status in Tier 1. CBM is then used to set individual education plan (IEP) goals, formulate individualized programs, and determine RTI in Tiers 2 and 3.

Linan-Thompson, Vaughn, Prater, and Cirino (2006) used RTI with L2 students at risk for reading difficulties identified at the beginning of Grade 1. Students were randomly assigned to an intervention group or control group. The intervention group received supplemental reading intervention provided daily for 50 minutes in small groups from October to April of the Grade 1 year, whereas the control group received the school's regular instructional program. Student progress was monitored at the end of Grade 1 and again at the end of Grade 2. Findings indicated that the students who participated in the intervention group had statistically stronger performance on reading-related measures as compared to their control group peers. The findings also demonstrated that the intervention group students met RTI criteria at the end of Grade 1 and Grade 2, indicating that they would likely not be referral candidates for special education support.

Overall, how the L2 learner responds to the intervention strategies and the degree of progress the student makes can indicate whether further intervention or support is necessary. As with L1 students with reading disabilities, L2 learners will need additional time and practice with decoding strategies and will need to work on their language development, such as vocabulary and listening comprehension skills. The L2 learner with a reading disability requires both continued support to help develop English oral language skills and focused instruction to develop word reading skills using intervention methods that have been found to be effective for L1 students with reading disabilities. Additional research is needed to explore reading difficulties, including word-level difficulties as well as poor comprehension and language impairment, in older L2 learners who begin their schooling in the higher grade levels.

CONCLUSION

The following two cases underscore some of the issues surrounding our growing understanding of reading difficulties in L2 learners. Ahmad's case highlights issues relating to word-level difficulties, while Naiara's case highlights those related to poor comprehension. Both Ahmad and Naiara are made-up, amalgamated cases. The following is a series of guiding questions to encourage deep reflection about the issues and an opportunity to apply what was discussed in this review chapter.

1 Are Naiara and Ahmad's word-level reading skills consistent with their language and reading comprehension skills?
2 Are there are any concerns with Ahmad or Naiara's oral language skills? If so, what are the specific concerns?
3 How does Naiara's progress compare to other children of a similar age and background? What are some "red flags" that Ahmad's progress is not on par with his peers?
4 What additional risk factors may play a role in Ahmad and Naiara's language and literacy development?

Case Study 1: "Ahmad"

Ahmad is a 12-year old boy in Grade 6. His parents immigrated to Canada the year before he was born. Since then he has lived for various periods of time in Canada and Sudan. He has missed weeks or even months of schooling in Canada on more than a few occasions when the family left for Sudan during the school year. He lives with both of his parents; however, his father is often out of the country on business. Arabic is the language spoken at home. His mother speaks only Arabic but has a rudimentary grasp of some basic English skills. Ahmad is the youngest of four children. He has two older brothers attending high school, and his older sister attends university. Ahmad has attended four different schools in the same large metropolitan city as a result of family moves.

Due to parent concerns about Ahmad's weak grades at school, he has attended 1-hour tutoring sessions once a week for the last 2 years. According to reports from Ahmad's older sister, his siblings often assist him with homework and assignments at home when necessary. Furthermore, his sister indicated that his oral language skills in Arabic are well developed and there were no concerns with his language acquisition. She indicated that he is a reluctant reader and rarely reads in Arabic, but as a young child he enjoyed being read to by his parents or older siblings.

His current teacher reported that her main concerns are with his reading and writing skills. Specifically, he is a slow, hesitant reader, he makes careless word reading errors, his spelling skills are weak, and his writing assignments are often incomplete and lack detail, despite his strong oral language skills. The teacher reported that it is hard for her to determine how much of Ahmad's weak academic work comes from lack of effort versus processing difficulties. Ahmad has not received ELL support due to the fact that almost all of his schooling has been in English. Furthermore, the frequent changes between schools have not allowed consistent tracking of his progress and he has received very minimal special education support.

Case Study 2: "Naiara"

Naiara is a 9-year old refugee from South America. Prior to her move to Canada 2 years earlier with her mother and three siblings, her family experienced considerable violence in their home country. Since this time, she and her family have been living in an economically underprivileged urban community in a large, metropolitan city in Canada. The language spoken at home is an indigenous language with no writing system, found in the northern areas of South America. The family also speaks Spanish fluently, but Naiara has spent very little time at school, and thus her reading and writing skills in Spanish are weak.

For the past two years, Naiara has spent 40 minutes per day in an English as a Second Language class, where her teacher has worked to increase her vocabulary and academic conversational skills, and to teach her English reading and writing. Naiara has responded well to the word-level reading strategies her teacher has implemented (e.g., sight word and phonics approaches). She can decode English words effectively and is performing on par with the class. That said, she is struggling in her vocabulary development and reading comprehension skills and has not progressed at the same rate as the other English L2 students in class. In particular, she seems to have persistent difficulties with language comprehension. She has difficulties making inferences when listening to stories, and cannot retell a story she has listened to. There are some inconsistencies in Naiara's progress: (1) She can read words in isolation with reasonable fluency but has great difficulties reading text orally with fluency and understanding what she has read; (2) she is a good speller but her overall writing skills are weak; and (3) she has good sight word vocabulary but has great difficulty remembering the meanings of words or making connections between words that are related (e.g., *heal* and *health*).

Otherwise, Naiara has acquired basic conversational skills, has several friends, and enjoys playing soccer with the other children at school. During class time, though, she sits at the back of the room and spends much of her time doodling. Because of her reading comprehension and language difficulties, Naiara is not progressing well academically.

Each of these cases illustrates some of the ongoing challenges associated with identifying, assessing, and providing interventions to L2 learners who are struggling to develop reading skills in their L1. Determining whether weak literacy skills are the result of a reading disability or the result of interrupted schooling is an added challenge for some L2 learners, as is highlighted in Ahmad's case. Often schools make the mistake of using the "wait and see" approach, which was the case for Ahmad, partly due to his frequent moves between schools and the fact that he displayed proficient oral language skills. Research has demonstrated that most children acquire L2 word-level reading skills relatively quickly. In fact, L2 learners who enter the school system in the primary grades should display word-level reading skills on par with their L1 peers after a couple of years, provided they were given proper instruction. Ahmad had been provided with English instruction since entering school in kindergarten; therefore the fact that he still had difficulty with his word-level reading skills in Grade 6 indicates that he is experiencing challenges beyond his L2 status.

The development of L2 proficiency and its impact on reading comprehension in children and adolescents with poor comprehension and language impairment are highly complex. Naiara's case study highlights some of those complexities and provides a springboard for thinking about poor reading comprehension in L2 learners. As is emphasized in the case study, some L2 learners have persistent reading and language difficulties that reflect deficits in development beyond their L2 status. These deficits can be indicative of true language impairments or specific learning disorders related to reading. The task of determining the root of poor reading comprehension is complex due to the confound with developing language proficiency. This task is made even more difficult when there are multiple risk factors to consider. The simple view of reading suggests that reading comprehension is the product of decoding and language comprehension skills. Thus, as we have seen with word reading difficulties, a child or adolescent who experiences difficulties with language will inevitably also have difficulties with reading comprehension. This is the case with Naiara, and with children and adolescents with poor comprehension and with language impairment. Regardless, both Ahmad and Naiara need to receive adaptive instruction that takes into account their difficulties and their strengths and that enhances their academic achievement.

To close, cognitive, linguistic, decoding, and to some extent comprehension profiles of L1 and L2 learners tend to follow similar developmental patterns, especially if they begin schooling in their L2 in the early grades. Additionally, L2 learners show similar profiles to their L1 counterparts whether they are typically developing or demonstrate persistent difficulties in the acquisition of reading skills. The available research suggests that educational strategies and interventions that work for L1 students can also be applied to L2 learners despite a lag in oral language skills. Therefore, when it appears that an L2 child or adolescent is not making appropriate progress, it is important to provide further assessment and intervention at the earliest time point possible in order to support L2 learners with reading difficulties. There is less available research on the developmental profiles of L2 learners who begin learning in their L2 in late childhood or in adolescence and who may have learning difficulties that cannot be easily attributed to their overall educational history. More research is required to determine how best to support the needs of struggling older L2 learners who have reading difficulties.

REFERENCES

Abu-Rabia, S., & Shakkour, W. (2014). Cognitive retroactive transfer (CRT) of language skills among trilingual Arabic-Hebrew and English Learners. *Journal of Modern Linguistics, 4*, 1–20.

Abu-Rabia, S., & Siegel, L. S. (2002). Reading, writing, orthographic, phonological, syntactic and memory skills of bilingual Arabic-English speaking Arab children. *Journal of Psycholinguistic Research, 31*, 661–678.

Adams, M. J. (1990). *Beginning to read: Thinking and learning about print.* Cambridge, MA: MIT Press.

Afflerbach, P., Pearson, P. D., & Paris, S. G. (2008). Clarifying differences between reading skills and reading strategies. *The Reading Teacher, 61*, 364–373.

Al Otaiba, S., Petscher, Y., Pappamihiel, N. E., Williams, R. S., Dyrlund, A. K., & Connor, C. (2009). Modeling oral reading fluency development in Latino students: A longitudinal study across second and third grade. *Journal of Educational Psychology, 101*(2), 315.

American Psychiatric Association. (2013). *Diagnostic and statistical manual of mental disorders (DSM-5).* Washington, DC: American Psychiatric.

Anthony, J., & Lonigan, C., (2004). The nature of phonological awareness: Converging evidence from four studies of preschool and early grade school children. *Journal of Educational Psychology, 96*(1), 43–55.

Arab-Moghaddam, M., & Sénéchal, M. (2001). Orthographic and phonological processing skills in reading and spelling in Persian/English bilinguals. *International Journal of Behavioral Development, 25,* 140–147

Artiles, A. J., Rueda, R., Salazar, J. J., & Higareda, I. (2002). English-language learner representation in special education in California urban school districts. In D. J. Losen & G. Orfield (Eds.), *Racial inequality in special education* (pp. 117–136). Cambridge, MA: Harvard Education Press.

August, D., & Shanahan, T. (Eds.). (2006). *Developing literacy in second language learners: Report of the national literacy panel on language minority youth and children.* Mahwah, NJ: Erlbaum.

Azimi, M., Geva, E., & Gottardo, A., (2015). *Beyond the simple view of reading: Early cognitive skills and reading fluency as predictors of subsequent reading comprehension in English Language Learners.* Manuscript submitted for publication.

Babayiğit, S. (2014). The role of oral language skills in reading and listening comprehension of text: A comparison of monolingual (L1) and bilingual (L2) speakers of English language. *Journal of Research in Reading, 37*(S1), S22–S47.

Baddeley, A. D. (1986). *Working memory*. Oxford, UK: Oxford University Press.

Baddeley, A. (2000). Short-term and working memory. In E. Tulving & F. Craik (Eds.), *The Oxford handbook of memory* (pp. 77–92). New York: Oxford University Press.

Beiser, M., Zilber, N., Simich, L., Youngmann, R., Zohar, A., Taa, B., & Hou, F. (2011). Regional effects on the mental health of immigrant children: Results from the New Canadian Children and Youth Study (NCCYS). *Health Place, 17*(3), 822–829.

Biemiller, A. J. (1977/78). Relations between oral reading rates for letters, words, and simple texts in the development of reading achievement. *Reading Research Quarterly, 13*, 223–253.

Biemiller, A. J. (1981). *Biemiller Test of Reading Processes*. Toronto, Canada: University of Toronto Press.

Biemiller, A. (1999). *Language and reading success*. Cambridge, MA: Brookline.

Bishop, D.V.M., & Snowling, M. J. (2004). Developmental dyslexia and specific language impairment: Same or different? *Psychological Bulletin, 130*(6), 858–886.

Cain, K. (2013). Reading comprehension difficulties in struggling readers. In B. Miller, L. E. Cutting, & P. McCardle (Eds.), *Unravelling reading comprehension: Behavioral, neurobiological, and genetic components* (pp. 54–65). Baltimore, MD: Paul Brookes.

Cain, K., & Oakhill, J. (2006). Profiles of children with specific reading comprehension difficulties. *British Journal of Educational Psychology, 76*, 683–696.

Cain, K., Oakhill, J.V., & Bryant, P. (2004). Children's reading comprehension ability: Concurrent prediction by working memory, verbal ability, and component skills. *Journal of Educational Psychology, 96*, 31–42.

Caravolas, M., Lervag, A., Defior, S., Seidlova Malkova, G., & Hulme, C. (2013). Different patterns, but equivalent predictors, of growth in reading in consistent and inconsistent orthographies. *Psychological Science, 24*(8), 1398–1407.

Carlo, M., August, D., McLaughlin, B., Snow, C., Dressler, C., Lippman, D., . . . White, C. (2004). Closing the gap: Addressing the vocabulary needs of English-language learners in bilingual and mainstream classrooms. *Reading Research Quarterly, 39*(2), 188–215.

Carver, R. P., & David, A. H. (2001). Investigating reading achievement using a causal model. *Scientific Studies of Reading, 5*, 107–140.

Catts, H.W. (1991). Early identification of reading disabilities. *Topics in Language Disorders, 12*(1), 1–16.

Catts, H., Adlof, S., & Ellis-Weismer, S. (2006). Language deficits in poor comprehenders: A case for the simple view of reading. *Journal of Speech, Language, and Hearing Research, 49*, 278–293.

Catts, H.W., Adlof, S.M., & Weismer, S.W., (2006). Language deficits in poor comprehenders: A case for the simple view of reading. *Journal of Speech, Language, and Hearing Research: JSLHR, 49*(2), 278–293.

Catts, H.W., Fey, M.E., Tomblin, J.B., & Zhang, X. (2002). A longitudinal investigation of reading outcomes in children with language impairments. *Journal of Speech, Language, and Hearing Research, 45*(6), 1142–1157.

Chall, J. S. (1996). *Stages of reading development* (2nd ed.). Fort Worth, TX: Harcourt Brace College.

Chiappe, P., & Siegel, L. S. (1999). Phonological awareness and reading acquisition in English- and Punjabi-speaking Canadian children. *Journal of Educational Psychology, 91*(1), 20–28.

Chiappe, P., Siegel, L. S., & Gottardo, A. (2002). Reading-related skills of kindergartners from diverse linguistic backgrounds. *Applied Psycholinguistics, 23*(1), 95–116.

Chiappe, P., Siegel, L. S., & Wade-Woolley. (2002). Linguistic diversity and the development of basic reading skills: A longitudinal study. *Scientific Studies of Reading, 6*, 369–400.

Chung, K., & Ho, C. (2010). Second language learning difficulties in Chinese children with dyslexia: What are the reading-related cognitive skills that contribute to English and Chinese word reading? *Journal of Learning Disabilities, 43*(3), 195–211.

Chung, K., Lo, J., Ho, C., Xiao, X., & Chan, D. (2014). Syntactic and discourse skills in Chinese adolescent readers with dyslexia: A profiling study. *Annals of Dyslexia, 64*, 222–247.

Cirino, P. T., Vaughn, S., Linan-Thompson, S., Cardenas-Hagan, E., Fletcher, J. M., & Francis, D. J. (2009). One-year follow-up outcomes of Spanish and English interventions for English language learners at risk for reading problems. *American Educational Research Journal, 46*(3), 744–781.

Cohen-Mimran, R. (2009). The contribution of language skills to reading fluency: A comparison of two orthographies for Hebrew. *Journal of Child Language, 36*, 657–672

Commeau, L., Cormier, P., Grandmaison, E., & Lacroix, D. (1999). A longitudinal study of phonological processing skills in children learning to read in a second language. *Journal of Educational Psychology, 91*(1), 29–43.

Crosson, A. C., & Lesaux, N. K. (2010). Revisiting assumptions about the relationship of fluent reading to comprehension: Spanish-speakers' text-reading fluency in English. *Reading and Writing, An Interdisciplinary Journal, 23*, 475–494.

Cummins, J. (1984). *Bilingualism and special education: Issues in assessment and pedagogy*. Cleveland, UK: Multilingual Matters.

Cummins, J. (2000). *Language, power and pedagogy: Bilingual children in the crossfire*. Clevedon, UK: Multilingual Matters.

Cummins, J. (2012). The intersection of cognitive and sociocultural factors in the development of reading comprehension among immigrant students. *Reading and Writing, 25*(8), 1973–1990.

Cutting, L. E., Materek, A., Cole, C. A. S., Levine, T. M., & Mahone, E. M. (2009). Effects of fluency, oral language and executive function on reading comprehension performance. *Annals of Dyslexia, 59*, 34–54.

Cutting, L. E., & Scarborough, H. S. (2006). Prediction of reading comprehension: Relative contributions of word recognition, language proficiency, and other cognitive skills can depend on how comprehension is measured. *Scientific Studies of Reading, 10*, 277–299.

Da Fontoura, H., & Siegel, L. S. (1995). Reading, syntactic, and working memory skills of bilingual Portuguese-English Canadian children. *Reading and Writing: An Interdisciplinary Journal, 7*, 139–153, 1995.

D'Angiulli, A., Siegel, L. S., & Serra, E. (2001). The development of reading in English and Italian in bilingual children. *Applied Psycholinguistics, 22*, 479–507.

De Jong, P., & Van der Leij, A. (1999). Specific contributions of phonological abilities to early reading acquisition: Results from a Dutch latent variable longitudinal study. *Journal of Educational Psychology, 91*(3), 450–476.

Deno, S. L. (1985). Curriculum-based measurement: The emerging alternative. *Exceptional Children, 52*, 219–232.

Deno, S. L., & Fuchs, L. S. (1987). Developing curriculum-based measurement systems for databased special education problem solving. *Focus on Exceptional Children, 19*(8), 1–16.

Droop, M., & Verhoeven, L. (2003). Language proficiency and reading ability in first- and second-language learners. *Reading Research Quarterly, 38*(1), 78–103.

Durgunoglu, A., Nagy, W., & Hanci-Bhatt, B. (1993). Cross-language transfer of phonological awareness. *Journal of Educational Psychology, 85*(3), 453–465

Durgunoglu, A., & Oney, B. (1999). A cross-linguistic comparison of phonological awareness and word recognition. *Reading and Writing, 11*(4), 281–299.

Erdos, C., Genesee, F., Savage, R., & Haigh, C. (2014). Predicting risk for oral and written language learning difficulties in students educated in a second language. *Applied Psycholinguistics, 35*(2), 371–398.

Everatt, J., Smythe, I., Adams, E., & Ocampo, D. (2000). Dyslexia screening measures and bilingualism. *Dyslexia, 6*, 42–56.

Farnia, F., & Geva, E. (2011). Cognitive correlates of vocabulary growth in English language learners. *Applied Psycholinguistics, 32*(4), 711–738. doi:10.1017/S0142716411000038

Farnia, F., & Geva, E. (2012). "Late emerging" language impairment in monolinguals and ELLs. In *Reading and language difficulties in clinical populations: Identification, development, and intervention perspectives.* Symposium conducted at the Society for the Scientific Study of Reading (SSSR) Annual Conference, Montreal.

Fender, M. (2008). Spelling knowledge and reading development: Insights from Arab ESL learners. *Reading in a Foreign Language, 20*(1), 19–42.

Fraser, C. (2015). *The identification of English language learners with reading comprehension difficulties* (Unpublished doctoral dissertation). University of Toronto. Manuscript in preparation.

Fraser, C., Adelson, V., & Geva, E. (2014). Recognizing English language learners with reading disability: Minimizing bias, accurate identification, and timely intervention. *Perspectives on Language and Literacy – The International Dyslexia Association, 40*(4), 11–17.

Fraser, C., Pasquarella, A., & Geva, E., Gottardo, A., & Biemiller, A. (2015). "Conjunction, junction, what's your function?": Exploring the role of conjunction knowledge in the reading comprehension of young English language learner (ELLs). Manuscript submitted for publication.

Fuchs, D., & Fuchs, L. S. (2006). Introduction to response to intervention: What, why, and how valid is it? *Reading Research Quarterly, 41*(1), 93–99.

Fuchs, L. S., & Deno, S. L. (1991). Curriculum-based measurement: Current applications and future directions. *Exceptional Children, 57*, 466–501.

Fuchs, L. S., Fuchs, D., Hosp, M. K., & Jenkins, J. R. (2001). Oral reading fluency as an indicator of reading competence: A theoretical, empirical, and historical analysis, *Scientific Studies of Reading, 5*, 239–256.

Genesee, F., Geve, E., Dressler, C., & Kamil, M. (2006). Synthesis: Cross-linguistic relationships in working memory, phonological processes, and oral language. In D. August &

T. Shanahan (Eds.), *Developing literacy in second-language learners: A report of the National Literacy Panel on Language-Minority Children and Youth* (pp. 153–174). Mahwah, NJ: Erlbaum.

Gersten, R., & Baker, S.K. (2003). English-language learners with learning disabilities. In H.L. Swanson, K.R. Harris, & S. Graham (Eds.), *Handbook of learning disabilities* (pp. 94–109). New York: Guilford.

Gersten, R., Baker, S.K., Collins, P., Linan-Thompson, S., Scarcella, R., & Shanahan, T. (2007, December). *Effective literacy and English language instruction for English learners in the elementary grades.* U.S. Department of Education. National Center for Education Evaluation and Regional, Institute for Educational Sciences. Retrieved from http://ies.ed.gov/ncee/wwc/pdf/practice_guides/20074011.pdf

Gersten, R., & Geva, E. (2003). Teaching reading to English learners in the primary grades: Insights into the new research base on teaching reading to English learners. *Educational Leadership, 60,* 44–49.

Geva, E. (2000). Issues in the assessment of reading disabilities in L2 children – beliefs and research evidence. *Dyslexia, 6*(1), 13–28.

Geva, E. (2006). Second-language oral proficiency and second-language literacy. In D. August & T. Shanahan (Eds.), *Developing literacy in second-language learners: Report of the National Literacy Panel on Language – Minority children and youth* (pp. 123–139). Mahwah, NJ: Erlbaum.

Geva, E., & Clifton, S. (1994). The development of first and second language reading skills in early French immersion. *Canadian Modern Language Review, 50,* 646–667.

Geva, E., & Farnia, F. (2012). Developmental changes in the nature of language proficiency and reading fluency paint a more complex view of reading comprehension in ELL and EL1. *Reading and Writing, 25*(8), 1819–1845.

Geva, E., & Herbert, K. (2012). Assessment and interventions in English language learners with LD. In B. Wong & D. Butler (Eds.), *Learning about learning disabilities* (4th ed., pp. 271–298). San Diego, CA: Elsevier.

Geva, E., & Lafrance, A. (2011). Linguistic and cognitive processes in the development of spelling in ELLs: L1 transfer, language proficiency, or cognitive processes? In A. Durgunoglu & C. Goldenberg (Eds.), *Language and literacy development in bilingual settings* (pp. 245–279). New York: Guilford Press.

Geva, E., & Massey-Garrison, A. (2013). A comparison of the language skills of ELLs and monolinguals who are poor decoders, poor comprehenders, or normal readers. *Journal of Learning Disabilities, 46*(5), 387–401.

Geva, E., & Ryan, E.B. (1993). Linguistic and memory correlates of academic skills in first and second languages. *Language Learning, 43,* 5–42.

Geva, E., & Siegel, L.S. (2000). Orthographic and cognitive factors in the concurrent development of basic reading skills in two languages. *Reading and Writing: An Interdisciplinary Journal, 12*(1), 1–31.

Geva, E., & Wade-Woolley, L. (2004). Issues in the assessment of reading disability in second language children. In I. Smythe, J. Everatt, & R. Salter (Eds.), *The international book of dyslexia: A cross-language comparison and practice guide* (2nd ed., pp. 195–206). New York: Wiley.

Geva, E., Wade-Woolley, L., & Shany, M. (1993). The concurrent development of spelling and decoding in different orthographies. *Journal of Reading Behavior, 25*(4), 383–406.

Geva, E., Wade-Woolley, L., & Shany, M. (1997). The development of reading efficiency in first and second language. *Scientific Studies of Reading, 1*(2), 119–144.

Geva, E., & Wiener, J. (2015). *Psychological assessment of culturally and linguistically diverse children – a practitioner's guide.* New York: Springer.

Geva, E., & Yaghoub-Zadeh, Z. (2006). Reading efficiency in native English-speaking and English-as-a-second-language children: The role of oral proficiency and underlying cognitive-linguistic processes. *Scientific Studies of Reading, 10,* 31–58.

Geva, E., Yaghoub-Zadeh, Z., & Schuster, B. (2000). Understanding individual differences in word recognition skills of ESL children. *Annals of Dyslexia, 50*(1), 121–154.

Gholamain, M., & Geva, E. (1999). Orthographic and cognitive factors in the concurrent development of basic reading skills in English and Persian. *Language Learning, 49*(2), 183–217.

Goodwin, A., & Ahn, S. (2010). A meta-analysis of morphological interventions: Effects on literacy achievement of children with literacy difficulties. *Annals of Dyslexia, 60*(2), 183–208.

Goswami, U., & Bryant, P. (1990). *Phonological skills and learning to read.* East Sussex, UK: Erlbaum.

Gottardo, A., Collins, P., Baciu, I., & Gebotys, R. (2008). Predictors of grade 2 word reading and vocabulary learning from grade 1 variables in Spanish-speaking children: Similarities and differences. *Learning Disabilities Research & Practice, 23*(1), 11–24.

Gottardo, A., & Mueller, J. (2009). Are first-and second-language factors related in predicting second-language reading comprehension? A study of Spanish-speaking children acquiring English as a second language from first to second grade. *Journal of Educational Psychology, 101*(2), 330.

Gottardo, A., Yan, B., Siegel, L., & Wade-Woolley, L. (2001). Factors related to English reading performance in children with Chinese as a first language: More evidence of cross-language transfer of phonological processing. *Journal of Educational Psychology, 93*(3), 530–542.

Gough, P. B., & Tunmer, W. E. (1986). Decoding, reading, and reading disability. *Remedial and Special Education, 7*(1), 6–10.

Graves, M., August, D., & Mancilla-Martinez, J. (2013). *Teaching vocabulary to English language learners.* New York: Teachers College Press.

Hamayan, E. V., Marler, B., Sanchez-Lopez, C., & Damino, J. S. (2007). *Reasons for the misidentification of special needs among ELLs.* Retrieved from LDOnline: http://www.ldonline.org/article/40715/

Harry, B., & Anderson, M. G. (1994). The disproportionate placement of African American males in special education programs: A critique of the process. *Journal of Negro Education, 63,* 602–619.

Hernandez, D. J., Denton, N. A., & Macartney, S. E. (2008). Children in immigrant families: Looking to America's future. *Social Policy Report, 22*(3), 16–17.

Hutchinson, J. M., Whiteley, H. E., Smith, C. D., & Connors, L. (2003). The developmental progression of comprehension related skills in children learning EAL. *Journal of Research in Reading, 26*(1), 19–32.

Jackson, N. E., & Donaldson, G. (1989). Precocious and second-grade readers' use of context in word identification. *Learning and Individual Differences, 1,* 255–281.

Jared, D., Cormier, P., Levy, B. A., & Wade-Woolley, L. (2010). Early predictors of biliteracy development in children in French immersion: A 4-year longitudinal study. *Journal of Educational Psychology, 103*(1), 119.

Jongejan, W., Verhoeven, L., & Siegel, L. S. (2007). Predictors of reading and spelling abilities in first- and second-language learners. *Journal of Educational Psychology, 99*(4), 835–851.

Kahn-Horwitz, J., Sparks, R. L., & Goldstein, Z. (2012). English as a Foreign Language spelling development: A longitudinal study. *Applied Psycholinguistics, 33*(2), 343–363.

Katz, L., & Frost, R. (1992). The reading process is different for different orthographies: The orthographic depth hypothesis. In R. Frost & L. Katz (Eds.), *Orthography, phonology, morphology, and meaning* (pp. 67–84). Amsterdam: Elsevier North Holland Press.

Keung, Y. C., & Ho, C. S. H. (2009). Transfer of reading-related cognitive skills in learning to read Chinese (L1) and English (L2) among Chinese elementary school children. *Contemporary Educational Psychology, 34,* 103–112.

Kintsch, W., & Rawson, K. A. (2005). Comprehension. In M. J. Snowling & C. Hulme (Eds.), *The science of reading: A handbook* (pp. 209–26). Oxford: Blackwell.

Kirby, J. R., Parrila, R., & Pfeiffer, S. (2003). Naming speed and phonological processing as predictors of reading development. *Journal of Educational Psychology, 95,* 453–464.

Kirby, J. R., & Savage, R. S. (2008). Can the simple view deal with the complexities of reading? *Literacy, 42*(2), 75–82.

Klingner, J. K., Artiles, A. J., & Barletta, L. M. (2006). English language learners who struggle with reading: Language acquisition or LD? *Journal of Learning Disabilities, 39*(2), 108–128.

LaBerge, D., & Samuels, S. J. (1974). Toward a theory of automatic information processing in reading. *Cognitive Psychology, 6,* 293–323.

Lado, R. (1964). *Language teaching: A scientific approach.* New York: McGraw Hill.

Lam, K., Chen, X., Geva, E., Luo, Y. C., & Li, H. (2012). The role of morphological awareness in reading achievement among young Chinese-speaking English language learners: A longitudinal study. *Reading and Writing, 25*(8), 1847–1872.

Larry P. v. Wilson Riles (1972, 1974, 1979, 1984, 1986). 343 F. Supp. 1306 (N.D. Cal. 1972) (preliminary injunction). Aff'd 502 F. 2d963 (9th Cir. 1974); 495 F. Supp. 926 (ND Cal. 1979) (decision on merits). Aff'd (9th Cir., No. 80–427, 1984) (order modifying judgment, C-71–2270 RFP, 1986).

Laurent, A., & Martinot, C. (2010). Bilingualism and phonological awareness: The case of bilingual (French-Occitan) children. *Reading and Writing: An Interdisciplinary Journal, 23,* 435–452.

Leonard, L. B. (1998). *Children with specific language impairment.* Cambridge, MA: MIT Press.

Lesaux, N., & Geva, E. (2006). Synthesis: Development of literacy in language-minority students. In D. August & T. Shanahan (Eds.), *Developing literacy in second-language learners: Report of the National Literacy Panel on Language-Minority Children and Youth* (pp. 53–74). Mahwah, NJ: Erlbaum.

Lesaux, N. K., & Kieffer, M. J. (2010). Exploring sources of reading comprehension difficulties among language minority learners and their classmates in early adolescence. *American Educational Research Journal, 47*(3), 596–632.

Lesaux, N. K., Lipka, O., & Siegel, L. S. (2006). Investigating cognitive and linguistic abilities that influence the reading comprehension skills of children from diverse linguistic backgrounds. *Reading and Writing, 19*(1), 99–131.

Lesaux, N. K., Rupp, A. A., & Siegel, L. S. (2007). Growth in reading skills of children from diverse linguistic backgrounds: Findings from a 5-year longitudinal study. *Journal of Educational Psychology, 99*(4), 821.

Lesaux, N., & Siegel, L. S. (2003). The development of reading in children who speak English as a second language (ESL). *Developmental Psychology, 39*, 1005–1019.

Li, M., & Kirby, J. R. (2014). Unexpected poor comprehenders among adolescent ESL students. *Scientific Studies of Reading, 18*(2), 75–93.

Limbos, M., & Geva, E. (2001). Accuracy of teacher assessments of second-language students at risk for reading disability. *Journal of Learning Disabilities, 34*, 136–151.

Linan-Thompson, S., & Hickman-Davis, P. (2002). Supplemental reading instruction for students at risk for reading disabilities: Improve reading thirty minutes at a time. *Learning Disabilities Research and Practice, 17*, 241–250.

Linan-Thompson, S., Vaughn, S., Prater, K, & Cirino, P. (2006). The response to intervention of English language learners at risk for reading problems. *Journal of Learning Disabilities, 39*(5), 390–398.

Lindsey, K. A., Manis, F. R., & Bailey, C. E. (2003). Prediction of first-grade reading in Spanish-speaking English-language learners. *Journal of Educational Psychology, 95*, 482–494.

Lipka, O., & Siegel, L. S. (2012). The development of reading comprehension skills in children learning English as a second language. *Reading and Writing, 25*(8), 1873–1898.

Lovett, W. M., De Palma, M., Frijters, J., Steinbach, K., Temple, M., Benson, N., & Lacerenz, L. (2008). Interventions for reading difficulties a comparison of response to intervention by ELL and EFL struggling readers. *Journal of Learning Disabilities, 41*, 333–352.

MacCoubrey, S., Wade-Woolley, L., Klinger, D., & Kirby, J. (2004). Early identification of at-risk L2 readers. *Canadian Modern Language Review, 61*(1), 11–29.

Manis, F., Lindsey, K., & Bailey, C. (2004). Development of reading in grades K–2 in Spanish-speaking English-language Learners. *Learning Disabilities Research & Practice, 19*(4), 214–224.

McBride-Chang, C., Liu, P. D., Wong, T., Wong, A., & Shu, H. (2012). Specific reading difficulties in Chinese, English, or both: Longitudinal markers of phonological awareness, morphological awareness, and RAN in Hong Kong Chinese children. *Journal of Learning Disabilities, 45*(6), 503–514.

McBride-Chang, C., & Suk-Han Ho, C. (2005). Predictors of beginning reading in Chinese and English: A 2-year longitudinal study of Chinese kindergartners. *Scientific Studies of Reading, 9*(2), 117–144.

McBride-Chang, C., Wagner, R. K., Muse, A., Chow, B.W.Y., & Shu, H.U.A. (2005). The role of morphological awareness in children's vocabulary acquisition in English. *Applied Psycholinguistics, 26*(3), 415–435.

Melby-Lervåg, M., & Lervåg, A. (2013). Reading comprehension and its underlying components in second-language learners: A meta-analysis of studies comparing first- and second-language learners. *Psychological Bulletin, 140*(2), 409–433. doi:10.1037/a0033890

Nakamoto, J., Lindsey, K. A., & Manis, F. R. (2007). A longitudinal analysis of English language learners' word decoding and reading comprehension. *Reading and Writing, 20*(7), 691–719.

Nation, K., & Snowling, M.J. (2000). Factors influencing syntactic awareness skills in normal readers and poor comprehenders. *Applied Psycholinguistics*, *21*(2), 229–241.

National Association of School Psychologists. (2007). *NASP position statement on identification of students with specific learning disabilities*. Bethesda, MD: National Association of School Psychologists. Retrieved from http://www.ode.state.or.us/teachlearn/conferencematerials/sped/sld_nasp.pdf

National Institute of Child Health and Human Development (NICHD). (2000). *Report of the National Reading Panel: Teaching children to read. An evidence-based assessment of the scientific research literature on reading and its implications for reading instruction* (NIH Publication No. 00–4769). Washington, DC: U.S. Government Printing Office.

National Reading Panel. (2000). *Report of the national reading panel: Teaching children to read*. Retrieved from http://www.nichd.nih.gov/publications/pubs/nrp/documents/report.pdf

Ndlovu, K. (2010). *Story-writing development from Grades 4 to 6: Do language status and reading profile matter?* (Unpublished doctoral dissertation). University of Toronto.

Ndlovu, K., & Geva, E. (2008). Writing abilities in first and second language learners with and without reading disabilities. In J. Kormos & E. Kontra (Eds.), *Language learners with special needs: An international perspective* (pp. 36–62). Toronto: Multilingual Matters.

Oakhill, J., & Cain, K. (2012). The precursors of reading ability in young readers: Evidence from a four-year longitudinal study. *Scientific Studies of Reading*, *16*, 91–121.

Paradis, J., Genesee, F., & Crago, M.B. (2011). *Dual language development and disorders: A handbook on bilingualism and second language learning* (2nd ed.). Baltimore, MD: Brookes.

Paradis, J., & Kirova, A. (2014). English second-language learners in preschool: Profile effects in their English abilities and the role of home language environment. *International Journal of Behavioral Development*, *38*, 342–349.

Pasquarella, A., Gottardo, A., & Grant, A. (2012). Comparing factors related to reading comprehension in adolescents who speak English as a first (L1) or second (L2) language. *Scientific Studies of Reading*, *16*, 475–503.

Patton, J.M. (1998). The disproportionate representation of African Americans in special education: Looking behind the curtain for understanding and solutions. *The Journal of Special Education, 32*, 25–31.

People for Education. (2013). *Mind the gap: Inequality in Ontario's schools: People for Education Annual Report on Ontario's Publicly Funded Schools 2013*. Retrieved from http://www.peopleforeducation.ca/wp-content/uploads/2013/05/annual-report-2013-WEB.pdf

Perfetti, C.A. (1985). *Reading ability*. New York: Oxford University Press

Perfetti, C., & Adlof, S.M. (2012). Reading comprehension: A conceptual framework from word meaning to text meaning. In J. P. Sabitini & E. R. Albro (Eds.), *Assessing reading in the 21st century: Aligning and applying advances in the reading and measurement sciences* (pp. 3–20). Lanham, MD: Rowman & Littlefield Education.

Petersen, D.B., & Gillam, R.B. (2013). Accurately predicting future reading difficulty for bilingual Latino children at risk for language impairment. *Learning Disabilities Research & Practice*, *28*(3), 113–128.

Pikulski, J.J., & Chard, D.J. (2005). Fluency: Bridge between decoding and reading comprehension. *The Reading Teacher, 58,* 510–519.

Prior, A., Goldina, A., Shany, M., Geva, E., & Katzir, T. (2014). Lexical inference in L2: Predictive roles of vocabulary knowledge and reading skill beyond reading comprehension. *Reading and Writing, 27*(8), 1467–1484.

Proctor, C.P., Carlo, M., August, D., & Snow, C. (2005). Native Spanish-speaking children reading in English: Toward a model of comprehension. *Journal of Educational Psychology, 97*(2), 246.

Programme for International Student Assessment (PISA). (2012). *Untapped skills: Realizing the potential of immigrant students.* [Preliminary version]. Paris: OECD. Retrieved from http://hdl.voced.edu.au/10707/217393

Puranik, C., Petscher, Y., Al Otaiba, S., Catts, H., & Lonigan, C. (2008). Development of oral reading fluency in children with speech or language impairments: A growth curve analysis. *Journal of Learning Disabilities, 41*(6), 545–560.

Quiroga, T., Lemos-Britton, Z., Mostafapour, E., Abbott, R.D., & Berninger, V.W. (2002). Phonological awareness and beginning reading in Spanish-speaking ESL first graders: Research into practice. *Journal of School Psychology, 40,* 85–111.

Ramirez, G., Chen, X., Geva, E., & Kiefer, H. (2010). Morphological awareness in Spanish-speaking English language learners: Within and cross-language effects on word reading. *Reading and Writing, 23*(3–4), 337–358.

Ramus, F., Marshall, C., Rosen, S., & van der Lely, H. (2013). Phonological deficits in specific language impairment and developmental dyslexia: Towards a multidimensional model. *Brain, 136,* 630–645.

Royer, J.M., & Carlo, M.S. (1991). Transfer of comprehension skills from native to second language. *Journal of Reading, 34*(6), 450–455.

Saiegh-Haddad, E., & Geva, E. (2010). Acquiring reading in two languages: An introduction to the special issue. *Reading and Writing: An Interdisciplinary Journal, 23*(3–4), 263–268.

Schatschneider, C., Fletcher, J.M., Francis, D.J., Carlson, C.D., & Foorman, B.R. (2004). Kindergarten prediction of reading skills: A longitudinal comparative analysis. *Journal of Educational Psychology, 96*(2), 265.

Seymour, P.H., Aro, M., & Erskine, J.M. (2003). Foundation literacy acquisition in European orthographies. *British Journal of Psychology, 94,* 143–174.

Shakkour, W. (2014). Cognitive skill transfer in English reading acquisition: Alphabetic and logographic languages compared. *Open Journal of Modern Linguistics, 4,* 544–562.

Shanahan, T., & Beck, I. (2006). Effective literacy teaching for English-language learners. In D. August & T. Shanahan (Eds.), *Developing literacy in second-language learners* (pp. 415–488). Mahwah, NJ: Erlbaum.

Share, D.L. (2008). On the anglocentricities of current reading research and practice: The perils of over reliance on an "outlier" orthography. *Psychological Bulletin, 134*(4), 584–615.

Shaywitz, S.E., & Shaywitz, B.A. (2005). Dyslexia (specific reading disability). *Biological Psychiatry, 57*(11), 1301–1309.

Snowling, M.J. (2000). *Dyslexia.* Oxford: Blackwell.

Solari, E.J., Petscher, Y., & Folsom, P.S. (2012). Differentiating literacy growth of ELL students with LD from other high-risk groups and general education peers: Evidence from Grade 3 to 10. *Journal of Learning Disabilities, 47*(4), 329–348. doi:10.1177/0022219412463435

Sparks, R. L., Patton, J.O.N., Ganschow, L., & Humbach, N. (2009). Long-term relationships among early first language skills, second language aptitude, second language affect, and later second language proficiency. *Applied Psycholinguistics, 30*(4), 725–755.

Stanovich, K. E., & Siegel, L. S. (1994). Phenotypic performance profile of reading-disabled children: A regression-based test of the phonological- core variable-difference model. *Journal of Educational Psychology, 86,* 24–53.

Statistics Canada. (2006). The evolving linguistic portrait, 2006 census: Findings. Retrieved October 1, 2011, from http://www12.statcan.ca/census-recensement/2006/as-sa/97–555/index-eng.cfm

Steacy, L., Kirby, J., Parrila, R., & Compton, D. (2014). Classification of a double deficit groups across time: An analysis of group stability from kindergarten to second grade. *Scientific Studies of Reading, 18*(4), 255–273.

Storch, S.A., & Whitehurst, G.J. (2002). Oral language and code-related precursors to reading: Evidence from a longitudinal structural model. *Developmental Psychology, 38*(6), 934.

Swanson, H.L., & Siegel, L. S. (2001). Learning disabilities as a working memory deficit. *Issues in Education: Contributions of Educational Psychology, 7*(1), 1–48.

Torgesen, J. K. (1998). Catch them before they fall: Identification and assessment to prevent reading failure in young children. *American Educator, 22,* 1–8.

Torgesen, J. K., Wagner, R., & Rashotte, C. (1999). *Test of word reading efficiency* (2nd ed.). Austin, TX: Pro-Ed.

U.S. Department of Education. (2003). *National Assessment of Educational Progress (NAEP) 2003 reading report card.* Washington, DC: National Center for Education Statistics, Institute of Education Sciences.

Van Dijk, T.A., & Kintsch, W. (1983). *Strategies of discourse comprehension.* New York: Academic Press.

Verhoeven, L. (2000). Components in early second language reading and spelling. *Scientific Studies of Reading, 4*(4), 313–330.

Verhoeven, L., Reitsma, P., & Siegel, L. S. (2011). Cognitive and linguistic factors in reading acquisition. *Reading and Writing, 24*(4), 387–394.

Verhoeven, L., & van Leeuwe, J. (2012). The simple view of second language reading throughout the primary grades. *Reading and Writing, 25*(8), 1805–1818.

Wade-Woolley, L. (1999). First language influences on second language word reading: All roads lead to Rome. *Language Learning, 49*(3), 447–471.

Wade-Woolley, L., & Siegel, L. S. (1997). The spelling performance of ESL and native speakers of English as a function of reading skills. *Reading and Writing, 9,* 387–406.

Wagner, R.K., & Torgesen, J.K. (1987). The nature of phonological processing and its causal role in the acquisition of reading skills. *Psychological Bulletin, 101*(2), 192.

Wagner, R., Torgesen, J., & Rashotte, C. (1994). Development of reading-related phonological processing abilities: New evidence of bidirectional causality from a latent variable longitudinal study. *Developmental Psychology, 30*(1), 73–87.

Wang, M., & Geva, E. (2003). Spelling performance of Chinese ESL children: Lexical and visual-orthographic processes. *Applied Psycholinguistics, 24*(1), 1–25.

Wang, M., Perfetti, C., & Ying, L. (2005). Chinese–English biliteracy acquisition: Cross-language and writing system transfer. *Cognition, 97*, 67–88.

Whitehurst, G., & Lonigan, C. (1998). Child development and emergent literacy. *Child Development, 69*(3), 848–872.

Wiederholt, J.L., & Bryant, B.R. (1992). *Gray Oral Reading Tests* (3rd ed.). Austin, TX: Pro-Ed.

Wise, N., & Chen, X. (2010). At-risk readers in French immersion: Early identification and early intervention. *Canadian Journal of Applied Linguistics, 13*, 128–149.

Wolf, M., & Bowers, P. (1999). The double-deficit hypothesis for the developmental dyslexias. *Journal of Educational Psychology, 91*(3), 415–438.

Wolf, M., & Katzir-Cohen, T. (2001). Reading fluency and its intervention. *Scientific Studies of Reading, 5*(3), 211–239.

Yaghoub-Zadeh, Z., Farnia, F., & Geva, E. (2012). Toward modeling reading development in young English as second language learners. *Reading and Writing: An Interdisciplinary Journal, 25,* 163–187.

Yeung, S., Siegel, L.S., & Chan, C. (2013). Effects of a phonological awareness program on English reading and spelling among Hong Kong Chinese ESL children. *Reading and Writing, 26*(5), 681–704.

Zehler, A. M., Fleischman, H.L., Hopstock, P.J., Pendzick, M.L., & Stephenson, T.G. (2003). *Descriptive study of services to LEP students and LEP students with disabilities* (No. 4). Arlington, VA: U.S. Department of Education, Office of English Language Acquisition.

9

Reading instruction in a technological age

Youngmin Park and Mark Warschauer

Abstract

This chapter explores how digital media can be integrated into L2 reading instruction to help learners improve their reading skills. Drawing on literature that outlines principles of L2 reading instruction, this chapter focuses on technological tools that can be used in activating background knowledge, enriching vocabulary, teaching for comprehension, improving reading fluency, and promoting extensive reading. Some of these tools are specifically geared to provide reading support, such as hypermedia annotation, text-to-speech, and text reformatting; others are more general, such as Internet resources, wikis, and blogs. We discuss findings from empirical studies that examine how effectively these tools facilitate cognitive processes integral to L2 reading, thereby assisting reading skills development. Limitations surrounding these studies are also addressed. We conclude by summarizing pedagogical implications for L2 instructors and offering suggestions to researchers who study the use of technologies in L2 reading.

INTRODUCTION

Advanced technology changes how we read. Literate engagement in the 21st century is not limited to reading paper-based texts but includes digital participation as well (Lankshear & Knobe, 2007). This change requires readers to orchestrate their knowledge and abilities to operate multiple streams of input, such as graphics, videos, and other content, as well as texts. These developments may pose a special challenge for second language (L2) learners, since it is already more cognitively burdensome to attend to and process L2 input than L1 input (VanPatten, 2004) and L2 readers tend to employ fewer cognitive and meta-cognitive strategies than do those reading in their L1 (Fitzgerald, 1995).

However, it is also the case that digital reading environments may afford resources to support the cognitive processes of L2 reading. To begin with, working memory overload (see Chapter 2 for further details) can be decreased by using multimodal presentations as linguistic input (Verhoeven & Perfetti, 2008) and presenting language chunks instead of individual words as the basic processing unit (Mayer & Moreno, 2003). In addition, technology can scaffold L2 readers in input processing and lead them to higher-order cognitive activities by supporting decoding (Parr, 2012) or providing sufficient time for thinking (G. Walker, 2005). There are also ways of assisting slow readers with efficient eye movements, such as forward and regressive saccades (Spritz, 2014; S. Walker, Schloss, Fletcher, Vogel, & Walker, 2005). In addition, an increasing number of platforms have become available for the ongoing evaluation of learning processes (e.g., Moodle).

From a pedagogical perspective, instruction that incorporates technology can enhance students' affective and cognitive involvement. Such instruction can facilitate learner-centered approaches that meet the specific linguistic needs of L2 readers with varied proficiency. Technology-enhanced instruction may also promote collaborative learning in the classroom since learners can share information on their particular interests online with others within or outside of the classroom. This type of collaboration promotes learning since, in keeping with interaction theories, language can be learned through noticing features of language while learners engage in communicating for meaning (Ellis, 2005). Perhaps most importantly, such collaborative learning environments may promote knowledge construction rather than rote learning as learners become better equipped to contribute to the knowledge economy, rather than passively consuming knowledge transmitted in an L2.

Finding mechanisms for evaluating and selecting digital resources or methodologies that work to the students' advantage is a new challenge faced by curriculum designers and instructors. There is a need for a comprehensive and detailed review of traditional curricular policies in order to incorporate state-of-the-art research findings on the role of technology in L2 language and literacy pedagogy. This chapter will focus on the advanced technological tools that are said to help facilitate L2 reading instruction. The critical components of L2 reading instruction provide the organizing framework for this chapter, which stresses the L2 reading skills that each tool or application benefits in instructional contexts. As some of the tools introduced in this chapter were recently developed, in some instances there might not be substantial empirical support for their positive impact on L2 reading instruction. In such cases, pedagogical and psycholinguistic foundations that may support the adoption of that technology will be discussed.

L2 READING INSTRUCTION

Before we discuss technology affordances in L2 reading, it is necessary to identify the areas where technology can best facilitate learning to read in L2. Drawing on both L1 and L2 research on reading theories and practices, a number of studies have attempted to identify principles for successful L2 reading instruction (e.g., Anderson, 2009; Grabe, 2004). For example, Grabe (2004) proposes instructional approaches that support 10 component abilities that learners need to develop for effective reading performance. Similarly, Anderson (2009) identifies six principles that inform the L2 reading curriculum development. There is substantial overlap between these two frameworks. First of all, both researchers emphasize the importance of *background knowledge, vocabulary knowledge*, and *reading strategy development*. While Grabe suggests that L2 reading instruction needs to ensure fluent *word recognition* and build *reading fluency* in general, Anderson highlights increasing overall reading rate. *Thinking about meaning* in Anderson's model is further divided into *acquisition of linguistic knowledge and general comprehension*, and *recognition of text structures and discourse organization in Grabe's model*. Three principles from Grabe's model – *extensive reading, intrinsic motivation*, and *coherent curriculum* – are not found in Anderson's framework. Instead, Anderson includes *progress evaluation* in his agenda. Guided by these successful instructional principles suggested by Grabe and Anderson, this chapter categorizes innovative technological tools into five pedagogical approaches that focus on promoting L2 reading skills. The first three categories correspond to three from Anderson's framework: (1) activating background knowledge, (2) enriching vocabulary, and (3) promoting reading fluency. Reading strategy development (from Anderson) and teaching about meaning (from Grabe) are combined in (4) teaching for comprehension skills. The fifth and final category (from Grabe) will discuss (5) extensive reading.

TECHNOLOGY IN L2 READING INSTRUCTION

Activating background knowledge

Readers bring their cultural and linguistic knowledge to a text. From a cognitive perspective, prior knowledge is essential for learning to take place: When new information is connected to background knowledge, working memory overload decreases, thereby becoming available for higher-order cognitive activities (Mayer & Moreno, 2003). Learners connect different types of input from separate channels (e.g., visual, verbal) with the help of prior knowledge (Mayer, 2002). In particular, activated background knowledge affects reading comprehension by helping readers anticipate the organization of the text and by providing clues to the meanings of unknown words.

L2 readers with limited prior knowledge need substantial instructional support. It is also likely that some readers will make an incorrect guess when they fail to omit unrelated information from their background knowledge (Yang, 2006). Thus teachers are advised to activate background knowledge prior to reading a text – for example, through classroom activities that highlight making predictions, knowledge of text structure, and pre-reading discussion (Anderson, 2009). Although there has been relatively little attention to how L2 readers utilize online resources to activate their background knowledge during their L2 reading (Chun, 2011), potential approaches have been tested, such as hypermedia use (Akyel & Erçetin, 2009; Sakar & Erçetin, 2005) and L1 resource use (Chang & Hsu, 2011; Park, Yang, & Hsieh, 2014). Hyperlinked multimedia commonly provides additional resources that can help readers make sense of a written text. L1 resources may help readers either to activate the knowledge that they already have to make sense of L2 or to learn complex concepts in L1 that they can later apply to L2 comprehension.

Hypermedia annotation. Sakar and Erçetin (2005) explored how intermediate L2 readers ($n = 44$) used annotations for reading an English hypermedia text and whether annotation use facilitated comprehension. The L2 readers were asked to read a 900-word hypertext for general comprehension followed by a recall task. A total of 104 textual annotations, which included lexical information, such as pronunciation and definition either in text or graphics, were provided within the body of text. In contrast, 26 extratextual annotations linked to background information about the topic were provided below the text in the form of text, graphics, sound, or video. Data were collected through a tracking tool, a reading comprehension test, a questionnaire, and interviews. The results from the tracking tool, which detected which annotations the reader had clicked and the order of the navigation, showed that the participants preferred visual annotations (e.g., video, graphics) significantly more than textual or audio annotations. In particular, the participants believed that the visual annotations certainly helped them understand the text better by providing background knowledge. However, based on the comprehension test result, auditory (e.g., pronunciation) and visual (graphics, video) annotations were found to negatively affect reading comprehension. The authors discussed potential reasons for such negative influence of such annotations on comprehension: (a) As video annotation and reading a text both require working memory in a visual channel, the participants might have experienced overload with visual information, which could have hindered reading comprehension, and (b) the participants gathered semantically similar information through several channels (e.g., visual, audio), which might have distracted them. It is also plausible that navigating hypertext was novel to the participants, who might have selected annotations that seemed interesting to them, but were not important to the topic. This interpretation is compatible with findings that poor comprehenders, compared to readers with good comprehension skills, are less likely to resist inhibitory factors while reading (Borella, Carretti, & Pelegrina, 2010).

A more recent small-scale study identified hypermedia annotation as being effective for L2 readers with limited prior knowledge. Akyel and Erçetin (2009) examined patterns of strategy use of 10 Turkish college students when reading English hypermedia texts. Data were collected from think-aloud protocols, text recall, a standardized reading test, an interview, and a tracking tool. The participants, advanced L2 readers, were divided into two groups – groups of low prior knowledge versus high prior knowledge – and the strategy use of the two groups was compared. While reading, these readers were able to access annotations that provided either word-level information (i.e., definitions of words) or topic-level information (i.e., background information about the topic). Strategies that were used in this study were compared to those which were identified by Anderson (1991) as being effective for printed texts. The findings indicated that most of the strategies used for reading printed texts were also employed for processing hypertexts (e.g., cognitive and metacognitive strategies). However, some strategies were used exclusively in this online context; the one most frequently employed was annotations used to retrieve background information about the topic. This strategy use accounted for 27% of all strategy occurrences. In particular, the group with low prior knowledge used this strategy more frequently (34.07%) than the high prior knowledge group (22.15%). The high-knowledge group tended to rely on their existing knowledge (9.03%) more than the low-knowledge group did (4.95%). The result of the recall test indicated that the high-knowledge group outperformed the low-knowledge group, but not at a significant level. Further research, with a larger number of participants and in a variety of contexts, could help determine whether hypermedia annotation of information pertaining to the topic could help L2 readers with limited prior knowledge to improve their reading comprehension in a definitive way.

Tools for matching L1 and L2 knowledge. Tools that provide access to L1 resources constitute additional ways of activating and enhancing the background knowledge essential for L2 reading comprehension. In three consecutive studies of intensive English reading, Chang and Hsu (2011) had their Taiwanese students use mobile devices with L1 translation annotation mode. This function automatically recorded the translation that students had annotated into their reading material. Instant L1 annotation and translation shared within a group enabled members to brainstorm and discuss their viewpoints. More than 70% of students found this instant translation annotation feature useful and easy to use either individually or collaboratively. Interestingly, the positive effects of this feature on learning outcomes were more pronounced when students worked collaboratively rather than individually.

Park, Yang, and Hsieh (2014) identified ways in which college-level L2 readers took advantage of additional resources they had prior experience with to fill in the gap in their background knowledge while reading online. Seven Asian college students in this study read two English texts online and were allowed to find information from the Internet in order to answer comprehension questions. The findings, derived from the observation, think-aloud protocols, and interviews, suggest that the participants used both L1 and L2 information while making sense of the texts. For example, some students retrieved content knowledge about a topic (e.g., Arctic melt) from Wikipedia, which helped them to compare their prior knowledge in L1 with what they did not know in L2. At other times, students resorted to resources written in their L1, such as online bilingual dictionaries, online encyclopedia, or blogs, to learn complicated concepts (e.g., currency exchange issues) dealt with in a text. Once students had L1 and L2 knowledge bases connected, they were able to unlock the meaning of the whole passage, not to mention one-to-one translation of unknown terminology.

Enriching vocabulary knowledge

Lexical items are the principal source that readers refer to when they try to make sense of L2 input (VanPatten, 2004). Research on the relationship between vocabulary and reading comprehension shows that readers need to be familiar with 95% or more of the words in a text if they are to be able to comprehend the text and infer the meanings of new words (Horst, 2009; Nation, 2001). Knowing a word is not simply one-to-one mapping of form and meaning. Schmitt (2000) reminds us that vocabulary knowledge should include semantic relations, such as synonyms, antonyms in terms of degree, antonyms in a hierarchical order, and whole and parts relations. (See Chapter 5 in this book for a discussion of the centrality of lexical knowledge during reading in an L2.) Technology indeed increases L2 vocabulary knowledge through learner- and community-centered learning practices, as in the following.

Multimodal vocabulary support. Web-based texts have additional information through hyperlinks to assist readers. Hyperlinked words in many multimodal gloss studies direct readers to written, audio, or pictorial information displays that contain definitions or pronunciations of those words. Proctor et al. (2009) went beyond this basic lexical information in their study of 240 fifth graders in the U.S., 49% of whom were L2 readers, over one school year. Their reading program conformed to Schmitt's (2000) notion about vocabulary knowledge in that its hyperlinked content and information provided potential exposure to a number of other semantically related words, as well as definitions and pronunciations. For example, when students learned the word *anxious*, they were possibly exposed to synonyms (nervous, agitated) and antonyms (calm and peaceful). There were additional audio supports that explained further linguistic information about a given word. L2 students, in particular, were able to tap into cross-linguistic information, such as L1 cognates (e.g., a Spanish word *ansiosamente* that is cognate with an English word *anxiously*). In their wrap-up activities, students were also encouraged to express themselves in multiple ways and were able to write or orally record their work. In comparison to a control group, the treatment group made significant gains on standardized measures of vocabulary knowledge.

Corpus-driven learning. Building vocabulary knowledge goes beyond just learning individual words. Learning L2 itself is often described as a process of learning linguistic *chunks*, such as L2 vocabulary and syntax (Ellis, 1996). Chunking is a way to improve one's working memory performance, thereby facilitating learning processes. Studies on the cognitive process have demonstrated that meaningful unit-based chunking of information has beneficial effects on learning, either by reducing repeated attention-switching between old and new information (Barrouillet & Camos, 2007) or by reducing the cognitive load that learners require to identify salient boundaries between information units (Schwan, Garsoffky, & Hesse, 2000; Wouters, Paas, & van Merriënboer, 2008). Corpus linguists propose the importance of multiword phrases as units of language by emphasizing the need for L2 learners to be exposed to semi-preconstructed lexical items (e.g., Sinclair, 1991). These linguistic chunks include collocations and formulaic expressions that appear more frequently than expected by chance.

Concordance software allows a fast corpus search and presents instances of a selected word or phrase in the center of a screen, along with the words that appear together to the left and right. A set of concordance lines, which are lines taken from a corpus, show lexical, syntactic, and semantic patterns in various reading passages and contexts (Constantinescu, 2007), so that L2 readers can become aware of such items in authentic contexts (Butler-Pascoe & Wiburg, 2003). For instruction, teachers collect language samples by using either existing corpora or their own written texts. There are free web-based corpora that contain large amounts of concordance, such as British National Corpus (http://corpus.byu.edu/bnc) or the Corpus of Contemporary American English (http://corpus.byu.edu/coca). In cases when concordance lines are to be obtained from classroom materials, concordance programs, such as AntLab Corpus Tools (http://www.laurenceanthony.net/software.html) and WordSmith Tools (http://www.lexically.net/wordsmith/), are available.

Liu and Jiang (2009) conducted a study with a sizeable number of participants (236 students and 8 instructors), which showed a positive effect of integrating corpus use in L2 instruction. In this study, instructors at a Chinese college and two U.S. colleges received detailed training on the importance of collocation in L2 learning and how to use corpus and concordance. Classroom activities included searching for desired ways in which target words or phrases (either errors in students' own papers or words assigned by instructors) were used. Data were collected both on learning and teaching, such as students' corpus search projects, reflections, lesson plans, teaching journals, and responses on a post-survey. Through these activities, students developed discovery learning skills, critical understanding of grammar, and understanding of inherent relationship between lexicon and grammar. At the same time, the students reported that it was challenging to effectively analyze a great number of search results (e.g., concordance lines) and to identify usages and patterns relevant to their tasks.

Teaching for comprehension skills

Efficient reading comprehension requires, but is not limited to, a sufficient amount of linguistic knowledge, recognition of text organization, and general comprehension skills. In particular, L2 readers' ability to extract meaning from text is closely associated with comprehension strategies, which should be taught (Anderson, 2009). A number of studies have shown that strategy training greatly benefits L2 readers (e.g., Wenden, 2002). Strategy-based reading instruction seems more effective in a constructivist approach than a traditional teacher-centered approach (Zhang, 2007). Constructivist learning environments emphasize collaborative knowledge construction rather than rote memorization (Plonsky, 2011; Sawyer, 2006). Cognitive linguistics also supports the view that humans learn language while processing input and using words to interact with others (Ellis, 2005). The experience of processing input during communication in social contexts may be obtained in reciprocal teaching, which encourages students to take the role of guiding group reading sessions by using such strategies as summarizing, question generating, seeking clarification, and making predictions (Spörer, Brunstein, & Kieschke, 2009). The following sections describe technological tools that help collaborative knowledge construction through reciprocal teaching.

Text-to-speech technology (TTST). TTST is geared to encourage weak readers to engage in collaborative and comprehensive reading approaches. As students read using TTST, they track along, listen carefully, apply their reading strategies to this experience, and, ideally, gain an understanding of the text (Parr, 2012). This assistive technology has been long explored mostly for students with impaired vision or dyslexia (e.g., Elkind, Black, & Murray, 1996; Stodden, Roberts, Takahashi, Park, & Stodden, 2012). TTST, however, has become much more available on smart phones, tablets, e-readers, and computers than in the past, potentially expanding its scope of instructional approaches. TTST not only helps those who struggle with word decoding and fluency, but also moves them forward to the next step in a reading activity. Al-Awidi and Ismail (2012) conducted a survey and interviews of 145 English as a Second Language (ESL) teachers in the U.S. to investigate their perception of the use of computer-assisted language learning, including TTSS. Teachers in this study reported that TTST helped ESL children learn to read by allowing them to make links between speech and print. More importantly, teachers were then able to encourage children to use effective reading strategies. In another recent study by Parr (2012), 28 high school students took advantage of TTST as a reading option and, furthermore, used a recording feature that enabled them to leave voice notes of their responses to texts. Parr found that these students were able to engage in a variety of interactive and collaborative reading activities, such as discussion of metacognitive strategies and of content they read. In addition, TTST helped foster self-efficacy and self-advocacy for those who might otherwise struggle to read.

Wikis. Wikis provide meaningful communicative context for language acquisition by allowing for collaborative posting and editing of information by its users. While this content management system is oftentimes used as a platform for collaborative writing (e.g., Lin & Yang, 2011), only a handful of studies have attempted to integrate wikis into L2 reading instruction and empirical evidence on their success is limited. For example, Wiseman and Belknap (2013) described how ESL students shared reading of bestselling novels and created online glossaries using wikis, which included definitions, etymology, synonyms, antonyms, and crosswords. Students also posted the research results of the author's background, themes, characters, a comprehensive overview, and critical analysis. However, no data was provided to support the effectiveness of this approach.

Survey results on the use of wikis in L2 reading instruction were provided by Ducate, Anderson, and Moreno (2011), who conducted two wiki projects involving reading activities. In the first project that lasted two months, 10 intermediate L2 French-students in a U.S. college were asked to create wikis containing key terms and personal stories and discussion questions relevant to a section of a novel that they were reading in class. For this project, student in groups compiled text, images, sounds, and videos to complete their assigned parts of the wiki page. The second project, to which 10 L2 German students devoted the first half of a semester (six weeks), focused on developing a pre-reading wiki page which the students could refer to while they read a text during the second half of the semester. Wiki entries on a brief history of an assigned topic and its current significance, as well as an annotated bibliography, were created by small groups. To increase the number of entries in their wiki page, the participants worked collaboratively with students at other universities. While the participants were reading in the second half of the semester, the instructor encouraged them to refer to the wiki by requiring them to complete a webquest regarding each topic entry. The survey results indicated that the wiki projects motivated the participants to use their L2 in a meaningful communicative environment. However, at the end, some students complained about difficulties in group communication and co-operation, whereas some students displayed satisfaction with this type of collaborative project.

Class blogs. Weblogs are regularly updated web pages, typically run by an individual or a small group. Class blogs can serve as a tool that encourages collaborative learning. This online learning resource has an *asynchronous* form of communication, allowing students to learn at their own pace by reflecting on the content. Given this feature, learners have sufficient time to process input (e.g., high-order cognitive questions) that requires critical thinking and develop responses to those questions. Such cognitive processes encourage learners to interpret, analyze, evaluate, explain, and edit (G. Walker, 2005). In a four-week study of 75 first-year college students in Taiwan, Wang (2010) examined how this blogging feature affected L2 readers' learning. The participating students, clustered into 12 groups, were required to finish three English reading selections. No instant online messenger services (i.e., forms of synchronous communication) were available. The students met face to face in a classroom for two hours a week. After finishing one reading, students were asked to post the main idea and summary and to answer three discussion questions relevant to the reading. In addition, they were encouraged to add a comment on other group members' postings twice a week and on another group's discussions at least once a week. Although, due to the short period of the study, the findings did not confirm that participants developed all of the targeted metacognitive and cognitive reading strategies, there was evidence of frequent online interaction with regard to task completion.

This asynchronous form in blogging is sometimes accompanied with a *synchronous* form of communication in which learners simultaneously participate. Zheng and Warschauer (2015) examined how synchronous online discussions on a class blog influenced L2 reading development. A total of 37 fifth graders participated in this study for one school year, 25 of whom were students with limited English proficiency. These students used real-time blogging for twice-a-week 20-minute sessions to complete reading-writing connection activities. A teacher first modeled how to facilitate thinking by asking questions in online discussion. This discussion session developed into reciprocal teaching, in which students took turns asking pre-reading and post-reading questions that helped develop deeper understanding of texts. The authors analyzed students' posts in the first and last two months of the school year, finding that the reciprocal teaching approach helped lead to a higher degree of interaction, develop cognitive comprehension strategies, and cultivate a sense of audience and authorship.

Reading fluency

Reading fluency is a set of skills that allows readers to rapidly decode text while maintaining a high level of comprehension (National Reading Panel, 2000). There have been many studies that reported a positive correlation between fluency and comprehension (Chard, Vaughn, & Tyler, 2002; Rasinski et al., 2005; Yovanoff, Duesbery, Alonzo, & Tindal, 2005). Klauda and Guthrie (2008) found that word-, sentence-, and passage-levels of fluency have a significant bidirectional relationship with reading comprehension. In terms of speed, research suggests an optimal reading speed for comprehension which varies from 180 to 300 words per minute (wpm) (Higgins & Wallace, 1989; Jensen, 1986). Combining accuracy with speed is important, with Anderson (2009) determining that 200 wpm with 70% comprehension reflected adequate reading fluency. L2 readers, however, have difficulties enhancing reading fluency because of a slow reading rate. There is a report that L2 reading rates of even highly bilingual readers are about 30% slower than L1 reading rates (Segalowitz, Poulsen, & Komoda, 1991). Specifically, in a study by Jensen (1986), advanced L2 students read only 100 wpm. This rate is only about half the number of wpm that research suggests as desirable.

Meta-analysis research of fluency development and instruction shows that instruction can enhance both reading fluency and comprehension skills (National Reading Panel, 2000). For promoting fluency development, it is necessary to understand the mechanisms that control eye movement during reading. Our eyes move, stop, or fixate on characters, and move again during reading. A rapid eye movement from one *fixation* to another is called a *saccade*. A reading activity consists of a series of fixation and saccades (see Chapter 2 for further details). While making saccades, readers may go back, instead of going forward, to words that have been previously read when they need to reread the words, which is referred to *regression*. Average readers fixate their eyes on a set of characters for about 250 ms (thousandths of a second) and make a saccade of seven to nine characters (Rayner, Foorman, Perfetti, Pesetsky, & Seldenberg, 2001). A saccade lasts 20 to 40 ms, and skilled readers make regressions about 15% of reading time (Rayner, Slattery, & Belanger, 2010). In contrast, slow readers tend to have longer fixation durations, shorter forward saccades, and more regressions (Hutzler, Kronbichler, Jacobs, & Wimmer, 2006; Rayner, Chace, Slattery, & Ashby, 2009).

Technology can assist readers by immediately affecting this visual processing of reading. For example, electronic texts are flexible so that readers can easily change the way written text is processed, such as font face, size, and colour, to meet their personal needs. However, innovative technology now goes beyond such simple changes. Yet, there is little research on how technology can influence L2 reading fluency. The following section discusses L1 research on how the layout of text on a screen influences eye movements since such findings have implications for L2 reading fluency.

Appearance of the text on a screen. Numerous recent studies have explored the relationship between reading fluency and simply reducing text width (Beymer, Russell, & Orton, 2005; Schneps, Thomson, Chen, Sonnert, & Pomplun, 2013; Schneps, Thompson, Sonnert, et al., 2013). Beymer et al. (2005), for example, found that when reading narrow-formatted paragraphs (4.5 inches), participants read faster, had fewer regressions, and retained more information from reading materials than when they read wider paragraphs (9 inches). Similarly, Schneps, Thompson, Sonnert, et al. (2013) found that reading from a small device (e.g., Apple iPod Touch) resulted in improved reading speed by 27%, decreased the number of fixations by 11%, and reduced the number of regressive saccades. In the subsequent study by Schneps, Thompson, Chen, et al. (2013), high school readers with dyslexia benefited from reading on an iPod with only a few words per line, as opposed to reading on paper, in terms of comprehension and reading speed.

Visualizing syntactic structure. Going beyond simple changes in line length, some studies have investigated dynamic text reformatting, addressing the relationship between reading speed and spatial extent of visual crowding (Spritz, 2014; S. Walker et al., 2005; Yu & Miller, 2010). For instance, *visual-syntactic text formatting (VSTF)* technology uses automatic parsing processing that analyzes each sentence using both visual and linguistic criteria and determines optimal positions for segment breaks and indentation patterns (S. Walker et al., 2005). As a result, VSTF creates cascading patterns that are meant to reflect syntactic hierarchies, similar to parse trees, as shown in Figure 9.1. When using a web-based program, users can copy and paste any digital text into VSTF converting software for automatic conversion and reading. S. Walker et al. (2005) examined whether VSTF enhanced reading fluency by reformatting a text in a way that visualized syntactic structures. In this study, a total of 48 college students read expository passages either in VSTF or in regular block format (approximately 70 characters per line). Average reading time of participants was 10% faster when reading in VSTF than in block format. This text format also positively affected comprehension as participants showed 40% higher scores on a reading test when reading in VSTF than in block format.

Adding space between sentences. A more recent study by Yu and Miller (2010) evaluated the usability of text reformatting in which spacing was added between sentences to reduce density of texts and to enhance web page readability. This format, shown in Figure 9.2, is named Jenga by developers. When a user clicks on a specific paragraph of a web page, the paragraph is converted

He let
  the Horse make free
    with his oats,
  gave
  the Ox an abundance
    of hay,
  and fed
  the Dog with meat
    from his own table.

Grateful
  for these favors,
  the animals
  determined
  to repay him
  to the best
    of their ability.

For this purpose,
  they divided
  the term
    of his life
      between them,
  and each endowed one portion
    of it
  with the qualities which
    chiefly characterized himself.

FIGURE 9.1 VSTF creates cascading patterns that are meant to reflect syntactic hierarchies.

A Horse, Ox, and Dog, driven to great straits by the cold,
sought shelter and protection from Man.
                                    He received them
kindly, lighted a fire, and warmed them.
                                    He let the Horse
make free with his oats, gave the Ox an abundance of hay,
and fed the Dog with meat from his own table.
                                    Grateful for
these favors, the animals determined to repay him to the
best of their ability.
                                    For this purpose, they divided the term of
his life between them, and each endowed one portion of it
with the qualities which chiefly characterized himself.

FIGURE 9.2 Jenga formatting of text.

into Jenga format and all sentences in the paragraph are highlighted in yellow
to help the reader focus on it. Another click turns the expanded paragraph
back to the original format. In order to not interrupt the continuous reading
of a given paragraph, Jenga format does not align sentences to the left margin;
instead, Jenga-formatted sentences connect to previous sentences with a space.
This paragraph shape of interlocking sentences resembles the Jenga game,

after which the developer named the text format. This way, the Jenga format may reduce the density of reading passages to enhance their readability. A total of 30 L2 readers read texts in three types of formats: regular block-shaped, VSTF, and Jenga. Despite the researcher's concern that reformatted texts might slow down reading speed due to readers' unfamiliarity with the format, there was no significant difference between reading block-shaped and two reformatted texts. Average reading comprehension scores were higher on sentence-spaced texts than on block-shaped or VSTF texts.

Removing regressions. Based on the idea that the more eye movements and regressions readers have, the slower reading speed becomes, an innovative reading tool called *rapid serial visual presentation (RSVP)* has been invented. It radically reduces the number of eye movements and regressive saccades (e.g., Spritz, 2014). RSVP presents one word at a time, enabling readers to fix their eyes on a small window while reading. Speed is prearranged from 100 to 1,000 wpm before readers start to read. However, to our knowledge, no study has been conducted to examine how RSVP affects reading performance. Instead, Schotter, Tran, and Rayner (2014) simulated a reading condition that approximated that of RSVP: the "trailing-mask condition," in which each word was masked and replaced with an X after a reader made a forward saccade. Forty college students participating in this study read sentences that were displayed either normally or in the trailing-mask condition. The findings show that readers were less accurate on a comprehension test when reading in the trail-masked condition than in the normal condition. In addition, regressions were not necessarily negative for reading comprehension, but, rather, were sometimes required for a more accurate interpretation of what was read. The authors suggest that RSVP could be appropriate only for reading short texts that rarely involve regressions.

Promoting extensive reading

Developing critical L2 reading skills inevitably requires repetitive exposure to a large number of written texts. Day and Bamford (1998) argue that extensive reading – that is, a large amount of reading in and outside the classroom, through both print and electronic sources – should be part of L2 reading programs, as it is an effective way of increasing various aspects of L2 reading proficiency. Their argument has been widely acknowledged and supported by continuing research efforts, including extensive reading studies on reading fluency (Grabe, 2004; Taguchi, Takayasu-Maass, & Corsuch, 2004), possible vocabulary development (Horst, 2005), and reading strategies (Zhang & Wu, 2009). Moreover, through extensive reading, L2 learners could consolidate linguistic items they have learned and deepen their knowledge about them (Laufer, 2003).

However, the extensive reading approach is not without criticism. Even advocates of the extensive reading admit that it may be unsuccessful if it is a short-term program (Krashen, 1993) and that the amount of reading required for vocabulary gains is unrealistic in instructed L2 teaching context (Laufer, 2003). From a practical perspective, indeed, it is challenging to make time for extensive reading in an already-crowded curriculum (Macalister, 2008). In English as a Foreign Language (EFL) contexts, it is even more difficult to implement extensive reading programs due to limited instructional time and input-poor environments (Al-Homoud & Schmitt, 2009).

Learning management system (LMS). LMS is a web-based technology that provides teachers with various ways to plan and administrate a course, deliver content, track students' learning, and assess students' performance. LMS allows for an individualized learning pace tailored to students' specific needs and enables students to constantly evaluate their own learning. Personalized learning paces and ongoing evaluation of knowledge help L2 learners with varying proficiency stay motivated in learning to read. The following LMS example focuses on motivating L2 learners to engage in extensive reading.

Recognizing the significance of extensive reading in EFL contexts, Thomas Robb launched MoodleReader (http://mreader.org/) to the standard Moodle course management system in the 2008–2009 school year. Although not including all LMS features, this LMS effectively supported the first-year students' English extensive reading (ER) program at a Japanese university. In his recent report (Robb & Kano, 2013), Robb described how this LMS encouraged a great number of Japanese students ($N = 2,500$ to $3,000$) to read extensively outside the classroom. This module provides quizzes on over 3,000 graded books for young readers so that students can simply assess their work. Students take short timed quizzes with randomized questions on their graded reading, and control the level of difficulty of the books on which they are quizzed, as well as the frequency with which they can access them. Instructors have a simple way to access information to verify their students' reading progress. Robb and his colleague examined the effect of the ER program on reading scores at the end of the school year by comparing the pre- and post-test results of two cohorts. The two cohorts in 2008–2009 and in 2009–2010 had the same curriculum, but only the 2009–2010 cohort (treatment group) participated in the ER program. Analysis of the data revealed that the treatment group had made significant gains in reading compared to the control group. The authors attributed the success of the ER program to the ease of MoodleReader's management system, which encouraged a high rate of participation among the instructors, thereby encouraging students to spend the requisite amount of time on reading outside of classroom.

LMS is not a magic wand to build a successful extensive program, but it can create supportive environments in which teachers can implement the program more easily than in traditional L2 classrooms. In addition to Moodle (https://moodle.org/), more and more LMSs have recently been developed to aid language classrooms, such as Schoology (https://www.schoology.com/home.php), Edmodo (https://www.edmodo.com/), and Eliademy (https://eliademy.com/).

IMPLICATIONS FOR L2 READING INSTRUCTION AND RESEARCH

This concluding section discusses implications for practice and practical applications of technology-assisted L2 reading. Teachers' roles in technology-incorporated classrooms are sometimes fundamentally different from those in traditional classrooms, especially since many of the technological innovations have not undergone large-scale testing. For one, L2 teachers need to make their own judgment calls when selecting digital tools that are appropriate for developing specific aspects of L2 reading for individual students. For example, such tools as TTST, VSTF, Jenga, and RSVP may help prompt students to read faster, but should not be universally recommended for all slow readers. TTST may be appropriate for those with decoding difficulties, while VSTF may support those who struggle with sentence structure. The teacher's role as a facilitator of collaborative learning is also important. Despite its advantages, a collaborative project is not necessarily always satisfactory. For example, there was some negative feedback on wiki projects, such as difficulty of group communication and role consensus. Group work needs to be carefully planned and monitored, because positive interactions do not always come naturally to collaborative learning situations in technology-enhanced classrooms.

Successful instruction also needs to balance innovative technology with sound content and pedagogy. As we know, it is not desirable either to use technology only as an add-on to existing lessons or to emphasize technical skills and digital resources over the language-related educational goals of a program. To this end, teachers first have to be equipped with digital skills that help them confidently and effectively use advanced technological tools, such as concordance software, wikis, or LMS, in classrooms, to allow for versatility in their pedagogical approaches (e.g., individualized, collaborative learning). To remove an undue "operational burden" in the use of technology, training may be necessary to integrate such tools into classrooms so that both teachers and students will not be frustrated, as was the case in some of the aforementioned studies. More importantly, teachers should become aware of how knowledge is constructed, prior to designing technology-incorporated lessons. Specific beliefs that teachers hold about learning indeed influence pedagogical approaches and integration of technology in classrooms (Jacobson et al., 2010). Such epistemological beliefs help teachers discern which resources are reliable and appropriate for their classrooms.

In concluding this chapter, it is worthwhile to briefly bring to the fore the implications for research in the field of L2 reading and technology. Given that technological tools are changing rapidly and unpredictably, the current speed of research and the speed of technological change may not be in sync. First of all, it is necessary to collect reliable data in this area using a variety of research methodologies. In fact, a number of teachers are satisfactorily using social tools, mobile applications, and new learning platforms in their classrooms, but they share their experiences via non-academic journals, blogs, and Facebook communities. However, studies either without learning outcome data (e.g., Al-Awidi & Ismail, 2012; Ducate, Anderson, & Moreno, 2011; John, 2001; Liu & Jiang, 2009) or without solid research designs (e.g., Robb & Kano, 2013) provide only limited answers. It is imperative to examine the effects of pedagogical tools within a theoretical framework and a research method with carefully controlled variables, and, furthermore, to widely disseminate new findings to benefit more L2 teachers and learners. We especially recommend research on the use of tracking eye movement (e.g., fluency studies), social network analysis (e.g., studies using social tools), and digital media literacy assessment (e.g., evaluating students holistically not just on L2 reading skills but also on digital skills that help them solve problems). Furthermore, it is required to replicate some of the aforementioned studies (e.g., Jenga study, hypermedia study) or to design studies that explore effects of tools (e.g., fluency tools) introduced in this chapter. As for those tools that have not existed for very long, they have either not been examined in an L2 context at all or else yielded conflicting results in L2 research. More theoretical and empirical evidence is needed to validate the use of those tools for specific L2 purposes.

REFERENCES

Akyel, A., & Erçetin, G. (2009). Hypermedia reading strategies employed by advanced learners of English. *System, 37*(1), 136–152. doi:10.1016/j.system.2008.05.002

Al-Awidi, H. M., & Ismail, S. A. (2012). Teachers' perceptions of the use of computer assisted language learning to develop children's reading skills in English as a second language in the United Arab Emirates. *Early Childhood Education Journal, 42*(1), 29–37. doi:10.1007/s10643–012–0552–7

Al-Homoud, F., & Schmitt, N. (2009). Extensive reading in a challenging environment: A comparison of extensive and intensive reading approaches in Saudi Arabia. *Language Teaching Research, 13*(4), 383–401.

Anderson, N. J. (1991). Individual differences in strategy use in second language reading and testing. *The Modern Language Journal, 75*, 460–472.

Anderson, N. J. (2009). ACTIVE reading: The research base for a pedagogical approach in the reading classroom. In Z.-H. Han & N. J. Anderson (Eds.), *L2 reading research and instruction: Crossing the boundaries* (pp. 117–143). *Ann Arbor, MI: University of Michigan Press.*

Barrouillet, P., & Camos, V. (2007). The time-based resource sharing model of working memory. In N. Osaka, R.H. Logie, & M. D'Esposito (Eds.), *The cognitive neuroscience of working memory* (pp. 59–80). Oxford: Oxford University Press.

Beymer, D., Russell, D., & Orton, P. (2005, September). *Wide vs. narrow paragraphs: An eye tracking analysis.* Paper presented at the 2005 IFIP TC13 International Conference on Human-computer Interaction, Rome, Italy.

Borella, E., Carretti, B., & Pelegrina, S. (2010). The specific role of inhibition in reading comprehension in good and poor comprehenders. *Journal of Learning Disabilities, 43*(6), 541–552. doi:10.1177/0022219410371676

Butler-Pascoe, M.E., & Wiburg, K. (2003). *Technology and teaching English language learners.* Boston, MA: Allyn and Bacon.

Chang, C.-K., & Hsu, C.-K. (2011). A mobile-assisted synchronously collaborative translation-annotation system for English as a foreign language (EFL) reading comprehension. *Computer Assisted Language Learning, 24*(2), 155–180. doi:10.1080/09588221.2010. 536952

Chard, D.J., Vaughn, S., & Tyler, B. (2002). A synthesis of research on effective interventions for building reading fluency with elementary students with learning disabilities. *Journal of Learning Disabilities, 35,* 386–406.

Chun, D.M. (2011). CALL technologies for L2 reading post Web 2.0. In N. Arnold & L. Ducate (Eds.), *Present and future promises of CALL: From theory and research to new directions in language teaching* (pp. 131–170). San Marcos, TX: Routledge.

Constantinescu, A.I. (2007). Using technology to assist in vocabulary acquisition and reading comprehension. *The Internet TESL Journal, 13*(2). Retrieved from http://iteslj. org/Articles/Constantinescu-Vocabulary

Day, R., & Bamford, J. (1998). *Extensive reading in the second language classroom.* Cambridge: Cambridge University Press.

Ducate, L.C., Anderson, L.L., & Moreno, N. (2011). Wading through the world of Wikis: An analysis of three Wiki projects. *Foreign Language Annals, 44*(3), 495–524. doi:10.1111/j.1944–9720.2011.01144.x

Elkind, J., Black, M.S., & Murray, C. (1996). Computer-based compensation of adult reading disabilities. *Annals of Dyslexia, 46*(1), 159–186.

Ellis, N. (1996). Sequencing in SLA: Phonological memory, chunking, and points of order. *Studies in Second Language Acquisition, 18,* 91–126.

Ellis, R. (2005). Principles of instructed language learning. *System, 33*(2), 209–224.

Fitzgerald, J. (1995). English-as-a-second-language learners' cognitive reading processes: A review of research in the United States. *Review of Educational Research, 65,* 145–190.

Grabe, W. (2004). Research on teaching reading. *Annual Review of Applied Linguistics, 24,* 44–69.

Higgins, J., & Wallace, R. (1989). Hopalong: A computer reader pacer. *System, 17,* 389–399

Hirvela, A. (2004). *Connecting reading & writing in second language writing instruction. Ann Arbor, MI: University of Michigan Press.*

Horst, M. (2005). Learning L2 vocabulary through extensive reading: A measurement study. *The Canadian Modern Language Review/La Revue Canadienne Des Langues Vivantes, 61*(3), 355–382. doi:10.1353/cml.2005.0018

Horst, M. (2009). Developing definitional vocabulary knowledge and lexical access speed through extensive reading. In Z.-H. Han & N.J. Anderson (Eds.), *Second language reading: Research and instruction* (pp. 40–64). Ann Arbor, MI: University of Michigan Press.

Hutzler, F., Kronbichler, M., Jacobs, A. M., & Wimmer, H. (2006). Perhaps correlational but not causal: No effect of dyslexic readers' magnocellular system on their eye movements during reading. *Neuropsychologia, 44*(4), 637–648. doi:10.1016/j.neuropsychologia. 2005.06.006

Jacobson, M.J., So, H.-J., Teo, T., Lee, J., Pathak, S., & Lossman, H. (2010). Epistemology and learning: Impact on pedagogical practices and technology use in Singapore schools. *Computers & Education, 55*(4), 1694–1706. doi:10.1016/j.compedu.2010.07.014

Jensen, L. (1986). Advanced reading skills in a comprehensive course. In F. Dubin, D.E. Eskey, & W. Grabe (Eds.), *Teaching second language reading for academic purposes* (pp. 103–124). Reading, MA: Addison-Wesley.

John, E.S. (2001). A case for using a parallel corpus and concordancer for beginners of a foreign language. *Language Learning & Technology, 5*(3), 185–203.

Klauda, S.L., & Guthrie, J.T. (2008). Relationships of three components of reading fluency to reading comprehension. *Journal of Educational Psychology, 100*(2), 310–321. doi:10.1037/0022–0663.100.2.310

Krashen, S. (1993). *The power of reading: Insights from the research.* Englewood, CA: Libraries Unlimited.

Lankshear, C., & Knobel, M. (2007). Sampling "the new" in new literacies. *A New Literacies Sampler, 29*, 1–24.

Laufer, B. (2003). Vocabulary acquisition in a second language: Do learners really acquire most vocabulary by reading? Some empirical evidence. *Canadian Modern Language Review, 59*(4), 565–585.

Lin, W.C., & Yang, S.C. (2011). Exploring students' perceptions of integrating Wiki technology and peer feedback into English writing courses. *English Teaching: Practice and Critique, 10*(2), 88–103.

Liu, D., & Jiang, P. (2009). Using a corpus-based lexicogrammatical approach to grammar instruction in EFL and ESL contexts. *The Modern Language Journal, 9*, 61–78.

Macalister, J. (2008). Integrating extensive reading into an English for academic purposes program. *The Reading Matrix, 8*(1), 23–34.

Mayer, R.E. (2002). Multimedia learning. *Psychology of Learning and Motivation, 41*, 85–139.

Mayer, R.E., & Moreno, R. (2003). Nine ways to reduce cognitive load in multimedia learning. *Educational Psychologist, 38*(1), 43–52.

Nation, I.S.P. (2001). *Learning vocabulary in another language.* Cambridge: Cambridge University Press.

National Reading Panel. (2000). *Teaching children to read: An evidence-based assessment of the scientific research literature on reading and its implications for reading instruction* (NIH Publication No. 00–4769). Washington, DC: U.S. Government Printing Office.

Park, J., Yang, J., & Hsieh, Y. (2014). University level second language readers' online reading and comprehension strategies. *Language Learning & Technology, 18*(3), 148–172.

Parr, M. (2012). The future of text-to-speech technology: How long before it's just one more thing we do when teaching reading? *Procedia-Social and Behavioral Sciences, 69*, 1420–1429. doi:10.1016/j.sbspro.2012.12.081

Plonsky, L. (2011). The effectiveness of second language strategy instruction: A meta-analysis. *Language Learning, 61*(4), 993–1038.

Proctor, C. P., Dalton, B., Uccelli, P., Biancarosa, G., Mo, E., Snow, C., & Neugebauer, S. (2009). Improving comprehension online: Effects of deep vocabulary instruction with bilingual and monolingual fifth graders. *Reading and Writing, 24*(5), 517–544. doi:10.1007/s11145–009–9218–2

Rasinski, T. V., Padak, N. D., McKeon, C. A., Wilfong, L. G., Friedhauer, J. A., & Heim, P. (2005). Is reading fluency a key for successful high school reading? *Journal of Adolescent & Adult Literacy, 49*, 22–27.

Rayner, K., Chace, K. H., Slattery, T. J., & Ashby, J. (2009). Eye movements as reflections of comprehension processes in reading. *Scientific Studies of Reading, 10*(3), 241–255.

Rayner, K., Foorman, B., Perfetti, C., Pesetsky, D., & Seidenberg, M. (2001). How psychological science informs the teaching of reading. *Psychological Science in the Public Interest, 2*(2), 31–74.

Rayner, K., Slattery, T. J., & Bélanger, N. N. (2010). Eye movements, the perceptual span, and reading speed. *Psychonomic Bulletin & Review, 17*(6), 834–839.

Robb, T., & Kano, M. (2013). Effective extensive reading outside the classroom: A large-scale experiment. *Reading in a Foreign Language, 25*(2), 234–247.

Sakar, A., & Ercetin, G. (2005). Effectiveness of hypermedia annotations for foreign language reading. *Journal of Computer Assisted Learning, 21*, 28–38.

Sawyer, R. K. (2006). Educating for innovation. *Thinking Skills and Creativity, 1*(1), 41–48.

Schmitt, N. (2000). *Vocabulary in language teaching.* Cambridge: Cambridge University Press.

Schneps, M. H., Thomson, J. M., Chen, C., Sonnert, G., & Pomplun, M. (2013). E-readers are more effective than paper for some with dyslexia. *PLoS ONE, 8*(9), e75634. doi:10.1371/journal.pone.0075634

Schneps, M. H., Thomson, J. M., Sonnert, G., Pomplun, M., Chen, C., & Heffner-Wong, A. (2013). Shorter lines facilitate reading in those who struggle. *PLoS ONE, 8*(8), e71161. doi:10.1371/journal.pone.0071161

Schotter, E. R., Tran, R., & Rayner, K. (2014). Don't believe what you read (only once): Comprehension is supported by regressions during reading. *Psychological Science, 25*(6), 1218–1226. doi:10.1177/0956797614531148

Schwan, S., Garsoffky, B., & Hesse, F. (2000). Do film cuts facilitate the perceptual and cognitive organization of activity sequences? *Memory & Cognition, 28*, 214–223. doi:10.3758/bf03213801.

Segalowitz, N. S., Poulsen, C., & Komoda, M. (1991). Lower level components of reading skill in higher level bilinguals: Implications for reading instruction. *AILA Review, 8*, 15–30.

Sinclair, J. (1991). *Corpus, concordance, collocation.* Oxford: Oxford University Press.

Spörer, N., Brunstein, J. C., & Kieschke, U. L. F. (2009). Improving students' reading comprehension skills: Effects of strategy instruction and reciprocal teaching. *Learning and Instruction, 19*(3), 272–286.

Spritz. (2014). Spritz reading. Retrieved from http://www.spritzinc.com/the-science/

Stodden, R. A., Roberts, K. D., Takahashi, K., Park, H. J., & Stodden, N. J. (2012). Use of text-to-speech software to improve reading skills of high school struggling readers. *Procedia Computer Science, 14*, 359–362. doi:10.1016/j.procs.2012.10.041

Taguchi, E., Takayasu-Maass, M., & Gorsuch, G.J. (2004). Developing reading fluency in EFL: How assisted repeated reading and extensive reading affect fluency development. *Reading in a Foreign Language, 16*(2), 70–96.

VanPatten, B. (2004). *Processing instruction.* Mahwah, NJ: Erlbaum.

Verhoeven, L., & Perfetti, C. (2008). Advances in text comprehension: Model, process and development. *Applied Cognitive Psychology, 22*(3), 293–301. doi:10.1002/acp.1417

Walker, G. (2005). Critical thinking in asynchronous discussion. *International Journal of Instructional Technology and Distance Learning, 2*(6). Retrieved from http://itdl.org/journal/jun_05/article02.htm

Walker, S., Schloss, P., Fletcher, C.R., Vogel, C.A., & Walker, R. (2005). Visual-syntactic text formatting: A new method to enhance online reading. *Reading Online, 8*(6). Retrieved from http://www.readingonline.org/articles/r_walker/

Wang, M. (2010). Online collaboration and offline interaction between students using asynchronous tools in blended learning. *Australasian Journal of Educational Technology, 26*(6), 830–846.

Wenden, A.L. (2002). Learner development in language learning. *Applied Linguistics, 23*, 32–55.

Wiseman, C.S., & Belknap, J.P. (2013). Wikis: A knowledge platform for collaborative learning in ESL reading. *TESOL Journal, 4*(2), 360–369. doi:10.1002/tesj.83

Wouters, P., Paas, F., & van Merriënboer, J.J. (2008). How to optimize learning from animated models: A review of guidelines based on cognitive load. *Review of Educational Research, 78*(3), 645–675.

Yang, Y.-F. (2006). Reading strategies or comprehension monitoring strategies? *Reading Psychology, 27*(4), 313–343. doi:10.1080/02702710600846852

Yovanoff, P., Duesbery, L., Alonzo, J., & Tindal, G. (2005). Grade-level invariance of a theoretical causal structure predicting reading comprehension with vocabulary and oral reading fluency. *Educational Measurement: Issues & Practices, 24*, 4–12.

Yu, C.H., & Miller, R.C. (2010, April). *Enhancing web page readability for non-native readers.* Paper presented at the SIGCHI Conference on Human Factors in Computing Systems, Atlanta, GA.

Zhang, L.J. (2007). Constructivist pedagogy in strategic reading instruction: Exploring pathways to learner development in the English as a second language (ESL) classroom. *Instructional Science, 36*(2), 89–116. doi:10.1007/s11251–007–9025–6

Zhang, L.J., & Wu, A. (2009). Chinese senior high school EFL students' metacognitive awareness and reading strategy use. *Reading in a Foreign Language, 21*(1), 37–59.

Zheng, B., & Warschauer, M. (2015). Participation, interaction, and academic achievement in an online discussion environment. *Computers & Education, 84*, 78–89. doi:10.1016/j.compedu.2015.01.008

Index

abjads 6, 7, 10–11
Aboriginal Head Start Program 202
abugidas 6, 7, 11–12
academic vocabulary 237;
    see also vocabulary
accommodation 54–5, 57, 237
achievement gaps 222
acoustic correlates 134
adolescents 168, 173, 218, 237–8, 240, 242,
    243, 248, 250–4, 258, 260, 261, 269–70
Akkadian 4
alphabets 6, 7, 8–10, 50, 80; Korean 9–10;
    Pinyin 23; Serbian 23; shared 138;
    Turkish 18
alphasyllabaries see abugidas
Amharic 7
Amish 202
Anki (website) 225
Arabic language 15, 35, 37, 51, 109, 211–12,
    240, 243, 267
Arabic script 10–11, 18, 23, 211–12
assimilation 54–5, 57
Atatürk, Kemal 18
automaticity theory 41–5, 249
automatization 135

background knowledge 162, 247, 284;
    activating with technology 284–7; and
    L1 reading comprehension 167; and L2
    reading comprehension 167–70; and
reading comprehension 160, 167–70,
    179; and schema theory 167–8; see also
    long-term memory; schema
backward digit span test 163–4
BIA (bilingual interactive activation) 140
BIA + 140
bigrams 1, 46
bilingual education: in Canada 202–3; in
    the United States 203–4
bilingual interactive activation (BIA) 140
bilingualism: advantage of 53; deficit
    model of bilingualism 199–200, 208,
    214, 223; in the United States 204
bilinguals: Arabic-English 243; Chinese-
    English 52, 53, 54, 109, 119; Czech-English
    105; Dutch-English 116; English-
    Chinese 54–5; English-French 101, 105,
    114; English-Hebrew 166; English-
    Italian 53; English-Spanish 50, 115;
    Farsi-English 112–13; Italian-English 53;
    Japanese-English 52; Russian-German
    52; Spanish-English 167, 204, 214
biliteracy 2; acquisition of 99; community
    support for 210–12; ecological approach
    199; emergent 214; home and community
    support of 206–7; socio-cultural context
    of 197–200; in the United States 204
bio-social factors: gender 220–1;
    immigration status 218–19; research on
    217–18; socio-economic status 219–20

blind spot 33, 36
blogs, class 291–2
Bosnia 22
Brāhmī script 11
brain: neuroimaging of 45–6, 52; physiology of 46–7; plasticity of 58
Broca's area 2, 46
Bulgarian language 23

Canada: bilingual education in 202–3; Chinese schools in 210; L2 English speakers in 251; writing systems in 11–12
Cantonese 107, 209, 242; *see also* Chinese language
Cherokee language 7, 203
Cherokee syllabary 12
children: bilingual 107, 108, 115, 198, 200, 202, 203, 208, 214, 217; with decoding problems 255, 256, 257, 264; early elementary 77, 138, 164, 165, 170, 171, 175, 176, 213; ESL 290; higher elementary grade 164, 168, 171, 173, 176, 243; immigrant 202, 208, 218–22; with language impairment 260–1, 264, 269; language minority 199–201, 203, 205, 212, 217, 218, 219, 222–4; with learning disabilities/reading difficulties 167, 237–8, 241, 246, 247, 251–2, 254–8, 261; monolingual 104, 105, 112; primary school 257; *see also* adolescents
Chilolla 225
China: early writing in 3, 5; immigrants from 222; printing in 17
Chinese language 7, 16, 17, 55, 79–80, 80–82, 88–90, 103, 105, 106–7, 108–10, 121, 140, 196, 208, 214, 242, 246; reading, 35, 36–7, 38, 39; *see also* Cantonese; Mandarin
Chinese writing system 5, 13–15, 49–50
chosongul 9
chunking 288
churches, immigrant and minority 211–12
class blogs 291–2
clay tokens 3

cognate awareness 100, 104, 121, 122, 124, 180; and transfer patterns 114–17
cognates 139–40, 288; research about 242
cognate strategy 122
cognition: and language 41–2; and reading 32–3, 45, 47–8, 52, 56, 58, 82, 100, 101, 102, 171, 173, 196
cognitive processes 17, 26, 41–3, 102, 236, 238, 240, 241, 245, 247, 253, 255, 256, 261–2, 282–3, 286, 292; automatic 43; higher-order 52, 58, 159–60, 259, 283–4, 291; *see also* metacognitive comprehension strategies
cognitive skills 1, 16, 17, 100, 159, 254, 258, 262; and cross-language transfer 245–7; *see also* metacognitive skills
cognitive skills transfer: cognate awareness 114–17; morphological awareness 108–11; orthographic processing 112–14; phonological awareness 104–8; reading fluency 118–20; working memory 117–18
cohesive devices 177, 183; *see also* conjunctions; connectives
collocation 74, 145, 147, 149, 250, 288, 289; congruent vs. incongruent 140
community/ies: Hispanic 136; Jewish 211–12; religious practices in 211–12; support for literacy in 195–7, 210–12
competencies, language-specific 86, 99, 100–5, 110
comprehension *see* reading comprehension
concordance software 288, 297
conjunctions 175–6, 241, 259, 264; *see also* cohesive devices; connectives
connectionist approach 76
connectives 177–8; *see also* cohesive devices; conjunctions
constructionist models 47
context 73, 78, 91, 249
contrastive perspective 242
Coptic language 5
Coptic Orthodox Church 5
corpus analysis 150
corpus-driven learning 288–9
cortical magnification 34

country of origin 221–3; *see also* cultural background
Cree languages 12
cross-language transfer 100, 240–1; of cognitive and word-level skills 245–7; contrastive (typological) perspective) 242; future directions 123–4; interdependence perspective 241; and phonological awareness 244; positive 101, 242; research on 120–3; theoretical frameworks of 101–3; underlying cognitive processes perspective 241–2
cross-linguistic interactions 89–91
cultural background 195; *see also* country of origin
cultural issues, in L2 acquisition 199
cultural knowledge 247
culture: Asian 222; and background knowledge 169; conflicts between L1 and L2 195; issues related to 148; relationship to scripts and power 17–26
Cummins, J. 102
cuneiform 4
curriculum, coherent 284
curriculum-based measurement (CBM) 266
Cyrillic alphabet/script; Russian 22; Serbian 19, 20–2
Czech language 105

decoding difficulties 255–9, 260, 262, 263–6, 297; and reading fluency 256–8
decoding skills 23, 43, 44, 45, 56, 58, 76, 83, 84–5, 87, 90, 91, 106, 107, 117, 118, 121, 139, 141, 142, 160, 161, 238–40, 243–50, 258, 260, 269, 283, 290; phonological 77, 80–1, 86; sublexical 134
deficit model of bilingualism 199–200, 208, 214, 223; double deficit hypothesis 256
demotic writing 4
diacritic marks 8, 10, 12, 51
Diagnostic and Statistical Manual of Mental Disorders (*DSM-5*) 236
digraphia, Serbian 20
direct letter instruction (Letter-Alph) 56
distributed feature model 142–3
Dominican Republic, immigrants from 222

double deficit hypothesis 256
dual route model 47
dyslexia 255, 260, 289; developmental 47

Easter Island 3
ecological approach 199
education: access to 18, 251; bilingual 106, 202–4; bilingual development in linguistically diverse classrooms 215–16; English classes for parents 216; heritage language schools 202, 209, 210–11; immersion programs 115, 203; intervention programs 216–17; minority language instruction 203; need for school and family alignment 214–16; of parents 195, 196, 197, 200, 220, 253
Egypt, early writing in 3, 4–5, 7
ELL students *see* English Language Learners (ELLs)
ELODiL 226
emergent biliteracy 214
emergent literacy 206–7
emergent writing 206
emoji icons 19
English as a Foreign Language (EFL) 296
English as a Second Language (ESL) 86, 88, 89, 90, 290
English classes, for parents 216
English language 7, 8–9, 15, 16, 17, 80, 81, 103, 105, 106–10, 112, 113, 116, 119–20, 121, 122, 140, 172, 196, 207, 209, 241, 242, 243, 245, 246, 257, 267–8
English Language Learners (ELLs) 108–9, 122, 195, 204, 261
"English plus" policy 203
Epi-Olmec script 5
episodic buffer 162
Eritrea, writing systems in 11
ERP *see* event-related potentials (ERP)
ESL *see* English as a Second Language (ESL)
Ethiopia, writing systems in 11
ethnography 200–1
Europe, printing in 17
event-related potentials (ERP) 46, 53

extensive reading (ER) program 296; promoting 284, 295–7
eye movement studies 32, 34–6, 39–40, 72, 292–3, 298
eye physiology 33–4

face recognition 46
facilitation 101, 102, 105
family language policies 197, 198
family literacy policies 208–10
Farsi 212
female advantage 221
Finnish 15, 245
First Nations 202–3
fixations 32, 35, 36–8, 39, 40, 292
fluency: in reading and language 41–5; native-like 45; research on 298; word-level 241, 261; see also reading fluency
forward digit span test 163, 165
fovea 33–4
frames 151
French language 37, 103, 106–7, 110–11, 112, 113, 119–20, 121, 208, 212, 241, 245, 257; in Canada 202
functional magnetic resonance imaging (fMRI) 46, 49, 52, 53, 54
funds of knowledge 196, 198–9, 204, 213, 215; see also knowledge

gender, influence on L2 acquisition 196
gender gap 220–1
general knowledge 134, 151
German language 19, 52, 242
glyphs, in Egyptian script 4
Google Translate 225
grain size 16, 81, 112, 140
grammar 166; through patterns 150
grapheme pairs (bigrams) 1, 46
grapheme-morpheme connection 80, 82
grapheme-phoneme correspondence 50, 80–1, 139, 206
graphemes 2, 5, 6, 7, 9, 10, 11, 12, 15, 22, 42, 46, 78, 80, 112
graphic organizers 183
Greek language 8, 9
Greeklish 19

hangul 9–10, 17–18
hànzì (Chinese characters) 13–15
Hawaiian language 203
Head Start program 217
Hebrew language 15, 35, 37, 51, 80, 81–3, 106, 109, 110, 207, 211–12, 242, 246, 257
Hebrew script 10–11, 51, 211–12
heritage country 221–3
heritage languages 136, 203
heritage language schools 209, 210–11
Herzegovina 22
hierarchical summaries 183
hieratic writing 4
hieroglyphic writing 4
higher-level processing skills and processes 159–60; deficits in 259; see also background knowledge; cognitive processes; cognitive skills; inferences, making; textual coherence; textual cohesion
Hindi 7, 23
hiragana 13
Hispanic communities 136
home literacy practices 205–6, 212, 217
home literacy support 196, 206–7, 254
homophones 49, 80
Hutterites 202
hypermedia annotation 285–6, 298

immersion programs 115, 203
immigration: advantages/disadvantages of 196; circumstances of 219; voluntary vs. refugee 253
Indian subcontinent 23; writing systems on 11
indigenous languages 204, 268
individual education plan (IEP) 266
Indonesian language 7, 17, 55
Indonesian-Chinese billboards 55
Indus Valley, early writing in 3
inferences: coherence 170; elaborative or extending 170; making 164, 181; and reading comprehension 160, 170–3
inferencing skills 247; deficits in 259
instruction methods see teaching
interdependence perspective 241

International Children's Digital Library 225
Internet access 18
intervention programs 216–17; for reading difficulties 263–6, 269–70
Inuit 202–3
Inuktitut (Inuttitut) 12, 151
Islam 211
Isthmian script 5
Italian language 50, 245

Jamaican Creole (Patois) 19–20, 24–6
Jamaican-English 19, 24–6
Japanese language 7, 13, 35, 55
Jenga 293–5, 297, 298
Jewish community 211–12
Judaism 211–12

kanji 13
katakana 13
Kharoṣṭhī script 11
knowledge: cultural 174, 247; funds of 196, 198–9, 204, 213, 215; general 134, 151; lexico-semantic 43, 149–51; linguistic 86–7, 134, 149, 284; matching L1 and L2 286–7; morphological 257; orthographic 12; print 206; prior 71, 72, 73, 99, 134, 135, 151, 160, 161, 168, 171, 172, 284–7; semantic 115; syntactic 149–51, 247; topic/general 142, 151; transfer of 136; vocabulary 74–5; of word meanings 73–4, 148; world 249; *see also* background knowledge; vocabulary knowledge
knowledge incorporation 71
knowledge transfer 136
Korea, printing in 17
Korean language 39, 88, 89, 90, 106, 109, 211
Korean writing system 9–10, 55

L1 language and literacy: effect of L2 development on 99, 106–7; influence of 87; relationship to L2 literacy 213–17
L1 reading: brain network involved in 45–8, 50; neuroimaging studies 52; and word-level reading 243; *see also* L1 reading comprehension; reading

L1 reading comprehension: background knowledge and 168; inference making and 171–2; relationship with L2 comprehension 178–9; and textual coherence 174; working memory and 164–6
L2 language and literacy: bio-social factors affecting 217–23; and the deficit model 199–200; ecological approach 199; effect on L1 99, 106–7; and family language policies 198; and funds of knowledge 198–9; language-general vs. language-specific development 102–3, 121; practices in schools 195; relationship to L1 literacy 213–17; socio-cultural context of 197–200; and Vygotsky's socio-cultural theory 197–8, 205
L2 proficiency 91, 247
L2 reading: accommodation and assimilation 54–5; and brain physiology 48–9, 50; differences between orthographies 49–51; difficulties in 44; dual language involvement and 89; educational implications 58; eye movements in 40; future research 56–7; instruction methods for 56; interactions with L1, 53–4; and the lexicon 137–43; neuroimaging studies 52; proficiency and effort 51–2; questions concerning 48–9; relationship with L1 reading 58; *see also* reading
L2 reading comprehension 159, 180–1; background knowledge and 168–70; inference making and 172–3; relationship with L1 comprehension 178–9; and textual coherence 174–5; working memory and 164–6
L2 reading development: and cross-language transfer 240–2; disabilities vs. difficulties 237–8; simple view of reading (SVR) 239
Labrador Inuttitut (Inukitut) 151
language: alphabetic 206, 246; automaticity and fluency in 41–5; and cognition 41–2; formulaic 147; indigenous 204, 268;

logographic 246; minority 136, 195–9, 201, 203–4, 207–8, 210, 212, 216–18, 223–4
language comprehension 164, 250
language impairment 258, 260–1
language processing 42; automatized 43; L1 43
language proficiency, L2 169
language threshold effect 169
language typology 241
languages: Arabic 15, 35, 37, 51, 109, 211–12, 240, 243, 267; Bulgarian 23; Cantonese 107, 209, 242; Cherokee 7, 203; Coptic 5; Cree 12; Czech 105; Farsi 212; Finnish 15, 245; German 19, 52, 242; Greek 8, 9; Greeklish 19; Hawaiian 203; Hebrew 15, 35, 37, 51, 80, 81–3, 106, 109, 110, 207, 211–12, 242, 246, 257; Hindi 7, 23; Indonesian 7, 17, 55; Inuit 202–3; Inuktitut (Inuttitut) 12, 151; Italian 50, 245; Jamaican Creole (Patois) 19–20, 24–6; Jamaican-English 19, 24–6; Japanese 7, 13, 35, 55; Korean 39, 88, 89, 90, 106, 109, 211; Mandarin 14, 23, 105, 196, 209; Norwegian 141–2; Punjabi 196; Russian 19, 212; Scottish Gaelic 15, 203; Semitic 51; Serbian 8, 20, 22; Serbo-Croatian 8, 15, 19–23, 80, 81; Sinitic 14; Sumerian 3–4; Swahili 7; Thai 7; Turkish 15, 240; Ukrainian 23; Urdu 23, 212; Yi 7; Zhuang 7; *see also* Chinese language; English language; French language; Spanish language
Latin alphabet, in the Serbian language 20
Latin America, immigrants from 203, 222
Latin script 8, 18
learning: collaborating 207; corpus-driven 288–9; declarative 43; procedural 43
learning disability (LD) 251–2; specific 236–7
learning management system (LMS) 296–7
lemmas 143, 150
Letter-Alph instruction 56
lexemes 143, 150
lexical access 16, 40, 45, 58, 79, 82, 88

lexical information 70–3, 75–6, 80–1, 86, 90, 285, 287
lexical knowledge 70, 151, 287; expansion of 135; and L2 reading ability 133–4; native-like 143; as predictor of reading ability 136–7; and reading comprehension 141–3, 152; studies on 147–51
lexical processing 35; L2 40
lexical restructuring 134
lexical semantic retrieval 48
lexical tones 103
linguistic ethnography 201
linguistic interdependence hypothesis 102
linguistic knowledge 86–7, 134, 149, 284
listening comprehension 247; deficits in 259
literacy: cultural support for 195–6; democratization of, 17–20; emergent 206–7; home support for 196, 206–7, 254; home practices 205–6, 212, 217; *see also* L1 language and literacy; L2 language and literacy
loanwords 124n1
logographic principle 5, 7
long-term memory 41, 42–3, 121, 161, 162, 244; *see also* background knowledge

magnetic resonance imaging (MRI) 45
Mamalisa's World 226
Mandarin 14, 23, 105, 196, 209; *see also* Chinese language
mapping: acoustic signal on phonology 43; grapheme to language 83; grapheme to phonology 81; of meaning 134, 239, 287; orthography to phonology 47, 50–1, 239; orthography to semantics 48; patterns of 103; referential 247; written forms to words 138
"Matthew effect" 136, 144
Mayan script 5–6
meaning representations 73; models of 142–3
memory: bilingual 118; declarative 43; enhancement of 146; integration of text information in 160; language-specific

underpinnings 121; lexical semantic 75; organization of 160; procedural 44; reading acquisition through 17, 33; and reading comprehension 100, 104, 160–1; representations of verbal information in 244; storage of schemata in 167; *see also* long-term memory; short-term memory; working memory

Memrise 225

mental lexicon, bilingual 40

Mesoamerica, early writing in 3, 5–6, 7

metacognitive comprehension strategies 239, 247, 290, 291–2

metacognitive skills 214, 258, 286; *see also* cognitive skills

metalinguistic awareness 91, 99, 114, 171, 205, 212; cross-linguistic contributions of 83–6

metalinguistic skills transfer 100, 103–4, 181; cognate awareness 114–17; morphological awareness 108–11; orthographic processing 112–14; phonological awareness 104–8; reading fluency 118–20; working memory 117–18

Métis 202–3

Mexico, immigrants from 222

microsaccades 35; *see also* saccades

monitoring: comprehension 161, 164, 165, 181; progress 165–6; response conflict 52; self- 42, 44

Montenegro 22

MoodleReader 296

moraic scripts 6, 7, 12–13

morphemes 4–7, 9, 13–15, 42, 49, 76, 77, 81–2, 84–6, 99, 108, 151, 205

morphograms 8, 15

morphographic principle 5

morphological analysis 39, 44, 70–2, 75, 76, 77–80, 86–7, 102, 263–4

morphological awareness (MA) 82, 84–6, 100, 108–11; transfer of 104, 108–12, 121, 123, 124, 259, 264

morphological difficulties 255

morphological fluency 58

morphological parsing 44

morphological processing 40, 58, 71, 77–8, 90–1

morphological progression 91

morphological segmentation 88

morphological skills 241, 247

morphological structures 4, 15, 37–8, 42–3, 72, 101, 123

morphological systems 139

morphology/ies 37, 39, 44, 45; deficits in 258; instruction 263–4; shared 138

morphophonemes 15

morphosyntactics 74

motivation 101, 102, 143, 215, 291, 296; intrinsic 284; of parents 200

multi-word items 148

My Languages 225

naming 80–1; *see also* rapid naming skills

National Association of School Psychologists 236

National Reading Panel 180

Native American communities 202

Native Americans, in Canada 202–3

Near East, early writing in 3

Neolithic symbols 3

neuroimaging studies 45–6, 52

neuronal recycling 2

No Child Left Behind policy 196, 204

non-word repetition test 163

North American context 196; Canada 202–3; United States 203–4

North Korea 9

Norwegian language 141–2

numerical notation systems 3

Olmec culture 5

Omniglot 225

online translators 225

onset-rime 105, 122

optic disk 33, 36

optimal viewing position (OVP) 37–8

oracle bone inscriptions 5

oral language proficiency 133–4, 137, 166, 241, 243–5, 250, 256–9, 260–2,

265–6; bilingual 58; comprehension 133–4; deficits in 259; and reading comprehension 247–8; and word recognition 87
oral traditions 19
orthographic depth, 15–16, 50–1, 86; shallow vs. deep 8, 9, 15, 16, 50, 80, 81, 82, 245–6
orthographic depth hypothesis (ODH) 16, 80
orthographic distance 87–8, 91
orthographic effects L1 91
orthographic knowledge L1 12
orthographic processing 47, 76, 100; transfer of 112–14, 123
orthography/ies 6, 43; alphabetic 8, 39, 50, 55; changes to 19; Chinese 55; differences between 49–51; English 8–9; etymological 25; of L2 writing systems 213; mapping to phonology 50; shared 138–9

parafoveal region 34, 37, 39
parental investment model 219
parents: education of 195, 196, 197, 200, 220, 253; English classes for 216; language minority 199–200, 210–11
Patois *see* Jamaican Creole
Persian script 23
Peru, early writing in 3
phonemes 9, 15, 22, 41, 42, 77, 104, 108, 112, 134, 205, 263; phoneme-grapheme relationships 245–6
phonemic awareness 263
phonics 56, 263, 268
phonological awareness (PA) 83–4, 100, 104–8, 144, 206, 241, 244, 246, 255–6, 258, 261–3; cross-language transfer of 122; teaching of 122; transfer of 105–8, 122
phonological information extraction 71
phonological loop 77, 162
phonologically based reading intervention program (PHAST) 263
phonological processing 77, 101, 102, 243, 258

phonological segmentation 55
phonological short-term memory (STM) 162–5, 166, 241, 256, 261
phonological skills 243, 258; poor 260
phonological systems 139
phonological units 42
phonology/ies 16, 43, 47, 74; mapping orthography to 50; shared 138
phonotactics 134
photoreceptors 33
phrasal boundaries 134
pictographs 4, 7
Pinyin alphabet 23
polysemes 148
poor comprehenders 165, 167, 172–3, 177, 240, 258–61, 275, 286; L2 259; *see also* reading comprehension, difficulties in
poor decoders 240, 256, 257, 259, 260
poor readers 72, 77, 84, 166, 182, 240, 256–8, 260
Poser, William 7
positron emission tomography (PET) 45, 50
pragmatics 250
Prakrit 11
predicting 181
preferred viewing location (PVL) 37–8
pre-readers 134, 179–80
priming 116, 118, 149, 151
print knowledge 206
printing presses 17
prior knowledge 71, 72, 73, 99, 134, 135, 151, 160, 161, 168, 171, 172, 284–7
progress evaluation 284
propositional level 135
psycholinguistic grain size theory 16, 81
psycholinguistic guessing game 72, 137
Punjabi language 196

qualitative research 200–1
quantitative research 201
question generation 181
Quizlet 225

rapid naming skills 102, 119, 241, 243, 244–5, 246, 255, 256, 261, 262 rapid serial visual presentation (RSVP) 295, 297

reader-text interactions 71–2

reading: automaticity and fluency in 41–5; basic mechanics of 35–6; eye movements during 34–5; interactions between L1 and L2 53–4; as interactive process 160; as metalinguistic endeavor 99; optimal viewing position (OVP) 37–8; preferred viewing location (PVL) 37–8; processes involved in 42; psycholinguistic grain size theory 16; and neurocognition 32–3; strategic 180–2; variability, change and adaption in 38–40; see also L1 reading; L2 reading

reading comprehension 107–8, 111, 114–22, 124, 134–7, 148–9, 160–1, 237–8, 263; and background knowledge 160, 167–70; conclusion 183–4; deficits in 259, 261; defined 247; difficulties in 258–60, 268; higher-order skills 159, 162, 264; and improving L2 vocabulary, 144; influence of text on 159–60; and inference making 160, 170–3; and L2 pedagogy and assessment 179–83; and lexical knowledge 141–3; monitoring 164, 181; and oral language proficiency 247–8; and reading fluency 249, 292; relationship between L1 and L2 comprehension 178–9; textual cohesion and coherence 160, 173–8; theoretical perspectives 139; using technology to teach 289–92; and working memory 160, 162–7; see also L1 reading comprehension; L2 reading comprehension; poor comprehenders; texts, comprehension of

reading development: and brain physiology 46–8; word-level reading in 243

reading difficulties 250; assessment of 261–3; case study (poor comprehension) 268, 269; case study (word-level difficulties) 267–8, 269; comprehension 258–60; decoding 255–6; decoding and reading fluency 256–8; identification of 251–4,

269–70; language impairment 260–1; remediation for 264–5; risk factors for 253–4; specific 254–61; treatment and intervention 263–6, 269–70

reading disabilities (RD) 236–7, 244; identification of 251–2

reading fluency 100, 118–20, 165, 257, 263, 284, 292–5; approaches to improving 265; and decoding difficulties 256–8; and lexical knowledge 136; and reading comprehension 249, 292; and technology 292–5; text 118–19; see also fluency

reading instruction: five components of 263; L2 137; strategy-based 289; technology-enhanced 282–3; see also teaching

reading processes: bottom-up 160–1; construction-integration (CI) model 161; continuum of 160; top-down 160–1, 249, 250

reading skills: higher-level 164; L1 16; L1 influence on L2 17; L2 243

reading strategy development 284

reading studies, developmental 116–17

reading to learn 258

reciprocal teaching 180–1

refixations 39, 40

regressions 35, 39, 40, 292, 293, 295; removing 295

religious practices, community 211–12

remediation, for reading difficulties 264–5

research: background knowledge and reading 167–70; on cross-language transfer 120–3; empirical 71; ethnographic 200–1; on factors in L2 acquisition 196; fluency studies 298; on home language and literacy practices 224; on inference making 170–3; interdisciplinary 197; on L2 reading 99; on lexical knowledge and reading 147–51; on lexical knowledge and reading comprehension 141–2; on phonological awareness 84; on poor comprehension 258; on reader-text interaction 71–2;

on reading 150; on the simple view of
   reading 239–40; on the socio-cultural
   context of L2 literacy and biliteracy 200–1;
   on textual coherence 174–5; on textual
   cohesion 174–5; on transferability
   120–1; on use of technology in L2
   reading instruction 298; on vocabulary
   development 145, 146; on working
   memory and L1 reading comprehension
   164–6; on working memory and L2
   reading comprehension 166–7
response to intervention (RTI) 253,
   265–6
revised hierarchical model (RHM) 142
RhinoSpike 225
Robb, Thomas 296
rongorongo 3
RTI *see* response to intervention
Russian language 19, 212
Russian Cyrillic 22, 23

saccades 35–7, 39, 40, 283, 292, 293, 295
saccadic suppression 36
sacred texts 211–12
Sanskrit 11
scaffolding 197–8, 205, 207, 283
schema/schemata 151, 167, 168, 179;
   see also background knowledge; schema
   theory
schema theory 167–8
Scottish Gaelic language 15, 203
script-dependent hypothesis 101
scripts 1–2, 151; alphabetic 246; Arabic
   10–11, 18, 23, 211–12; *Brāhmī* 11;
   Chinese 5, 13–15, 49–50; Cyrillic 8,
   22; Epi-Olmec 5; Hebrew 10–11, 51,
   211–12; hieroglyphics 4–5; indigenous
   18; Isthmian 5; *Kharoṣṭhī* 11;
   Mayan 5–6; in Mesopotamia 3; Persian
   23; relationship with literacy 26; Russian
   Cyrillic 22; Serbian Cyrillic 19, 20–2;
   and transfer of orthographic processing
   112–13; types of, 6–17; variations in
   42; Vietnamese 18; Zapotec 5; *see also*
   writing
self-regulation 241

semantic abilities 165
semantic alignment 70
semantic category judgments 53, 75, 89
semantic complements 4–5, 6
semantic extension 4–5
semantic fields 152
semantic grammar 150
semantic information 39
semantic maps 183
semantic patterns 288
semantic-phonetic compounds 14
semantic processing 47–9, 52, 71, 77, 78–9,
   81, 87, 89–90, 108, 116–17, 140, 143, 145,
   148, 150–1, 160
semantic relations 159, 173, 175–7,
   180, 287
semantics 39, 239, 260
semantic-semantic compounds 14, 15
Semitic abjad 8
Semitic languages 51
sentences, adding space between 293
Serbia 3, 22
Serbian alphabet 23
Serbian Cyrillic alphabet 19, 20–2
Serbian language 8, 20, 22
Serbo-Croatian 8, 15, 19–23, 80, 81
shallow structure hypothesis 137
shape filters 2
short-term memory (STM) 41, 43, 121,
   245; phonological 162–5, 166, 241,
   256, 261
simple view of reading (SVF) 239–40
Sinitic languages 14; *see also* Chinese
   language; Chinese writing system
situation model building 71
social media posting 19
social network analysis 298
social support 254
socio-cultural theory: and the deficit
   model 199–200; and the ecological
   approach 199; family language policy
   198; and funds of knowledge 198–9;
   Vygotsky's theory 197–8, 205
socioeconomic status 195, 196, 208,
   219–20; as high-risk factor 252, 253
software, concordance 288, 297

sound units, sub-syllabic 104; *see also* phonemes

South Korea 9

Southeast Asia, writing systems in 11

Spanish language 9, 50, 106, 108–9, 112, 113, 115, 116, 121, 122, 196, 204, 207, 241, 243, 246, 268; religious practices in 211

special education programs 251, 252, 263, 266, 268

specific learning disabilities *see* learning disability (LD)

speech errors 151; *see also* oral language proficiency

spelling 6, 8, 15, 19, 25, 47, 50, 53, 76, 87, 90, 100, 101, 105, 107, 114, 206, 213, 241–2, 249

spelling difficulties 255, 267

spelling patterns 79, 88, 112, 246, 265; *see also* orthographic processing

spoken language *see* oral language proficiency

studies *see* research

sub-lexical information 70, 71, 73, 86

Sumerian language 3–4

summarizing 180–2, 289

support networks 254

Swahili language 7

syllabaries 6, 7, 12–13

syllables 4, 5, 7, 9, 10, 12, 13, 14, 16, 17, 42, 76, 81, 86, 99, 104, 107, 122, 138; complexity of 16

synergy 207

syntactic awareness, deficits in 258

syntactic knowledge 149–51, 247

syntactic processing, L2 40

syntactic skills 262

syntactic structure, visualizing 293

syntax 43, 45, 150; parsing 135

teachers: resources for 225–6; role of in technology-incorporated classrooms 297

teaching: of comprehension skills 289–92; method for L2 reading 56, 282–4; pre-reading 179–80; reading pedagogy 137, 263, 282–3, 289; reciprocal 180–1;

vocabulary instruction 264; whole-word instruction 56

technology use 282–3; activating background knowledge 284–7; enriching vocabulary knowledge 287–9; promoting extensive reading 295–7; for reading fluency 292–5; teaching for comprehension skills 289–92

textbase construction 71

texting 19

text reading fluency *see* reading fluency

texts: appearance of on screens 293; children's understanding of 107; comprehension of 74–5, 142; electronic 292–3; information about 170; mental representations of 159–61; processing of 164; sacred 211–12

text structures 182–3, 247

text-to-speech technology (TTST) 289–90, 297

textual coherence, and reading comprehension 170, 173–5

textual cohesion, and reading comprehension 160, 173, 175–8

Thai language 7

thinking about meaning 284

tracking eye movement 32, 34–6, 39–40, 72, 283, 292–3, 298

trailing-mask condition 295

transfer: bidirectional 110–11, 119, 136; cross-language (*see* cross-language transfer); of knowledge 136; language specific vs. language general elements of 120; reverse 103, 107, 110, 115, 123; theoretical and educational implications of 120–3; *see also* cognitive skills transfer; cross-language transfer; metalinguistic skills transfer

transfer patterns: and cognate awareness 114–17, 122; of metalinguistic and cognitive skills, studies of, 103–104; morphological awareness 108–11, 123; orthographic processing 112–14, 123; phonological awareness 104–8, 122; and reading fluency 118–20; and working memory 117–18

transferability 112, 120, 121
translation "equivalents" 143
tree diagrams 183
triangulation 195
TTST (text-to-speech technology) 289–90
Turkey, literacy in 18
Turkish 15, 240
Turkish alphabet 18
typesetting 17
typological perspective 242

Ukrainian language 23
underlying cognitive processes perspective 241–2
Unicode 19
United States: bilingual education in 203–4; bilingualism in 204; biliteracy in 204
Urdu 23, 212

ventral occipito-temporal cortex (vOT) 46, 47, 50, 54
verbal abilities 165
verbal efficiency theory 249
video annotation 285
Vietnamese script 18
Vinča culture 3
vision impairment 289
visual cortex 34
visual field 34
visual object recognition 46
visual representations 183
visual spatial processing, global 50
visual system 33–4; eye movements during reading 34–40
visual word form area (VWFA) 1, 46
visual word recognition see word recognition, visual
visual-syntactic text formatting (VSTF) 293, 295, 297
visuo-spatial sketchpad 162–3
vocabulary 262–3; academic 237; cross-language transfer of 116; deficits in 258, 259; improving L2 143–7; multimodal support for 287–8
vocabulary development 134, 144–5, 264; direct strategies 146; through reading

145; traditional methods 145; word building exercises 263
vocabulary knowledge 74–5, 142, 160, 165, 166, 169–70, 247–8, 262, 284, 287–9; and reading comprehension 74–5, 178; enriching with technology 287–9
vocabulary tests 147–9
vocabulary through reading hypothesis 146

Wernicke's area 2, 46
whole-word instruction 56
wikis 290–1
women and the female advantage 221
Word-Alph and Word-Arb instruction 56
word associations 151
word building exercises see vocabulary development
word decoding see decoding skills
word extraction 71
word identification 134
word identification span 38–9
word-level reading skills 262; cognitive processes involved in 243–5; and cross-language transfer 245–7; difficulties with 255, 267–8
word list reading 262
word meanings: context-specific 91; knowledge of 73–4; retrieval of 71, 72; see also vocabulary development; vocabulary knowledge
word reading see reading; reading fluency; visual word recognition
word recognition 17, 36, 38, 42, 51, 139, 142, 145, 159, 165, 166, 243, 246, 249–50, 257, 258, 284; automatic 118, 137, 248; component operations of 76–9; cross-linguistic interactions 89–90; cross-linguistic variations in 79–82; development in L2 82–3; effect of scripts on 15–16; future research on 90–2; grapho-semantic 134; inaccurate 258; and L1–L2 orthographic distance 87–8; in L2 70–1; linguistic knowledge 86–7; and metalinguistic awareness 83–6; and morphological processing

77–8; and orthographic processing
76, 86; and phonological processing
77; and reader-text interactions 71–2;
relationships among vocabulary
knowledge, vocabulary learning, and
text comprehension 74–6; and semantic
processings 78; relationships among
word forms, word meanings, and prior
knowledge 72–4; skillful 141, 249;
and text meaning construction 71–6;
variations in development of 86–90;
visual 1, 45, 47, 133–5, 137–40; visuo-
phonological 134
words, with fuzzy boundaries 148
word span test 163, 165
working memory 41, 43, 44, 77, 100, 101,
102, 159, 183–4, 239, 241, 245–7, 258,
259, 261; and cross-language transfer
117–18; deficits in 165, 258, 259;
improving 288; and inferencing ability
135; and L1 reading comprehension
164–6; and L2 comprehension 166–7;

lexical semantic 75; overload of 283–5;
and reading comprehension 160, 162–7;
revised model 163; semantic 45, 48, 75;
verbal 150, 163, 165, 262; visual-spatial
165; weakness in 256; and word-level
reading 244, 356
writing: emergent 206; history of 2–6;
see also scripts
writing skills, deficits in 259–60
writing systems: Chinese 13–15; Korean 55;
hieratic 4; hieroglyphic 4; logographic
49, 50; morphographic 6, 7–8, 13–15,
23; phonographic 6, 7–13, 23; see also
alphabets; scripts
written word form area 46

Yi language 7
Yousafzai, Malala 18

Zapotec script 5
Zhuang language 7
zone of proximal development 197–8, 207